Illustrated
Encyclopaedia
of World Coins

Burton Hobson and Robert Obojski

ROBERT HALE & COMPANY
63 OLD BROMPTON ROAD
LONDON, S.W.7

ACKNOWLEDGMENTS

The authors are indebted to the following individuals and institutions for photographs and information: Charles R. Hoskins, National Bank of Detroit Money Museum; I. G. Spasski, Numismatic Department of the Hermitage Museum, Leningrad; the Cleveland Museum of Art; Hans M. F. Schulman, New York; Jacques Schulman, Amsterdam; Gene Hessler, Chase Manhattan Bank Money Museum; Stack's, New York; B. A. Seaby Ltd., London; *Coin World*, Sidney, Ohio; *Numismatic News*, Iola, Wisconsin; the American Numismatic Association, Colorado Springs; The American Numismatic Society, New York; the Maritime Museum and Warship Vasa, Stockholm; Q. David Bowers, Santa Fe Springs, California; the Trustees of the British Museum; Jack Friedberg, Coin and Currency Institute, New York; William A. Pettit, Rarcoa, Chicago; the Smithsonian Institution, Washington, D.C.; Mr. Louis Eliasberg, Baltimore; and the Avesta Steel Works of the Axel Johnson Group.

Contents

How to Use This Book

The Illustrated Encyclopedia of World Coins is intended to be an easy-to-use mine of information covering many aspects of coins and coin collecting. You will find entertainment in just reading through the articles at random. This Encyclopedia may answer all sorts of questions you have wondered about—and many that may not even have occurred to you. Illustrating many of the articles are photographs which relate to the text.

The articles in this Encyclopedia are arranged alphabetically so that you can look up any subject in its proper alphabetical place, just as you would look up a word in the dictionary. Many subjects, however, are touched upon in several articles. If you do not find the subject you want by looking through the Table of Contents, be sure to check the Index at the end of the book for all the appropriate references, and for places where a subject may be covered in part under a different heading.

Typical of Afghanistan's 20th century coins, this 1929 silver 1 afghani features the country's national emblem, a throne room.

Afghanistan

The nation of Afghanistan enjoys a certain distinction for being always the first country to appear in alphabetically arranged coin catalogs. Besides this, however, its issues are interesting in many ways and in spite of the remoteness of the land, many of its coins are readily available to collectors at modest prices.

Afghanistan, a mountainous inland country in Southwest Asia, achieved its independence from Persia in 1747. Afghanistan's early coinage was hand struck by the hammer method at provincial mints with little control from the central government of the Shah. The obverses of the copper pieces which are mostly on irregular planchets portray various objects such as animals, swords, leaves, etc. The reverses have an Arabic inscription giving the date according to the Moslem calendar and the name of the mint city.

Modern coin making machinery was installed at the Kabul mint in 1890 and from then until 1961, the national emblem, a throne room, was a feature on nearly every coin.

King Mohammed Zahir Shah appears on Afghanistan's first portrait coin, a nickel-steel 5 afghani first issued in 1961.

Afghan coins have been inscribed in Arabic and Persian, but Pushtu (a form of Persian) has been used exclusively since 1950. Dates were given according to Mohammedan reckoning (A.H.) up to 1920 (and briefly again in 1929–31), with solar calendar dates (S.H.) being used since that time.

Afghanistan ❧ 9

Two of Africa's oldest independent nations are represented by this Ethiopian ¼ talari of 1894 showing the Emperor Menelik II (1889-1913) and the Liberian cent of 1896 with a head of Liberty.

Africa

During the past half century, the make-up of Africa has changed from a continent of European colonies and protectorates to a land of independent republics. In 1900, Africa had only two sovereign countries—Ethiopia, or Abyssinia, an ancient kingdom in northeast Africa, and Liberia, a country on the continent's west coast inhabited mostly by Negroes.

Egypt, whose history can be traced back to at least 3400 B.C., was under Turkish rule at the turn of the century, was made a British protectorate during World War I, regained its independence in 1922, and became a republic in 1953.

King Fuad I (1922-36) played a major role in the reestablishment of Egypt's independence in 1922. He is portrayed on the bronze ½ millieme of 1924.

Ethiopia, which was brought under Italian control in 1935, was occupied by a friendly Great Britain during World War II, and in 1945 Emperor Haile Selassie once again became undisputed ruler of the ancient country. The end of World War II marked the start of the redrawing of

(Left) King Idris of Libya (1951-69) shown on a 1952 2 piastres and (Right) King Mohammed V of Morocco (1957-61) on a 1960 silver dirhem. These two North African countries gained independence after World War II.

the map of Africa. By 1970 there were over two score independent republics on the continent with a mere handful of colonies and protectorates remaining. In 1958, the first Conference of Independent African States was assembled at Accra, capital of Ghana (formerly the British Crown Colony of the Gold Coast). Nine countries were free by that time: Liberia, Ethiopia, Egypt, Libya, Sudan, Tunisia, Morocco, Ghana, and South Africa, though the latter did not attend the conference.

The portrait of Kwame Nkrumah, prime minister and then president of Ghana (1957-66), is featured on the first independent coinage of 1958.

Within two years 18 names were added to the growing list of free African nations: Guinea, Mauritania, Mali, Senegal, Ivory Coast, Upper Volta, Niger, Dahomey, Togo, Cameroon, Chad, Central African Republic, Gabon, the Congo (capital, Brazzaville), the Congo (capital, Kinshasa), the Somali Republic, and the Malagasy Republic.

Somalia's coins feature jungle animals native to the country, the lion and elephant.

Sierra Leone was added in 1961, along with Tanganyika. The island of Zanzibar achieved independence in 1963, and in the following year united with Tanganyika to form the United Republic of Tanzania. The following countries complete the current list of independent republics: Rwanda, Burundi, Algeria, Uganda, Kenya, Malawi, Zambia, Gambia, Rhodesia . . . however, Rhodesia's declaration of independence from Great Britain did not receive international recognition, Botswana (formerly Bechuanaland), and Lesotho (formerly Basutoland). Swaziland became a fully independent constitutional monarchy within the British Commonwealth in 1968.

Thus, only a few African territories now remain under European rule. They are: the Spanish Equatorial Guinea, Sahara, and Ifni; the Portuguese Guinea, Angola and Mozambique; and the French Somaliland.

French Somaliland and Portuguese Mozambique are among those few African territories to remain under European rule. Somaliland's 1949 aluminum 2 francs has the bust of Republic, with an antelope head on the reverse; Mozambique's 1960 copper-nickel 5 escudos shows the Portuguese arms on a cross on the obverse, the arms of the colony itself on the reverse.

While the new republics are technically sovereign, many are economically dependent upon their former colonial masters. The Congo, for example, still relies heavily upon Belgium for technical assistance, while most of the small and underdeveloped states in West and Equatorial Africa are bound to France by strong economic ties. The fact remains, however, that the days of colonialism and paternalism in Africa are largely a thing of the past.

Africa's remarkable transformation from a continent of colonies to a continent of republics has naturally meant great changes in its various monetary systems. Colonial coinages have been largely replaced, of course, by coinages struck independently by the new nations.

FRENCH AFRICA

Former Colonies　　　　　　　　　　　　New Nations

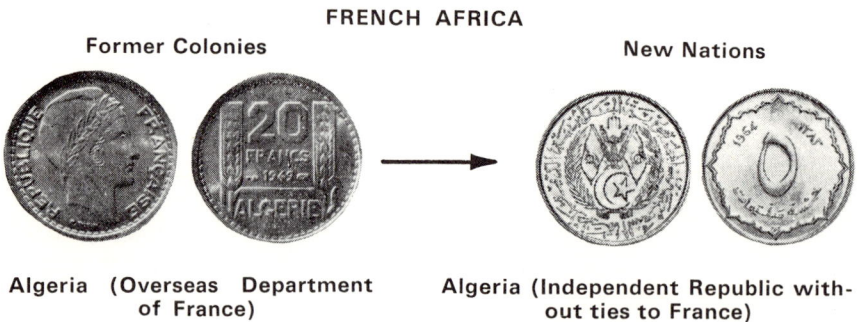

Algeria (Overseas Department of France)　　　Algeria (Independent Republic without ties to France)

Madagascar → Malagasy Republic

Cameroun

Chad
Gabon
Middle Congo
Ubangi-Shari
(Central African
Republic)

French Equatorial Africa

Equatorial
African States

Togo

Dahomey
Ivory Coast
Mauretania
Niger
Senegal
Upper Volta
*French Guinea
**French Sudan

French West Africa

West
African States

*Now Republic of Guinea with its own coinage.
**Now Republic of Mali with its own coinage.

Africa ◈ 13

BRITISH AFRICA

Former Colonies

New Nations

Union of South Africa

Republic of South Africa

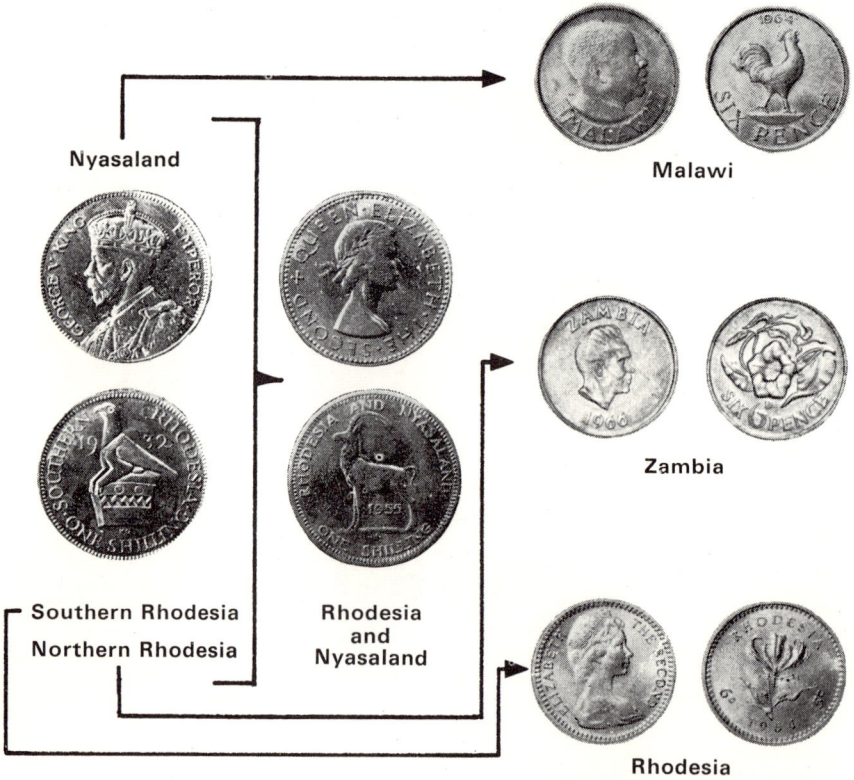

Nyasaland

Malawi

Southern Rhodesia
Northern Rhodesia

Rhodesia
and
Nyasaland

Zambia

Rhodesia

14 ◈ Africa

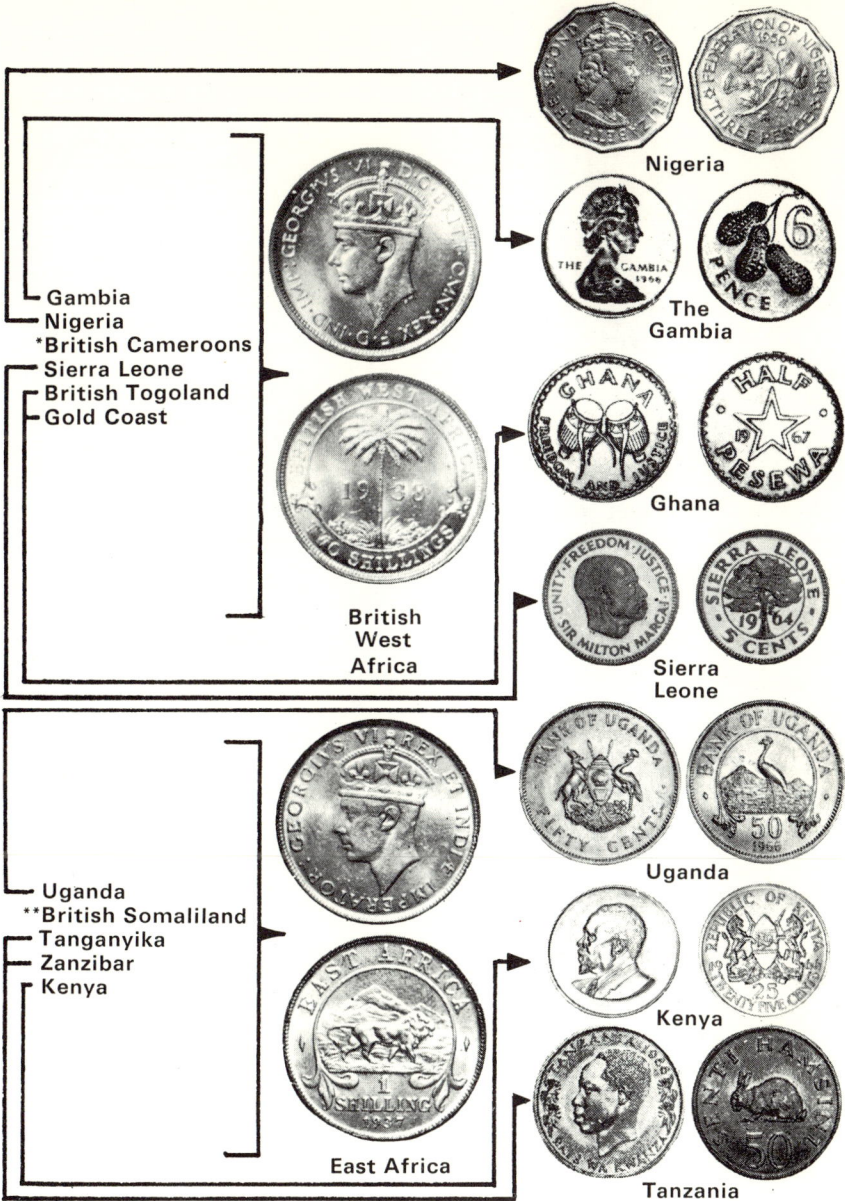

Gambia
Nigeria
  *British Cameroons
Sierra Leone
British Togoland
Gold Coast

British
West
Africa

Nigeria

The
Gambia

Ghana

Sierra
Leone

Uganda
  **British Somaliland
Tanganyika
Zanzibar
Kenya

East Africa

Uganda

Kenya

Tanzania

*Northern Cameroons merged with Nigeria, Southern Cameroons merged
with French Cameroons to form Cameroon Republic.
**Merged with former Italian Somaliland to form Somali Republic.

Africa ● 15

The African country with the longest history of independence is Ethiopia. The Emperor of Ethiopia claims descent from Solomon and the Queen of Sheba, and styles himself "the Lion of Judah." The history of Ethiopian coinage dates back at least to the Axumite kings of Abyssinia who issued small gold pieces as early as the second half of the third century A.D. The gold coins were supplemented by bronze issues and by

In the third century A.D., Ethiopia became the first African nation to issue coins independently. Illustrated is a 1/3 gold solidus of the Axumite King Ezanas struck c. 330.

an occasional series in silver. After the Moslems subjugated Egypt in 650, they also took control of Ethiopia . . . and from then until the 1850's Ethiopia lost virtually all contact with the mainstream of Western Civilization. During this period in the country's history, especially from 900 on, the use of coinage lapsed almost completely.

The history of modern Ethiopia begins in 1855 with the accession to the imperial throne by Theodore, a military man of vision. Menelik II (1889–1913), who defeated the Italians decisively at the Battle of Adowa in 1895, issued a variety of handsome portrait coins in gold and silver.

Haile Selassie I, long-reigning emperor of Ethiopia (since 1930), is seen on the current silver 50 cent piece. The crowned Lion of Judah is on the reverse.

Haile Selassie I, who has ruled Ethiopia since 1930, has struck a wide range of coins bearing his portrait on obverse and the historic Lion of Judah on reverse.

Liberia was established in 1816 when American abolitionists founded the National Colonization Society of America to set up a homeland in Africa for freed Negroes. The first settlers arrived on the Society's land in 1820. The Society surrendered its title to the land in 1847, when Liberia was recognized as an independent republic.

Liberian currency has been modelled after the U.S. system with 100 cents equal to one dollar. The first coinage, issued by the Colonization Society in 1833, consisted of a series of copper cent tokens showing a naked figure planting a palm tree. Later 19th century issues of one- and two-cent bronze coins had a Liberty Cap obverse reminiscent of early U.S. coins, with a palm tree reverse.

A set of three silver coins (10, 25 and 50 cent values) minted in 1896 and again in 1906, also bear the head of Liberty. Modern coinage has the head of a native girl on the higher denominations, an elephant and coastal scene on the lower values.

South Africa became a factor in world history for the first time when the Dutch succeeded in rounding the Cape of Good Hope in 1487. Settlers from Holland arrived in 1652 and founded a settlement at what was to become Capetown. Following the Napoleonic wars, British settlers began to take up residence. The South African Republic was formed in 1853 by the Boers (Dutch colonists, the term means "farmers" or "peasants") who lived in the Transvaal area. In 1877 Great Britain annexed the Transvaal, but the Boers regained their independence in 1883.

A few gold pieces (now extremely rare) were struck for the Transvaal in the 1870's, but the first substantial series of coins were issued in the 1890's by "Oom" ("uncle") Paul Kruger (1883–1902), the crusty Boer president of the South African Republic.

Paul Kruger, the president of the South African Republic for nearly 20 years, is portrayed on this 1892 bronze penny.

British victory in the Boer War put an end to the South African Republic in 1902. In 1910, the Cape of Good Hope, Natal, and the Orange Free State (and later Transvaal) were formed into the Union of South Africa, a self-governing dominion of the British Commonwealth. All coins of the Union carry the Afrikaans spelling "Zuid-Afrika" ("Suid-Afrika after 1930) as well as the English "South Africa."

In 1961, the country became the Republic of South Africa and withdrew from the British Commonwealth. In this same year the new republic went on the decimal system, with 100 cents equalling one rand (formerly 10 shillings). Current coinage has either English or Afrikaans spellings with approximately equal quantities in each language issued for each denomination.

COLONIAL COINS

The English vied with the French in colonizing Africa during the last half of the 19th century. As late as the first decades of the 1800's the map of most of Africa's interior was not even drawn. Much of the continent remained unexplored. Cecil John Rhodes (1853–1902) was obsessed with the idea of adding a vast domain to the British Empire and establishing a north-south chain of British colonies to be linked by a Cape-to-Cairo railroad. It was due to the daring initiative and fiery ambition of Rhodes that the British established themselves in Northern and Southern Rhodesia.

Southern Rhodesia's 1953 silver crown was issued for the centennial of the birth of empire builder Cecil Rhodes.

Coins of the British colonies in Africa almost always carried the monarch's portrait on the obverse: Queen Victoria, Edward VII, George V, George VI, and Elizabeth II.

British West Africa's copper half-penny of 1936 was issued in the name of Edward VIII who abdicated later that year.

A common coinage for the British West African colonies (Gambia, Sierra Leone, Gold Coast, and Nigeria) and East African territories (Kenya, Tanganyika, Uganda, British Somaliland and Zanzibar) was issued for many years (see chart). Several varieties of these coins were holed.

France, like Great Britain, once maintained a vast system of colonies in Africa. Most of them have now gained their independence. At one time, France's holdings in Africa encompassed several million square miles, much of which, however, was desert and waste land. The French were responsible for many technical achievements in their colonies and they tried to familiarize the natives with French institutions and French culture.

Remaining loyal to the Free French movement during World War II, French Equatorial Africa's 1942 50 centimes portrays a Gallic cock and the Cross of Lorraine.

In 1941, when many governors of French colonies were proclaiming their allegiance to the Nazi-oriented Vichy government, Felix Eboue, brilliant administrator and governor of French Equatorial Africa, refused to follow their example. By his enthusiasm and organizing ability he raised a Free French force of 50,000 men and increased the colony's war production four-fold. Interestingly enough, Eboue, who played such a key role in saving France's African empire during World War II, was a Negro from French Guiana; his soldiers were all African natives. This is one of the key reasons why the new French Constitution of 1946 extended full French citizenship to all inhabitants of French Africa. Under Charles de Gaulle, France allowed most of their African colonies to peacefully achieve their independence.

The great majority of the French colonial coins circulated in Africa were designed and struck at the Paris Mint, often utilizing the same designs for several issues (see chart).

A crowned bust of Italian King Umberto I (1878-1900) is portrayed on Eritrea's dollar-size 5 lire piece dated 1891, one of the handsomest of all colonial coins.

Germany, Italy, and Portugal also produced coins for their African colonies. The money circulated in the Spanish possessions has been a mixture of regular Spanish issues and foreign currencies.

A walking elephant fills the obverse of this Belgian Congo 2 franc piece of 1943.

Germany lost her African possessions after World War I. Nevertheless, the German East African coins issued in the early 1890's under Wilhelm II have the distinction of being the first coins struck by a European power for use in Africa. Coins for German East Africa were produced until 1916, mostly at the Berlin and Hamburg Mints.

Coins issued for German East Africa in the early 1890's were the first coins struck in Africa by a European power for circulation. The gold 15 rupees actually struck at Tabora in Africa features an elephant against the background of Mt. Kilimanjaro. A helmeted Kaiser Wilhelm II appears on the 1910 silver rupee minted in Germany at the Hamburg mint.

Kenya, 1966 2 shillings
President Jomo Kenyatta

Zambia, 1968 20 ngwee
President Kenneth David Kaunda

Rwanda, 1964 5 francs
President Gregoire Kayibanda

Lesotho, 1966 50 licente
King Motlotlehi Moshoeshoe

Guinea, 1959 10 francs
President Sekou Toure

Malawi, 1964 florin
President Hastings Banda

Tanzania, 1966 20 cents
President Julius Kambarage Nyerere

Africa has produced new leaders during the past two decades and many of
them are portrayed on the coinages of the new nations.

Africa ❀ 21

George IV, both King of England and King of Hanover (1820-30), struck this portrait ⅔ taler for Hanover in 1822-29.

Anglo-Hanoverian Coinage

None of the children of Queen Anne of Great Britain survived her and, on her death in 1714, the throne went to Georg Ludwig (1698–1727), elector of Hanover and duke of Brunswick-Luneburg. In addition to their British coinages, the five Hanoverian kings—George I, II, III, and IV and William IV—struck coins for use in their German possessions, Brunswick-Luneburg until 1807, the kingdom of Hanover from 1813 until 1837.

Many of the coins have the portrait of the king and the British coat-of-arms though the style is distinctly German. Sometimes the king's monogram or coat-of-arms appeared on the obverse rather than his portrait. The value is shown on the reverse and the denominations are pfennigs, groschen, gulden and talers.

When Queen Victoria came to the British throne in 1837, the German possessions passed to her male relatives, since the Salic Law in effect in Germany stated that no female could rule.

This 1836 Hanover Taler shows the combined arms of Great Britain and Hanover. William IV (1830-37), used the same arms and portrait on his British gold and silver pieces.

Arab States

IRAN (PERSIA)

Located in Western Asia on the Persian Gulf between the Tigris and Indus Rivers, Iran was known as Persia until 1935. One of the oldest countries in the world, Persia maintained a mighty empire in ancient times. A constitutional monarchy since 1906, the country is now important for its large oil reserves.

The coinage of Iran is dated according to the Mohammedan calendar. In 1877–78, a monetary reform was effected by Shah Nasir-ad-Din (1848–96) and milled coins were issued for the first time; previously, all Persian coins were struck by hammer. Between 1500 and 1877, about 120 provincial mints operated at various times throughout the country, many of them being almost completely independent of central government control. The number of coin varieties produced in Persia during this period runs into the tens of thousands. As part of the monetary reform, the Imperial Persian Mint at Teheran, the capital, was modernized and some coins were struck at European mints, including Berlin, Birmingham and Brussels.

The lion with sword badge of Iran appears on the reverse of Mohammed Riza Pahlevi's portrait 10 rials of 1966.

In accordance with Moslem tradition, the Persian Shahs did not picture themselves on their coinage until recent times, the first portrait piece being a gold 2 tomans minted by Nasir-ad-Din, in 1854.

After Ahmed Shah Mirza (1909–25), the last ruling member of the Kajar Dynasty, was overthrown by Riza Khan, who founded the Pahlevi Dynasty, a new coinage was instituted. The new currency is based on 100 dinars equalling a rial with 20 rials to the pahlevi.

Riza Shah Pahlevi (1925–41) appears on both his gold and silver coins, but his son, Mohammed Shah, is portrayed on gold pahlevis only from 1952 onwards.

A child portrait of young King Faisal II (1939-58) appears on Iraq's scalloped edge 10 fils of 1943.

IRAQ

Iraq, known to the Greeks and Romans as Mesopotamia, corresponds to ancient Assyria and Babylonia, the area encompassing the oldest world civilizations. Part of the Turkish Empire until World War I, Iraq became a British Mandate in 1920. The Mandate ended in 1932 when Iraq became independent. It was a monarchy from 1921–58 when an army revolt and the assassination of King Faisal II resulted in the creation of a republic.

This silver 100 fils showing the Iraqi arms is part of a new regular coinage issued in 1959 under the military republic.

JORDAN

Jordan, part of the Ottoman Empire from the 16th century until 1918, came under a League of Nations Mandate in 1922 as Transjordan. In 1923, Great Britain recognized Transjordan as an independent state under British tutelage within the League of Nations mandates system. Full sovereignty was achieved in 1946.

Jordan issued its first coinage in 1949 based on 1000 fils to the dinar or pound. Its coins have been struck at the London Mint.

Jordan's first series of coins, six values from 1 to 100 fils minted in 1949-66, show the values in both Arabic and Western numerals. The bronze 5 fils portraying King Hussein I (1952-) is part of the new 1968 series.

24 ❧ Arab States

The famous Cedars of Lebanon are represented on this Lebanese 50 piastres of 1929, with a cornucopia shown on the reverse.

LEBANON

Lebanon, in Asia Minor on the Mediterranean coast, was formerly part of the Turkish Empire, and came under French mandate from 1920 until 1944 when it became an independent state.

The piastre was adopted as Lebanon's monetary unit with 100 piastres equalling one lira or pound.

An ancient galley with banks of oars is featured on the reverse of Lebanon's 1925 5 piastres. Lebanon, at the eastern end of the Mediterranean, was once part of ancient Phoenicia.

MUSCAT AND OMAN

Muscat and Oman, an independent sultanate at the southeastern tip of the Arabian peninsula, was under Portuguese rule from 1508 and fell under Persian influence after 1648. The Persians left in 1741, and Muscat and Oman is now independent under British protection.

Sultan Fessul Bin Turkee issued a copper coinage in the 1890's, but coinage then lapsed until 1940. The present monetary system is based on 200 baizah (a Muscat pice) equalling 1 ryal. The ryal is also equivalent to the Maria Theresa taler which circulated for many years in the sultanate.

The square-shaped 20 baizas of 1940, issued by Sultan Sa'id Ben Taimur (1932-) carries the crossed dagger arms of Muscat and Oman.

Arab States ❧ 25

SAUDI ARABIA

Although for centuries the Ottoman Turks nominally controlled the Arabian peninsula, much of the land was actually governed by local potentates. Ibn Saud III, Sultan of Nejd, succeeded in overthrowing the last of the Turkish rulers in 1913. By 1926 he completed the conquest of the Kingdom of Hejaz and thereupon consolidated his gains, forming the Kingdom of Saudi Arabia which occupies most of the Arabian peninsula.

Arabia's coins are all dated according to the Moslem calendar. The kingdom's monetary system since 1926 has been based upon the silver ryal, which is divided into 22 girsh. Coins bearing girsh values are struck in copper-nickel.

Since Saudi Arabia does not have a mint of its own, its coins have been struck at various world mints, including Birmingham, London, Philadelphia, Bombay, and Mexico City.

The kingdom's modern gold coins include the guinea (or Saudi pound) values issued in 1951 and 1957–58. In 1945–47, the Philadelphia Mint also struck gold discs for Arabia, equal to one and four British sovereigns in weight.

Saudi Arabia's intricately designed silver ryal of 1928 (A.H. 1346) has Arabic inscriptions with swords and pine trees. Arabian coins do not carry portraits.

(Left) Syria's 1929 50 piastres, struck under French mandate, bears the obverse inscription "Etat de Syrie," State of Syria. (Right) The 1950 lira of the independent nation displays an eagle.

SYRIA

Syria, in Western Asia and bordered by Turkey in the north, was ruled by the Ottoman Turks from 1517 to 1918. Syria was placed under French mandate in 1920 and joined with Lebanon in a customs union. On January 1, 1944, Syria became an independent republic and the customs union was cancelled in 1950. Syria joined Egypt as part of the United Arab Republic on February 21, 1958, but broke away and declared itself independent again on September 29, 1961.

Yemen's 1963 1 ryal (imadi) has the same amount of silver as the Maria Theresa taler.

YEMEN

Yemen, formerly an independent feudal kingdom on the Red Sea, became a republic in 1962. Since 1923 the major unit of coinage has been the imadi of 40 bogaches. Forty bogaches also equal one Maria Theresa taler, a coin that has circulated in the country for many years, especially in the mountain regions. Yemen maintains its own mint at Sana, one of its two capitals (the other is Taiz). All coins are dated according to the Moslem calendar.

Arab States ⊛ 27

Argentina's first coin as an independent state is this interesting 8 reales of 1813 showing a beaming sun face. The reverse has the country's new coat-of-arms, two hands holding a staff surmounted by the Cap of Liberty.

Argentina

.Argentina achieved independence between 1810–16, but conflicts between the Federalists and the Centralists persisted until 1880, resulting in a widely varied provincial coinage. The first coins for an independent Argentina were struck at the Potosi Mint in 1813 and were inscribed "Provincias del Rio de la Plata." The gold escudos and silver reales portrayed the radiant sun with human features on the obverse, the Nation's arms on the reverse.

General Manuel de Rosas, dictator of Argentina in 1835-52, is portrayed on this silver 2 reales coin of 1842.

A few years after liberation, the notorious General Juan Manuel de Rosas, a Federalist, became dictator of Argentina as "protector of the poor and persecutor of the rich." The period from 1835 to 1852 is known as the era of "Bloody Rosas." Becoming more and more tyrannical, he was finally deposed in the latter year. In 1836, Rosas changed the name of the state to "Republica Argentina Confederada." Rosas' portrait was carried on both gold and silver coins during this era.

The striking of a national coinage stopped almost completely after Rosas' overthrow until a new decimal coinage was decreed in 1881. During those 30 years, banknotes filled the gap as the chief circulating medium. The new decimal coins were struck at a modern new mint in Buenos Aires. The basic unit was the silver peso equalling 100 centavos.

Argentina's 5 pesos gold piece of 1885 bears a representation of Liberty similar to that on several French coins.

Argentina's last gold coins, $2\frac{1}{2}$ and 5 peso values, were produced in the 1881–96 period. They portray the head of Liberty on the obverse. The country's last fine-silver pieces were minted in 1881–83. No coins of either gold or silver have been struck at Buenos Aires during the 20th century. In 1896, the 5, 10 and 20 centavo values, struck in copper-nickel, had the Liberty head and value. These were the chief coins until 1942. In that year they were modernized and minted in aluminum-bronze until 1950.

The design of the 1813 8 reales coin is repeated on this 25 pesos piece of 1964.

The centennial of San Martin's death was marked in 1950 by an issue of 5, 10 and 20 centavos pieces bearing the general's portrait. Since the early 1950's, steel has been used in most of Argentina's coins, first copper-nickel-clad steel, and then nickel-clad steel. In the early 1960's, 12-sided 5, 10 and 25 pesos values were added. The sesquicentennial of the declaration of Argentina's independence was marked by the issue of a 10 peso commemorative in 1966.

Argentina's current 5 and 10 peso pieces depict the sailing frigate *President Sarmiento*, and a gaucho, one of the famous cowboys of the pampas.

Argentina ❧ 29

Asia Minor

LYDIA

The Kingdom of Lydia, which lay at the edge of the Aegean Sea along what is now the coast of Turkey in Asia Minor, issued the world's first coins sometime between 700 and 650 B.C. The Lydians hit upon the idea of shaping precious metals into convenient-sized pieces of fixed weight and purity and stamping them with official symbols. This overcame the time-consuming practice of weighing and testing the purity of the metal every time it changed hands. The earliest pieces were crude, bean-shaped lumps of electrum, a pale yellow, natural alloy of gold and silver found in the sands of rivers.

This lump of electrum from Lydia is attributed to the 7th century B.C. Stamped with symbols, it is an example of the world's first known coinage.

Writing about 430 B.C., Herodotus, the Greek historian, acknowledged the Lydians as "the first people we know of to strike coins of gold and silver." Lydia was an important focus of trade, being just at the head of caravan routes to India toward the East and having access by sea to all of the lands bordering the Mediterranean. The Lydian kings were fabulously rich, their wealth coming from the country's natural resources of gold and silver, as well as from the profits of commerce.

Pure gold stater issued by the fabled King Croesus of Lydia (560-546 B.C.), whose reputation for great wealth is still with us in the expression "rich as Croesus."

The first pure gold coins were minted during the reign of King Croesus of Lydia (560–546 B.C.) whose name is still used as a standard for great wealth. Croesus' coins show the facing heads of a lion and a bull, symbols of royal power. The reverse had just the simple indentation of a rectangular punch.

These early coins were made by placing a heated lump of metal, adjusted to the proper weight, on top of an anvil engraved with a die for the obverse design. A punch, held by hand against the piece of metal, was hit with a hammer forcing the metal into the die. The impression left by the lower die in the anvil was the obverse design standing out in relief on the coin; the rough end of the punch produced the incuse mark on the reverse.

PERSIA

Croesus lost his throne around 546 B.C. to the Persians led by Cyrus the Great who took over his mint as well. Ancient Persia was perhaps the first major power to issue gold and silver coins for wide circulation. Darius the Great, who ruled from 521 to 485 B.C., in his efforts to consolidate his empire established a standard coinage based principally upon gold.

The gold daric (after Darius, from the Persian *dara*, a king) shows on the obverse a kneeling bearded figure of the king with a spear, bow and a quiver of arrows on his back; the reverse is a rough incuse square.

Gold daric (left) and silver siglos (right) of King Darius the Great of Persia (521-485 B.C.). Production ran into the millions and the silver pieces are still available to today's collectors at modest prices.

The silver version of the daric is called a siglos. One gold daric is believed to have been a month's pay for a Persian soldier. The production of this coin was enormous as records show one military expedition alone was provided with 4 million gold darics! The output of the silver siglos also ran into the many millions. These two coins dominated the economy of Asia Minor for two centuries until the next conquest of Persia by Alexander the Great. Not too many ancient Persian coins have come down to us, however, as they were melted down and recoined by the conquering armies.

IONIA

In this early period of coinage history, the coins of Asia Minor are generally included under the broad heading of Greece. The issues of Greece proper (or Ionia as it was called in ancient times) were really autonomous coinages however. Ionia was that portion of the west coast of Asia Minor, adjoining the Aegean Sea and bounded on the east by Lydia. It consisted basically of a narrow strip of land near the coast, which together with the adjacent islands, was settled by immigrant

Greeks. Originally, there were 12 Ionian cities. They were (from south to north): Miletus, Myus, Priene, Ephesus, Colophon, Lebedus, Teos, Erythrae, Clazomenae and Phocaea, together with Samos and Chios. All of them minted coins although in some cases not until many years after their founding.

Ionia's earliest coins, minted in the late seventh and early sixth centuries B.C., are electrum specimens, usually uninscribed. Electrum issues were replaced by a silver coinage that continued down toward the end of the fourth century B.C., when small bronze coins gradually replaced the silver.

Chios: silver tetradrachm c. 400-336 B.C., showing sphinx, amphora and grapes. In Greek mythology, the sphinx is an enigmatic monster with wings, a lion's body and the head and bust of a woman.

Clazomenae: silver tetradrachm c. 400-336 B.C. displaying a remarkable, full face head of Apollo. Apollo was the god of sunlight, prophecy, music, poetry and manly beauty.

Colophon: silver drachm c. 480-400 B.C. with profile head of Apollo. The reverse pictures a lyre in an incuse square.

Ephesus: silver tetradrachm c. 400-336 B.C. carrying a life-like representation of a bee. The reverse has a stag representing Artemis, sister of Apollo, the virgin huntress and patron goddess of the city.

Erythrae: silver tetradrachm c. 336-280 B.C. portraying Herakles (or Hercules) in a lion's skin headdress. A bow in its case, a club and an owl are on the reverse.

Lebedus: silver tetradrachm c. 190-100 B.C. with the helmeted head of Athena, an owl on the reverse.

Miletus: silver didrachm c. 280-190 B.C. showing Apollo. On the reverse is a lion looking backward at a star.

Samos: silver tridrachm c. 400-336 B.C. bearing a lion's scalp. The reverse scene shows the infant Herakles strangling serpents.

Teos: silver stater c. 544-394 B.C. depicting a griffin with forepaw raised above a bearded mask. The griffin is a mythological creature having the head and wings of an eagle on the body of a lion.

Australia

Australia, the "Land Down Under," has a colorful history as a nation, a history that has been graphically portrayed on its coins. This huge island continent nearly the size of the United States, was sighted by Portuguese sailors as early as the 1530's, but there are no records of actual landings. The generally accepted year for the beginning of Australian history is 1606 when a Spanish navigator, Luis Vaez de Torres, sailed through the island-dotted strait, between Australia and New Guinea, that still bears his name. No serious exploration was done, however, until the time of Captain James Cook, one of the greatest navigators of all time. Captain Cook, in 1770, charted much of the Australian coast and claimed the eastern part of the sub-continent for his King, George III.

The only people populating the island were wild bands of aborigines living under Stone Age conditions. Captain Cook and his men were even more fascinated by the many kinds of strange animals living in Australia. Some of these strange creatures appear on Australian coins. Foremost among these is the kangaroo which, like many Australian animals, carries its young in a pouch. Kangaroos come in many sizes and varieties and can outrun all but the fleetest horses and have been known to jump 40 feet.

Associated with the kangaroo on the Australian coat-of-arms is the emu, an ostrich-like bird almost six feet tall. Unable to fly, it can reach a speed of 40 miles per hour with its long muscular legs. The Australian coat-of-arms consists of the kangaroo and emu standing on either side of a shield. The shield itself has six devices, each representing one of the original colonies. This unique coat-of-arms has been inscribed on many of the country's coins.

Australia's numismatic history begins in 1788 when England officially opened New South Wales as a penal colony. Free settlers came also and the need for circulating coins and banknotes grew. The currency circulating in Australia in those early days was very "cosmopolitan." Spanish silver dollars were brought over in large quantities because they were regarded as a kind of international currency. British and Irish banknotes were used, together with coins from many parts of the world, including Portuguese joannas, Indian mohurs and rupees, Ceylonese pagodas, Dutch guilders and ducats.

Nevertheless, all these currencies combined were not adequate to serve the country's growing economy. England was hard pressed to supply the colony with sufficient coin because of a shortage of its own due to the wars against Napoleon. Promissory notes, or I.O.U.'s, were tried for a time, but these were often misused. Finally, in 1812, England sent over 40,000 Spanish dollars. Previously, many of the coins brought into Australia had gone out again in trading ships and thus lost to the colony as a circulating medium of exchange.

Governor Lachlan Macquarie was determined that these coins stay in Australia. He ordered, therefore, that the middle of each dollar was to be punched out, leaving a ring and a "dump" (the center of the original coin). The two new pieces were valued at 5 shillings and 15 pence respectively so that together they were worth 6s. 3d. compared to the dollar's original value of 4s. 9d. This was profitable to the government and the new pieces easily identifiable in the event of any attempt at exportation.

The Australian "Holey Dollar," a Spanish piece of eight with the center cut out, was used as a necessity coin. The cut out piece, known as a "dump" or "bit," was overstruck with new designs and inscriptions and valued at 15 pence.

The ring dollar, later named the "holey dollar," was overstruck with the inscription "New South Wales 1813" on the obverse and "five shillings" on the reverse. This same scheme for making ring dollars was used in other British colonies as well.

Gold discoveries in Australia during the second half of the nineteenth century attracted thousands of new settlers. One result was the establishment of three new mints. While their function at first was to mint gold coins only, they later struck silver and copper pieces as well. The Sydney Mint, Australia's first coin-striking facility, was opened in 1855 and operated for 71 years. The gold sovereign struck at Sydney in 1855 is the first coin to have actually been produced in Australia. The Melbourne Mint was established in 1872, and the Perth Mint in 1899, following the Western Australian gold rush in the South Kalgoorlie region.

Australia • 35

Australia's two shillings (or florin) struck in 1910 shows the national coat-of-arms supported by a kangaroo and an emu.

One of Australia's rarest coins, the 1930 penny, catalogues for nearly $500.00. Only about 1,500 specimens were released.

Over the years, however, Australian mint facilities were often not able to meet the demands for coins and officials had to call on foreign mints to satisfy the country's full requirements. Coins were produced for Australia at the Bombay and Calcutta Mints in India, at London's Royal Mint, and at the Denver and San Francisco Mints in the United States. In early 1965, Australia opened an ultra-modern mint at Canberra, a facility that has been designed to produce over 300 million coins per year. The Melbourne and Perth Mints continue to operate as branches of Canberra. The earlier mint facilities were classified as branches of the Royal Mint of Great Britain but the Canberra Mint is being operated independently by the Australian Parliament. Australia remains a Dominion of the British Commonwealth.

A rider on horseback adorns the reverse of the George V 1935 silver florin commemorating the 100th anniversary of settlement at Melbourne, Victoria.

36 ❧ Australia

Leaping kangaroos are shown on the George VI pennies and halfpennies of 1938-52. Using his powerful hind legs and long thick tail, the kangaroo makes leaps of more than 40 feet. The head of a merino ram is depicted on the silver shillings.

Australia changed to decimal coinage in February 1966, with 100 cents equal to 1 dollar. The Canberra Mint struck six new coins for the occasion. Queen Elizabeth II, the British sovereign, is featured on the obverses. The reverses show the following designs: 50 cents, Australian coat-of-arms; 20 cents, platypus; 10 cents, lyre bird; 5 cents, spiny anteater; 2 cents, frilled lizard; and 1 cent, feather-tail glider or flying mouse.

Australia minted six new values when decimal coinage began in 1966. All the obverses show Queen Elizabeth II wearing a diamond tiara. The reverses show some of Australia's unusual animals: 50 cents, kangaroo and emu; 20 cents, platypus; 10 cents, lyre bird; 5 cents, spiny anteater; 2 cents, frilled lizard; and 1 cent, feather-tail glider or flying mouse.

Australia ❧ 37

Undated gold gulden of Albert II, 1330-58, Austria's first gold coinage.

Austria

Now a relatively small republic in central Europe, Austria was for centuries one of the major European powers. The region of Austria was inhabited by uncivilized tribesmen many centuries before the birth of Christ. Roman authority penetrated here early in the second century B.C. The Romans founded a series of military camps within the present boundaries of Austria, one of them at "Vindobona," the site of modern Vienna.

Later, as an eastern rampart of the Carolingian realm established about A.D. 800, this mid-Danubian area guarded against pagan marauders from the East. The region was known as "Marca Orientalis," (the eastern mark) to the Romans or the "Osterreich" (Austria) in the Germanic tongue of the inhabitants.

Under Leopold I, who was appointed ruler of Austria in 976 by Holy Roman Emperor Otto II, Austria began its rise to power. In the meantime, an obscure Swiss family, named Hapsburg for its home, Habichtsburg ("hawk's castle") first appeared in European history in about 900. By means of advantageous marriages to royalty, the family kept adding to its holdings. In 1282, Austria was acquired by the House of Hapsburg and became the center of its domains. Rudolf I, head of the family at the time, was the first Hapsburg to become Holy Roman Emperor, reigning from 1273 until his death in 1291. And from 1438 until 1806, all of the Holy Roman Emperors were Hapsburgs.

A distinct Austrian coinage began toward the end of the eleventh century in the form of uninscribed deniers, often in semi-bracteate form

Undated silver groschen struck at Hall in the Tyrol by Archduke Sigismund (1446-90).

and frequently of a distinctive square shape with rounded corners. A variety of birds, dogs and crosses were represented on these early coins of Austria.

Austria had its first gold coinage when Albert II (1330–58) issued a series of undated goldguldens. The obverse had a standing portrait of St. John, while the reverse bore a lily. Rudolph IV (1358–65) also struck a similar goldgulden coinage.

During the early Middle Ages and the early Renaissance, the Hapsburgs enlarged the boundaries of Austria, of which they were hereditary archdukes. Some of them were also elected Kings of Bohemia and Hungary, and in time the Hapsburgs incorporated both these countries into their empire.

Maximilian I, Holy Roman Emperor 1493-1519, and his bride, Marie of Burgundy, are portrayed on their famous Wedding taler struck in 1479. This unusual coin proclaims the ages of the bride and groom— Maximilian was 19, Marie 20.

Austria issued some of Europe's earliest silver talers and Europe's first dated coins. Crown-sized silver coins made their first appearance in Tyrol, bearing in Arabic numerals the date, 1486. These coins, along with some smaller, thicker trial specimens dated 1484, are the first example of dating on European coinage. The obverse portrays a standing figure of Archduke Sigismund while the reverse displays a mounted figure of the archduke in armour within a border of shields of the Hapsburg possessions.

Maximilian (1493–1519) is credited with having introduced Austria's modern coinage with the goldgulden and silver talers forming the foundation. The gold pieces usually portray St. Leopold (early ruler of Austria and benefactor of the church) on the obverse and arms consisting

of five shields on the reverse. The talers have a reverse similar to the gold coins, but the obverse shows the half-length portrait of Maximilian crowned, holding a sceptre and sword.

The Hapsburgs reached the height of their powers when they intermarried with the ruling family of Spain. Through his Hapsburg father and Spanish mother, Charles V in 1516 inherited the rule of Spain, Austria, the Netherlands (modern Holland and Belgium), Burgundy, and parts of Italy, as well as colonies in Africa and the Mediterranean, and the vast colonial empire of Spain in the New World. He was elected Holy Roman Emperor in 1519. Never had so much widespread power been concentrated in one man but holding together this enormous Empire taxed even his considerable abilities. Charles V is represented on many coins, and on all of them he looks weary.

Parts of Austria were under the control of princes of the Church. Salzburg's archbishops issued coins from the 11th until the 19th century. Many such as this 1513 klippe ¼ taler of Leonard Keutschback (1495-1519) show St. Rupert, the founder of the bishopric, with the Archbishop's arms on the reverse.

This undated taler carries an armored bust of Ferdinand I, Holy Roman Emperor 1556-64. Ferdinand also ruled as King of Austria 1527-56 during which time Vienna was beseiged by the Turks under Sultan Suleiman the Magnificent. The coin at right is a 1529 6 kreuzer emergency issue clipped from silver plate and crudely stamped to provide money to pay the defending troops.

In 1522, Charles V placed his energetic brother Ferdinand I in charge of the eastern part of the Empire, which included Austria. Ferdinand issued a wide variety of gold pieces, including square klippe types that were struck in 1529 during the Turkish siege against Vienna. From 1526 to 1560, he struck portrait pieces (2, 6, 8 and 12 ducat values) with the double eagle on reverse. When Charles V retired because of sheer exhaustion in 1556, Ferdinand replaced him as Holy Roman Emperor (see "Holy Roman Empire" for succeeding rulers).

The local rule of various Hapsburg lands was often parceled out to brothers of the Holy Roman Emperors. This 1626 double taler from Tyrol was struck by Archduke Leopold (1619-32), youngest brother of Emperor Ferdinand II, who also carried the title Archduke of Austria.

Austria ❧ 41

This Vienna Mint taler of 1751 shows a youthful portrait of Empress Maria Theresa. The Austrian coat-of-arms, a silver fess (bar) on a white shield, is surrounded by the arms of her other territories on the reverse.

Maria Theresa (1740–80) ranks as one of the greatest of all Austrian rulers. Daughter of Emperor Charles VI, wife of Emperor Francis I, she was also the mother of Emperors Joseph II (1780–90) and Leopold II (1790–92). While she was a reigning monarch for no less than 40 years, she still found time to become the mother of 16 children! One of her daughters was the ill-fated Marie Antoinette of France. At her father's death, Maria Theresa was crowned ruler of Austria-Hungary and Bohemia. Her reign, however, was marked by almost continuous conflict, including her involvement in the War of the Austrian Succession and the Seven Years' War.

Although dated 1780, the coin illustrated here was actually struck in the 20th century. Maria Theresa's silver taler has been struck for almost 200 years without change.

Maria Theresa's taler dated 1780 is the most famous of all the Austrian crowns—in fact, it is one of the world's most noted coins. They were circulated all over the Levant, the Middle East, and north and east Africa, particularly Ethiopia. They were so popular, that up until recent times natives of these countries refused to accept any other coin. The Austrian Mint continued to strike the Maria Theresa talers long after the abdication of the last Hapsburg Emperor; nevertheless, all the talers have been dated 1780 regardless of the year in which they were minted. While the Vienna Mint has struck the majority of the Maria Theresa talers, they have also been produced at mints in London, Brussels and Bombay. Italy's Rome Mint also issued the famous taler for use in Ethiopia after the conquest of that country by Mussolini's forces in the mid-1930's.

Maria Theresa issued numerous other types of silver and gold coins during her long reign. She is reputed to have been an avid numismatist herself and helped to build Austria's national numismatic collection at Vienna into one of the world's finest.

Francis II, last of the Holy Roman emperors (1792-1806), is portrayed on Austria's silver 20 kreuzer dated 1806.

Napoleon's victory at Austerlitz in 1805 ended the Holy Roman Empire of which Austria had been the central force. Despite the heavy losses suffered during the Napoleonic Wars, the Hapsburgs were still left with sizable domains. They controlled a large number of Magyars, Czechs, Italians, Ruthenians, Poles, Slovaks, Croats, Rumanians, and Slovenes. At the Congress of Vienna in 1815, Austria became the leading power in a new German confederacy. However, she faced constant opposition from Prussia and was forced to withdraw from the confederacy after the Seven Weeks' War of 1866. In the following year, Austrian Emperor Franz Joseph I reformed his empire into the Dual Monarchy of Austria-Hungary. In 1882, he played a major role in establishing the Triple Alliance of Austria-Hungary, Italy and Germany.

1854 double taler
Marriage Commemorative

1879 2 florins
Silver Wedding Anniversary

1887 2 florins, Reopening of the Kuttenburg Silver Mines

1900 5 corona
Older Portrait

1908 5 corona
60th Year of Reign

44 ❧ Austria

World War I was set off in the summer of 1914 when Archduke Francis Ferdinand was assassinated in Sarajevo, capital of Bosnia. Since the assassin was a Serbian student, Austria believed this to be part of a conspiracy and sent an ultimatum to Serbia, an ultimatum that Serbia could not accept. The Dual Monarchy declared war, and within a short time most of Europe was in a state of conflict.

Austria's eagerness for war turned out to be folly. At the end of the conflict in 1918, Austria was reduced to about the size of Maine, with all its former subject peoples established in independent nations of their own. The Hapsburg dynasty, which had endured for nearly 650 years, came to an end, and Austria, now little more than a hinterland surrounding the great city of Vienna, became a republic.

A series of commemorative silver 2 schilling pieces honoring Austria's great men was produced during the 1928-37 period. Here are the composers Mozart, Schubert and Haydn.

In 1938 Hitler's Germany absorbed Austria by force and made it a federal division, known as "Ostmark," of the Third German Reich. The country was liberated and occupied by the Allies in May 1945. A decade later in 1955 Austria regained its sovereignty and independence (by the Austrian State Treaty signed by the United States, Great Britain, France, Russia, and Austria) and the last occupation troops left the country. Austria became a member of the United Nations in 1955.

Austria's modern coinage shows a young girl in peasant headdress, one of the famous Lipizaner stallions and some edelweiss flowers.

Austria ❧ 45

Austrian coinage was stopped with the loss of independence in 1938, but was resumed in 1946 after the restoration of the republic. With the resumption of coinage after the war, the Austrian eagle returned as the standard obverse on the zinc 10 groschen, as well as on the aluminum 50 groschen and 2 schilling pieces.

Austria's coins graphically reveal the turbulent history of the past century. Franz Joseph I, the dignified Hapsburg emperor whose 68-year reign (1848–1916) stands as one of the longest in world history, is portrayed on many varieties of coins. Special commemoratives were struck in 1898 to mark the 50th anniversary of his accession to the throne and again in 1908 to celebrate the 60th year of his reign.

An annual series of commemorative 2 schilling coins issued from 1928 through 1937 honored many of Austria's great men. Since 1955, 25 and 50 schilling pieces recalling a wide variety of people and events have been issued regularly.

1955, Reopening of the Bundes-theater.

1956, 200th Anniversary of Birth of Mozart.

1964, Olympic Winter Games at Innsbruck.

1967, 100th Anniversary of the Blue Danube Waltz.

Austrian commemorative 25 and 50 schilling pieces have been issued regularly since 1955. The examples above are representative of the wide range of people and events honored.

The Balkans

The ancient Romans as well as the Byzantines regarded the Balkan Peninsula as an important objective for expansion. This region was also overrun by nomadic tribes pressing out from central Asia. One of these invading peoples, the Ottoman Turks, had the necessary military power and governing skill to conquer virtually all of the Balkans and to rule the area for centuries. It wasn't until after the Balkan Wars of 1912–13 that Turkey was finally driven from most of the peninsula. The countries occupying the Balkan Peninsula today are Albania, Bulgaria, Greece, Rumania, and Yugoslavia, as well as the small remaining part of European Turkey.

Ahmed bey Zogu, a young tribal chieftain, rose to power in Albania after World War I, proclaimed himself president in 1925, and king, as Zog I, three years later.

ALBANIA

Although Albania achieved independence from Turkey in 1912, the outbreak of World War I prevented the immediate establishment of a sovereign state. Albania existed as a republic from 1925 to 1928, as a kingdom under Zog I from 1928 to 1939, and has been a Communist People's Republic since 1946.

During his 11 years on the throne, Zog I issued a series of artistic coins which were struck mostly at the Rome, Vienna and London mints. Since 1946, Albania's coinage has been almost strictly utilitarian in design.

Albania fell under Italian domination at the beginning of World War II. Victor Emmanuel III, King of Italy, is portrayed in a battle helmet on Albania's 1939 2 lek coin.

BULGARIA

The first Bulgarian kingdom was founded in the 7th century, and during the 11th and 12th centuries Bulgaria was part of the Byzantine Empire. The second Bulgarian kingdom flourished until 1396 when the country was brought under Turkish control. Though Bulgaria was liberated from absolute Turkish rule in 1878, it remained a principality under Turkish suzerainty until 1908 when it was again declared an

The Cavalier of Madara, a legendary knight, appears on this 10 leva coin. The date 814 is the year when medieval Bulgaria reached its height of power.

independent kingdom. Boris III (1918–43) ruled as an absolute monarch toward the end of his reign. After World War II, Bulgaria became a Communist People's Republic.

After Bulgaria commenced an independent coinage in 1881, its coins were struck at various European mints, including those at Vienna, Kremnitz, Brussels, Paris, Budapest, London and Belgrade.

The current coins of Bulgaria feature the Bulgarian lion as the central design.

48 ⚬ The Balkans

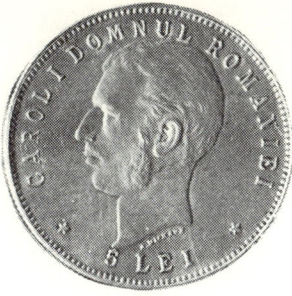

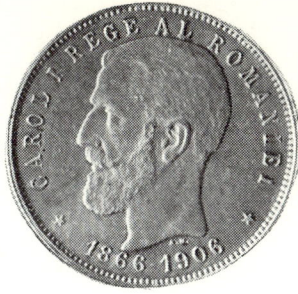

This unusual double-headed coin was issued in 1906 to mark the 40th year of the reign of King Carol I of Rumania. The obverse shows him as he appeared in 1906, the reverse portrays him as he looked in 1866.

RUMANIA

Part of the Roman Empire in ancient times and known as Dacia, Rumania was overrun by Barbarian tribes from the 6th to the 12th centuries. The principalities of Wallachia, founded about 1290, and Moldavia, founded about 1340, were united in 1859 to form Rumania. Independence from Turkey was declared in 1877, the Turks having dominated the affairs of Rumania since the late Middle Ages.

Karl Eitel Friedrich, Prince of Wallachia and Moldavia (1866–81), ascended the throne of the newly-recognized Kingdom of Rumania in 1881 and reigned until his death in 1914. The country suffered heavily in both world wars. After World War II Rumania became a "People's Republic" within the Russian orbit.

Wallachia's first coins consisted of silver groschen struck by Wladislav I of Bessarabia (1360–73). The issues of Moldavia begin with Bogdan I (1348–55), who struck coins in imitation of Polish silver pieces.

Coins of modern Rumania were first issued by Carol I in 1867 while he was still a prince. During the past century Rumanian coins have been produced at a number of European mints, including Brussels, London, Paris, Hamburg and Birmingham.

The current steel 3 lei of Rumania shows an oil refinery on the reverse. The country is a major oil producer in Europe.

The Balkans ❧ 49

Alexander I, King of Yugoslavia (1921-34) and his Queen, Marie, appear in a conjoined portrait on the 4 ducat gold piece of 1932. Alexander, a Serb, was fatally shot by a Croat assassin at Marseilles in 1934.

YUGOSLAVIA

Yugoslavia ("land of the South Slavs") is a good example of the extraordinary intermingling of Balkan cultures and peoples. The South Slavs arrived in this region about 650, and in the course of time were split up among several different rulers. The Kingdom of Serbs, Croats and Slovenes was formed after World War I from Serbia, Montenegro and parts of the former Austro-Hungarian Empire, but did not take the name Yugoslavia until 1929.

After World War II, in 1945, Yugoslavia became a republic headed by Marshal Tito who had led the resistance against the invading Germans. Although a Communist state, it remained outside the Soviet orbit. The country took its new name, Socialist Federal Republic of Yugoslavia, in 1963, when a new constitution was adopted.

Some of the earliest coins produced in the territories now comprising modern Yugoslavia were the silver pieces struck by the Serbian kings Vladislav I (1234-40) and Stephan Uros I (1240-72).

The heads of male and female workers form the design for the reverses of the aluminum-bronze 50, 20 and 10 dinars values of the series of 1955. The obverses all show Yugoslavia's new national arms.

50 ❧ The Balkans

A mounted knight appears on Lithuania's silver ½ groschen of 1549 and again on its modern bronze 5 centai piece of 1936. The ½ groschen was struck for Lithuania by Poland's Sigismund II (1548-72) when Lithuania was a Grand Duchy united with Poland.

The Baltic Countries

Lithuania enjoyed its golden age in the 15th century when it was about three times the size of Poland, sweeping south to the Black Sea and east almost as far as Moscow. In 1795, Lithuania became a province of the Russian Empire.

Most of the Baltic lands were under Russian domination until the time of World War I. For several centuries, however, Lithuania and Poland were closely associated.

Along with Latvia and Estonia, Lithuania was established as an independent nation following the first World War. In 1940 they were all absorbed by the Soviet Union.

The short-lived Republic of Lithuania honored three national heroes on its coins—Grand Duke Vitatas, 15th century military leader; Dr. Jonas Basanivicius, World War I freedom fighter; and Antanas Smetona, its President.

A young girl in peasant costume is shown on Latvia's silver 5 lati of 1931. The coin's reverse has the Latvian arms with lion and griffin supporters.

Latvia flourished as an important trading center on the Baltic, coming under Polish, Swedish and Russian control over the centuries. Russian domination became complete in 1795 and has continued with the exception of the 20 years of independence beginning in 1918.

Estonia marked the 300th anniversary of the University of Tartu in 1932 with a silver 2 krooni piece.

A Viking ship with a dragon head extending from its prow is featured on the aluminum-bronze kroon of 1934.

The Estonians are related to the Finns and their languages are very similar. Sweden, Poland and Russia also contested for possession of Estonia, the Russians gaining complete control in 1721. Estonia, too, became a free nation in 1918, only to be reabsorbed by Russia in 1940.

52 ❧ The Baltic Countries

Belgium

Wedged in by the North Sea and the Netherlands on the north, Germany on the east, and France on the south and west, Belgium has often been caught in the middle during armed conflicts among its bigger and more powerful neighbors.

Belgium's history covers a period of more than 2,000 years. Julius Caesar conquered the Belgic tribes which were probably of Celtic origin . . . he called their country "Gallia Belgica." Belgium formed part of Roman Gaul and then portions of the Merovingian and Carolingian states. During the Middle Ages it was divided into the county of Flanders

This silver gros for the Duchy of Brabant was struck at the Brussels Mint (MONETA BRVXELIENCIS inscribed on the obverse) by Jean I (1272-94). The Duke's title, JOHANNES DVX BRABANTIE, is on the reverse.

and the duchies of Hainaut and Brabant. Flanders was part of the Kingdom of France, while Hainaut and Brabant belonged to the Holy Roman Empire. In the 1300's all these feudal states fell under the control of the Valois dukes of Burgundy and in 1477 they were acquired through marriage by the powerful House of Hapsburg. They remained in the hands of the family, controlled by the Spanish branch until 1700, then by the Austrian branch, until their conquest by Napoleon Bonaparte. During this period, Belgium was known as the "Spanish Netherlands," and subsequently as the "Austrian Netherlands."

Joseph II, Holy Roman Emperor (1765-90), and ruler of all the Austrian dominions, struck this copper liard for Belgium, then known as the Austrian Netherlands, in 1788.

After the Napoleonic Wars in 1815, the Congress of Vienna joined Belgium with Holland to form the Kingdom of the Netherlands. The present state came into being fifteen years later when the Belgians revolted and proclaimed their independence on October 16, 1830, and elected Prince Leopold (of Saxe-Coburg) King of the Belgians.

After Belgium declared its independence from the Netherlands in 1830, Prince Leopold of Saxe-Coburg was elected King of the Belgians. Leopold I, who reigned for 34 years (1831-65) appears on this silver 5 francs dated 1849.

Since two languages are spoken in Belgium, coins issued from 1886 carry both French and Flemish inscriptions or both French and Flemish varieties are struck in approximately equal numbers. Under Leopold III (1934–51) a handsome 50 franc silver piece was struck in 1935 to promote the Brussels Exposition of that year. This coin also commemorated the centennial of the Belgian railway system. Leopold III abdicated the Belgian throne in 1951 in favor of his son Baudouin I.

This 1935 50 franc piece marks the centennial of the Belgian railway system. St. Michael and the dragon are on the obverse.

This silver 100 franc piece of 1948 is dedicated to the Belgian dynasty and shows the heads of four kings: Leopold I, Leopold II, Albert I, and Leopold III.

Perhaps the most outstanding single coin of Baudouin's reign thus far is the 50 franc silver piece minted in 1958 in connection with the Brussels World's Fair. King Baudouin's portrait is on obverse, while the reverse shows the famous Brussels Town Hall and the nuclear symbol of the fair.

Baudouin's marriage to Fabiola De Mora y Aragon in 1960 was marked with a handsome 50 franc silver piece struck at the Brussels Mint in that year. The obverse has the king and queen in dual portrait; the reverse shows the crowned arms of the two royal families.

50 franc silver coins were struck in 1958 on the occasion of the Brussels World Fair. King Baudouin is on the obverse, Brussels' city hall on the reverse. This coin comes in two varieties, one with the legend in French (left), the other with the legend in Flemish (right).

BELGIAN CONGO

From 1887 to 1960, Belgium also struck many coins for the Belgian Congo, its huge African colony. In the latter year, the colony gained its independence and became known as the Republic of the Congo (capital city Kinshasa, formerly Leopoldville). Leopold II founded the Congo Free State as his own personal domain in the early 1880's. Leopold, who was severely criticized for exploiting the natives, gave up his interest in the area in 1908 and allowed the Congo to be annexed to Belgium. The Belgian Congo had an area more than 80 times as great as that of the mother country.

This hexagonal planchet coin with its walking elephant design was struck at the Philadelphia mint during World War II.

Biblical Coins

Both the Old and New Testaments of the Bible have numerous references to money. For example, passages in the Old Testament clearly indicate that the ancients relied on ornaments both as decoration and as a measure of value. When the Israelites left Egypt they took the only portable wealth known to them, ornaments . . . these objects probably had a distinctive weight and possibly were so inscribed. We can read in Exodus 12: 35—*And the children of Israel did according to the word of Moses; and they borrowed of the Egyptians jewels of silver and jewels of gold, and raiment.*

The shekel issued by the Jews during their first revolt against the Romans in A.D. 66-70 shows the golden cup which held manna, the food miraculously supplied to the Israelites in their journey through the wilderness. The reverse has a branch with three pomegranates.

Old Testament references to money are generally expressed in silver or gold by weight. The term "shekel" is found in many sections of the Bible. The shekel as a unit of weight equalled about 9 pennyweight troy or ½ ounce avoirdupois, slightly more than an American silver half dollar. As a unit of weight, the shekel was first used in Assyria and Babylonia, and later adopted by the Phoenicians, Hebrews and other Semitic races. Still later it became the principal silver coin of the Jews.

As a Hebrew coin, it was probably struck at the time of the first revolt in the reign of Nero, in A.D. 66. The obverse bears a chalice, ornamented with gems, and the Hebrew inscription "Shekel of Israel," with the year of the Revolt (one to five). The reverse has a three-branched flower, or rather buds (the supposed "Aaron's rod"), and the Hebrew inscription "Jerusalem Kedushah" (Jerusalem the Holy). Half-shekels were also minted with similar designs.

This silver denarius of the Roman emperor Tiberius, A.D. 14-37, is the "tribute penny" of the Bible.

One of the Roman provinces was Judea, and Octavian, the founder of the Roman Empire, is well known to Bible students as Caesar Augustus from whom in Luke 2:1: "There went out a decree . . . that all the world should be taxed." The tax was payable in Roman coin and the so-called "penny" of the Bible is really the standard Roman denarius. (In England, "d" still stands for "penny" or "pence.") The scholars who prepared the King James version of the Bible in the early 1600's substituted English names for Biblical coins.

A specific reference to money is found in Matthew 22: 15–22 in the story of the Pharisees seeking to entangle Jesus in His own words by asking whether it was lawful to pay tribute to Caesar. Jesus asked them to show Him the tribute money and they brought Him a penny (denarius). Holding it in His hand, He asked them, "Whose image is this and whose superinscription?" They replied, "Caesar's." Then He said to them, "Render therefore unto Caesar the things which are Caesar's; and unto God, the things which are God's." The "tribute penny" was almost certainly a silver denarius of the emperor Tiberius who was ruler of Rome in that year of A.D. 30.

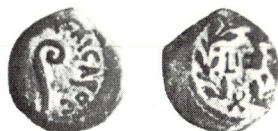

Small bronze coins such as this one attributed to Pontius Pilate c. A.D. 30, are the so-called "widow's mites." This piece shows a wine ladle and three ears of grain.

The most fascinating of the New Testament coins is the "widow's mite." The "mite," or "lepton," was the smallest of the bronze coins known to the Jews. These moneys were frequently mentioned in the New Testament manuscripts as we can read, for example, in Mark 12: 41–44: "And He sat down over against the treasury, and beheld how the multitude cast money into the treasury: and many that were rich cast in much. And there came a poor widow, and she cast in two mites, which make a farthing. And He called unto Him his disciples, and said unto them, Verily I say unto you, This poor widow cast in more than all they that are casting into the treasury: for they all did cast in of their superfluity; but she of her want did cast in all that she had, even all her living."

Pontius Pilate was the Roman governor of Judea at this time so the coins could have been those with his inscription showing a simplum, a ladle used at Roman sacrifices to pour wine into a cup. Similar coins of earlier rulers were undoubtedly still in circulation in the Holy Land during the first century A.D. so the two coins were not even necessarily the same.

For this same reason, the variety of coinage in circulation, the thirty pieces of silver paid to Judas for betraying Christ are thought to have been of more than one type. The most widely used were the silver shekels (also called a tetradrachm) from the Phoenician city of Tyre. This coin with the head of a pagan god, Melkarth, is almost certain to have made up at least part, if not all, of the payment. The thirty pieces of silver probably also included the silver tetradrachm of Antioch.

In connection with the payment of Judas for the betrayal of Christ, the Biblical passage reads: Matthew 26: 15—*And said unto them, what will ye give me, and I will deliver him unto you? And they covenanted with him for thirty pieces of silver.*

The tetradrachm or shekel of Tyre, a large silver coin circulated in Judea during Jesus' time, is believed to have made up at least part of the 30 pieces of silver paid to Judas for his betrayal of Christ. The obverse portrait is of Melkarth, also known as Hercules.

Harsh persecution of the Christians began under the notorious emperor Nero (54–68), who needed someone to blame for the fire which burned Rome in the year 64. Stories of Christians being fed to wild beasts or burned alive are true enough. The Christians were hunted down and often martyred until the reign of Constantine the Great, who in 313 issued the Edict of Milan securing toleration throughout the empire. The legend of Constantine's conversion to Christianity is that before an important battle, a flaming cross appeared to him in the sky with a message, "By this sign, thou shalt conquer." In gratitude for his victory, he embraced the new religion and repealed the cruel decrees against the Christians.

Bolivia's silver 8 sueldos of 1838 shows Simon Bolivar, the country's first president and one of the greatest heroes in Latin American history.

Bolivia

After Peru threw off Spanish rule in 1825, the southern part split off to form a new state, named for the Liberator, Simon Bolivar. The new republic's first silver coins, ½ sol through 8 sueldos values, were struck at the Potosi Mint. Gold pieces were also produced at Potosi. The first set, issued in 1831–40, featured the uniformed bust of Bolivar, while a second set, 1841–47, had a small laureate head of the Liberator.

A new mint at La Paz was finished in 1853 to supplement the work of the Potosi facility. Decimal coinage was introduced in 1863 with the basic unit being the silver peso, or boliviano, divided into 100 centavos. Since 1860, part of Bolivia's coinage has been produced at various world mints, including Birmingham, London, Vienna and Philadelphia.

Many Bolivian coins of the past century feature obverse designs having an oval shield, flanked by flags and surmounted by a condor. Copper centavo specimens minted in 1878 have the condor only on the obverse. A new currency system was introduced in 1961 in which 1000 old bolivianos were made equal to 1 new peso boliviano. The new bronze 10 boliviano of 1951 has the bust of Bolivar. Since 1965, Bolivian coins have been struck in steel. The 5 and 10 centavos values are being produced in copper-clad steel, and the 20 and 50 centavos in nickel-clad steel.

A radiant sun with a human face casts a glow upon a mountain and a llama on Bolivia's nickel 50 centavos of 1965.

Bolivia ə 59

Obverse and reverse of a bracteate denier of Emperor Frederick II (1215-50), struck at Saalfeld in Thuringia. The bracteates were manufactured by hammering a thin piece of silver against a form that stood out in relief. The reverse thus had an incuse mirror image.

(Left) Bracteates of Archbishop Ulrich von Reinstein of Halberstadt (1149-60) and (right) Archbishop Wichman von Seeburg of Magdeburg (1152-92).

Thuringia
1190-1217

Landgrave
Hermann I

Three Medieval bracteates issued by: (left) Henry the Lion (1152-90), Duke of Saxony and Bavaria; (middle) the state of Sigmaringen-Helfenstein, about 1250; and (right) Frederick Barbarossa, Holy Roman Emperor (1152-90), for Thuringen-Altenburg.

60 ❧ Bracteates

The bas relief obverse of this bracteate shows Otto I of Brandenburg (1170-87) holding a sword. The incuse mirror-image reverse (right) shows the sword apparently in his left hand.

Bracteates

Thin silver pennies called "bracteates" appeared in Germany during the early 12th century and circulated widely in Europe until the early part of the 14th century. The name comes from the Latin *bractea* meaning a thin piece of metal. The bracteate planchets were so thin that the design stamped in relief on one side appeared as an incuse mirror image on the other. The metal was hammered between two interlocking dies which may have been made of wood, more easily shaped than metal and strong enough for the extremely thin planchets. The term bracteate itself did not come into general use until the 18th century . . . while the coins actually circulated, they were merely regarded as a form of the denar or silver pfennig.

Bracteates originated in Thuringia and Hesse and though they were also issued in Bohemia, Hungary, Switzerland, Poland and the Scandinavian countries, bracteates are particularly associated with districts that were part of the medieval Holy Roman Empire.

Because of debasement, the regular denar was growing smaller about the time the first bracteates appeared. They may have been intended to look as large as the older coins although no really conclusive explanation

Bracteate designs are of finer artistic style than other coins of their time. The dies may have been of wood, more easily shaped than metal—a good possibility, since they would have been strong enough for the extremely thin planchets. The coin illustrated, of Herman I of Thuringia (1190-1217), is about the maximum width used.

for the issuance of these unusual thin coins is known. They may have been produced for another profit motive, the difference between the intrinsic metal value and the official value of these coins. If the issuing authority refused to redeem damaged coins or accepted them at a discount, the profit would have been considerable. Thus, the bracteates may have been struck so fragiley thin on purpose, in hope of their becoming damaged! Another explanation of their widespread use might be the ease with which they could be made in an age when every coin had to be hammered out by hand.

The artistic appearance of the bracteates is due perhaps to the wider planchets—the die-maker had more space to work out his design. The figures on the bracteates are stylized—there is no attempt to produce a likeness of the person in whose name the coin was issued. The engravers often used a crown and a sceptre to represent a king or a mitre and a crozier to indicate a bishop. Bracteates were issued by emperors, barons, dukes, counts, palatine electors, and by ecclesiastics, churchmen, as well. In the latter case they are known as *pfaffen-pfennige* ("parsons' pennies").

(Left) Silver bracteate of Bishop Adelhog (1170-90) of Hildesheim. (Right) A lion walking appears on a coin of Bernhard III, Duke of Anhalt (1170-1212).

Saints are liberally portrayed on bracteates, either in portraits or as participants in scenes from legends associated with them. Scenes from the scripture as, for example, Adam and Eve in Paradise are also featured on bracteate types. The most common motif on these coins, however, is architecture, chiefly church buildings and city walls and towers. Heraldic designs are also common on these coins.

An interesting proof that, as expected, the coins did not wear well is the fact that no bracteate hoards have been found with more than a thirty-year maximum span between the earliest and latest issued. The bracteates did not completely displace the regular two-sided pfennigs and both styles were often struck simultaneously by the same authorities. By about 1350, the standard coinage had taken over again.

The B in the center of the obverse shows that this 960 reis coin of John, Prince Regent (1799-1816) was struck at the Bahia mint in Brazil. The inscription, SUBA SIGN NATA STAB, means "The land discovered under this sign shall prosper."

Brazil

In 1493–94, Pope Alexander VI assigned to Portugal all unclaimed lands, including those not yet discovered, that lay east of 51 degrees west longitude. Consequently, when Pedro Alvares Cabral, a Portuguese navigator, discovered Brazil in 1500, the region already belonged to Portugal. In 1532 the Portuguese made their first permanent settlement in Brazil, and shortly thereafter King John III granted large tracts of land to Portuguese nobles. Apart from the seizure of several coastal areas by the Dutch between 1624–54, the whole of Brazil remained firmly in Portuguese hands for over three centuries. During the early period of colonization, Brazil's currency requirements were met by use of coinage from Portugal. Toward the end of the 17th century, Spanish colonial coins were countermarked for use in Brazil. The countermarks usually consisted of a small crown with new values. Portuguese coins were also specially countermarked for circulation in Brazil. Brazil's worth as a colony increased considerably when gold was discovered there in 1690.

In 1694, a new coinage for Brazil was decreed by Pedro II. In the following year, a mint was established on the east coast at Bahia, the oldest

A bearded Dom Pedro II (1831-89) appears on this silver 500 reis coin dated 1868. Though personally popular, he was forced to abdicate in 1889 and a republic established.

The 400th anniversary of the discovery of Brazil by Portuguese navigator Pedro Alvares Cabral is commemorated on Brazil's 1900 silver 4,000 reis coin. The reverse displays the shields of Portugal and Brazil.

city in Brazil. This new coinage, consisting of both gold and silver, was modelled after the Portuguese monetary system. In 1699, a good part of the minting operation was transferred to Rio. The first gold pieces struck at the Brazilian mints came in 1000, 2000 and 4000 reis values. The coins bore the arms of Pedro II, while the reverses had the dates (1695 to 1702) and a plain cross in a quadrilobe.

When Napoleon Bonaparte invaded Portugal in 1808, Prince Regent John (later Emperor John VI) fled with his court to Rio de Janeiro. In 1821 he returned to Portugal, leaving his son Dom Pedro (lived 1798–1834) as regent of Brazil. Dom Pedro sympathized with the people's desire for independence and was instrumental in declaring Brazil an independent empire in 1822. He was crowned emperor in that year. Dom Pedro abdicated in 1831 and turned the government over to his five-year-old son, Dom Pedro II, who ruled under a regent until he reached the age of 15 in 1840. Dom Pedro II reigned until 1889 when a republic was formed through a bloodless revolution.

The head of Liberty in a cap is featured on this 1889 coin struck to mark the establishment of the republic in Brazil.

| Santos Dumont Pioneer Aviator | Luiz Alves Duke of Caxias | Father Anchieta Missionary | Diogo Feijo Prince Regent |
| Oswaldo Cruz Microbiologist | Carlos Gomes Composer | Viscount Maua Railroad Builder | Admiral Tamandare Sailor |

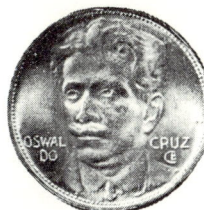

Several of Brazil's outstanding men were honored on the obverses of the coinage issue of 1935-38.

Many of Brazil's modern coins recall the country's long history. A set of four silver pieces minted in 1900 (400, 1,000, 2,000 and 4,000 reis values) commemorate the 400th anniversary of discovery. Another set of four coins, struck in aluminum-bronze in 1922 (two varieties of 500 and 1,000 reis values) mark the centennial of independence. A set of three (100, 200 and 400 reis) produced in copper-nickel in 1932, commemorates the 400th anniversary of colonization by the Portuguese.

Brazil has experienced a number of monetary crises within the past three decades. A currency reform was introduced in 1942 whereby 100 centavos equal 1 cruzeiro. In recent years the value of the cruzeiro has often fallen so sharply that coins have had little value in trade. Paper money in relatively high denominations has had to be utilized even in making "small change."

The map of Brazil is shown on the aluminum 20 cruzeiros of 1965. Brazil covers half the South American continent.

Brazil ❧ 65

Burma's silver rupee, series of 1852-78, shows a peacock, symbol of pride and immortality, with tail outstretched in a fan-like position.

Burma

Burma fell under British influence during the 19th century although native kings were allowed to remain on the throne until 1916. Coinage of the kings of Burma began in 1852 although the actual date on the coins, given in Burmese numerals, was 1214 according to the Chula-Sakarat (C.S.) system which dates from A.D. 638. To convert C.S. to A.D. dates, it is only necessary to add 638 (1214 + 638 = 1852).

Following World War II, Burma became a completely independent republic.

The Burmese lion appears on the scalloped and square planchet pya coins of the 1952 series.

General Aung San, a resistance hero of World War II, is portrayed on the aluminum 50 pyas of 1966. In recent years, Burma's government has been dominated by military leaders.

Byzantine Coinage

The Byzantine Empire survived for more than a thousand years, from the reign of Constantine I the Great (324–37) to the fall of Constantinople in 1453. In A.D. 330, the Roman emperor Constantine moved the seat of the Imperial Government from Rome to Byzantium (from "Byzas," a hero in Greek mythology), which he re-named Constantinople. This divided the Roman world into two empires—the West and East, sometimes called the Greek Empire because its language and culture were Greek. Constantine made the move because of increasing barbarian attacks on Rome.

Byzantine emperors like Anastasius (491-518) used the figure of Victory holding a long cross on the reverses of their gold solidi as a symbol of resistance against the barbarians who threatened the frontiers of the Empire.

A distinct Byzantine coinage dates from the reign of Anastasius I, who ruled from April 11, 491 to July 1, 518. Prior to that time, coins produced in Constantinople are ordinarily considered a part of the Roman coinage. Coins of such emperors as Arcadius (395–408), Theodosius II (408–50) and Leo I (457–74) are arbitrarily listed by dealers as Roman or Byzantine.

The Byzantine Empire varied in its boundaries over the centuries . . . at one time it stretched from Spain to Persia, but its heartland consisted of Asia Minor, Greece and other Balkan countries. By 1050, during the Byzantine era of glory, the Empire included virtually all of the Balkan peninsula, Asia Minor, Crete, Cyprus and southern Italy. Holding back the invading tribes from Asia after the fall of the Western Roman Empire to barbaric invaders, Constantinople kept classical Greek culture alive during the Dark Ages, and it helped to arouse the renaissance of learning in the West.

The greatest of the early Byzantine emperors was Justinian, "the Great" (527–65), who codified the Roman law. The Justinian Code forms the

The gold solidus of Justinian I (527-65) shows a facing portrait of the emperor, typical of Byzantine coinage.

Two bronze coins of Tiberius II (578-82): (left) the 40 nummia and (right) the 30 nummia. The M on the reverse stands for 40, while each of the 3 X's stand for 10. In Byzantium where symbols represented numbers, K equalled 20; IS, 16; IB, 12; H, 8; S, 6; and E, 5.

foundation for modern civil law. He had two great generals: Belisarius, who defeated the Persians and Africans, and Narses, who accomplished the conquest of the Ostrogoths in Italy. The great age of Byzantine art also flourished under Justinian. During his reign the famous church of Hagia Sophia at Constantinople was erected with beautiful marble walls and floors and wonderful mosaics. The Turks later turned this church into a mosque which is still standing today.

Justinian was a master of finance and his activities in this area were made easier since he had a large supply of gold at his disposal. Justinian's gold solidus, a denomination first struck by Constantine the Great, circulated throughout the Empire and beyond it. Its obverse bears the head of the Emperor, while reverse shows victory holding a long cross. As in most Byzantine art, there is an unnatural stiffness about these figures.

The Justinian solidus was struck in such large quantities at the Constantinople Mint that it is easily obtainable today on the numismatic market. The solidus continued as the chief gold coin for centuries, later called a *nomisma* by the Byzantines and known in the West as the *bezant*. This was *the* coin of Byzantium; it was the dollar or pound of the Middle Ages. Additional denominations based on a unit called the "nummia" were introduced at the beginning of the 6th century.

Justinian's coins from 538 to his death in 565 are of great interest since they were almost literally "dated." In 538, the twelfth year of his reign, he ordered that the regal year be placed to the right of the reverse denomination mark and the word "ANNO" (year) to the left. The numerals, therefore, run from XII through XXXIX, when his tenure in office ended in 565. This is significant in the history of numismatics for, actually, the first European coins were not dated until the 14th century.

Though the Empire's chief mint was located at Constantinople, a variety of other mints operated through its long history. Since each of these coin-striking facilities put its own distinctive mint marks on many of their issues, especially bronze coins, individual specimens can be attributed to specific mints as well as emperors. The following table identifies the mints and their marks:

AAE	Alexandria	NC	Nice
ANT	Antioch	NE	Naples
CAR	Carthage	NI	Nicomedia
CAT	Catania	R	Rome
CON	Constantinople	RA	Ravenna
ISAUR	Isauria	SCL	Sicily
KVIIP	Cyprus	TC or TES	Thessalonica
KY or KVZ	Cyzicus	THEV	Theopolis
ML	Milan	XEP	Cherson

A religious atmosphere prevailed in the Byzantine Empire. The sacred emblems of the Christian Church such as the cross and Christogram (intertwined letters X and P, equivalent to CH and R in Greek, the beginning letters of Christ's name) are frequently found on the reverse of the coins. Justinian II (685–711) first used the portrait of Christ on his coins, and the Virgin Mary appears on later issues.

The Virgin Mary appears with the ruler on these gold solidi of Theodora (1055-56) and Romanus III (1028-34). On the reverse sides Christ is seen standing and enthroned.

Byzantine bronze coinage degenerated steadily during and following the reign of Phocas (602–10) and many of the issues are extremely crude. John F. Lhotka, a specialist on the series, states: "Legends are corrupted (misspelled), unintelligible, and frequently off the flan."

The Greeks and Romans centuries earlier had minted coins of extraordinary beauty, but by the seventh and eighth centuries, many of the coins issued were back to primitive levels. It must be noted, however, that there were numerous periods in Byzantine history in which coins of high aesthetic quality were struck. If it had not been for Byzantine scholars, many of the Greek and Roman literary classics would have been lost forever because they were not preserved by Western Europe during the centuries after the fall of Rome.

Although Christ's portrait on the coins of Justinian II (685–711) resembled a line drawing, it was improved upon in later centuries. One of the most famous of all the Christ portrait coins is the gold solidus struck in 869–79 while the emperor Basil I, "The Macedonian," was in power. Christ is shown seated on a throne, the right hand raised in benediction; the left hand holds a book of the Gospels. The full-face pose, rare in most coinage, is characteristic of Byzantine issues. This particular specimen was produced in such great numbers and so many have been preserved that it can be easily obtained even today for about $25.00. The heads of Christ and the Virgin resemble the mosaics in the church of St. Sophia.

Basil II (976-1025), the "Bulgar-Slayer," is seen in dual portrait on this gold solidus with his co-ruler and brother Constantine VIII. Christ is on the reverse.

Basil II (976–1025), called the "Bulgar-Slayer," is considered the greatest ruler of medieval Byzantium. He expanded the Empire's borders considerably by annexing part of Armenia, and in the Balkans he subjugated the Bulgarian Empire by completely crushing the Bulgarian army. Since he was in power for nearly a half-century, he struck a great many coins. One of the most interesting is a gold piece showing Basil in a dual portrait with his brother Constantine VIII who was his co-emperor at the time, later succeeding him to the throne. The American Numismatic

Society Museum in New York City has this specimen on display . . . in fact, the A.N.S. research collection of Byzantine coins is one of the largest in the world.

During the 11th century, a new saucer-shaped or "scyphate" coin came into use. The gold planchets were quite thin, providing maximum diameter for the given weight. These were struck between two dies, one concave, the other convex. The unusual shape gave rigidity to the thin planchets, besides allowing them to be stacked easily so that many coins could be fitted into small packages.

The scyphates remained in circulation for at least 200 years. While gold was used almost exclusively for the earlier scyphates, electrum and bronze were employed later for this type of coinage. Byzantine coins are unique in this respect for no other empire or country ever made coins in such an unusual shape.

The unusual saucer shape of this scyphate nomisma of John II (1118-43) gave strength to the thin planchet on which it was struck.

The Empire was under constant pressure from Turkish invaders for several centuries. By 1356 these invaders crossed into Europe and gradually conquered the Balkan Peninsula except for Constantinople and a small region around it. On May 29, 1453, Constantinople itself was captured by the Ottoman Sultan Mohammed II, and the last emperor, Constantine XI himself fell in the fighting. The final Byzantine emperor to have struck coins was John VIII (1425–48) as Constantine XI is not known to have produced any coinage.

The quantity of coins struck by the Byzantine emperors was so tremendous that great hoards of these coins are still being uncovered in our time, which makes many of these centuries-old coins available to collectors for very little cost. Most of the freshly unearthed coins find their way to the famous Grand Bazaar in Istanbul (the Turkish name for Constantinople) and from there to all parts of the world.

Canada

In 1497, only five years after Christopher Columbus' first voyage, his fellow Genoese John Cabot discovered Newfoundland ("new-found-land"). Cabot, who was a merchant as well as an explorer, sailed in British service, and thus Newfoundland became the first colony ever acquired by the British Empire, although the English did not immediately follow up the discovery with the establishment of permanent settlements. Cabot, like Columbus, mistakenly thought he had reached the domains of the Great Khan of China.

In the meantime, the French arrived on the scene. In 1534 Jacques Cartier discovered the St. Lawrence River and founded New France. He began serious trading with the Indians with the result that the enormously profitable fur trade became the keystone of Canada's early economy. Beaver skins were one of Canada's first exchange media. Other "primitive" currencies used in Canada include skins of various animals, copper shields, wampum, flints, spears, arrows, just about any object with a utilitarian value.

A French *voyageur* and an Indian guide are seen paddling a canoe on Canada's first silver dollar struck in 1935 to mark the 25th year of the reign of King George V. In the background are some pine trees and in the sky, the *aurora borealis*, or northern lights.

From the very beginning, the French treated the Indians better than any other Europeans did. Instead of looking down on the Indian, the French admired his prowess as a hunter and fighter, his skill in the woods, and his masterly handling of the fragile-looking canoe. This sentiment is reflected even now on Canadian coins. Most issues of Canadian silver dollars portray on their reverse sides a French *voyageur* and an Indian paddling a canoe.

Samuel de Champlain (1567–1635), the first governor of New France, succeeded in 1608 in founding a permanent colony at Quebec. Montreal

("Mount Royal"), the headquarters of the fur trade, was not founded until 1642. Governor Champlain liked the Hurons and the Algonquins, and they reciprocated his affection. He encouraged his Frenchmen to live in the Indian villages, to study their methods of survival in the Canadian wilds, to learn their language, and to intermarry with them. He was enchanted with the birchbark canoe, quickly realizing that it was the best means of transportation through otherwise trackless forests. New France grew unspectacularly but steadily.

The first coins struck for Canada under the French Regime were the copper 20 deniers, and the silver 5 and 15 sols specimens of 1670. The two silver pieces bear the portrait of King Louis XIV on obverse and his arms on reverse. All the 1670 varieties are rare.

The French issued coins only intermittently for use in Canada. The 9 deniers copper pieces struck in 1721–22, inscribed "Colonies Francoises," saw limited circulation . . . the bulk of the issue was returned to France by Governor Vaudreuil in 1726. The billon "marques" and "half-marques" of the 1738–60 period were produced mainly for use in France itself, but they were widely circulated in Canada.

A wide variety of jetons, or counters, were also struck for use in French Canada. These were distributed to aid in the reckoning of sums in the old French fractional currency.

The English, sensing that Canada was a land with a real future, organized the Hudson's Bay Company in the 1660's. King Charles II's royal charter, issued in 1670, gave the Company title to all rivers emptying

Canada ❧ 73

The Bank of Montreal copper penny token of 1842 provides a view of the bank.

into the bay and to all the land drained by the rivers. No man living then could know that this gave the Hudson's Bay Company title to a vast area amounting to 1,480,000 square miles! From the start, the Company realized huge profits in the fur trade.

Though the Crown did not ask for any share of the profits, it provided for a unique symbol of its authority over the Company. The charter stipulated that when the British King or his successors entered the Company's domains, they were to receive "two Black Beavers." Such presentations were actually made to the Prince of Wales (the present Duke of Windsor) during his Canadian tour in 1927, and to King George VI during his 1939 visit.

The Hudson's Bay Company is still operating today on a major scale, three centuries after it was founded. Over 200 trading posts are maintained but motorboats have replaced the old-time canoe. The airplane and short-wave radio are also liberally used. Silver fox and mink rather than beaver are now the high profit items. The Company is the only business organization in the British Commonwealth that is allowed to fly its own ensign. This consists of the letters "HBC" in white on a red field, and is seen on the Company's ocean liners, freighters, and Arctic icebreakers.

The letters "NB" on this Hudson's Bay Company token of the 1850's should have been "MB," signifying "Made Beaver," a prepared beaver skin, the standard trading unit.

74 ❧ Canada

The British and the French battled on and off for more than two centuries for possession of Canada. Finally, the British gained control during the French and Indian Wars (also known as the Seven Year War). In 1759, a British expedition led by General James Wolfe scaled the rock of Quebec under cover of darkness and defeated the French on the Plains of Abraham. Both Wolfe and Louis de Montcalm, the French general, were killed in the action. The English completed the conquest of Canada in the following year. French culture, however, is still of great importance in the country today, especially in Quebec. French and English are both official languages, and nearly one-third of the population is of French extraction. Banknotes are inscribed in both languages. Many of the coin inscriptions are in Latin.

The colonies of Upper (Ontario) and Lower (Quebec) Canada were unified in 1841 to form the Province of Canada. Adopting a decimal currency in 1858, the Province's first coins of 1858 were decimal twenty, ten, five and one cent pieces.

Canadians longed for some measure of self-government and reforms gradually widened the scope of Canadian self-determination. These reforms culminated in the establishment of the Canadian Confederation in 1867. The Federation, which originally included only Quebec, Ontario, New Brunswick, and Nova Scotia, was patterned on the parliamentary government of Great Britain. The handling of foreign affairs still remained with the British.

Canadian troops fought gallantly on the side of Great Britain and the Allies in both World War I and World War II. After the first World War, Canada joined the League of Nations as an independent member, and in 1926 it became a self-governing Dominion, completely free of control by Great Britain, although its nominal head is the British Crown. Today,

Canada is regarded as one of the key members of the British Commonwealth of Nations. The British sovereign's portrait appears on virtually all Canada's coins, stamps and banknotes.

Modern Canadian coinage began in 1858, the year in which a decimal coinage, based upon a dollar of 100 cents, became the official exchange medium in the Province of Canada. The decimal coins replaced British sterling and a bewildering variety of foreign and private issues. In this year sizable quantities of large bronze cents, and silver 5, 10 and 20-cent pieces inscribed "Canada" were shipped over from London's Tower Mint. This shipment, together with 9 million more cents dated 1859, provided sufficient coin to meet the Province's requirements until after Confederation. The first coins of the federal union were struck in 1870 and they resembled the 1858–59 provincial issues. However, the 20-cent piece ("the silver fifth") was dropped in favor of a 25-cent coin, and a 50-cent silver piece was added.

Nova Scotia and New Brunswick joined the Province of Canada in 1867, forming the Dominion of Canada. Their one cent coins portraying Queen Victoria are similar in design. Prince Edward Island, which joined the Dominion in 1873, struck its only regular issue coin in 1871, a bronze cent, unique among Canadian coin types since it is the only one having the royal title in English.

Nova Scotia and New Brunswick had their own decimal and token coinages up to the time of the Confederation, but these gradually disappeared from circulation as the new national coins replaced them. Prince Edward Island which did not join the Dominion of Canada until 1873 issued a bronze cent in 1871. This cent is unique insofar as it is the only coin issued anywhere in Canada with the royal title in English.

British Columbia issued two coins in its pre-Dominion days, $10 and $20 gold pieces dated 1862. They were struck by order of the provincial government during a gold rush in British Columbia's Cariboo district, but were disallowed for circulation by the British authorities who maintained that the right of coinage belonged exclusively to the Crown. The

Canada's $5 and $10 gold pieces of 1912-14, bear the portrait of George V, with a reverse shield inscribed with the emblems of the four original provinces—Quebec, Ontario, New Brunswick, and Nova Scotia.

pieces are considered patterns rather than regular issues and specimens are now very rare.

Since Newfoundland did not join the federation until 1949, it issued its own coins including two dollar gold pieces over a long period of time. Newfoundland's last coins were the 1, 5 and 10 cent pieces dated 1947. It is interesting to note that Newfoundland continued to issue 5¢ pieces of silver right up to the end even though Canada switched to larger nickel coins for this denomination in 1922.

Canada's decimal coins produced prior to 1908 were struck at either London's Royal Mint (the Tower Mint), or at the Heaton Mint in Birmingham, a private coin-striking facility with which the Royal Mint subcontracted. In 1908 a new Canadian mint at Ottawa began full-scale operations. All of Canada's coins since that time have been struck at Ottawa. Canadian coins carry no mint marks with the exception of the British gold sovereigns at Ottawa struck in the 1908–19 period. These were inscribed with a "C" on the reverse.

Five cent pieces of tombac (a copper and zinc alloy) were struck because of a severe nickel shortage during World War II. The 1951 issue of pure nickel, also 12-sided, marked the 200th anniversary of the isolation of the metal by a Swedish chemist in 1751.

British Columbia's centennial as a crown colony was marked by a 1958 silver dollar featuring a totem pole.

The Royal Canadian Mint also struck a set of $5 and $10 gold coins in 1912–14. The obverse has the portrait of King George V, while the reverse has an ornate shield surrounded by maple leaves.

Canadian silver dollars were first struck in 1935 to commemorate the 25th year of the reign of King George V. The Ottawa Mint has struck silver dollars regularly ever since except during the war years of 1940–44. Canadian silver dollars, especially the commemoratives, are popular with collectors the world over.

The Ottawa Mint struck seven coins, including a $20 gold piece to commemorate the Confederation's centennial in 1967. This is popularly called the "Wildlife Set" since aside from the gold piece animals, birds and fish native to Canada are portrayed on the reverses.

Because of rapidly increasing prices in silver throughout the world, Canada in 1968 switched from silver to pure nickel for much of its coinage.

For over a century, Canadian coins have portrayed the bust of the reigning monarch on the obverse. The reverses of the regular issues show a *voyageur* and Indian guide, Canada's coat-of-arms; a fishing schooner; maple leaves; a beaver; and a caribou.

78 ❧ Canada

Central America

Central America is the slender neck of land more than 1,200 miles long that connects the continents of North and South America. Smaller in land area than the state of Texas, Central America includes six republics—Guatemala, Honduras, Salvador, Nicaragua, Costa Rica and Panama. This area was settled long ago by the Maya Indians, who established one of the world's notable civilizations during the first thousand years of the Christian era.

Columbus is known to have reached Honduras and may have landed in Guatemala in 1502. Settlement followed, the first Spanish city being founded in 1524. Spain controlled Central America for the next three centuries, calling it the Captaincy General of Guatemala. Spanish rule was often harsh, with the natives exploited for slave labor on the plantations and in the mines.

After they achieved independence from Spain in the 1820's, the Central American nations (Guatemala, Honduras, Salvador, Nicaragua and Costa Rica—the sixth country, Panama, was still a part of Colombia at this time) tried to unite as "The Central American Federation" or "Republic of Central America." But the experiment did not succeed, and the confederation broke up in less than 20 years. Even unity within the remaining small countries has been difficult to achieve, and revolutions even today are not uncommon.

The "G" mint marks on the obverse of this 1769 silver 8 reales identify it as a product of the Guatemala mint.

GUATEMALA

The Spaniards opened the first mint in Central America at Guatemala City in 1733 and all coins struck there bore the "G" mint mark. In 1773 the capital was destroyed by an earthquake and in 1776, upon the rebuilding of the city, it was called New Guatemala. The mint mark

Guatemala's silver 8 reales of 1810 is unusual because it bears the bust of Charles IV (1788-1808) with the legend of Ferdinand VII (1808-22). News of Charles' death reached the mint before the new portrait punch which was prepared in Spain.

became "NG." Under Spain, Guatemala's coins strongly resembled those of Mexico—the main difference is the mint mark.

Since independence, Guatemala's coins have been struck at various world mints, including Philadelphia, London, Birmingham and Hamburg. Guatemala as a republic has issued a wide variety of coins in gold, silver and base metals. The quetzal bird forms the central design on the country's national emblem and appears on many of the coins.

The "White Nun" orchid, Guatemala's national flower, appears on the 1962 silver 50 centavos, while the reverse arms feature the brilliantly plumed quetzal bird.

HONDURAS

Honduras became independent of Spain in 1821, was part of Mexico briefly, next a state in the Central American Federation until 1838, and since then has been an independent republic. To relieve a coin shortage following the wars of independence, a temporary mint was set up at Tegucigalpa, the capital, which struck silver 2 real pieces in 1823. These coins, which are now rare, were inscribed with the Spanish arms between two pillars. The Tegucigalpa Mint also struck silver real pieces with a "T" mint mark in 1830–31 for the Central American Federation. Foreign mints supplied Honduras with coins until 1878 when a regular mint was established, producing coins until 1920.

80 ◦ **Central America**

The Honduras silver 4 reales of 1853 shows the "T" mint mark of the Tegucigalpa mint.

The coinage decree of April 6, 1926 instituted a new monetary unit, the lempira, which equals 100 centavos. The silver 20 centavo (1931–58), 50 centavo (1931–51), and 1 lempira (1931–37) obverses all portray Lempira, the Indian chief who led the resistance against the Spaniards. All of the recent Honduran coinage has been struck at the U.S. Mint in Philadelphia.

The silver lempira of Honduras is named for a courageous Indian chief who defied Spanish rule in Central America.

BRITISH HONDURAS

British Honduras is a Crown Colony on the Yucatan Peninsula. Shipwrecked English sailors landed there in 1638, the basis for Britain's claim to the area. Britain and Spain contested the area until 1783 when the British finally won supremacy. Until early in the 20th century, the colony was known as Belize.

British Honduras' scalloped edge bronze 1 cent piece, current since 1956, portrays Queen Elizabeth II.

Though British Honduras achieved colonial status in 1862, its administration was combined with Jamaica and its first distinctive coinage was not struck until 1885. Since that time its coins have been the standard British colonial type produced at the Birmingham and London mints.

Christopher Columbus appears on Salvador's silver pesos issued 1892-1914. In 1919, the peso was renamed the colon (Spanish for Columbus) in honor of the great navigator.

SALVADOR

Salvador, or "El Salvador" ("The Saviour") is the smallest of the Central American countries. After Salvador declared its independence from Spain in 1821, it was a part of Mexico for a brief period, then belonged to the Central American Federation until 1839, when it became completely independent.

Although some crude emergency coins were struck in Salvador in 1833–35, regular coinage did not begin until 1889. During much of the 19th century, Spanish colonial coins and coins of the other American republics were counterstamped with the coat of arms of El Salvador.

El Salvador's gold 20 colones of 1925 with a dual portrait of Conquistadore Pedro de Alvarado and President Alfonso Quinonez Molina marks the 400th anniversary of the founding of San Salvador, the capital.

An interesting pair of coins issued in 1925, a 20 colones gold piece and a silver 1 colon, commemorate the 400th anniversary of the founding of the city of San Salvador. The obverse has the conjoined heads of conquistador Pedro de Alvarado (1525) and President Alfonso Quinonez Molina (1925). The reverse of these beautiful coins, of which only 200 gold and 2,000 silver specimens were struck at the Mexico City Mint, bears the national arms enclosed in a wreath. A new monetary unit, the colon (the Spanish form of Columbus) which is still in use, was instituted with these coins. Columbus himself appears on some issues of 1892–1914 but the monetary unit in those days was the peso. In addition to Mexico City, coins of Salvador have been struck at the Brussels, Birmingham, Hamburg, Philadelphia and San Francisco mints.

NICARAGUA

Taking its name from Nicarao, an Indian chief of the 1500's, Nicaragua is the largest of the Central American countries. After gaining its independence from Spain in 1821, Nicaragua too was united for a short period with Mexico, then with the Central American Federation, finally becoming an independent republic in 1838.

Nicaragua's coinage begins with the issue of the 1 centavo copper-nickel piece of 1878. Before this point, Nicaragua relied on the use of foreign coins and banknotes. The peso was the basic monetary unit until 1912, when the name was changed to the cordoba for Francisco Hernandez de Cordoba (1475–1526), the Spanish explorer of Nicaragua. Cordoba is portrayed on many of Nicaragua's coins.

Since the country has never had its own mint, all of Nicaragua's coins have been ordered from other mints—most recently from Philadelphia and the Royal Mint in London.

Francisco Hernandez de Cordoba is portrayed on the Nicaragua 1912 silver cordoba. The inscription EN DIOS CONFIAMOS means "In God We Trust."

COSTA RICA

Costa Rica ("rich coast"), following the pattern of the other Central American countries, gained its independence from Spain in 1821, was joined to Mexico for a brief period, then, a part of the Central American Federation, achieved independence in 1838 and adopted a Republican constitution in 1847.

A Costa Rican mint at San Jose struck a number of coins during the Federation period. One of these specimens is the silver 8 reales, dated 1831, showing on obverse mountains and sun; reverse has a tree. The mint mark is "CR." After 1838, the San Jose Mint struck a similar coinage of fractional values, as well as a coinage of gold escudo values.

From 1841 until about 1857, Costa Rica suffered from a shortage of coin. As in some of her sister republics, Costa Rica counterstamped

Central America ⚜ 83

Costa Rica's silver 8 reales of 1831 features a sun and mountains design, a popular device on Latin American coins of the period. The "CR" initials on the reverse indicate the coin was struck at a local mint in San Jose.

older Spanish colonial and other Latin American coins to legalize their circulation. Many of the counterstamped coins have small holes punched in them and it is thought that these silver plugs were removed to pay for the expense of the counterstamp.

Columbus, who discovered Costa Rica on his fourth voyage in 1502, is portrayed on the gold 20 colones of 1897-1900.

During the 1865-96 period, 1 peso equalled 100 centavos, but under the new coinage system adopted in 1896, 1 colon equals 100 centimos. The head of Columbus is shown on the 2 colones gold coins of 1897–1928, as well as on the 5, 10 and 20 colones gold pieces of 1897-1900. These coins were struck at the Philadelphia Mint, along with most other modern coins of Costa Rica. Contemporary 5 and 10 centimos and 1 and 2 colones coins are being minted in stainless steel.

Costa Rica's arms show three volcanoes separating two oceans, recalling its location between the Atlantic and Pacific Oceans.

Vasco Nunez de Balboa appears on many Panamanian coins, including the tiny silver 2½ centesimos, the so-called "Panama Pill." The largest of the 1904 series is the crown-sized 50 centesimos.

PANAMA

Some geographers don't consider Panama an integral part of Central America, but rather as an isthmus connecting Central and South America. Collectors, however, have traditionally included its coins with the Central American series.

Panama was formerly a Department of the Republic of Colombia until it broke away in 1903, declaring its independence. Immediately thereafter, the Republic of Panama concluded a treaty with the United States allowing the Panama Canal to be constructed. The Panama Canal, completed in 1914, is situated in the Canal Zone, a ten-mile-wide strip of land leased to the United States, that divides the country.

Panama's first coins, issued in 1904, are a set of five values bearing the bust of Vasco Nunez de Balboa (1475–1517), the Spanish conquistador, who in 1513 discovered the Pacific Ocean by crossing the isthmus of Panama. The Panamanian monetary system is based upon 100 centesimos equalling 1 balboa. The Panamanian balboa is closely pegged to the U.S. dollar. Most of Panama's coins have been struck at the Philadelphia and San Francisco mints, but a few varieties have also been produced at London and Mexico City.

Panama, host country for the 1970 Central American & Caribbean Games, issued a large sterling silver 5 balboas coin (equal to $5 U.S.) to mark the event.

After the sudden death of Charles IV in 1808, the Santiago mint went ahead with a coinage for the new monarch, Ferdinand VII, without having the new portrait dies from Spain. They used a "fantasy" head of their own on the 1808 8 reales. Ferdinand VII's true likeness is shown on the 1815 coin.

Chile

Chile, one of the world's longest countries, stretches some 2,635 miles from Arica in the north to Cape Horn in the south, with an average width of only 110 miles. Though Santiago was founded in 1541, a mint was not established there until 1750. Some of the earliest coins struck at Santiago were the famous Spanish gold doubloons. The doubloons and other gold denominations were struck there until 1817. These gold pieces as well as the silver reales were similar to the ones produced during the same period at the Mexico City Mint.

After Bernardo O'Higgins, with the aid of Jose de San Martin and his troops, succeeded in driving out the Spanish in 1818, an efficient national government was established and Chile has maintained a relatively stable political structure throughout most of its history. Except for the brief period between 1835–53 when copper coins were produced in England

Chile's gold 100 pesos shows Liberty with coiled hair. On the reverse, the star shield of Chile is supported by a llama and a condor.

and the United States, all Chilean coins have been struck at Santiago's Casa de Moneda. On occasion the Santiago Mint has also manufactured coins for other Latin American countries.

Despite its political stability, Chile has experienced economic crises. Thus, its silver coinage is marked by frequent changes in size and fineness brought about because of continual inflation. On January 1, 1960, a

Bernardo O'Higgins, Chile's national hero, became the country's first president in 1818 after he drove out the Spaniards with the aid of Jose de San Martin. O'Higgins appears in military uniform on this aluminum peso of 1957.

currency revaluation went into effect, with the new monetary unit, the escudo, equalling 100 centesimos. The previous monetary system was based on the peso equalling 100 centavos.

Bernardo O'Higgins has been portrayed on a number of Chilean coins. The great flying condor has been portrayed on a wide variety of coins, including on the aluminum 5 and 10 peso values, series of 1956.

The giant condor, shown on many Chilean coins, has a wingspan of up to ten feet and thrives near the peaks of the Andes that stretch along the Chile-Argentina border.

Chile ⊛ 87

A 1st century B.C. "knife coin" looked more like a key. Eventually, only the round handle called a "cash" was circulated, representing the trading value of the original knife.

The obverse of this cast cash coin of Emperor Kao Tsu (618-27) is inscribed with the Chinese characters K'ai Yuan T'ung Pao—"current money of the Kai Yuan era."

An ancient Chinese bronze tao or "knife coin" from about 700 B.C. Cast in the shape of a knife, the tao had the same trading value as a real knife.

China

The numismatic story of China covers a greater span of time than that of any other country in the world. While the ancient Lydians in Asia Minor made the first *coins* in about 700 B.C., the Chinese had been using a variety of objects for *money* even before that. Some authorities on ancient China place the use of a metallic coinage in China as early as the 20th century B.C. Numismatic historians, however, have not been able to confirm the existence of a true coinage in Chinese civilization much earlier than the eighth century B.C.

One of the first known examples of Chinese metallic currency is the bronze tao or "knife coin" of about 700 B.C. Cast in the shape of a knife, the coin had the same trading value as a real knife. The Chinese made replicas of such useful articles as knives, hoes, spades and shirts and these replicas were used instead of the real object as media of exchange. These unusual bronze pieces are actually the forerunners of round coins. Real knives were usually hung from the belt or wrist on a thong passed through a hole in the handle so, in making a replica, the round handle with its central hole was copied on the "tao" knife coins. This enabled a person to string pieces of knife money together for large transactions. Over the centuries, the blade part of the "tao" was made smaller and smaller until the coins looked more like keys than knives. Finally, only the handle with its central hole, the so-called "cash" coin, was produced.

These round cash coins first appeared about the time of Confucius, China's greatest philosopher (*c.* 551–479 B.C.), and large quantities were in circulation by the time the Great Wall was being constructed late in the 3rd century B.C.

The term "cash" used for these Chinese bronze coins has no connection with the English word "cash," which comes from the French *caisse*, a box or treasure chest. The Chinese word is from the Tamil *Kas*, a small Indian coin. The name given to the coin in China is *tsien*.

Strangely enough, once the cash-type coin was established, it continued almost without change for nearly 2,500 years. In fact, the first minting of orthodox silver coins in China did not occur until 1889. The cash coins issued during those 25 centuries were cast in molds of various substances, including: stone, bricks, earthenware, tamped clay, bronze, and perhaps iron. Arthur Braddan Coole, one of the greatest students of Chinese coins, said they were cast singly, in pairs, or in clusters which remind one of the skeleton outline of the veins of a serrate leaf. Coole also pointed out that the numerous variants in sizes of coins are sometimes attributed to counterfeiters who would use the original coins in the making of their molds.

Most Chinese cash type coins are of one cash value, the basic exchange unit. They have four characters on the obverse, those at top and bottom being the ruler's name and those at the sides meaning "precious coin." The reverses of the one cash pieces were sometimes left blank, but often they were inscribed with two characters, one at each side, indicating the location of the mint.

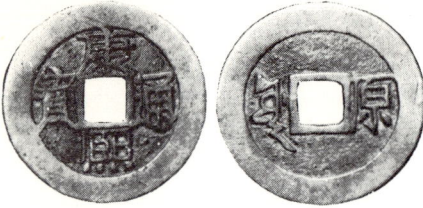

Ch'ing Dynasty, one cash piece of Emperor K'ang-hsi (1662-1722) from the T'ai Yuan mint in Shansi province.

It is convenient to classify the cash pieces and miscellaneous other types of currencies by dynasty. The major dynasties during which coins were produced in China were the: Chou, 1122–255 B.C.; Han Empire, 206 B.C.–A.D. 220; Wei, 386–557; Sui, 581–618; T'ang, 618–906; Northern

Ch'ing Dynasty, cast bronze 50 cash coin of Emperor Hsien-feng (1851-62) from the Board of Public Works mint.

Sung, 960–1126; Southern Sung, 1126–1260; The Mongol (Yuan) Dynasty, 1260–1368; Ming, 1368–1644; Ch'ing (Manchu) Dynasty, 1644–1912. The gaps are due to minor dynasties, disturbed and transitional periods. Through most of China's dynastic period, gold and silver were current by weight only, the latter in the form of boat-shaped ingots.

Silver crowns of foreign origin were widely circulated in China for many years. The first Spanish dollar-size coin was minted about 1497, and soon afterward the Spaniards, who maintained trading bases in the Philippine Islands, brought these silver pieces into China. During the 1600's and 1700's, the British East India Company paid for tea purchased in Canton with Spanish dollars. During the era of American clipper ships this same currency was brought in by American merchants.

Some of the South American countries, too, especially Bolivia, Chile and Peru, produced silver dollars which found their way to China. These coins usually had a slightly higher proportion of base metal in their alloy than their Spanish counterparts and were not as readily accepted by Chinese businessmen. The Mexican peso, with its design featuring the spread-winged eagle standing on a cactus with a serpent in its beak began arriving in China in 1854. Its high silver content made it very popular among the Chinese and until the period of the Republic, it was undoubtedly the most widely circulated dollar in China.

To compete with the Mexican peso in China and the rest of the Orient, the United States issued a series of special trade dollars in the period 1873–83. These trade dollars had a weight of 420 grains compared to $412\frac{1}{2}$ grains, the standard weight for regular dollars.

Foreign silver dollars which circulated in China have special appeal to numismatists because most of them were impressed with "chopmarks" by the Chinese businessmen. The native merchants and money dealers impressed their private marks on all the silver pieces that passed through their hands, as a guarantee of genuineness and full weight. A coin so marked is called a "chopped" coin, while an unmarked coin is known as "clean."

Various attempts were made to institute a native silver coinage during the 1800's but it wasn't until near the end of the 19th century that mints were established in the provinces to strike silver and copper coins of European style.

The first modern provincial series was struck for Kwantung (Canton) in 1889, followed by issues in other provinces. The obverse design of these provincial coins usually gives the name of the province and the

Kiang Nan Province of China, undated dollar (struck 1897), issued by Emperor Kuang Hsu (1875-1908). The Chinese characters in the central part of the reverse read from right to left in Chinese fashion, "large money," and from top to bottom, "Kuang Hsu."

value in Manchu characters, while the reverse carries the imperial emblem, a flying dragon, and a circular inscription in English giving the name of the province and the value.

China became a Republic in 1912 after a successful revolution led by Dr. Sun Yat-sen toppled the feeble and corrupt Manchu Dynasty, ending the Empire which had survived for more than 2,500 years. Under the Republic, coins were at once struck with the portraits of the great political leaders, including Dr. Sun and Yuan Shih-kai, and various generals who had been fighting for the Chinese Republic. Many of the leading generals had coins personally struck with their portraits. Many of these new coins were in gold, the first time in Chinese history that gold pieces were produced on any large scale.

Kweichow Province in 1928 struck the world's only coin featuring a motor car. This silver "automobile dollar," which is inscribed on reverse with a combination of Chinese characters, is a highly popular coin among collectors.

China's Kweichow Province issued this remarkable "Automobile Dollar" in 1928, the only coin ever struck to feature a motor car. The coin's popularity among collectors has caused its value to rise steadily.

Dr. Sun Yat-sen appears on the Chinese silver dollars of 1932-34 with the sailing junk reverse. The birds over the junk and the rising sun were omitted after the first year because of hostilities with Japan. The birds apparently looked like warplanes.

Japan became increasingly aggressive in its relations with China, and in 1931 the Japanese army marched into Manchuria and set up the huge puppet state of Manchukuo. Japan attacked China with full force near Peiping in 1937 and Peiping and Tientsin soon fell.

When World War II came to an end in 1945, China was freed from Japanese domination, but the country was left in the throes of a civil war between the Kuomintang government headed by Chiang Kai-shek and the Communist government headed by Mao Tse-tung. General Mao's forces gained control of the mainland in 1949, and on October 2nd of that year, Mao proclaimed the People's Republic of China. The Nationalists of Chiang retired to the island of Formosa.

American collectors cannot legally import coins produced by Mao's Communist government, but coins struck at Formosa's national mint at Taipei, the capital, are popular in the U.S. and throughout the world. The monetary unit of Nationalist China is based on 10 cents equalling 1 chiao, and 100 cents equalling 1 yuan or dollar. Many Formosan coins of the Republic of China feature the portrait of Sun Yat-sen on obverse and a map of the island on the reverse.

This aluminum 2 chiao of 1950 is typical of Nationalist China's coins. Dr. Sun Yat-sen is on the obverse, a map of Formosa on the reverse.

Cob Money

Cob Money (from the Spanish *Cabo de barra*, "cut from a bar") is a term used to describe crude silver coins issued in the Spanish colonies of the New World. The Spanish colonial mints at Lima, Potosi and other cities were primitive affairs. Because of economic necessity they converted the raw silver into coins as rapidly as possible. The term "cob" is also an apt description of the rough appearance of their early issues.

In the minting process, raw silver was refined and cast into bars. Planchets for coins were crudely sliced or chiseled off the end of the bar. The irregular planchets were then roughly trimmed to the right weight. The planchets were heated up and hammered between two dies. The dies carried a complete design and inscriptions but the surfaces of the blanks were never perfectly flat so, in stamping them, the design and lettering were impressed only on the highest parts. Moreover, by the time enough metal was clipped away to bring the planchet to the proper weight, it was usually smaller than the dies, so even when the legends do show, they run off the edge of the coin.

The history of the cob pieces is a long one since they were minted for nearly 250 years. The first cob moneys were issued about 1600 during the reign of Philip III (1598–1621); the last ones were produced in Argentina in 1823–24.

The 8 reales or "pieces of eight" cobs of Philip II bear the royal arms, quartered lions and castles on the obverse. The reverse is inscribed with two crowned pillars, the value in Roman or Arabic numerals and the initials of the mint and the assayer.

Many varieties of cob pieces were struck in the reign of Charles II (1665–1700) at Bogota, Potosi, Lima and other cities as well. Even on a better than average Charles II specimen, the legend and design can barely

Early 18th century cob 8 reales recovered off Florida from the wreckage of a 1715 Spanish treasure fleet that sank in a hurricane.

This crude 8 reales cob was struck at Mexico City in 1600-18 during the reign of Philip III (1598-1621).

be made out. The portion of the design that is weak on one coin may be strong on another, however, so by examining many specimens, specialists in this series can tell us what the full legend would be if it did appear on any one coin. Charles II cob 8 reales minted at Lima in 1688 are especially sought after by collectors because many of these specimens have unusually clear legends.

Besides being crudely struck to begin with, many of the cobs were further cut into halves and quarters (conveniently marked off by the arms of the cross) to make small change. Since crude implements were used, the quartered or halved pieces frequently came out as highly irregular shapes. Many cobs were cut into triangular pie-shaped pieces. Many of the fractional pieces as well as some of the full 8 reales coins have also been counter-stamped, sometimes years later to signify either a change in value, a change in rulers or to authorize their circulation in some other country.

Since so little of the design is clear on many of its cob coins, it often takes a specialist to determine the date in which any individual coin was struck. Sometimes the only attribution that can be made is the approximate period of issue based upon the general appearance and style of the specimen.

This cob piece struck at Lima, Peru in the late 1600's carries the "91" of the date and the "L" mint mark in the bottom line of the obverse inscription, the denomination "2" reales at the top.

Collecting Coins

The best kind of collection, certainly, is the kind that interests you most. Before you can decide about this, however, you must know what the possibilities are. Here are the most popular kinds of collections and a discussion of what is involved in each of them. There is no "one way" or even "best way" to collect. Any of these basic plans can and should be adapted to suit your particular taste and interest.

Collectors everywhere are likely to start with coins of their own countries because they can build their collection with coins from their day-to-day pocket change. The lower-denomination coins receive the most attention because the face-value investment is low and everyone handles more of them every day.

In collecting coins from circulation, the goal is to complete a set of a given series of coins—U.S., Lincoln Head cents, Canadian small cents, British farthings, or modern Mexican centavos. To complete the series you try to collect one coin of each different date and from each different mint. This method is best for current or recently issued coins.

To begin a collection, have a separate pocket or purse where you can put each coin you get during the day to be checked later. The secret of finding coins with scarce dates in circulation is to be consistent. If you are watching your coins, watch all of them. If you only look at the date when you "think it might be a good one," you are bound to let most of the scarcer ones slip right by.

When you are ready to check the accumulated coins against your collection, sit down near a strong light. Pick up one of the coins and read the date and mint mark. Turn to your check list or the space provided in your album for that particular coin. If the space is empty, you have made a "find" and you place the coin in it. If the space is already filled, compare the condition of the new coin with the one already there and keep the better of the two.

You may wish to search through more coins than come your way in daily change. It is possible to purchase rolls of coins from banks and you may also be able to arrange to go through coins taken in at local stores, from parking meters, vending machines, etc. A few duplicates of each issue can be saved for trading stock although it is pointless to save too many of any one issue. For instance, if you are able to find 25 or 50 pieces of the same variety, you can be sure that any potential trader you meet will have found at least one of that issue for his own set. If you do save duplicates for trading, remember always to save the ones in best

The two most popular American series for beginners collecting from circulation are Lincoln cents (left) and Jefferson nickels (right). New collectors usually start with the lower denomination coins and work up to the higher.

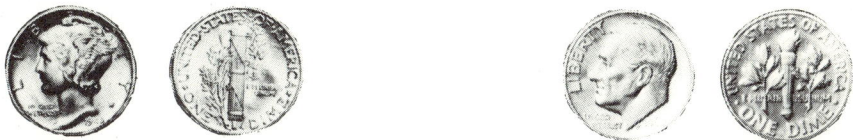

It is still possible to complete a set of Roosevelt dimes (right) from coins found in circulation but many of the pre-1964 dates are scarce. Mercury dimes are not often seen in daily change.

Washington quarters can be found in change and occasionally some of the standing Liberty issue turn up. The dates of most of them have been completely worn off, however, making them valueless to collectors.

The large size of Walking Liberty, Franklin and Kennedy half dollars makes them attractive in collections. All half dollars have just about disappeared from circulation, however, and there are some really scarce dates in these series.

Collecting Coins ❧ 97

UNCIRCULATED: New condition, all lettering, the date and details of the design are extremely clear. An UNC coin shows no signs of wear or damage at any point.

EXTREMELY FINE: The very highest points of the design show the slightest signs of wear or rubbing. All fine detail is still clear and coins in EF condition often have a little mint luster left.

VERY FINE: Design still quite clear but VF coins begin to show definite signs of wear, smooth spots on the highest points. Lettering may be worn but the outline of every letter must be clear.

The photographs on these two pages show the same type coin, a Queen Victoria veiled head penny, in six grades of condition. The uncirculated specimen is worth about 50 times as much as the poorest coin illustrated, as collectors nearly always want coins in the best possible condition.

condition. If you are fortunate enough to find extras of any of the really scarce dates, you can easily sell them to a coin dealer at a good price.

In nearly every series of coins, certain dates are scarcer than others. The British pennies of George VI provide a good example of this. The usual quantity minted of the dates between 1937 and 1948 was in excess of 50 million pieces of each issue. Coinage dropped off to 14 million in 1949, plunged to 240,000 in 1950 and to only 120,000 in 1951. Consequently, while the earlier George VI pennies (none coined in 1941, 1942, or 1943) can still be easily found in circulation, the 1949 date requires more patience or good luck and it is virtually impossible to find a 1950

FINE: Considerably worn but still desirable coins, on which the basic outline is still clear but much of the detail is lost. On F coins portions of some of the lettering may be worn away.

VERY GOOD: Much worn but not altogether unattractive coins. A coin in the VG condition should be free of serious gouges or other mutilations but it may be somewhat scratched from use.

GOOD: A really minimum condition coin. The date and mint mark must be at least recognizable on a G coin and major portions of the design distinguishable.

or 1951. In fact, these now sell for a premium of about $7.50 and $20.00 respectively, depending upon condition.

In the United States, date and mint mark sets of the Lincoln Head cent series have been by far the most popular. Since 1909 these coins have been issued in most years from three different mints ("D" for Denver, "S" for San Francisco, no mint mark for Philadelphia). The San Francisco mint operated as an assay office only from 1955 to 1967, resuming full-scale coinage operations in 1968. No "D" mint marks were inscribed on any Denver mint coins during the coin shortage of 1965–67.

Next in popularity are the Jefferson nickels and Roosevelt dimes. It is still possible to find an assortment of dates and mint marks in circulation, including some of the older issues, but the billion-coin mintages of the past few years have so diluted the proportion of older coins in circulation that they are becoming increasingly difficult to find. Since the introduction of the base-metal "sandwich" planchet quarters in 1965, the fine silver

Collectors building a collection by types, choose one coin, usually the commonest variety, to represent all of the coins of similar design. The major types of U.S. cents are represented by the illustrations on these two pages.

issues of 1964 and earlier have just about disappeared from circulation. Half dollar coins are no longer in regular day-to-day use.

In England the decimal "new pence" coins are taking the place of the older shillings and pennies. Decimal coins have replaced the older issues in Australia and New Zealand as well. Canada, like the U.S., has had to discontinue fine silver coinage. The result of such changes has been to make it difficult to find coins more than a few years old still in circulation almost anywhere in the world. Collectors, consequently, are abandoning the idea of assembling whole series of coins in favor of collecting by type.

Major design types of U.S. cents: 1a. 1793 only, Liberty head with flowing hair, chain reverse; 1b. 1793 only, wreath reverse; 2. 1793-1796, Liberty head with cap on pole; 3. 1796-1807, draped bust of Liberty; 4. 1808-1814, turban head of Liberty; 5. 1816-1857, Liberty head with coronet; 6. 1857-1858, flying eagle; 7a. 1859 only, Indian head, olive wreath, no shield; 7b. 1860-1909, oak wreath, with shield; 8a. 1909-1958, Lincoln head, wheat spray reverse; 8b. 1959-, Lincoln Memorial reverse.

The plan of a type collection is to let one coin represent many others. Usually this means that one of the commonest and thus least expensive dates or varieties is used to represent all the other coins, including expensive rarities, that are of the same design or "type." The collection is thus limited to "face different" varieties. The type collection approach can be applied to portraits of rulers as well as design types.

A collector may decide to get one coin from each of as many different countries as possible, or he may concentrate on coins from a certain group of countries, or coins of a particular era. He may specialize in ancient coins (Greek, Rome, Byzantium), or in crowns (dollar size coins), commemoratives, medals, tokens or oddities and errors. He may want to form a topical collection of animals, fish, birds, plants, ships or religious themes on coins.

Collecting Coins ❧ 101

Bull

Wolf

Moufflon

Giraffes

Beaver

Polar bear

Elephant

Antelope

Dog

Kangaroo

Tiger

Lion

Jaguar

Turtle

Moose

Squirrel

Horse

Hare

Camel

Brahma bull

Wolfhound

Stag

Merino sheep

Caribou

Lioness

Sow and piglets

Springbok

Cow

Buffalo

Fish on coins

Mackerel

Dolphin

Flounder

Salmon

Bonga fish

Cod

Collecting Coins ❧ 103

Birds on coins

Grouse

Bird of paradise

Condor

Quetzal

Wren

Tui

Eagle

Peacock

Rooster

Owl

Huia

Woodcock

Dove

Kiwi

Sparrows

Hen

Pope Paul VI

Maori tiki

Martin Luther

Buddhist prayer
wheel and temple
bell

Menorah

Indian totem pole

Ecumenical
Council

Christ and apostles
in boat

Moslem Mosque

St. George

St. John
the Baptist

1627 2 escudos of the mint of Santa Fe del Nuevo Reino de Granada (Bogota), the first gold piece coined in the Americas.

Colombia

Named after Christopher Columbus, Colombia, which was part of New Granada under Spanish rule, formed with Venezuela, Panama and Ecuador the Confederacy of Greater Colombia shortly after independence was achieved in 1819. The Confederacy collapsed in 1830 when Venezuela and Ecuador withdrew. It wasn't until 1886 that the present name Republic of Colombia ("Republica de Colombia") was adopted. The Department of Panama broke away from Colombia and declared its independence in 1903. During the twentieth century Colombia has become unified through an effective central government despite the country's great physical diversity.

Colombia's silver 2 reales of 1816 was struck at the Bogota mint under Ferdinand VII (1808-24), though it has the bust of Charles IV (1788-1808).

After gaining independence from Spain, Colombia issued silver coins from ¼ to 8 reales values as the chief circulating media. During this early period in the country's history, gold pieces were struck in values from 1 to 8 escudos. Both the silver and gold coins were produced at the Bogota and Popayan mints.

This silver 2 reales was struck in 1843 when Colombia was known as "Republica de la Nueva Granada," Republic of New Granada.

Colombia ⚬ 107

The 400th anniversary of the discovery of America was marked on this Colombian 50 centavos piece of 1892 bearing the bust of Christopher Columbus.

Mints at Popayan and Medellin continued to produce coins regularly throughout most of the 19th century, but at the beginning of the 20th century, the Bogota facility remained as the only working mint in Colombia. From 1881 to 1946, various issues of Colombian coins were struck at a number of world mints, including Birmingham, Brussels, Philadelphia and San Francisco. Today, however, the enlarged Casa de Moneda at Bogota is able to supply the country with almost all its coinage requirements. The beautiful Spanish colonial mint building dating from the 17th century still stands, used now as a museum.

Colombia's 1967 cupro-nickel peso with the portrait of Simon Bolivar was struck at the Bogota mint on 10-sided planchets imported from England.

Bolivar has been portrayed on many Colombian coins. Included among these are the silver 10 and 20 centavos, series of 1911–42; and the 50 centavos, series of 1912–33. He also appears on the current copper-nickel regular issues: 20 centavos, series of 1956; and 50 centavos, series of 1958.

The *p/m* on the reverse of Colombia's copper-nickel 5 pesos of 1907 stands for *papel moneda* (paper money) . . . this token coin was similar to a banknote, indicating a promise to pay, but without any intrinsic value of its own.

One of the most interesting Colombian issues is the 5, 2 and 1 peso *p/m* series of 1907–16. These were token coinages of copper-nickel issued at a time when the regular issue silver coins contained full face value of precious metal. The *p/m* stands for *papel moneda* (paper money), a notice that the coins were, like banknotes, a promise to pay but without intrinsic value of their own.

A 1 peso coin was struck in 1956 to mark the 200th anniversary of the Popayan mint. The coin's obverse shows the huge door of the Casa de la Moneda in Bogota, which was founded in 1620.

The 200th anniversary of the mint building at Bogota was commemorated in 1956 with a 1 peso silver piece. The reverse bears the national arms, with the obverse showing the huge door of the Casa de Moneda. The Bogota Mint, whose history goes back to 1620, also struck a special 5 peso cupro-nickel coin to mark the 39th Eucharistic Congress held at the Colombian capital in the summer of 1968. The coin's reverse is inscribed with the value within a circle of laurel leaves, while the obverse has the emblem of the Eucharistic Congress.

Colombia issued a 5 peso coin to commemorate the 39th International Eucharistic Congress which was held at Bogota in 1968. The coin's obverse has the Congress' emblem, a cross of fish representing the four corners of the earth.

This contemporary counterfeit of a sixth century B.C. silver stater of the Greek Island of Aegina is one of the world's oldest counterfeit coins. A crack at the coin's edge reveals a copper core that has been plated with silver. The technical accomplishment is amazing, considering that coining had just been introduced.

Counterfeiting

Counterfeiting probably began soon after the first coins were minted. In fact, the story of world coinage is closely bound up with the ceaseless struggle between the safeguards of the authorized coinmakers, and of the cleverness and skill of the counterfeiters. Ancient Greek and Roman coins were frequently counterfeited, as we know from many substandard specimens still existing as well as from references in centuries-old records. The penalties for counterfeiting were severe in ancient times—oftentimes death, although the Greeks were usually more lenient . . . they merely had the hands of the counterfeiters amputated so he could no longer practice his craft.

In England the counterfeiter was already at work in the days of the Roman occupation. At Halton Chesters, near a fort on the Roman Wall, the remains of a Roman coiner's den have been discovered; many forged

Roman coins were found here, together with a mold for manufacturing them. In the days of the Saxons, Athelstan, King of Wessex (925–35) ordained that the penalty for forgery should be the loss of a hand. In spite of this, matters steadily got worse. In the reign of Henry I it was so rife that in 1125 the King summoned nearly a hundred of the mint officials to his castle in Winchester and had them all mutilated!

In China things were done differently. On one occasion during medieval times, after a long and futile struggle between the government and the counterfeiters, the most skillful of the forgers were rounded up and offered highly paid jobs at the Imperial Mint.

The forgery of gold or silver coins, an infringement of the exclusive prerogative of the Crown, was formerly held by English law to be treason; the penalty for such a crime was transportation (banishment to a penal colony) or death by hanging. The striking of copper coins, however, was not a regal prerogative, and counterfeiting these was, therefore, merely a misdemeanor. As a consequence, the cautious 18th century forger concentrated his energies on producing false copper coins. This was done to an enormous extent since the forger's profit was in proportion to quantity he could turn out. By the middle of the 18th century, more than half of the copper coins in circulation in England were counterfeit.

Perhaps the most famous counterfeiter of all time was Karl W. Becker (1772–1830), a highly-skilled engraver who devoted most of his energies to forging ancient and classical coins sought by collectors. The forgery of coins became a fine art in the hands of Becker, who spent most of his working life in Offenbach, near Frankfurt, Germany. After failing as a wine merchant, he became an antiquarian. He received extensive training as a die cutter at the Munich Mint and used to amuse himself by copying ancient Greek coins in gold. Soon the story spread that, though his collection was small, it contained some superb pieces that might well grace the cabinets of princes and dukes.

Early in Becker's career, a nobleman of Munich sold him a coin which turned out to be a fake. When he complained of the deception, the Baron merely laughed at him and chided him for not knowing his business. So here Becker saw a chance to get back—he would fleece others as he had been fleeced. He eventually succeeded in duping the very Baron who had tricked him. Revenge was so sweet—and so profitable—that Becker decided to make coin forgery his profession.

Karl Becker's work is exhibited in a special display case at the "Munzkabinett" in the Berlin Museum. A large number of his dies and coins are shown, and the visitor may compare Becker's work with genuine examples of the pieces he so expertly copied. As expert as he was, Becker is clearly exposed at the Berlin Museum for even the neophyte collector can easily learn to distinguish between his forgeries and authentic ancient coins.

Counterfeiters produce forgeries by three different methods: (1) making casts, (2) electrotypes, and (3) false dies.

Casting is a cheap and common method of making forgeries. A cast is produced by making a mold from a genuine coin. Molten metal is then poured into the mold which is usually made of sand. Cast pieces can be distinguished from struck coins by the blunt and blurry edges of the design where the metal does not completely fill the mold. This is especially noticeable in lettering. In the angles of the letters, and on the whole surface of the field, little pitmarks left by the sandy surface of the mold can nearly always be discerned.

Another more sophisticated form of casting, said to have been developed in Egypt, involves placing the poles of an electro-magnet on either side of the mold. This pulls the molten metal into the finest parts of the design. Forgeries produced in this way are known as "pressure casts" and are often difficult to detect.

Though this counterfeit of a Mexican gold 8 escudos bearing the portrait of Charles IV, and dated 1807, was expertly done, the lack of sharp detail in the portrait and arms and the reddish color of the gold makes it recognizable as a fake. Such fake coins are passed off on unsuspecting tourists the world over.

Whichever casting method is used, however, the surface of a cast coin feels "soapy" when rubbed between thumb and finger. Frequently there are signs of filing on the edge where any rough ridges left at the point where the two halves of the mold come will have been removed.

An electrotype is a replica of a coin or medal made by a process somewhat resembling silver-plating, or electrolysis. As in casting, a genuine coin is used as a model. An electrotype is usually made in two pieces, filled with lead and soldered together. Electrotypes are the easiest copies to detect since it is almost impossible to hide the join, seen as a thin line running around the edge of the coin. An expert forger can plate over the join, but the plating often wears off.

Not all electrotypes have been made to deceive the public. The British Museum Department of Coins and Medals at one time had many varieties of their Greek, Roman, Byzantine, English and Continental coins reproduced as electrotypes for use in schools and in exhibits. All of these "coins" are inscribed on the edge with the initials of the electrotypist, or "MB" (Museum Britannicum). The danger is that even on such marked specimens, the letters are sometimes rubbed out, and the coins passed off as originals. In any case the join should be clearly visible.

Of all the forgeries, those produced from false dies are the most difficult to detect. At one time duplicate dies had to be cut free hand, with the result that the "style" of the copy differed slightly from the original. Karl Becker used the false die method almost exclusively in making his forgeries . . . but even in his best work, his "style" differed slightly from the original Greek, Roman and other classical coin engravers. When an expert says that a coin "does not look right," you should take it seriously and investigate further.

Governments and other official bodies authorized to strike coins have tried hard to make the counterfeiter's work difficult. Over the centuries we see the introduction of milled edges, lettering around the edges, and projecting rims. Some countries have used scalloped edge planchets or unusually shaped coins which, of course, are more difficult to reproduce. A counterfeiter today would be hard pressed to faithfully reproduce the U.S. clad or "sandwich" dime and quarter since the inner core of pure copper is so clearly visible in the genuine article.

Perhaps the only reason that the counterfeiting of circulating coins has diminished is bound up in the phenomenon that coinage has generally declined in value throughout the world, paper money being used for all but the lowest denominations of money. Today, the counterfeiter concentrates on printing false banknotes and checks or produces false credit cards.

Although there is no longer much need to be wary of getting counterfeit coins in your daily change, the collector of rare coins needs to double his guard. The most talented counterfeiters have now turned their attention to reproducing the most widely sought after and rare numismatic items.

At present, forgers are more expert than ever at making false dies. Many of the dies used today for striking forgeries are made partly by a

A counterfeit 1765 2 *Frederick d'or* of Frederick the Great, King of Prussia.

A 2½ times magnification exposes the *Frederick d'or* as a counterfeit. Lack of detail in the hair, poorly formed letters and the grainy surface of the planchet are the giveaway clues.

photographic process, a method that makes possible the faithful transcription of the most minute details of the original coin onto the false die.

The issue of counterfeit coins has become one of the most serious problems facing numismatics today. Forgeries are being made literally in every corner of the world. Many forgeries coming into the United States have been made in Europe, with most types of U.S. gold coins having been abundantly counterfeited.

An individual collector can protect himself from being exposed to counterfeit coins by trading only with reputable dealers. Reputable dealers will back up the authenticity of the coins they sell. If the dealer himself unwittingly makes a mistake, he will make good on the error immediately. All of the established numismatic organizations are making serious efforts to combat the flood of counterfeit coins pouring into the market place.

An 8 reales cob struck at Potosi in **1684** was counterstamped in **1849-51** with a sun over three volcanoes design for use in Guatemala. At the same time the counterstamp was applied, a plug of silver was removed to "pay for the work."

Countermarks and Counterstamps

Countermarks—devices, lettering, numerals, etc.—are stamped on a coin subsequent to its issue to give it a fresh or further guarantee, to alter the value of the coin, or to make it officially current in some country other than the one of issue. After declaring their independence from Spain, the new republics of Central America counterstamped Spanish colonial coins to indicate their new authority.

Countermarking was extensive in Russia during the 17th century, especially under Czar Alexis Mihailovich (1645–76). Foreign taler-type coins were countermarked, converting them into silver rubles. Two marks were stamped on Mihailovich's rubles of 1655: an oval punch produced the mounted figure of the czar, and an oblong punch impressed the date. This 1655 date was the first appearance of Christian-era dating on Russian coins.

This 4 reales of Spanish king Charles III was countermarked with a small portrait of the British king George III for circulation in England.

Spanish 8 reales counterstamped with Portuguese arms for use in Brazil.

1875 Chilean peso counterstamped in 1894 for circulation in Guatemala.

The counterstamped Portuguese arms on this Brazilian 40 reis of 1786 indicates a reduction to half value of 20 reis.

1831 8 soles of Bolivia counterstamped with monogram of the Spanish king for use in the Philippines.

116 ❧ Countermarks and Counterstamps

The "GR" countermark indicates that this Mexican 8 reales of Mexico was circulated in Jamaica.

The flowing M and bow counterstamps were applied to this coin by the Mexican revolutionary leader Morelos.

This 1792 French ecu was revalued by counterstamp at 40 batzen value for Berne, Switzerland.

This 1808 30 sueldos for the Balearic Islands was created by smoothing off the old design and counterstamping the resulting planchet.

Countermarks and Counterstamps ❧ 117

Among the most interesting countermarked coins are the Spanish dollars which circulated in England during the time of George III. Owing to the scarcity of silver at the end of the 18th century, both Spanish dollars and half-dollars were made legal tender in Great Britain in 1797. They were countermarked with the stamp of the Goldsmith's Company—a small oval stamp with the king's head. The value of this token dollar was set at 4s. 9d., somewhat higher than the actual bullion value. As a result, the counterstamp was quickly forged and fraudulently used to unofficially raise the value of Spanish dollars. In 1804, a new octagonal countermark was brought into use and in the same year, an official issue of Bank of England dollars replaced the countermarked coins.

This 1818 8 reales piece of the Chihuahua, Mexico mint was overstruck on an older coin. Portions of the previous design show on both obverse and reverse. Since the coin looks so crude, it was countermarked with a "T" representing Royal Treasury authentification as genuine.

Many counterstamps were applied to coins issued in Mexico during the country's War of Independence against Spanish rule, 1810–21. Some colonial mints resorted to casting coins in molds rather than striking them with dies. The resulting official coins looked so much like crude counterfeits that the officials countermarked them with a "T," representing Royal Treasury authentication for the coins.

Mexican coins were also counterstamped by a number of other countries. Its 8 reales pieces, for example, were counterstamped by Portugal for use in its possessions and by Japan for use as trade dollars. Portugal counterstamped Mexican 8 reales pieces of the 1740–64 period with an "MR" for use in Mozambique, and in the 1810–21 period with the crowned letters "G.P." for circulation in the Azores. In the 1890's, Japan counterstamped Mexican 8 reales coins dated 1858–59 with a series of four characters for use as trade dollars.

Brazil's 1828 80 reis coin was counterstamped in 1836 with the numeral in value to 40 to reduce its value.

Most instances of countermarking to change a coin's value represent increases. During much of its early history, most of the coins circulated in Brazil were counterstamped. Large quantities of various denominations were counterstamped in Portugal in the early 1640's for use in Brazil. The purpose of this counterstamping was to increase the value of the coins by 20 per cent.

Again, during the turbulent 1809–22 period, Brazil's coins were counterstamped to raise their face value. In an unusual switch, however, 20, 40 and 80 reis denominations minted between 1824–30, were counterstamped in 1836 to reduce their values!

Counterstamped coins also saw service in other countries of the Western Hemisphere, including: Argentina, Bolivia, Chile, Colombia, Costa Rica, Curacao, the Danish West Indies, Dominica, the Dominican Republic, French Guiana, Grenada, Guadeloupe, Haiti, Honduras, Martinique, Nicaragua, Paraguay, Peru, Puerto Rico, San Salvador, Uruguay, Venezuela, as well as most of the islands of the British West Indies. One of the rarest of all Latin American counterstamped coins is the Argentine gold doubloon (8 escudos) dated 1828, that has been specially countermarked for use in the Philippine Islands. This specimen, thought to be unique, has an estimated value of more than $2,500.00.

The Spaniards counterstamped this 1828 Argentine gold doubloon for use in the Philippine Islands. It is one of the rarest of all counterstamped coins.

Countermarks and Counterstamps ❧ 119

The piece of eight was often cut up for change in the American colonies since low value silver coins were scarce. The cut sections illustrated are "four bit" and "two bit" pieces with counterstamps showing they originated from islands in the West Indies.

Cut Money

Cut money refers to the fractional parts of the 18th century Spanish dollars (or "pieces of eight") which were literally cut into pieces to make small change. This so-called "sharp money" circulated freely in the West Indies, parts of Latin America, even the colonies which became the United States. When regular small coins were lacking, a Spanish dollar was broken up into as many as eight pieces (the denomination was 8 reales). Most common were the quarter piece ("two bits") and the half.

On the island of St. Lucia the dollar was usually cut into three portions, each stamped with the name of the island. Other countries cut up the dollar in various ways, or stamped out small portions of a peculiar shape until they were hardly recognizable as coins. Some of the cut pieces were counterstamped with values higher than their worth as bullion and the holed pieces circulated in their own area at full value in spite of the fact that some metal had been removed. This effectively kept the coins in circulation as it meant a loss to anyone taking them to another place where they would be worth only metal value. Though bits were most widely used in the 1700's, they were still used in the British Virgin Islands as late as 1892.

These Spanish cut pieces represent a challenge to the collector who seeks to accurately identify a partial coin. The bits have only a part of the Spanish monarch's portrait, only a part of the reverse arms designs, and just a portion of the inscription, etc. The shape of the cut piece and the countermark are usually sufficient to establish the area for which the cut piece was intended. The illustrations and the following table of countermarks and piercing of the cut coins should enable you to identify most specimens:

Countermarks Found on
Coins of the West Indies

Curacao

C—Curacao
C and anchor—Santo
   Domingo (Le Cap)
D (script)—Dominica
E.D. or E & D—British
   Guiana (Essequibo &
   Demerara)
G—Grenada, Guadeloupe
G (crowned)—Guadeloupe
G.L.D.—Guadeloupe
   (Isle Desirade)
GR—Jamaica
GR (script)—Trinidad
GR and crown—British
   Honduras
G.T. or GT—Guadeloupe
   (Grande Terre)
H—Tortola
I-lis-D—Guadeloupe
   (Isle Desirade)
I.G.—Guadeloupe (Les
   Saintes)
I.H.—Trinidad
L.C.—Santo Domingo
   (Le Cap)
L.S.—Guadeloupe (Les
   Saintes)
M—Montserrat
N crowned—Santo
   Domingo

Guadeloupe

British Guiana

St. Lucia

Jamaica

St. Lucia

St. Vincent

St. Bartholomew

O crowned—St.
 Bartholomew
O/TB—Tobago
P—St. Eustatius
RF—Guadeloupe
S—St. Vincent
SD or S:D—Santo
Domingo
SE—St. Eustatius
S/IV½/B—St. Vincent
S.K.—St. Kitts
SL monogram—St. Lucia
S:Lucie—St. Lucia
SM—St. Martin
SP or SP monogram—
 Martinique (St. Pierre)
St. M.—St. Martin
St. PE—Martinique
 (St. Pierre)
SV monogram—St. Vincent
T—Tobago, Tortola,
Trinidad
TB—Tobago
TIRTILA—Tortola
TOB—Tobago
TR—Trinidad

Tortola

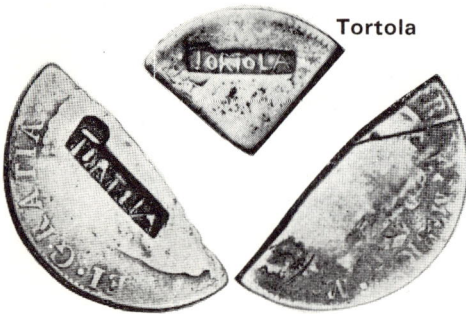

Numeral Countermarks

2.6—Montserrat
3—Curacao
5—Curacao
9—Curacao
18—Curacao
20 (in square)—St. Martin
20 (eagle)—Martinique
21 and rosace—Curacao
22 (in square)—British
 Guiana

Curacao

Montserrat

22 (in rectangle)—St.
  Martin
22 (eagle)—Martinique
25—Haiti

Object Countermarks

Arrows (bundle)—St.
  Martin
Crown—St. Bartholomew
Crowned heart—
  Martinique
Fleur-de-lis—Guadeloupe,
  Puerto Rico, St. Martin
Head in rectangle—St.
  Martin
Heart—Martinique
Lattice—Trinidad
Lion's head in square—
  St. Martin
Ring—St. Lucia
Star—Curacao

Guadeloupe

Martinique

Central Holes and Plugs

Heart-shaped—
  Dominica, Martinique
Hexagonal—Tobago
Octagonal—Guadeloupe,
  Tobago, Trinidad
Round (smooth)—
  Dominica, Puerto Rico,
  St. Kitts, St. Vincent
Round (scalloped)—
  British Guiana, Dominica,
  Guadeloupe, Trinidad

Tobago

Cyprus

Cyprus, a Mediterranean island off the coast of Turkey, was colonized by the ancient Greeks and Phoenicians and it later became part of the Persian and Roman empires. The island changed hands several times after 644, until 1571 when the Turks wrested it from the hands of the Venetians.

The imposing George V silver 45 piastres was struck in 1928 to mark Cyprus' 50th anniversary as a British colony.

In 1878, Turkey was forced to cede the island to the British who began a distinctive coinage by striking bronze 1, $\frac{1}{2}$ and $\frac{1}{4}$ piastres in 1879, and the territory became a British Crown Colony in 1925. Cyprus switched to decimal currency in 1955 and became an independent republic within the British Commonwealth in 1960.

The copper-nickel 100 mils of 1963 features the new emblem of the Republic of Cyprus. A moufflon (wild sheep) is on the reverse.

Czechoslovakia

The modern state of Czechoslovakia was established after the first World War from territory made up of ancient Bohemia, Moravia (incorporated into Bohemia in 1029) and part of Hungary. The Czechs trace their origins to Bohemia; the Slovaks are historically linked with the kingdom of Hungary, which absorbed Slovakia in the 11th century.

The first known coinage was struck by Boleslav I, Duke of Bohemia, in about A.D. 950. The coins were silver pennies of crude workmanship—the inscriptions are almost unintelligible, the prominent designs being swords and birds.

One of the major events in the history of medieval coinage occurred when the mint at Prague, capital of old Bohemia, began striking a U.S. quarter-size silver piece, the gros (meaning "great" or "big") to serve the needs of expanding trade. First struck under Wenceslas II (1278–1305), the gros was the forerunner of a whole series of silver coins struck throughout Europe—the grosso, the groschen and the groat.

On the Slovakian side, the Kremnica Mint, which is the center of Czech coinage operations today, was established about 1335 under King Charles of Hungary. In the Middle Ages Kremnica was a "Free Town" and since the area was one of Europe's chief producers of gold and silver, so it was practical to construct a mint there. Because of the mint Kremnica became an important city.

While the famous gros was struck mostly at Prague, a new Hungarian-type groat was designed and was first produced in Kremnica in the late 1330's, following the same basic style of the Prague silver piece. The city's name in Hungarian is "Kormoczbanya" and a "KB" mint mark appears on many of its issues.

During the fourteenth and fifteenth centuries, Hungary was unquestionably one of the most powerful nations in Europe. Her rich silver and gold mines contributed much to this greatness. These precious metals were sent to the mints for the production of a coinage that was used to pay a large standing army and the considerable number of civil servants. The Hungarian gold ducats from Kremnica were respected throughout

The first large quantities of dollar-size silver coins were struck in 1516-26 in Joachimstal (Joachim's valley) in Bohemia. Called a Joachimsthaler, it was popularly referred to as a "thaler," a name that was then applied to any large silver pieces. The Joachimsthaler illustrated was struck by Count Schlick of Bohemia in 1526, with the Bohemian lion on the obverse, a portrait of St. Joachim above the coat-of-arms on the reverse.

Europe, the Middle East and points beyond. In design, they closely resembled the Florentine ducat or florin.

The Hungarian throne passed to Vladislav II of Bohemia in 1490. Upon the death of his son Ludwig, who died in 1526 fighting against the Turks, Ferdinand I, Archduke of Austria, was elected King of Bohemia and Hungary. From this date until the 20th century, both thrones were hereditary to the House of Hapsburg. The coins issued during this period resemble other issues of the Holy Roman Empire but can be distinguished by their mint marks and/or differences in the coats-of-arms.

With the establishment of Czechoslovakia as an independent republic following World War I, the Kremnica Mint was entirely revitalized, becoming the Czech national mint. During the past half-century, zinc, bronze, copper-nickel, aluminum, silver and gold coins have been struck at Kremnica. The Czech monetary system is based on 100 Haleru equalling 1 Koruna or "Crown."

One of the first Czech coins, the 2 Haleru piece of 1923–25, was struck in zinc. The first Czech commemorative was the 10 Korun silver specimen with the portrait of Thomas G. Masaryk struck in 1928 to mark the tenth anniversary of Czech independence. Dr. Masaryk (1850–1937), a university professor, became the spokesman for the cause of Czech independence during the early years of the twentieth century. Another commemorative, the 20 Korun silver of 1937, was minted as a memorial after the death of Dr. Masaryk.

Dr. Thomas Masaryk, first president of Czechoslovakia, appears on this silver 10 korun piece struck as a memorial to him in 1937.

The Kremnica Mint also produced gold commemoratives in the 1920's and 1930's. The 1 ducat piece of 1923 marked the fifth anniversary of the Republic. The three denomination set of 1929 paid tribute to 1,000 years of Christianity among the Czechs. The four value set of 1934 with mining scenes on the reverse commemorated the reopening of the mines in the Kremnica region.

The puppet states of Slovakia and Bohemia-Moravia struck this aluminum 20 halierov (left) and zinc 20 haleru (right) during the German occupation of Czechoslovakia in 1939-45.

During the German occupation of 1939–45, the nation was split along the old lines into the so-called Slovakian Republic and the protectorate of Bohemia and Moravia. Each area had its own coinage and although some silver commemoratives were struck for Slovakia, the coins issued for circulation were all of base metal.

During the past two decades the Czech coins produced at Kremnica have ranked among the finest and most artistic struck anywhere in Europe. Starting with the 50 Korun silver of 1947 recalling the August 29, 1944 Slovak uprising against the Nazis, the Czechs have released a whole series of 10, 25, 50 and 100 Korun commemoratives.

The centennial of Prague's National Theatre was marked by a silver 10 korun in 1968. The design features a triga and the national arms, a rampant lion.

Czechoslovakia ✤ 127

This 1375 groschen is dated in Roman numerals, MCCCLXXV, on the reverse. The obverse carries a bust of Charlemagne.

Dating on Coins

Most countries today indicate the date of issue prominently on their coins, but with respect to world coinage history as a whole, dates are a relatively new phenomenon. Regular dating of coins begins only with the dawn of the Modern Era. While a few coins dated according to the Christian Era are known from the late 14th century, the years are shown in Roman numerals. Arabic numeral dates did not appear until a hundred years later, toward the end of the 15th century.

The first regular-issue coin inscribed with a full Arabic numeral date is a silver 1 gulden-groschen of 1486 struck at the Hall mint in the Tyrol region of Austria under Archduke Sigismund (1439–89). A smaller size coin from the same mint dated 1484 is considered a pattern. From this point on, the practice of dating coins spread to all the mints of the world. Nevertheless, as late as the 19th century some coins, especially gold pieces, were still issued without dates.

In England, the first coin to bear a date is the shilling of Edward VI, which is inscribed in Roman numerals MDXLVIII (1548). Three years

This guldiner issued by Maria of Burgundy for Brabant has the date 14-77 in Gothic numerals above the crowned shield on the reverse. The coin's obverse portrays Mary Magdalena, representing Maria of Burgundy, with Christ child on her arm; at the sides are St. Andreas and St. Sebastian.

later a silver crown of Edward VI was inscribed "1551," marking the first appearance of an Arabic numeral date on an English coin. Although dates are frequently found on coins from the time of Elizabeth I, it was not until 1662 that all English coins were regularly dated.

A curiosity of dating appears on the silver sixpence of George V, fourth issue (1927–36), where the letters "A.D." appear. The "A." appears to the left of the reverse date, while the "D." is at the right.

One of the coin dealers' favorite stories is the one of the lady who changed her mind about buying the coin of Alexander the Great struck in 323 B.C. (*before* Christ) because the date wasn't on the coin! In most instances, ancient coins can only be assigned approximate years of issue based on a study of their overall style or at best a range of years when the name of the ruler who issued the coin can be determined. In some instances, however, exact dates can be given to certain Greek coins that do

The earliest coin to carry a full year date in Arabic numerals is the silver 1484 half guldengroschen struck in Tyrol by Archduke Sigismund of Austria.

carry dates, not according to our system of reckoning of course, but numerals that show the regnal year of the monarch or the number of years after some remarkable event. The fixed date most often used is 312 B.C., the founding of the Seleucid empire in Syria.

On Roman Imperial coins, the abbreviation "Tri Pot," signifying TRIBUNITIA POTESTATE is one of the keys to exact dating. The tribunitian power, the right of veto over the Senate, was one of the many offices taken over by the emperors from the earlier and more democratic government of Rome. It was conferred annually by the Senate and the number of the year in which the office was conferred is often indicated in the legend on coins (TRI. POT. III, etc.) so, knowing from history the year in which a reign begins, the specific year of issue can be worked out.

Another title, "Cos," the Latin abbreviation for consul, is also helpful in determining the date of issue as it indicates that the emperor held the

Nuremburg, ⅓ klippe with a lamb and legend CHRISTO DUCE VERBO LUCE —"Christ, the leader, the Word, the Light." Above the arms on the reverse is the inscription EST VBI DVX IESVS PAX VICTO MARTE GVBERNAT— "Where Jesus is the leader, war is conquered and peace restored." The reverse legend is a chronogram, an inscription in which certain letters, more prominent than others, express the date when added together as Roman numerals. (In this case we have 1M, 1D, 1C, 2X's, 5V's, 3I's = 1648.)

office of Consul in the year the coin was struck. The emperor was not always one of the two consuls of the state but may have held the office more than once during his reign. The abbreviation "Cos" is often followed by a numeral which shows the number of times he had been consul. By reference to a dated list of consuls available in many history books about the Romans, it is usually possible to pinpoint the coin to the years of that particular term.

Some coins of the Byzantine Empire struck in the sixth and seventh centuries were also "dated." The period of dating embraces ten reigns from Justinian I "The Great" (527–65) to Constantine IV (668–85). Justinian I introduced dating in the twelfth year of his reign (A.D. 538) when he ordered that the regal year be placed to the right of the reverse denomination mark and the word "ANNO" (year) to the left. His dates start in 538 with the numeral "XII," the same year in which the obverse type was modified from a bust right (on the major bronze values) to a facing bust. Similarly, the numeral XIII represents the "regal year" 539; XIV is 540, XV is 541, etc.

Tiberius II (578–82) actually began dating his coins with the year V because his predecessor, Justin II, had gone violently insane during the last years of his reign. In 574, the real powers of government passed to Tiberius who had been raised to the rank of Caesar. Consequently, numeral V represents 578, the first year of his "official" reign after the death of Justin.

Constantine III, also referred to as Constans II (641–68), followed the same general dating system established by earlier Byzantine emperors, commencing with I for 641, and closing with XXVII for 668. However, the appearance of the coinage degenerated markedly during his long reign.

Dating of coins was irregular under Constantine IV. The dating is missing on a great many specimens, even on coins struck at the main Constantinople Mint. Some years are unknown from any of the mints.

The Moslem date A.H. 1321 on Morocco's bronze 5 mazunas is equivalent to 1903 of the Christian Era.

Dates on coins of Middle Eastern and Far Eastern countries present the collector with some problems. Those countries which are predominantly Moslem, located mostly in North Africa, the Middle East and parts of the Orient, set their dates according to the Mohammedan calendar. The Mohammedan Era, also known as the Era of the Hegira (flight) begins in A.D. 622, the year in which Mohammed fled from Mecca to Medina. The Era of the Hegira is abbreviated "A.H." (from the Latin *anno Hegirae*) and is the Moslem counterpart of the Christian "A.D." (*anno Domini*).

The complication in comparing Mohammedan with Christian dates is that the Moslems use a lunar calendar on which a year is eleven days shorter than the solar year. To convert a Mohammedan date to its equivalent on our own calendar, you must deduct 3 per cent (for difference in length) and add 622 (for different starting point) to the A.H. figure. This will give the A.D. year.

Afghanistan is the only country in modern times to use a calendar of solar years dating from Mohammed's hegira in A.D. 622. Thus, to convert S.H. dates to A.D., it is only necessary to add 622 without making the 3% adjustment.

On coins of Thailand, the dating systems of two eras have been used. The Buddhist Era (B.E.), which began in 543 B.C., can be converted into our Christian Era A.D. dates by simply subtracting 543. The Bangkok Era (R.S.) starts in A.D. 1782, the year in which the present Chakri Dynasty line of rulers established itself at Bangkok. The A.D. equivalent dates can be determined by adding 1782 to the Bangkok date.

Debasement

World economic crises are reflected on coins from the time of the ancient Romans right up to coins now in circulation in some parts of the world. Over the centuries, governments have reacted to financial difficulties by reducing the intrinsic value of their coins while attempting to maintain the face value purchasing power.

In ancient Rome, supposedly "silver" coins were made by putting a thin silver coating over a bronze core. This was originally the work of forgers, but was also done at times by the State. Roman coins were regularly debased from the time of Caracalla (211–17), when the *antoninianus* of base silver (heavily diluted with bronze) was introduced.

In medieval Europe, Philip IV ("The Fair") of France was one of the first monarchs of his era who deliberately debased his coinage—to meet the expenses of his Flemish campaign in 1302 he debased the coinage to such an extent that he got three times the amount of coins out of the same amount of precious metal.

"Silver" shillings of Henry VIII were badly debased . . . this 1544 specimen was 2/3 copper and only 1/3 silver. The coin gave Henry the nickname "Old Coppernose" because the copper began to show through at the highest point of the design.

English silver coins, from the earliest times until the reign of Henry VIII (1509–47), maintained their purity. The first official debasement of English coinage took place in 1526 when, to enrich his treasury and to provide for his lavish expenditures, the gold crown and half-crown were reduced to "crown gold" of 22 carats fineness; later in his reign the gold coins were further reduced to 20 carats. Silver coins were struck of one-third alloy, then half (1544), and finally the silver content was reduced to only one-third (1545). In modern times, British silver coins were reduced to 50 per cent silver in 1920 and in 1947 silver was completely eliminated from the coinage.

Due to the increasing price of raw silver during the 1960's, the few nations still maintaining fine silver coinage have been forced to seek substitute metals. Most have adopted copper-nickel alloy, Canada has turned to pure nickel and the U. S. has developed a new "sandwich" planchet—a copper core banded between two layers of nickel.

Denmark

Denmark's first coinage was produced in about A.D. 825 during the time of King Hardecanute (824–55). In the course of the next three centuries Denmark's economy was based in large part on booty brought back from overseas adventures, especially from England. Medieval Denmark reached its greatest heights under Cnut (1016–35), who ruled over Norway and England as well as Denmark. In the medieval era, Danish coins often closely resembled Anglo-Saxon issues. Further, certain English types have been found in much greater quantity in Denmark than in England. The reason is quite simple—these coins were used to pay the annual tribute. Under Harthacnut (1035–42), Magnus the Good (1042–47) and Sven Estridsen (1047–74), the continuing English types were influenced by designs derived from Byzantine models, and sometimes a Runic script indicates the name of the mint and engraver.

The successors of Cnut saw Danish military power decline . . . England was lost in 1042 and Norway in 1047. Succession to the Danish throne was in almost constant dispute from the later 11th century. Coinage suffered as a consequence, both in respect to debasement and poorer engraving. The 13th century was a period marred by bloodshed and civil war. However, Danish fortunes rose steadily in the 14th century, especially under Valdemar IV Atterdag (1340–75) considered the greatest of the medieval Danish kings. Among many achievements, he seized control of the Ore Sound, a chief entrance to the Baltic Sea, and imposed dues on ships passing through it.

When Denmark, with Norway and Sweden, formed the Union of Kalmar in 1397, the most powerful and populous of the three states was

Silver penning of Valdemar II, King of Denmark (1202-41). The inscription reads WALDEMARVS REX DANORVM.

Denmark which became the dominant partner in the Union. Proud of its pre-eminence, Denmark adopted a coat-of-arms with three lions.

Under Eric VII, Duke of Pomerania and first ruler under the new union, coinage reform was introduced and a form of taxation was put into effect. During Eric's long reign (1396–1439) silver pieces in 3 and 6 pence values replaced the base metal billon coinage of the 14th century. Eric's coins are distinguished by the letter "E" inscribed in the field or at the center of the crown.

In 1448, with the extinction of the Estrith dynasty (which had ruled Denmark since 1047), the Danes elected Christian I, Count of Oldenburg, to the throne. The Oldenburg family kept the throne until 1863. Denmark's first gold coins were struck under Hans I (1481–1513). His 1, 2 and 3 noble specimens show the king seated on a throne with the arms on reverse.

Denmark lost Sweden in 1521, when the Swedes under Gustavus Vasa declared their independence. This was a great blow to Danish power and for the next several centuries the Danes found themselves involved in wars with larger nations. The reign of Christian II (1513–23) marks the beginning of Denmark's modern period of coinage. The large silver

Denmark's first gold coins were struck under King Hans (1481-1513). This gold noble of 1496 shows the King seated on his throne holding a sceptre.

134 ⦾ Denmark

These necessity coins, 2 mark and 2 skilling silver klippings, were struck during the Seven Years War with Sweden (1563-70) by Danish King Frederick II (1559-88). The klippings were so unpopular that the King had to threaten death to anyone who refused to accept them.

gulden, struck for the first time, shows the enthroned king and a crowned shield. Christian II also produced a variety of gold pieces.

From this point on, gold coins were struck by Danish monarchs in profusion. Frederick II (1559–88) produced a number of square-shaped

1618 silver krone of Christian IV (1588-1648). This long-reigning monarch introduced trade with the East Indies and sent expeditions in search of a northwest passage in the Pacific.

pieces, while Christian IV (1588–1648) also struck a variety of squared gold pieces—in 3, 4, 6 and 8 daler values. The last of the famous "klippe" gold pieces were minted under Frederick III (1648–70). "Klippe" came in six major varieties ranging in value from a half-ducat to five ducats.

The armored Christian IV is shown standing. The reverse of this 1644 gold ducat has the words IUSTUS JEHOVAH IUDEX—"The Lord is a Righteous Judge." The word "Jehovah" is written in Hebrew and the gold and silver coins in the series are known as Christian IV's "Hebrew coinage."

Denmark ✪ 135

1723 silver krone or 4 marks of Frederick IV (1699-1730) showing the King mounted on horseback.

Frederick V (1746-66) struck this undated triple taler in 1746 to mark his accession to the throne. The new king's father, Christian VI (1730-46) appears on the reverse . . . it was customary on the accession coins to portray the preceding monarch. An interesting sidelight to Danish coinage is that since 1513 the kings have been alternately named Frederick and Christian.

This 1769 portrait specidaler of Christian VII shows the badge and ribbon of the Order of the Elephant around the shield of arms.

136 ⬡ Denmark

During the Napoleonic Wars, Denmark was driven by circumstance to
support the French, and was punished by having to turn Norway over to
Sweden in 1814. A half-century later, Prussia seized Denmark's southern
provinces of Schleswig and Holstein in a lightning war. Thus, Denmark
became the "tiny" Denmark of today with an area of just under 17,000
square miles.

The 1906 accession 2
kroner of Frederick VIII
(1906-12), also portrays
the King's father,
Christian IX (1863-1906),
on the reverse.

No gold coins have been produced by Denmark since 1931, while none
have been issued for circulation since 1917. Twenty kroner gold pieces
were minted as late as 1926–27 and 1930–31 under Christian X, but
were not released. They are being held by the National Bank of Denmark
at Copenhagen as backing for the country's paper money. Under Danish
monetary law, coins, as well as gold bullion, must be used for this purpose.

Christian IX's 20 kroner gold piece of
1873 displays Dania, a seated female
figure holding a sceptre and shield on
the reverse.

Since the end of World War II, the Copenhagen Mint has produced an impressive array of commemorative pieces. Christian X's 75th birthday was marked with a 2 kroner silver coin in 1945. Frederick IX, son of Christian X, who has been on the Danish throne since 1947, has been portrayed on a variety of coins since his accession. He and his Queen, Ingrid, were honored with a dual-portrait 5 kroner silver piece in 1960 on the occasion of their silver wedding anniversary.

A special issue of the silver 2 kroner specimen in 1958 with the portraits of Frederick IX and Princess Margrethe was struck on the occasion of the declaration of the Princess as heir to the throne.

Denmark's recent commemoratives mark important events in the life of the Royal family: (top) the 25th wedding anniversary of King Frederick IX and Queen Ingrid; (left) 18th birthday of Princess Margrethe; (center) wedding of Princess Benedikte; (right) wedding of Princess Anne-Marie.

This 1953 Danish 2 kroner with its Greenland map was sold to raise funds to combat tuberculosis in Greenland. Greenland, long a Danish colony, became a part of the Danish Commonwealth in 1953.

Greenland

The Copenhagen Mint struck distinctive money for Greenland in the early 1920's. They were tokens for use by the Cryolite Mining and Trading Co. at Ivigtut. In 1926 official government coins were released for use throughout Greenland. During World War II, when Denmark was occupied by Nazi Germany, brass 5 kroner pieces for Greenland were minted at Philadelphia. However, all coins for Greenland are now produced at Copenhagen. Current Greenland coins in circulation are two varieties of 1 krone pieces, one struck in aluminum-bronze and the other in copper-nickel.

This 1944 Greenland 5 kroner piece was struck at the U.S. mint in Philadelphia as Denmark was then under wartime occupation. The polar bear appears on all of Greenland's coins.

Iceland

Some historians maintain that Iceland was known to mainland Europeans as early as 300 B.C. and that Irish monks visited the island beginning about A.D. 500. In about 870, Iceland was settled by Vikings, some of whom had lived in Ireland. In 930, they established the Althing, oldest existing legislature in the world.

Iceland remained an independent republic until 1264, when the island passed into Norwegian hands. In 1381, Iceland came under Danish rule along with Norway. When Norway was separated from Denmark in 1814, Iceland remained under the Danish king. Finally, in 1918, Iceland was recognized by Denmark as a sovereign state, bound to Denmark only through a common king. When the Germans overran Denmark at the

outset of World War II, the island dissolved its union with Denmark, and on June 17, 1944, the Republic of Iceland was proclaimed.

Foreign coins were extensively circulated in Iceland from the Middle Ages up to the 20th century. Coins of the other Scandinavian countries were especially utilized, along with a good measure of British and Spanish issues. The first coins inscribed with Iceland's name are the rare Danish trade coins (piasters) dated 1771 and 1777. However, Iceland did not have its own separate coinage until 1922. Since Iceland was still included in the union with Denmark this was a regal coinage struck at the Copenhagen Mint.

The monetary unit was the krona, divided into 100 aurrar, and the ordinary coinage until the early 1940's consisted of 10, 5, 2 and 1 krona, and 25, 10, 5 and 2 aurar. There was also a 1 eyrir piece struck in bronze from 1926 to 1942, and again from 1946 until the present day. Under the Republic, the basic monetary unit has remained the same with 100 aurar equalling 1 krona.

Under Denmark the coins had the Icelandic arms crowned and flanked by the monogram "Cx-R" of King Christian X of Denmark. A set of three silver commemorative pieces (2, 5 and 10 kronur values) was struck in 1930 to mark the one-thousandth anniversary of the Althing.

On June 17, 1961, Iceland released a handsome 500 kronur commemorative gold piece to mark the sesquicentennial of the birth of Jon Sigurdsson (1811–79), regarded as the father of modern Iceland. This was the first gold coin issued by any Scandinavian country since 1931, when all went off the gold standard. Sigurdsson's portrait adorns the obverse, while the reverse has the Icelandic arms and value.

Though not intended for circulation, this 1961 Iceland 500 kronur gold piece portraying Jon Sigurdsson was officially issued by the government.

A bracteate issued at the Nunnery of the Holy Cross in Nordhausen, Germany by the Abbess Cecilia (1135-60). Cecilia is portrayed holding a crozier (symbol of office) and a palm branch.

Ecclesiastical Coins

Ecclesiastical mints, striking coins in the name of prelates of the church, operated in Europe for over a thousand years—from the fall of the Roman Empire until into the 19th century. Since the right to mint coins yielded a profit (the difference between the face value and the intrinsic worth of the metal) it was a much sought after privilege controlled by the Holy Roman emperors. Since the empire was founded as a working union between Church and State, the emperors over the centuries did grant the mint rights to many ecclesiastical authorities as well as to secular rulers.

Cologne, one of Germany's oldest and greatest cities, was the site of a Roman colony as early as A.D. 50. Raised to the status of an archbishopric by Charlemagne, the city was the site of an imperial mint that struck coins in his name. Bruno I, brother of Emperor Otto I, the Great, became Archbishop of Cologne in 953 and during his reign imperial coins were issued carrying his name and the reverse inscription SANCTA COLONIA (the Latin name for Cologne). A century later, the archbishops began to issue coins on their own authority, establishing archiepiscopal mints in the surrounding towns as well. During the 14th century, the coinage of the Cologne archbishops was one of the most important of Germany and all of Europe.

1680 silver piece issued by Peter Philipp of Dernbach, Duke of Eastern Franconia (1672-83), for the archbishopric of Bamberg. The coin portrays St. Henry, patron of Bamberg, with the Duke's crowned arms on the reverse.

The city itself became independent of church rule in 1288, although the archbishops continued to have strong influence over the city's affairs. A city mint was established in 1474 and for the next three centuries, Cologne had two separate coinages—one issued by the city's municipal authorities, the other by the church authorities—a situation not unusual in those areas with ecclesiastical coinages. The coinage right was not limited just to archbishops—in some instances even abbots and abbesses issued coins.

In Switzerland during the Middle Ages, various emperors granted coinage rights to ecclesiastical foundations as a means of gaining support in the prolonged conflicts between the emperors and the popes. Coins were struck in the name of church prelates at Lausanne and Geneva beginning in the tenth century.

Another early Swiss ecclesiastical coinage came from the Benedictine monastary at St. Gall which first issued pfennigs during the 11th century. At Zurich the nunnery established about 850 struck bracteates during the 12th, 13th and 14th centuries. The early coinages of the ecclesiastical mints, like the issues of the secular authorities, were mostly bracteate pfennigs or silver deniers.

In England, even during the early days of the Saxons, archbishops, certain bishops, and abbots were permitted to issue coins by privilege of the king. The coins were of their own design and inscribed with their own names. In fact, the archbishops were allowed to use their own portraits. The earliest known issues are the coins of Archbishop Ecgberht (734–66), and Jaenberht, Archbishop of Canterbury (766–90).

At the Council of Greatley held in 928, it was decreed by Aethelstan, King of Wessex, that there should be only one kind of money throughout the realm; henceforth, though coins from ecclesiastical mints were issued (mainly from Canterbury, York, Durham, and London) they resembled those from the Royal Mint. The name of the prelate was dropped in favor of the king's inscription, but there is some significant letter, mint mark, or symbol to distinguish them from the regal coins. In many cases it is a bit difficult to distinguish regular issue regal coins of England from episcopal issues. For example, the Edward I silver penny struck at the Royal Mint in York Castle in about 1280 differs from the episcopal coinage of York, struck by order of the Archbishop, only in that the latter issues have a quatrefoil in the center of the reverse.

By the 1270's and 1280's England's ecclesiastical mints ran into difficulties. The abbots, bishops and archbishops operated their mints for the purpose of making profits, which came from the difference between face value and intrinsic worth of the metal. By this time, however, the London Mint and associated royal coin striking facilities in other cities were by then able to supply most of the country's circulating currency. During the mid-14th century, the supply of silver bullion ran so low that the ecclesiastical mints had difficulty in getting sufficient amounts for coinage. The Royal Mint at London made increasingly strong demands for all available supplies. The shortage of silver bullion provided the king with an excuse for permanently closing the abbots' mints at St. Edmunds and Reading and of bringing the mint at Canterbury to a standstill for a long time. By the end of Edward III's long reign (1327–77), the near monopoly of the coinage passed to the London Mint.

Ortenburg, 1656 taler portraying Christoph Cardinal Widmann wearing the hat and robes of his clerical office. The coin's reverse shows Cardinal Christoph's ornate arms surmounted by a flat red hat, the traditional emblem of a Prince of the Church.

The right for ecclesiastics to issue coins was abolished by Henry VIII, the last of these mints being that of Thomas Cranmer, of Canterbury (1533–56). One of the final issues was that of Thomas Cardinal Wolsey, Archbishop of York, who struck a silver groat during the 1514–30 period. This notorious coin figured in Wolsey's impeachment since stamping his archiepiscopal signature on a coin with the high value of a groat was deemed a flagrant infringement of the royal prerogative.

No gold coins were permitted and, in fact, the ecclesiastical mints confined themselves almost exclusively to the silver penny.

The fact that ecclesiastical coins were issued in such great quantities over so long a period indicates the enormous power of the church in both spiritual and temporal matters.

Ecclesiastical Coins ❧ 143

These similarly designed coins, both minted at Quito, were struck in 1834 while the country was still united with Colombia, and in 1836 as an independent republic.

Ecuador

After the period of Spanish rule, Ecuador, whose name in Spanish means "equator," was united with Colombia upon its liberation in 1819. Ecuador achieved its independence in 1836 and became a republic. Coins were minted at Quito, the capital, from 1833 to 1862. Since the Quito Mint closed, Ecuadorian coins have been struck at a variety of world mints, including Birmingham, Lima, Mexico City, Philadelphia and Santiago.

When Ecuador was still technically part of Colombia, a coinage of gold escudos and of silver reales was produced at the Quito Mint in 1833–35. Both the silver and gold coins were of the same basic type. The obverse had fasces between two cornucopiae inscribed "EL EGUADOR EN COLOMBIA", and the mint name, while the reverse had a sun above two mountain peaks. A similar silver coinage of ½ to 4 reales values was struck after the establishment of Ecuador as a separate republic in 1836— the only alteration was in the obverse inscription which now read "REPUBLICA DEL ECUADOR."

General Antonio Jose de Sucre (1795-1830), Bolivar's lieutenant in the fight for South American independence, appears on Ecuador's silver 5 sucres of 1943. The coins were struck for Ecuador at the Mexico City mint.

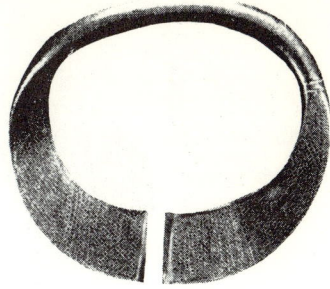

Egyptian gold money-ring (c. 1680-1350 B.C.).

Egypt, Ancient

Ancient Egypt, which endured as an advanced civilization for several thousand years, never used coins as currency. Barter was the general form of exchange. Services were paid for in goods and the same was true of taxes. The Egyptians developed credit and bookkeeping to a high level; they had ample supplies of metal; yet for centuries they had no coinage.

Egypt was a self-contained economy. What foreign commerce existed was a monopoly of the Pharaoh. All the mines belonged to him. The vast majority of the people were tillers of the soil. Craftsmen worked for the temples or the nobles or the Pharaoh. The government scribes got their pay from the Pharaoh. The priests received huge donations and much of the best land belonged to the temples.

In barter transactions in the early period, the Egyptians used sacks of corn of standard weight. Linen was another favorite as a medium of exchange. Finally, about 2000 B.C., the Egyptians began to use metal rings and copper utensils of standard size and weight, as a medium of exchange. From this time on, they recorded business deals in terms of copper bowls, pitchers, dishes, etc. To get a rough idea of "money" proportions, it has been determined that silver was worth 40 times as much as copper, and gold as much as silver.

In the period 1500–1200 B.C., the civilization of Egypt began to decline. Gradually the provinces in Asia Minor slipped away from Egyptian control. Egypt's domains shrank steadily, foreign tribute decreased and large-scale building slowed down.

In 605 B.C., Nebuchadnezzar, king of the rising Babylonian Empire in the East, defeated the Egyptians in battle. From 525 B.C. on, Egypt was a province of Persia. Then, in 332 B.C. Alexander of Macedon (then

Ptolemy I (323-285 B.C.), Alexander the Great's successor as ruler in Egypt, broke all tradition when he issued a tetradrachm (left), c. 320 B.C., showing the undisguised likeness of the dead Alexander. Ptolemy went a step further c. 300 B.C. by using his own realistic portrait on a tetradrachm (right), establishing a custom followed by rulers down through the centuries.

northern Greece) conquered Egypt and founded the city of Alexandria at the mouth of the Nile.

With the Greek conquest, coinage came at last to Egypt, and Alexandria became the site of one of the greatest mints of the ancient world. At Alexander's death (323 B.C.), Ptolemy, one of his ablest generals, made himself ruler of Egypt and established a dynasty there. (Actually, it was not until 305 B.C. that he gave himself the formal title of "king.") All the kings who followed had the same name—Ptolemy—and are distinguished only by their numbers and nicknames.

The Ptolemies had a monopoly of commerce, banking, land and mines. Throughout the life of the dynasty, they continued to issue excellent coinage. Alexandria, with its far-flung commerce and its importance as a center of Greek culture, was second only to Rome. After the first five

For general circulation, Ptolemy II (246-221 B.C.) issued this large cast bronze coin showing the head of Zeus and the traditional eagle and thunderbolt on the reverse.

146 ॰ Egypt, Ancient

The finely detailed portrait of Arsinoe, wife of Ptolemy II, is shown on this rare gold octodrachm struck in 266 B.C.

Ptolemies, the dynasty deteriorated and it finally came to an end with the famous Cleopatra (51–30 B.C.).

Roman Egypt, which Octavian had won from Cleopatra in 30 B.C., was considered the personal possession of the emperor himself rather than a province of the Empire. Octavian instituted a coinage at Alexandria based on the debased silver tetradrachms of his predecessors, the Ptolemies. The coins of Roman Egypt show the head of the emperor as on the issues of Rome, but the legends are in Greek in deference to the local population.

Cleopatra VII (51-30 B.C.), Egypt's last queen, is best known in history as the woman whose beauty captivated Julius Caesar and Mark Antony.

The tetradrachms were very thick in relation to their diameter. They were equivalent in value to one Roman denarius and, like the denarius, they suffered a constant reduction in silver content under each succeeding ruler until by the time of Diocletian (A.D. 284) the tetradrachms had only about 1 per cent silver to 99 per cent base metal. Coins containing enough silver to appear white are called "billon" tetradrachms, and the alloys that look like bronze are called "potin."

Among the least expensive Roman coins available today are the issues of the Imperial Mint at Alexandria, Egypt. The eagle on this potin (base, mixed metal) tetradrachm of Probus (276-82), is a forerunner of the type of birds inscribed on United States coins centuries later.

Egypt, Ancient ✿ 147

King Farouk (1936-52) wearing a fez appears on this 10 milliemes scalloped planchet bronze coin of 1943.

Egypt, Modern

After the passing of its great kingdoms of the ancient era, Egypt was conquered in turn by the Greeks, the Romans, the Arabs, and the Ottoman Turks. During the four centuries of Turkish rule, all Egyptian coins carried the *Toughra*—the Sultan's calligraphic emblem. The dates, inscribed in Turkish figures, are given according to the Moslem calendar (see Dates on Coins).

Early in the 19th century, Mehemet Ali, a swashbuckling Albanian officer in Turkish service, seized power as Pasha of Egypt, although he still paid nominal allegiance to Turkey. Under his successors, the khedives, Egypt came more and more into the sphere of British influence, especially after completion of the Suez Canal in 1869. Made a British Protectorate in 1914, Britain in 1922 declared Egypt an independent kingdom.

Egypt's greatest pharaoh, Rameses II (1292-1225 B.C.), is shown in a chariot on this 1 pound gold piece struck in 1955.

The Egyptain monarchy was overthrown in 1952 when an army revolt led by General Mohammed Naguib deposed playboy King Farouk (Farouk, incidentally, was an avid collector of gold coins). Colonel Gamal Abdel Nasser succeeded Naguib as a leader of Egypt in 1954 and has been in power ever since. Egypt's coins of recent years reflect quite clearly the country's fierce national pride.

Egypt's colossal Sphinx, shown on the coin series of 1954-59, is several thousand years old and still stands near the Great Pyramids of Gizeh.

Under the Russian czars, coins of the markkaa denomination were first issued for Finland. The obverses have the Russian Imperial eagle with the Finnish lion in the shield on its breast.

Finland

Finland, the "land of the fens," although settled in the north by the Lapps, who are related to the Eskimos, and in the south by emigrants from the Baltic countries and the Urals, became linked to Scandinavia in 1155, when the Swedish King Erik "The Good" invaded Finland as a crusader and completed the Christianization of the country. Eventually, Finland became a part of the Kingdom of Sweden. Finland was to remain under Swedish influence and rule for more than six centuries.

King Gustavus I Vasa of Sweden founded Helsinki in 1550; the capital of Finland is famous for its distinguished architecture and spotless streets. During the 16th century, Sweden made Finland a Grand Duchy, and Swedish became the official and literary language. Even today there are two official languages in Finland: Swedish and Finnish. Many postage stamps, coins and banknotes are inscribed in both languages. (The country is "Suomi" in Finnish and "Finland" in Swedish.)

After centuries of fighting for control, Sweden surrendered Finland to Russia in 1809 and Czar Alexander I made the country an autonomous Russian Grand Duchy. When the Russian Revolution broke out in 1917, the Finns revolted and set up their own government. Under the leadership of the great General Gustav von Mannerheim (b. 1867–d. 1951), Finland formally declared independence on December 6, 1917.

During the 19th century, Finnish coins followed Russian coins and were technically issued under the ægis of the various Russian czars. However, beginning in 1864, coins of distinctively Finnish denomination—with markkaa values—were struck. Gold 20 and 10 markkaa coins with the

Issued for Finland under Alexander II (1855-81), this 1873 copper coin shows the Russian Czar's monogram.

Finland ❧ 149

names "Finland" and "Suomi" on them were first issued in 1878. The crowned eagle design was used until 1913.

The Markkaa denomination was retained when Finland became a republic in 1917, but the coat-of-arms of Finland, a rampant lion with uplifted sword, replaced the Russian eagle on the obverse. A handsome set of two gold coins, 100 and 200 markkaa values, was issued in 1926.

In 1941–43, during World War II, holed 5 and 10 pennia pieces were issued in both bronze and iron. A commemorative 500 markkaa silver piece was issued in 1951–52 to mark the staging of the International

Finland's currency reform of January 1, 1963, revalued 100 old markkaa at 1 new markkaa worth 100 pennia. Thus the 1953 50 markkaa coin (left) and the 1963 50 pennia piece (right) are of equal value.

Olympic Games in Helsinki. This coin should have been dated "1952" only, but through a mint error the "1951" date appeared on some of the coins first produced.

On January 1, 1963, a monetary reform went into effect in Finland: 100 old markkaa were revalued at one new markkaa. As a consequence, a new series of coins were introduced, the 1, 5, 10, 20 and 50 pennia values. A new one markkaa coin in the base metal billon was introduced in 1964.

On December 6, 1967, the Bank of Finland released a silver 10 markkaa coin to commemorate the country's 50th year of independence.

1967 silver 10 markkaa commemorative struck to celebrate Finland's 50th anniversary of independence. Five flying ospreys symbolize the decades. The reverse design refers to the nation's architectural advances.

150 ❧ Finland

France

The land we call France today is the *Gallia* or *Gaul* of Julius Caesar's time. Even while Rome declined, Gaul remained its most flourishing and civilized province. France began to emerge as an independent nation during the fourth and fifth centuries A.D. During its fifteen centuries of historical change and development, France has strongly influenced the rest of the world in art, music, literature, philosophy, political theory, fashion, and in many other ways.

The first true coinage in France after the Roman period consisted of currencies issued by the Merovingian kings. Their coins of the fifth and sixth centuries are relatively crude and were minted mostly in silver and billon with very little gold. Merovingian deniers were at first imitations of Roman silver coins and later, by the sixth century, they were imitations of Byzantine silver coins of Justinian I.

Dagobert I (628-39), a Frankish king of the Merovingian Dynasty, struck this gold tremissis in imitation of similarly designed Byzantine gold pieces.

The Visigoths and Burgundians, two other barbarian tribes who shared France after the Roman period, also maintained coinages. The Visigoths, a Teutonic people, settled in southern Spain and France. The Burgundians, also a Germanic tribe, invaded the region of the Rhone and Saone rivers in about A.D. 400. Both these tribal kingdoms were comparatively short-lived. Nevertheless, the two kingdoms managed to strike some of France's earliest and most interesting coins. The Visigoths maintained mints at Burdigala (Bordeaux) and Tolosa (Toulouse). The Burgundians struck several varieties of solidi and tremissis—some of them bear the inscriptions of their kings, Sigismund (516–24) and Gundobald II (C. 524).

Of the three barbarian kingdoms the Merovingians were by far the most important. Merovingian coins are generally very difficult to classify since several kings often bore the same name with no ordinal number inscribed on the coins. The Merovingians existed in the heart of the so-called "Dark Ages," and the quality of their coinage declined steadily. By the seventh and eigth centuries their imitations of Byzantine silver pieces are almost unrecognizable and the inscriptions meaningless.

In about 628, the actual ruling power in France passed from the Merovingian kings to the mayors of the palace, or chief ministers, who

Pepin the Short (741-51), the first of the Carolingian kings, began a new issue of silver deniers. The denier illustrated bears the initials "RP" for *Rex Pipinus*, while the reverse is inscribed with the name of the Lugdunum (Lyon) mint.

were the first of the Carolingians. The Merovingian kings continued to occupy the throne until 751, however, the last of their kings being Childeric III (741–51).

The name Carolingian (from the Latin *Carolus*, or Charles) is derived from either Charles Martel, father of Pepin the Short, or from Charlemagne, Pepin's son.

When the Moors threatened to overrun Western Europe, it was the Franks who drove them back in 732 near Tours in what historians now consider one of the greatest decisive battles of all history. Charles Martel ("Charles the Hammer") was the Frankish chieftan who succeeded in rallying his divided people and who led them to victory. Charles' son, Pepin the Short, deposed Childric III to become the first Carolingian ruler in name as well as in fact. The Carolingian dynasty (from the Latin *Carolus* for Charles) is derived from Charles Martel.

Pepin replaced the deteriorated Merovingian coinage with a new issue of silver deniers. The obverse bore only the initials "RP" (for Rex Pipinus) while the reverse was inscribed with the name of the mint.

Charlemagne (from Carolus Magnus, "Charles the Great") who reigned for 46 years as Carolingian emperor (768–814) continued the denier coinage of Pepin, but because of competition from the Arab dirhem circulating in Spain he raised the coin's weight with the planchet becoming thicker and flatter. Charlemagne reached the apex of his career when Pope Leo III crowned him "Emperor of the Romans" on Christmas day in 800.

Early in the Carolingian dynasty coinage had been a royal prerogative, but Charlemagne and his successors began granting the mint right to abbeys. As the power of the Carolingian kings declined, feudal counts issued their own currencies, mostly in imitation of the royal deniers. The

This denier of Charlemagne (768-814), struck at Dorestadt in Lorraine, is inscribed CAROLVS on the obverse and has the name of the mint on the reverse.

(Left) Pepin the Short, King of the Franks (751-68), struck this denier at Lugdunum (Lyon). (Right) A century later Pepin II, King of Aquitania (839-65), struck a similar denier at Toulouse. The obverse reads PIPINVS REXE, the reverse TOLOSA CIVI.

Carolingians continued to rule France until the reign of Louis V who died without heirs in 987.

Louis V was succeeded by Hugh Capet (lived 938-96), the founder of the Capetian dynasty that held the French throne until 1328. Hugh was also a lay abbot and the family name was taken from his abbot's cape of gray wool, called a *capet*. The Capetians were succeeded by the Valois and Bourbon branches of the family. Thus, after the Carolingians, all French kings except the Bonapartes are descended from Hugh Capet.

Hugh Capet struck coins inscribed not only with his title as king, but separate feudal issues carrying his title, for instance, as Count of Paris or Count of Sens. Although the king himself did issue an important currency, it was still one of many as feudal lords and bishops by the dozen struck their own coinages.

Philippe II Auguste (1180–1223), one of the greatest of the French medieval kings, extended the royal domains and expanded the power of the monarchy at the expense of the feudal lords. He struck a denier with the king's name and title occupying the whole obverse in a circular inscription, while the reverse is a simple cross with the name of the mint, Paris. He also struck deniers at other mints, including Arras, Montreuil, and Saint Omer. The silver deniers and half deniers constituted the chief coinage of this entire period—for the monarchy as well as for the feudal lords and ecclesiastics.

During the period from Louis IX to Charles VIII,· 1226-1498, the regal coinage became clearly dominant over the feudal issues. Because of

Charles the Bald (843-77), King of the West Franks, struck silver deniers at Paris. The design features a cross and the inscription CAROLVS REX; the king's monogram and PARISII CIVITAS are on the reverse.

France ❧ 153

The silver gros tournois ("big coin of Tours") was first minted during the reign of Louis IX (1226-70). The obverse legend reads BHDICTV (Benedictum) SIT HOME (Nomen) NRI (Nostri) DEI JHV (Jesu) XPI (Christi), Latin for "blessed be the name of our Lord, Jesus Christ." The name of the king and his title LVDOVICVS REX fills the inner circle around the cross. On the reverse is a castle representing the abbey at Tours where these coins were first struck.

improved economic conditions in France and the rest of Western Europe during the 13th century, larger silver coins and gold pieces were minted. Louis IX (1226–70) introduced the silver gros tournois valued at four deniers. This coin was extensively copied by other European countries. Louis IX, who was noted for his piety and charity, was canonized by Pope Boniface VIII in 1297, and is now known to history as "St. Louis." At the end of his reign, in 1266–70, he introduced the first of France's regal gold pieces, the *ecu d'or*, showing on obverse the royal shield in lobed circle; the reverse has a floriated cross.

Philip VI (1328–50) was the first French monarch of the House of Valois, a dynasty that ruled until 1589. Though the power of the French crown was great at this time, Philip was a frivolous king and the Hundred Years' War against England began in 1337 with disastrous results for France. Philip's coinage is rich in variety, especially in the gold issues. The *ecu d'or* (golden shield) was first struck by Philip. It shows the king beneath a canopy, with the motto XPS VINCIT XPS REGNAT XPS IMPERAT (Christ conquers, Christ reigns, Christ commands) which was repeated on many subsequent issues. Prominent on the reverse is a shield with the fleur-de-lis arms of France.

Ecu a la Couronne of Charles VII (1422-61), named for the crowned shield (ecu) that fills the obverse of the coin.

154 ❧ France

Henry V (1415–22) of England and Henry VI (1422–53) of England both struck coins for France during this period when England controlled large areas of French territory. In 1415 Henry V invaded France and won the great battle of Agincourt.

Charles VII (1422–61) was not crowned king until 1429 at Reims with Joan of Arc standing by his side. Under Henry VI, the English controlled much of northern France, but by 1453 the French drove the English from all their possessions in the country except Calais. Charles struck a new type of silver coin, a double gros, at Tournai.

Louis XI (1461–83), a master of diplomacy and intrigue, strengthened the French kingdom which was now free of English incursions. He

These ornately engraved 14th-century gold coins are (left) a gold leopard of Edward the Black Prince of Aquitaine (1355-75), and (right) a gold mouton (lamb). They take their names from the animals shown on them.

simplified the monetary system, producing his coins in a relatively few basic denominations. His *ecu a la couronne* was the major type of gold piece; this coin features the crowned arms on obverse and the floriated cross on reverse.

During the last years of the 15th century and early years of the 16th, France made the transformation from feudalism to the modern age. The House of Valois continued to rule until 1589 when, at the death of Henry III, the Bourbons in the person of Henry IV of Navarre acceded to the throne. Louis XII (1498–1515), who attempted throughout his reign to expand French borders at the expense of Italy, succeeded in establishing regular banking procedures for the crown. He issued an interesting *ecu d'or* featuring his crowned arms flanked by two porcupines. He was also the first French king to issue the teston which replaced the gros tournois.

France ꙮ 155

Francis I (1515–47), who was thwarted in his attempts to be placed at the head of the Holy Roman Empire by Charles V, spent most of his reign carrying on wars with his successful rival. He made a number of administrative reforms in coinage production. One of the reforms included the placing of letter mint marks on all coins—"A" for Paris, "B" for Rouen, "K" for Bordeaux, etc.

Henry II (1547–59) recovered Calais, the last English possession in France. He further modernized French coinage and placed the royal portrait on gold coins. His silver testons carried a variety of portraits including the laureate head type done in the Roman imperial manner.

Charles IX (1560–74), second son of Henry II and Catherine de Medici, was troubled with a series of civil-religious wars between Catholic and Protestant factions in his kingdom—these difficulties were to last for a half century. He omitted the royal portrait on gold coins, though it still appeared on almost all his silver testons. Under Charles most coins were dated regularly for the first time with Arabic numerals.

Henry IV of Navarre (1589–1610), the first of the Bourbon kings, re-established internal order in France. His *ecu d'or* shows his crowned arms on obverse and floriated cross on reverse. His silver pieces, including the half and quarter francs, carry the royal portrait in armor.

The H mint mark below the shield (left) and the K mint mark (right) indicate that these testons of Henry II (1547-59) dated 1554 and 1558, were struck at the La Rochelle and Bordeaux mints respectively.

This teston portraying Charles IX (1560-74) is dated in Roman numerals on the reverse.

1586 silver franc of Henry III (1574-89) struck at the Toulouse mint (letter M).

By 1640, under Louis XIII (1610–43) the Paris Mint had coverted almost wholly from hammer-struck gold and silver to machine-produced coinage. Louis XIII introduced a new gold unit, the *louis d'or*, which features the royal portrait on its obverse. One of his most famous single coins is the large 10 *louis d'or* showing on obverse the king's draped laureate bust; the reverse has a cross of 8 "L's."

New equipment at the Paris mint made it possible for Louis XIII to introduce the machine-struck, crown-sized silver ecu and a companion ½ ecu piece.

France ❦ 157

1644 ½ ecu, Paris mint (A)

1656 ¼ ecu, Paris (A)

1711 ecu, Rouen (B)

Louis XIV issued coins bearing different portraits during his 72-year reign, one of the longest in world history. On the three coins above, he is shown as a child, a teenager and as an old man.

Louis XIV (1643–1715) was the first French king who could be truly considered an absolute monarch. He carried the crown to new heights and raised France to Europe's leading power. The nobles no longer presented any danger to the Crown. The King acted as his own Prime Minister and did not dream of convening the States-General. The "Sun-King" regarded France as his private property.

Everything Louis XIV did was in the grand manner—from politely lifting his hat to a chambermaid to building his enormous palace at Versailles in 1685. Louis XIV had a mania for enlarging French territory and for 40 years he carried on a complicated series of foreign wars. His reign, the longest in the country's history, was splendid, but at his death in 1715, the French crown was perilously near bankruptcy.

Gold and silver coinage constituted the heart of the currency system and during his 72-year reign, Louis used no fewer than ten different portraits ranging from a "Child's Head" to the "Old Laureate Head."

The Sun King also introduced a new denomination in copper, the *liard,* with the reverse consisting of the inscription *liard de France* in three

In 1650, Louis XIV introduced the copper liard, a minor coin worth ¼ sol.

Originally a gold piece, the *sol* became a silver coin under Louis XI, and by the time of Louis XV (1715-74), it was a copper coin.

lines. This copper piece, representing the fourth part of a sol, was current until 1793.

Louis XV, the great grandson of Louis XIV, who became king at the age of 5, also issued a variety of portraits in the course of his reign. A new denomination in copper, the sol, was issued with the reverse having the crowned shield of France.

Louis XV struck *louis d'or* specimens in great variety at a number of mints during his long reign. (Left) the 1722 *louis d'or* from the Lille (W) mint portrays the king as a boy. (Right) the 1739 specimen from Perpignon (Q) shows the king as a young man.

The heron below the bust on this 1757 Paris mint ecu is the mark of the engraver, Charles Norbert Roettiers.

Louis XVI (1774-92), silver ecu, 1790. Both Louis XVI and his queen, Marie Antoinette, were executed in 1793 during the Revolution which toppled the French monarchy.

Louis XVI (1774–92), grandson of Louis XV, was obliged to summon the States-General for the first time since 1614, and when the Revolution erupted in 1789, Louis at first appeared to concur with the desires of the people for a change of government but, having attempted to escape from France, he was arrested, and publicly guillotined in Paris on January 21, 1793. His glamorous Austrian-born queen, Marie Antoinette, daughter of Maria Theresa, was frivolous, erratic, and wholly without understanding of the people. She too was guillotined.

Coinage of Louis XVI falls into two series: a regal series which contains royal portraits in the tradition of the previous Bourbon kings; and the constitutional series of 1791–93. The *louis d'or* specimens of 1775–84 are particularly handsome coins—they have on their obverse the king's uniformed bust and on the reverse the crown over two oval shields. Louis' ecu of 6 livres of 1792–93 has the monarch's bareheaded portrait on obverse, and on reverse an angel writing on a tablet.

The French Revolution with its call for "Liberty, Equality and Fraternity" followed on the heels of the American Revolution.

French coinage was altered considerably soon after the Revolution's outbreak and even more so after the execution of King Louis XVI in 1793. The winged angel (symbolic of liberty) now began to appear on

Copper 12 deniers of 1791, struck during the Constitutional Period, shows a fasces topped with a liberty cap.

The silver 5 francs, struck in 1796 during the Directory period, was dated according to the Revolutionary calendar that began when the new Republic was declared in September, 1792. *L'An 5*—"the fith year," is thus 1796. The obverse portrays Hercules and personifications of Liberty and Equality with the legend, "Union and strength."

the obverse of many varieties of coins. One of the most startling reforms ushered in by the Revolution was a new calendar starting on September 22, 1792, the formal opening date of the new Republic. There were twelve months of thirty days each, plus five feast days to fill out the year. The new era was numbered from the Year I.

In 1795, a thorough reconstruction of French coinage was effected. In place of the fluctuating gold *louis* and the silver *ecu*, the decimal system was introduced, based on the silver *franc* as the monetary standard. French inscriptions took the place of the old Latin legends. Modifications have been made from time to time, but the basic decimal system has been continued to this day with 100 centimes equal to 1 franc.

When the Bourbons were restored to the French throne in 1814, it was foreign pressure, not the will of the French people that placed Louis XVIII on the throne. He ruled for ten years until his death in 1824. Charles X (1824–30), younger brother of Louis XVI, was deposed during the July, 1830 Revolution, and Louis Philippe (1830–48) was forced to abdicate during the Revolution of 1848. Louis Napoleon was first president of the Second Republic (1848–52) and then elected Emperor of the Second Empire (1852–70).

The 1798 (year 7) five centimes portraying Liberty is similar in appearance to the U.S. large cent of the same era.

France ❧ 161

The name "Napoleon" for 20 franc coins originated with the portrait pieces struck by Napoleon I in 1803-15. This 1808 specimen is from Toulouse (M).

The restoration of the French monarchy occurred under Louis XVIII (1814-24) whose portrait appears on this 1818 40 franc gold coin from Lille (W).

Both Charles X (1824-30) and Louis Philippe I (1830-48) were forced off their thrones by revolutions.

An angel, the "genius" or spirit of France, appears on the 20 franc gold piece struck in 1848 at the formation of the Second Republic.

Louis Napoleon, nephew of the Emperor, served as president of the Second Republic and then, in 1852, declared himself Emperor of France. He was deposed in 1870 during the disastrous war against Prussia.

The head of Republic or Liberty, as she is often called, is shown wearing a cap on these issues of the 1930's.

The Third Republic, which came into being at the time of France's devastating military defeats in the Franco-Prussian War of 1870–71, weathered innumerable crises and survived German aggression in two World Wars. The new coinages of the 1920's and 1930's featured the various stylized heads symbolizing the Republic on the obverses.

During World War II, the Vichy Government issued a coinage with German permission. Significantly, the old Republican motto of "Liberty, Equality, Fraternity" disappeared in favor of "Work, Family, and Fatherland." Subsequent coinage has restored the old motto.

Coins of France's Third Republic feature a portrait of Ceres, the goddess of Agriculture, the head of Republic and a Gallic cock.

The copper-nickel 100 francs of 1954 graphically illustrates the depreciation of French currency over a century's time. In the 1850's 100 francs was a gold coin about the size of a U.S. $20 gold piece.

The Fourth Republic (1946–58) was relatively unstable because new premiers rose and fell with great rapidity. Finally, Charles DeGaulle, France's World War II hero, formed his more durable Fifth Republic in 1958. Inflation following World War II depreciated the value of the franc and base metal coins up to 100 franc denominations were issued. A new heavy franc standard introduced in 1960 restored the franc to its former value by making one new franc equal to 100 of the old. The new coin designs are revivals of former issues, the Hercules group shown on the 10 franc piece having been first used in 1795, the Sower dating back to 1898. The Paris Mint has used chrome steel to strike the low denomination 1 and 5 centime pieces of the 1960's.

Under the Fifth Republic a new heavy franc standard was instituted with a new franc equalling 100 of the old. Familiar designs were used on the new coinage.

1608 silver ¼ ecu issued by Prince Charles II of Gonzaga for the principality of Nevers-Rethel.

Silver ½ franc struck by Maurice, Prince of Orange (1618-25), with the ruler's armored bust.

(Left) ½ teston of Charles III, Duke of Lorraine (1545-1608) and (right) 1614 liard of Francis de Bourbon, Prince of Chateau-Renaud (1603-14).

Henri de la Tour, Prince of Sedan, issued this ornate silver ecu in 1614. Feudal lords controlled large estates in France from the middle of the tenth century up to the time of the Revolution. Many were granted the right to issue their own coinages.

France ❧ 165

Declared a free city of the Empire in 1188, Lubeck maintained its own coinage for many centuries. Charles V, Holy Roman Emperor (1519-56), is shown on this taler struck in 1528.

Free Imperial Cities

The numerous divisions of the Holy Roman Empire included the so-called "Free Cities." These communities paid the Emperor a generous sum for the privilege of self-government and freedom from the control of envious princes. The free cities were extremely proud of their status, and were permitted to continue their own coinage even after the unification of Germany.

One of the most famous free cities was Lubeck, founded on the shores of the Baltic during the 12th century by a group of German grain merchants. Lubeck prospered, for its port, on the Baltic Sea at the mouth of the Trave River, was ideally located for handling east-west traffic along the Baltic. The city prided itself on the excellence of its coinage. In the 13th century, Lubeck began to band together with other cities to form the Hanseatic League. At its height the League had ninety member-cities, the majority of them German. Like the Hudson's Bay Company and the East India Company of later times, the Hansa established distant agencies. The League maintained, for example, a trading station in

Besancon, a free city in western France, issued this $\frac{1}{4}$ testone in 1623 with the portrait of Charles V who died in 1556. He had granted Besancon its mint right in 1526 and the city continued to use his name and title long after his death.

Coins of the imperial city of Bremen are inscribed with the key badge of the city and the imperial double eagle. This 1624 taler was issued under the aegis of Holy Roman Emperor Ferdinand II (1619-37).

London on the Thames known as the "Steelyard." Agencies were also maintained in Venice, Bruges (Flanders), Bergen (Norway), Visby (Sweden), and Novogorod (Russia). Chief cities in the League, besides Lubeck, were Hamburg, Bremen, Danzig, Rostock and Kiel.

The main purpose of the Hanseatic League was to control the exchange of raw materials from the north and east for finished goods from the south and west. It established codes of fair business practice which were binding on all Hanseatic merchants. Wherever necessary, the League brought suit in foreign countries for damages suffered by its members. And—perhaps most important of all—it came to the aid of members in case of attack, and raised fleets to clear the Baltic of pirates.

The suppression of the pirates, the discovery of the New World, the growing importance of trade with the Indies, and England's steadily improving ability to process her own raw materials, all contributed to take from the Hanse cities a substantial part of their business. Finally, the Thirty Years War brought the League's activities almost to a complete standstill.

Gaining minting rights in 1428, the free city of Frankfurt-am-Main struck coins almost continuously until 1866. This 1863 taler, commemorating Prince Day (Furstentag), shows a view of the city square.

Free Imperial Cities ❧ 167

1573 taler of Aachen, issued in the name of Maximilian II (1564-76), showing Charlemagne seated on his throne. Although struck more than 700 years after his death, Aachen continued to honor the man who had made the city the capital of his Empire.

Germany

The story of the Germanic people can be traced back as far as 113 B.C. when the Teutonic tribes (Teutones) defeated an army of invading Romans. The history of Germany as a nation however and the closely associated Holy Roman Empire both date from the reign of Charlemagne who reigned as King of the Franks from 768 until 814. Germany was an integral part of the Holy Roman Empire for nearly a thousand years. This long-lived empire was theoretically the political counterpart of the Holy Catholic Church. Charlemagne received the crown of emperor from Pope Leo III in 800. Many of the greatest succeeding German rulers were also Holy Roman Emperors and in later centuries the Germanic influence was so strong that the Empire was simply called the German Empire.

Usually considered the greatest of all rulers during the Middle Ages, Charlemagne minted and circulated silver denier coins throughout his empire which included France and Italy as well as Germany. In German

Silver deniers struck during the reign of Charlemagne (768-814) at the Bonn and Trier mints. The obverses have the Latin form of the Emperor's name, CAROLUS, the reverses the names of the mint cities BONA and TREVERIS.

territory Charlemagne maintained mints at Aachen, Bonn, Cologne, Mainz and Trier. His capital was Aachen and his magnificent palace there lasted into modern times.

Charlemagne's successors quarreled among themselves, eventually dividing up his empire. The history of Germany as a nation may be said to commence in 843 when the Treaty of Verdum established separate kingdoms for Charlemagne's grandsons. Louis I (Ludwig the German) became King of Germany with Lothair and Charles the Bald taking Italy and France.

Silver denar of Henry II, the Saint (1002-1024), last of the Saxon emperors. Henry permitted the feudal lords wide latitude in striking their own coins, a privilege that had previously been reserved for the Emperor.

Following the Carolingian kings, Henry the Fowler, Duke of Saxony (912–36) became Emperor and King in 919, founding a line of Saxon kings that was to last for more than two centuries. Henry's deniers have a cross on the obverse with a representation of a church and the name of the mint on the reverse. His chief mints were at Metz and Strasburg.

The major accomplishment of the House of Saxony came under Otto I (936–73), called "the Great." When he came to the throne, Germany was a small country lying along the shores of the Rhine. Otto greatly increased the size of Germany during his long reign by adding Bavaria, Bohemia, northeast Prussia and other territory to his dominions. It was Otto who first took the title "Kaiser," the Germanized form of the Roman "Caesar."

Silver denier of Emperor Conrad II (1024-39). Conrad brought the Holy Roman Empire to the zenith of its power and glory in the medieval period.

Germany ❧ 169

During the period from about 1120 to 1350, the bracteate coinage circulated widely through German lands, largely replacing the silver deniers. Although they were very thin, many of them were large enough in diameter to contain nearly as much silver as the regular coins and they were often done in a finer artistic style than other coins of the period.

Albert I the Bear, Margrave of Brandenburg (1134-70), a state that later became the kingdom of Prussia, is seen on this silver bracteate.

The bracteate coinage originated in Thuringia and Hesse and were especially popular in Franconia, Swabia and Brandenburg. They were issued not only in the name of the emperor but by innumerable dukes, barons, counts, palatine electors and by the ecclesiastics, many of whom were granted the mint right.

Frederick Barbarossa is portrayed on this silver denier from the Aachen mint. A church building appears on the coin's reverse. During his reign this was one of the most productive mints of medieval Europe.

At this point in German history we encounter that familiar hero, Frederich Barbarossa ("Red Beard"). According to legend, Barbarossa, bewitched, sits in a mountain cave at a stone table, through which his beard has grown, waiting to come forth to again lead the German people. During his reign (1152–90), he did bring the German states into closer harmony than ever before. This was the time of the great Crusades to free the Holy Land and Barbarossa lost his life as one of the leaders of the Third Crusade.

Gold augustale of Frederick II (1220-50) struck at Brindisi in Italy. The German emperor is shown with a laurel wreath dressed in the style of the ancient Roman emperors.

A grandson of Barbarossa, Frederick II, called "Stupor Mundi" (The Wonder of the World) was crowned Holy Roman Emperor in 1220. Byzantine, Saracen, and Jewish scholars were welcome at his court, and he read widely in Arabic philosophy, science, mathematics and literature. He spoke nine languages, including Greek and Latin. His gold augustales picture Frederick as a Roman Emperor of ancient times. These are among the first gold coins of Germany and are one of the finest examples of medieval coins.

The House of Hapsburg put its first emperor, Rudolf I, on the throne in 1273. After the death of Rudolf, a total of five different houses took turns at ruling for the next century and a half, but from 1438 until the Empire came to an end in 1806, the Emperor was always a Hapsburg.

By the end of the 13th century, coins had taken on greater importance in the entire economic structure of Europe. The bracteates and deniers were simply not adequate to meet the demands of Europe's growing economy. To fill the need, "nummi grossi" or "grossi denarii," called groschen in Germany, came into being. The first of these larger pieces. were struck in Bohemia but the French "gros tournois" (large coin of Tours) was the most influential type. The French gros was widely imitated in Germany, especially in Rhineland and Westphalia. The groschen of Meissen and Saxony were inspired by the famous Bohemian groschen struck by Wenceslas II in 1300. The Meissen type groschen also was used extensively in Hesse and Brunswick.

During the late Middle Ages, the Holy Roman Empire began to change form. Gradually Italy and Burgundy withdrew from its influence and

Silver groschen of the archbishopric of Cologne issued by Walram of Julich (1332-49).

The first of the large dollar-size silver coins were struck in Tyrol but their use soon spread throughout Germany as well. This undated Saxon taler of Elector Frederick the Wise and his brothers, Dukes George and Johann, was one of the earliest, made sometime between 1500 and 1507.

even the title was changed to "Holy Roman Empire of the German Nation." The last ties with the papacy were broken in 1493. Even within Germany, the powers of the individual princes and dukes increased at the expense of the emperor. Charles IV (1347–78) issued a proclamation in 1356 (The Golden Bull) by which a constitution was established and the Empire became a federation of independent states.

With the discovery of rich silver mines in Bohemia, silver talers, coins much larger than the groschen, began to be struck in great quantities and circulated throughout Europe. The silver talers seemed to have the right size, weight, and metallic content for both local and international trade. They were copied all over Europe and in the New World, where they became the Spanish dollar ("Piece of Eight"). Talers became the currency foundation for many countries, especially Germany. Special

An armored bust of Augustus I, Elector of Saxony (1553-86), is shown holding a sword and sceptre on this taler of 1562.

172 ❧ Germany

1579 Saxe-Weimar taler of Johann III issued jointly with Friedrich Wilhelm I (shown on the reverse), two brothers who ruled jointly. Their descendants founded separate lines with capitals at Altenburg and Weimar.

1579 taler of Saxony portraying three fraternal Dukes of the Electoral Line—Christian, Johann George and August.

In Saxony, territory was sometimes divided among sons, creating many new dukedoms. At other times, brothers ruled jointly. The greatest number of fraternal rulers to appear on a single coin are on this "Eight Brothers" taler of 1615.

Germany ❧ 173

talers were often struck to commemorate outstanding events such as battles and peace treaties; others were issued for the weddings, anniversaries, birthdays or deaths of minor princes.

Though the right of coinage remained theoretically in the hands of the Holy Roman Emperor and the seven prince-electors, all of the component states, large and small, within the Empire were permitted to issue coins. Countless specimens were issued by petty states as a matter of local pride. During the Renaissance and modern periods, Germany and associated states have issued more varieties of coins than any other single country or region. The number of varieties struck in all metals runs into the many tens of thousands.

1516 Cologne city taler depicts The Three Magi, the "Wise Men of the East," who visited the Christ-child in the manger.

1561 taler of the town of Jever carries a scene of the prophet Daniel in the lion's den.

St. George on horseback, slaying a dragon, appears on this 1804 taler of Friedberg issued by Johann, Count of Waldbott-Bassenheim.

1632 taler of Hameln, city of the legend of the famous piper and children who disappeared into a hillside.

An open Bible is featured on this 1617 taler of Worms issued to mark the centenary of the Reformation. The date is given on the obverse in the form of a chronogram LVMEN EVANGELII PERENNA DEVS NOSTER—"Eternal light of the Gospels of our Lord."

Germany ❧ 175

The Thirty Years War (1618–1648), the struggle between Catholics and Protestants which followed the Reformation with Martin Luther (1483–1546) were the two great events of the early modern age which deeply influenced German history. Reminders of both of these events can be found on coins, especially in the many siege pieces issued by beleagued cities during the fighting. The Peace of Westphalia signed in 1648 left Germany split up into 350 parts!

The 1622 "Parson's Foe" taler issued by Duke Christian of Brunswick-Luneburg (1611-33), who supported the Protestant cause in the Thirty Years War.

Hesse-Cassel, 1629 broad double taler showing a palm tree in a storm issued by Landgrave William V, "the Constant " (1627-37) who received his nickname for his steadfast support of the Protestant cause.

176 ☙ Germany

Mecklenberg, Friedland and Sagan, 1632 taler portraying Albrecht Wenzel
Eusebius von Wallenstein, general in command of the Imperial armies during
the Thirty Years War.

Issued by Duke Johann Ernst of Saxony-Saalfeld, this taler commemorates
the 200th anniversary of Martin Luther's famous 95 theses. The date of issue,
1717, is given on both sides in the form of a chronogram, an inscription in
which certain prominent letters, also Roman numerals, reveal the date when
added together.

1643 so-called "Bell Taler" of Brunswick with legend TANDEM PATIENTIA
VINCIT—"Patience at length prevails." The ringing of the church bells symbolizes the withdrawal of the Imperial troops during the Thirty Years War.

Germany ❧ 177

During the years following the tremendous struggle of the Thirty Years War, one of the German states managed to rise above the others in military, political and economic power.

From the era of the Great Elector, Frederick William (1640–88), the Margravinate of Brandenburg assumed increasing influence among the Protestant German states. A milestone was reached when the Elector Frederick assumed the title King of Prussia in 1701 . . . this was even recognized by the Holy Roman Emperor Leopold I. Prussia promoted German nationalism and worked toward eroding Hapsburg domination of the German states.

Frederick William, "the Great Elector" of Brandenburg (1640-88) appears on this 1646 taler struck at the Berlin mint. Welding a number of diverse territories into a strong single state, he gained full sovereignty as Duke of Prussia.

It was Frederick II, "the Great" (1740–86) who made Prussia into a potent European military power by transforming the Prussian army into a force feared by the rest of Europe. Inheriting a well-trained army and an ample treasury, he snatched Silesia from Austria in 1740; invaded Saxony in 1756 without warning; and engineered the first partition of Poland in 1772. Thus, Frederick set the pattern for later Prussian or German lightning invasions ("blitzkriegs").

178 ❧ **Germany**

1786 taler of Frederick II the Great (1740-86). The letter A below the date denotes the Berlin mint. Frederick began the system, still in use on German coins today, of using a single letter to identify the mint of issue.

The Prussian military machine weakened after Frederick's death and was no match for Napoleon's armies. However, a great national revival and a surge of patriotism was responsible for the army's being revitalized, and with the help of other German armies it played a major role in the Battle of Leipzig in 1813—the "Battle of Nations"—which assured Napoleon's downfall.

The Holy Roman Empire collapsed with Napoleon's smashing victory at Austerlitz. The last emperor, Francis II, abdicated in 1806. After the downfall of Napoleon, a Germanic Confederation with Austria at its head was formed at the Congress of Vienna in 1815. However, such a union was doomed to failure because of the continuous friction between Prussia and Austria. Prussia gradually became the leading power in this Confederation, which amounted to a loose group of 38 states.

Napoleon had not only aroused German nationalist feeling; he had in effect stimulated the unification of Germany by wiping out a great many principalities. This unification took time, because Prussia strove mightily

Frederick William III (1797-1840) in military uniform appears on this taler dated 1786. The eagle on the reverse is flanked by flags and cannon.

Germany ∙ 179

1871 taler issued by the Kingdom of Prussia to mark the victorious conclusion of the Franco-Prussian War.

to be the supreme power in the new Germany. The other states wanted to keep their automomy, and were fearful of coming under Prussian domination.

After three quick and victorious wars, the Prussians succeeded in their ambitions. In 1864 they took Schleswig and Holstein from the Danes; in 1866 they defeated Austria in seven weeks, removing their last rival for German domination; and in 1870–71 they electrified the world by defeating France. All the German states took part in this war, under an agreement whereby they turned their armies over to Prussian leadership but retained their other powers. At the end of the Franco-Prussian War, the various states formed the German Empire, with the King of Prussia becoming the German Emperor (Kaiser). Prussia at this time annexed the states of Hanover, Nassau, Electoral Hesse and the Free City of Frankfurt.

The silver 5 marks of 1901, commemorating the 200th anniversary of the founding of the Kingdom of Prussia, has the dual portrait of Friedrich I (1701-13) and Wilhelm II (1888-1918).

1776 so-called "Blood Taler" of Hesse-Cassel, home of the Hessian soldiers who fought for the British side in the American Revolution.

Hesse was noted in the 18th century as the source of mercenary soldiers, many of whom fought on the British side during the American Revolution. In 1567, on the death of Philip I (the "Magnanimous"), the original Landgraviate of Hesse was divided up among his four sons. Each founded a new Hessian line named for the city from which they ruled. Two of the sons died without heirs but the Hesse-Cassel line lasted until 1866 and the Hesse-Darmstadt line endured until 1918. In Germany, titles and lands did not necessarily pass intact to the oldest son and, under the Salic Law, females were excluded from succession to any throne.

Hesse-Cassel,
1858 taler

Hesse-Darmstadt,
1847 2 gulden

Originally a single landgraviate, Hesse was divided into two major lines, Hesse-Cassel and Hesse-Darmstadt, named for their capital cities.

Maximilian I, Elector of Bavaria (1623-51), struck this ornate taler in 1626. The coin's obverse shows the elector's crowned arms, while the reverse portrays the Madonna and Child.

Bavaria, now Germany's largest and southernmost state, existed as a separate duchy, electorate or kingdom for over 1,000 years until 1918, when it became a part of the new Republic. Duke Henry XII the Lion (1156–80) established a mint at Munich as early as 1158, and from that point Munich grew steadily in importance. During the 13th century, the dukes of the Wittelsbach dynasty selected Munich as their residence and capital city. The House of Wittelsbach, founded in 1180, ruled Bavaria to the time of King Ludwig III who abdicated in 1918.

Ludwig II, King of Bavaria (1864-86), is shown as a clean-shaven young man on the 1868 taler, as an older man with a goatee on the 1875 5 marks.

Friedrich August II held the joint thrones of Saxony and Poland for thirty years (1733-63). His 1742 portrait taler shows the crowned conjoined arms of Saxony and Poland.

At the time of the Reformation early in the 16th century, one of the most powerful states in central Europe was the Duchy of Saxony. The duchy was greatly weakened during the Thirty Years War and its strength was further sapped by the cost of supporting two of its dukes as kings of Poland. Prussia gained half of Saxony's territory in 1815 at the Congress of Vienna and for the rest of the 19th century, Saxony was forced to maintain a secondary position in German affairs. Nevertheless, Saxony produced hundreds of varieties of coins over the centuries attesting to the region's wealth.

Saxe-Altenburg

Saxe-Coburg-Gotha

Saxe-Meiningen

Saxe-Weimar

Gold 20 marks pieces of four separate Saxon duchies were issued during the time of the German Empire, 1871-1918.

Germany 183

Brunswick-Wolfenbuttel's 1662 double taler displays a handsome equestrian figure of Duke August II (1635-66). The mark of value "2" was punched onto the coin after it was struck. Thus the same pair of dies could be used for even thicker, higher value coins.

Brunswick is another state that issued an extensive coinage, with gold and silver coming from the rich Harz mines located within the territory. The first coins struck for Brunswick were the silver bracteates issued by Henry the Lion who held the title Duke of Saxony and Bavaria until 1180, but who ruled in Brunswick until his death. The House of Brunswick split up into numerous divisions, the two most important lines being those of Brunswick-Wolfenbuttel (later Brunswick) and Brunswick-Luneburg (later Hanover). Luneburg was one of the chief commercial centers in North Germany and in 1293 the Dukes of Brunswick granted it the right to mint its own coins. "Luna" is the Latin word for moon and some of the cities show the face of the "man in the moon."

Brunswick-Luneburg, 1547 taler with an ornately dressed Duke Heinrich, the Younger (1514-68).

Brunswick-Wolfenbuttel, 1665 taler of Duke August II, the Younger (1635-66). The "Wild Man" device, a common feature on Brunswick's coins was first used in 1539, in reference to the silver mine of that name in the Harz Mountains.

Brunswick-Luneburg, 1710 taler of Elector Duke George Ludwig (George I, King of England, 1714-27). The coat-of-arms is crowned with an Elector's cap; the reverse shows the full-length figure of St. Andrew.

Baden
50th Year of Reign

Anhalt
25th Wedding Anniversary

Saxe-Meiningen   **Death of Duke**

Wurttemburg   **Hesse**
25th Year of Reign   **25th Year of Reign**

Saxe-Weimar
100th Year of Grand Duchy

Mecklenburg-Schwerin
Grand Duke's Marriage

During the period of the Empire, the Second Reich (1871-1918), a wide variety of coins were issued in gold and silver to commemorate anniversaries of reigns, weddings, marriages and deaths. The reverses were all similar, a crowned double eagle.

186 ❧ Germany

Aluminum 50 pfennig of 1921, picturing a shock of wheat, refers to the revitalization of agriculture after World War I.

This aluminum-bronze 50 rentenpfennig of 1923 was part of a new coinage issued in an effort to combat the disastrous post-war inflation.

After Napoleon and the formation of the Confederation, the extreme proliferation of German coin issues disappeared but not until 1917 was there a purely national coinage. The Weimar Republic which followed World War I lasted until 1933. One of its immediate problems was to deal with the disastrous inflation of 1919–23 which wiped out the savings of millions of Germans. During and after World War I, thousands of varieties of base necessity coins, called "Notgeld" were issued by cities

German leather currency of 1923. Because of the inflation, metal coins disappeared from circulation. Emergency "money" of all sorts including pieces of shoe leather stamped with various denominations circulated in place of regular currency.

Germany ❧ 187

and towns throughout Germany. The inflation was so rampant that Saxony in 1923 issued an aluminum coin in a one million mark value, while Westphalia released a coin with the highest denomination ever— one billion marks! In its short life, the Weimar·Republic issued a number of handsome commemorative coins.

1930 5 mark piece honors the 1929 world flight of the Graf Zeppelin (the LZ-127). The Zeppelin remained in service until 1937, making some 590 commercial flights.

Albrecht Durer (1471-1528), Germany's great Renaissance artist, is portrayed on the 1928 3 marks recalling the 400th anniversary of his death.

1932 3 marks noting the centenary of the death of German writer Johann Wolfgang von Goethe (1749-1832).

The 175th anniversary of the birth of Friedrich von Schiller (1759-1805), philosopher, poet and dramatist, is commemorated on this 1934 3 mark coin.

188 ❧ Germany

Issues of Germany's several mints are distinguished by the mint marks inscribed on them. On these two silver 5 marks of 1951, the G (for Karlsruhe) and D (for Munich) appear below the date.

Following World War II, Germany was again dismembered. The former East Prussia has been annexed by Poland and the Soviet Union, though the finality of this annexation is disputed. Germany proper is divided into a German Federal Republic (West Germany) and the German Democratic Republic (the eastern portion, under Soviet influence). Berlin, deep inside East Germany, is still divided into American, British, French and Russian zones.

West Germany's coins are struck at four major mints: at Munich, Stuttgart, Karlsruhe and Hamburg. East Germany's coins are produced at the sprawling old mint in East Berlin. The issues of the various mints can be recognized by the mint marks D, F, G, J and A placed on the coins.

Wilhelm von Humboldt (1767-1835) and his brother Alexander (1769-1859), one of Germany's greatest naturalists, appear in dual portrait on West Germany's 5 marks of 1966.

Wilhelm von Humboldt, portrayed on East Germany's 20 marks of 1967, was both a statesman and linguist.

Germany ❧ 189

Crude, uninscribed imitations of gold staters of Macedon were the earliest coins struck in England. The imitations themselves were copied again and again, with each successive issue looking less like the original design.

Great Britain

The history of English coinage covers a period of more than 2,000 years and it is one of the richest and most varied coinages of any nation in the world. The earliest coins struck in England were the crude uninscribed imitations of the gold staters of Philip II of Macedon (359–336 B.C.). These imitations were produced in the first quarter of the first century B.C. of debased gold and have the laureate head of Apollo with a crudely copied horse on the reverse.

During this same period, 100–50 B.C., various sizes of ring money in gold also circulated in England. These were of course also used for ornamentation.

This interesting gold stater struck in the style of the Greeks was issued by the Celtic King Cunobelin struck c. A.D. 20.

Julius Caesar achieved preliminary conquests in Britain about 55 B.C. and the Romans under Claudius in A.D. 43 succeeded in occupying Britain. Thus, Roman imperial coins supplanted the native imitations of Greek types. For the next five hundred years, the currency of the Roman Empire was the only coinage of the British Isles; therefore, no representative collection of British coinage is complete without Roman coins.

The first coins classified as those of Roman Britain are the silver denarii of Julius Caesar, with and without portrait, struck in 44 B.C. The abbreviation, "d," used today for British pence, comes from the Latin "denarius."

Struck in Rome, this gold aureus of Claudius (A.D. 41-54) depicts the triumphal arch constructed there in the year 44 to commemorate the Emperor's personal role in the conquest of Britain.

The bronze sestertius of Antoninus Pius (A.D. 138-61) with the Britannia reverse commemorates the emperor's achievements in Britain. Britannia was later introduced on English coins in the time of Charles II.

Claudius commemorated the conquest of Britain with a series of aurei and denarii showing his triumphal arch at Rome. The reverse shows an equestrian statue of the emperor between trophies and an arch bearing the legend DE BRITANN. Hadrian (117–38) celebrated the building of his wall between the Tyne and Solway by striking bronze coins showing a seated figure of Britannia with her right foot resting on a pile of stones. A similar type was issued by Antoninus Pius (138–61), celebrating his more northerly defenses between the Forth and the Clyde. This coin seems to have been the prototype of the reverse of the modern English penny.

The Romans established a mint at London under Carausius (287–93). It was closed about 337, though it was probably reopened for a brief period under the mint name of Augusta, in the reign of the usurper Magnus Maximus (383–88). The Romans also operated a mint at Colchester and possibly at other English towns as well.

The Roman rule came to an end in 410 when the people, feeling that the emperor was neglecting them, revolted against Constantine II and expelled his governors. The remaining Roman legions withdrew from Britain, and soon the Angles, Saxons, and Jutes—Germanic peoples— driven westward by the barbarian tribes, began to settle on the island. By 600 they were masters of what is now modern England (land of the

The PLM inscription on the reverse of this bronze coin of the Roman emperor Constantine the Great (307-37) indicates that it was struck at the London Mint. The P stands for pecunia, "money" in Latin.

Great Britain ❧ 191

Angles). Seven Anglo-Saxon kingdoms emerged; East Anglia, Mercia, Northumbria (mainly Angles), Essex, Wessex, Sussex (mainly Saxons), and Kent (Jutes).

Discoveries of Roman coins are regular occurrences in modern England. In these hoards, coins of the Republic are found as well as the more common ones of the Empire, mixed with native coins of Britain. During the past century alone hundreds of thousands of Roman coins have been dug up in Great Britain.

When the Romans departed, Britain was left without any regular supplies of coinage and a "coinage of necessity" developed. These necessity coins, degenerate copies of Roman types, were small, often minute, bronze specimens which served local requirements. About 650, a more regular coinage was resumed with small silver sceats modeled after the Frankish coins which found their way to England in commerce. The majority of the sceats do not have legends and the specific kingdoms that issued them cannot be identified.

During the period from about 650 to 800, coinage in Britain was largely of silver sceats, modelled after Frankish coins which were themselves copies of Roman coins.

The first of a long series of English medieval silver pennies was introduced during the reign of Offa, King of Mercia (757–96). The new coins were of standard weight and quality and the king's name clearly stated the authority for their issue. Mercia was the most powerful of the kingdoms at this time and Charlemagne recognized Offa as a ruler of importance. Offa also struck a gold dinar in the style of the contemporary Arabian dinars.

The kings of Kent, Wessex and East Anglia followed Offa's example and issued silver pennies. Some show portraits of the ruler with a reverse design including the name of the moneyer and the mint. Many issues before 1000 are without a portrait, having a cross on both sides, the names of the ruler, mint, and moneyer in the legends.

The Archbishops of York and Canterbury also issued coins during the eighth and ninth centuries. Ecclesiastics continued to strike their own coins until the 16th century when this privilege was abolished by Henry VIII.

Mercia declined in power after Offa's death, and Wessex took the lead against frequent invasions by the Danish Vikings. King Alfred of Wessex

Offa, king of Mercia
(757-796)

Alfred, king of Wessex
(871-907)

Cuthred, king of Kent
(798-807)

Aethelstan I, king
of East Anglia (825-40)

(871-99) extended his rule over Mercia and issued one coin with the title, REX ANGLOR (King of England), though full control of the country did not fall under one monarch until the time of Edgar (959–75). Edgar drove out the Danes who had occupied part of the country, but the coast was still ravaged by frequent raids. Aethelred II (978–1016), sometimes called "The Unready," tried to buy off the raiders by payment of tribute or "Danegeld" and many more of his coins have been discovered in Scandinavia than in England!

As to design, the "long cross" reverse, with the arms of the cross being extended to the edge of the coin, was frequently used as it facilitated cutting the coin into halves and quarters, making half pence and farthings (fourthlings), for use as small change.

The moneyers, generally blacksmiths, whose names appear on the reverse of the coins, were appointed by the king to strike coins at the local mint. Dies for the coins were sent out from the capital and the moneyers had to pay the king for the privilege of using the dies, receiving their profit through a commission charged those bringing bullion for conversion into coins. Under Aethelred II, who had great need for coins

King Aethelred II (979-1016) paid huge sums of tribute to the Danes in an effort to stop Viking raids on England. The reverse on his silver penny carries a "long cross" which facilitated cutting the coins into halves and quarters for small change.

Great Britain ❧ 193

to pay the Danegeld, the number of mints rose to more than a hundred. The king ordered frequent changes of design, ostensibly to make it difficult for the counterfeiters, but incidentally, bringing him a considerable revenue for new dies alone.

In 1016, the Danes under Cnut II took over all of England. Cnut, who was an exceptionally able monarch, founded a Scandinavian empire with London as its capital and commercial center. It broke up soon after

(Left) Silver penny of Edward the Confessor (1042-66), showing the monarch seated on his throne. (Right) Harold II, the last Anglo-Saxon king of England, who ruled for only a few months in 1066, was slain at the Battle of Hastings.

his death in 1035, however, and a representative of the exiled Saxon dynasty, Edward III ("the Confessor"), ruled England from 1042 to 1066. On his death, the English nobles elected Harold, son of Earl Godwin, as King Harold II. His reign of a few months ended with his defeat and death at the Battle of Hastings, and William, Duke of Normandy, called "The Conqueror," was crowned in Westminster Abbey as William I of England on Christmas day, 1066.

Although the Norman conquest altered the entire political life of England, it had little effect upon the coinage. The Saxon coins were better than those of Normandy and the rest of Europe; thus the new king kept

Silver penny of William the Conqueror (1066-87). The obverse inscription reads PILLELM REX (Norman coin legends use the Runic form of W which looks like the Latin P). On the reverse are the letters PAXS (Peace).

194 ⊛ Great Britain

the Saxon moneyers to carry on their work. The style, workmanship, weight and value of the coins remained the same although, of course, there were new legends as would be the case with any new king. The best known example of William's coinage is the PAXS pennies (pointing out peace either achieved or hoped-for under the new ruler). This type was once considered rare, but it is now the commonest variety because so many were among a hoard of some 8,000 silver pennies unearthed in 1833 at Beaworth near Winchester, seat of William the Conqueror's government.

Henry I (1100-35) passed severe laws against the moneyers who persisted in forging and clipping silver pennies, but despite harsh penalties Henry's coinage became rather poor. Although most of the coins were produced at the official mints, they were struck in base silver or of low weight. The coinage disorder grew worse when Stephen (1135-54) engaged in Civil War with the Empress Matilda. Both warring factions struck pennies, which their followers countermarked or copied. Several barons, including Robert de Stuteville and Eustace Fitzjohn of York, issued coins with their own portraits.

The "short cross" pennies, first issued by Henry II (1154-89) (left) all carried the name HENRICVS even though they were struck in the reign of Richard I (1189-99), John (1199-1216) as illustrated (right), and finally Henry III (1216-72). The issues can be differentiated by slight variations in the design.

Henry II (1154-89) restored some semblance of order in 1180 when he issued his "short cross" pennies (named from their reverse design). He ended the practice of constantly changing types and the short-cross penny remained essentially the same in design throughout the reigns of Richard I (1189-99), John (1199-1216) and through part of Henry III's (up to 1247). Toward the close of the short-cross issue, clipping of coins had again become so widespread that Henry III (1216-72) changed

Silver penny of King Henry III (1216-72). On the reverse is the name of the moneyer, RICARD ON LVND (Richard at London) around a long cross. Extending the arms of the cross to the edge of the coin was intended to discourage clipping.

Great Britain ❧ 195

the silver penny type to the long-cross. With the reverse cross now extended to the edge of the coin, pennies ceased to be legal tender if more than one end of the arms of the cross were missing.

Henry III (1216–72) also introduced a gold penny, worth 20 silver pennies, in 1257, but it proved to be unpopular. The obverse portrays the king on his throne, while the reverse has the long-cross. This gold piece today is extremely rare.

The groat, equal to four silver pennies in value, was introduced in England during the reign of Edward I (1272-1307). The legend on this coin includes DEI GRATIA (by the grace of God) for the first time on an English coin.

Edward I (1272–1307) restructured the coinage operations when he abolished the system of moneyers and appointed a mint master to supervise the coinage of the entire country. The mint master maintained headquarters at London and had a personal deputy at each branch mint. An engraver was appointed to design the coins, dies being sent from London to their respective mints. Edward also introduced the "Trial of the Pyx" in which a sampling of gold and silver coins were carefully weighed and assayed annually.

Edward ordered the striking of round halfpennies; previously small change had been cut from pennies. Finally, this able monarch introduced a new four penny denomination, the groat. This coin was copied from the continental *gros tournois*. In type it was not unlike the penny, though more ornate and of finer workmanship. Very few were struck in this reign, but in the reign of Edward III, the groat became a common coin.

Edward III was the first English monarch to strike gold coins in quantity. His gold issues include $\frac{1}{4}$, $\frac{1}{2}$, and 1 florin pieces, along with $\frac{1}{4}$, $\frac{1}{2}$, and 1 noble values. The obverse of the florin portrays the king on his throne, while the noble has the ruler in a ship.

On the accession of Richard II (1377–99) no attempt was made to make new dies and his earliest coins are struck from dies used in the previous reign. Even when new dies were engraved later, they were similar in style to Edward's.

196 ❧ **Great Britain**

This gold noble of Edward III (1327-77) shows the king standing in a ship, with an ornate cross on the reverse. Since relatively primitive tools and production methods were used in the 14th century, the coin is remarkable for both its beauty and intricacy of detail.

For nearly 400 years after the Conquest, the English kings tried to gain control of France. They fought many wars, including the famous Hundred Years' War, in the attempt to achieve this goal. Not until 1453 did the English finally give up these attempts.

In 1399 Henry, Duke of Lancaster, forced Richard II to abdicate and, supported by the nobles, was acclaimed king as Henry IV (1399–1413). The undervaluing of English currency in the early 1400's led to the export and melting down of silver coins so that Henry was compelled to issue a new coinage of reduced weight both in gold and silver.

During the Middle Ages, the heads on coins were merely symbols representing the monarchy. The issues of Henry VI (1422–61 and 1470–71), for example, show the same type of crowned, impassive, unaging head on all his coins even though he became king at the age of 9 months and held the throne for a span of nearly 50 years!

The Wars of the Roses began in 1455 and the subsequent defeat in 1461 of the Lancastrian army at Mortimer's Cross in Herefordshire by Edward Duke of York, enabled the Yorkists to proclaim Edward king. Edward IV (1461–70 and 1471–83) introduced a new gold coin, the "angel," to replace the old noble denomination. Edward's gold angel

Edward IV (1461-70 and 1471-83) introduced the gold "angel" to replace the noble. The coin shows St. Michael slaying the devil in the form of a dragon.

The gold sovereign of Henry VII (1485-1509) shows the king enthroned, holding sceptre and orb; on the reverse, the shield of arms is centered upon a Tudor rose. The reverse legend in Latin, IHESUS ATVEM TRANSIENS PER MEDIVM ILLORVM IBAT, means "But Jesus passing through the midst of them, went His way" (Luke iv, 30).

shows St. Michael killing the Devil in the form of a dragon, while the reverse has a ship with cross and the English shield.

The first of the Tudor line, Henry VII (1485–1509), was an outstandingly able ruler, working unceasingly to unite his land, devastated by the War of the Roses. He took great interest in coinage. One of his innovations was a magnificent new gold coin, the sovereign. The obverse shows the king on his throne, while the elaborate reverse has the famous Tudor Rose—combining the roses of Lancaster and York representing the new, peaceful era. Like the old noble, this coin has Biblical texts around the edge to discourage clipping.

Henry VII also introduced the shilling, a silver coin often called a "testoon." The name comes from the Italian *testa* ("head") and reflects the influence of the Italian Renaissance in England. Designed by the master engraver Alexander de Brugsal, this is the first English coin to bear a realistic portrait of a monarch. Henry's shilling was also the first English profile coin to be struck in about 300 years and from this time on, virtually all British coins have the profile style.

Henry VIII (1509–47), one of England's most colorful and controversial kings, was forced to debase his coinage in the middle 1520's. He reduced the amount of gold and silver in his coins in order to compete with the vast number of sub-standard foreign pieces circulating throughout England. Once the King realized that debasing was profitable in itself, his coinage deteriorated even more rapidly. His later "silver" coins (an alloy of one-third silver and two-thirds copper) are usually found in poor

Henry VIII (1509-47) used his father's portraits on his coinage until 1526 when he switched to his own youthful portrait as on this groat.

condition with the copper showing through on the highest part of the design, earning Henry the nickname "Old Coppernose."

Attempts were made during the brief reign of Edward VI (1547–53) to restore gold and silver coins to standard. Edward struck England's first dollar-sized coins (called crowns) in 1551. The completely new design on the crown has a representation of the king astride a galloping horse, dressed in mail and holding a sword. Below the horse is the date, 1551, the first appearance of an Arabic numeral date on an English coin. (Henry VIII issued a shilling in 1538 with the date in Roman numerals.)

The first English crowns, dollar-size coins, were produced during Edward VI's reign (1547-53). The date below the horse, 1551, is the first appearance of an Arabic numeral date on an English coin.

Great Britain ☙ 199

Mary, Queen of England (1553-58), ruled jointly with her husband, Philip II of Spain, during the last four years of her reign.

Elizabeth I (1558-1603) reigned during the period when England emerged as a world seapower. Here she appears on a silver shilling.

Philip II of Spain (1556-98) and Elizabeth became bitter antagonists. Matters came to a dramatic climax in 1588 when the English navy decisively defeated the supposedly "invincible" Spanish Armada.

During the reign of Henry VIII's daughter, Queen Elizabeth I (1558–1603), English sea power began to grow. The great captain, Sir Francis Drake, successfully challenged Spanish primacy on the high seas. When the English navy defeated the supposedly "invincible" Spanish Armada in 1588, England for the first time was recognized as a true world power.

Elizabeth's coins were issued with a greater variety in the legends, designs and denominations than were ever issued before. Threepences, threehalfpences, and three-farthing pieces were struck for the first time. The latter, despite its small size, carries a portrait of Elizabeth on the obverse.

The most important development in coinage under Elizabeth was the introduction of machinery. Eloye Mestrelle, a worker from the Paris Mint, was brought to the Royal Mint at London where he produced coins with a mill that rolled metal to the desired thickness, cut out the blanks, and stamped them. Power was supplied by horses. Despite the fact that these coins are better struck than the old hammered issues, they were discontinued after ten years, as the mint workers, fearing for their jobs, raised objections to the new machinery. Mestrelle fell from favor and the former coining methods were restored in 1572. It wasn't until 1662 that hammered coinage gave way completely to milled coinage.

(Left) 1562 machine-milled sixpence and (right) 1594 hand-hammered sixpence coined under Elizabeth I. During Elizabeth's reign, coin-making machinery was introduced from France. Although the machine-made coins were better, protests from the Royal Mint workers forced a return to hand-hammering.

When James I (1603–25) ascended the English throne, he had already been King of Scotland for 36 years. He succeeded to the Scottish throne at the age of one due to the forced abdication of his mother, Mary, Queen of Scots. His coins claim the kingship *Magnae Britanniae* ("of Great Britain.") Scotland became an integral part of the United Kingdom in 1707. Under James I values of English and Scottish coins were adjusted so that one English shilling equalled twelve shillings in Scottish money. Thus, the Scottish sixty-shilling piece was current for five shillings English, the thirty shillings was current for 2s 6d and the half shilling equalled the English halfpenny. The Scottish coins are the same size and design as their English equivalents, but they can be identified as being either from the thistle which appears on the trappings of the horse on the Scottish sixty and thirty shillings and by the rose on the English crown and half-crown.

James authorized the first copper pieces in English coinage in 1613 when he granted a special license to Lord Harrington to issue copper farthings. One of James' most beautiful coins is the 1 rose gold ryal showing the king on his throne and arms on a large rose.

Gold half laurel of James I (1603-25). James was the first to use the title King of Great Britain (MAG BRI).

Charles I (1625–49) continued to strike gold and silver coins at London's Tower Mint until 1642, when he moved to Oxford, Parliament taking over the Tower Mint and issuing coins in Charles' name. During the Civil Wars (1642–49) the king struck gold and silver coins at a number of emergency mints, including Oxford, Bristol, Chester, Exeter, and Shrewsbury.

The noteworthy 3 pounds gold piece (called a "Triple Unite"), struck at Oxford in 1642–44, is a handsome coin showing the crowned king holding a sword and olive branch. Its reverse inscription in Latin reads, "the Protestant religion, the laws of England, the liberty of Parliament," this declaration being the avowed policy of the Royalist Party. These are the first English gold coins to have dates.

Charles I (1625–49) declared he would defend the "Protestant religion, the laws of England and the liberties of Parliament" against the faction opposing him in the English Civil War. This inscription appears on many coins of his reign, including this 1643 silver pound struck at Oxford.

Years of struggle between the monarchy and Parliament reached a climax in 1649 when the army of Charles I was overwhelmed by Oliver Cromwell's Puritan troops. Charles was captured, tried and beheaded. A Commonwealth was established with Cromwell as its Lord Protector (1653–58). Richard Cromwell succeeded his father as Lord Protector in 1658–59.

During the Interregnum, Parliament struck gold and silver coins in the name of the Commonwealth of England with the arms of England and Ireland. These are the only English coins with legends in English rather than Latin.

Silver 5 shillings of the Commonweath, 1652, bears the shield of St. George; on the reverse are the shields of St. George and Ireland. Early Commonwealth specimens are the only British coins with legends in English rather than Latin.

This pattern 5 shilling piece portrays Oliver Cromwell, the Lord Protector of the Commonwealth.

The Commonwealth period was followed by the Restoration, when Charles II (1660–85), son of Charles I, was recalled from France to assume the throne. Under Charles II, in 1662, hammered coins were abolished altogether in favor of a milled—or a machine-made—coinage. Hammered coins ceased to be legal tender after 1697.

When milled coinage was inaugurated, a new gold denomination, the guinea, took the place of the united. Fixed at a value of 20 shillings in 1662, and raised to 21 shillings in 1717, the guinea was struck until 1813.

Britannia made her first appearance on English coins in 1672, when copper coinage was established. Hundreds of types of private copper tokens were issued in the 1600's because the official coppers were not issued regularly. During the gaps of official coinage, merchants and

The famous "Petition Crown" was made in 1663 by Thomas Simon as a protest against his replacement as mint engraver by the Flemish medalist Jan Roettiers. The edge of the coin bears a minutely engraved appeal to King Charles II.

manufacturers in order to carry on their businesses, produced their own private tokens which they pledged themselves to redeem on demand. Even greater numbers of these tokens were issued toward the end of the 18th century.

The figure of Britannia appeared for the first time on this 1673 copper halfpenny of Charles II. Her pose is almost the same as the figure portrayed on a bronze sestertius of the Roman emperor Antoninus Pius (A.D. 138-161).

James II (1685–88) maintained virtually the same denominations as his predecessor. The most impressive coin issued during this period was the five guinea portrait piece, with a cross of four shields on the reverse. Under James II, it became traditional to alternate right and left facing regal portraits for successive reigns. Thus, the portrait of Charles II looked to the right, James II to the left, William and Mary, right, etc.

William III and his wife Mary assumed the throne after the abdication of James II, and they were crowned at Westminster Cathedral on February 13, 1689. Until Mary died in 1694, their conjoined busts were depicted on all coins. William III ruled alone until his death in 1702.

1687 shilling of James II (1685-88)

1693 shilling of William and Mary (1689-94)

1704 shilling of Anne (1702-14)

Beginning with James II it became customary to alternate right and left facing regal portraits for successive reigns.

An extensive recoinage took place under William since the hammered and badly-clipped money had to be withdrawn. New coins were minted not only at London, but at branches in Bristol, Chester, Exeter, Norwich, and York. Sir Isaac Newton, the great mathematician and physicist, was Master of the Mint from 1696 to 1727, and he was particularly zealous in his hunt for clippers and counterfeiters.

Under Anne (1702–14), the kingdoms of England and Scotland were joined permanently through the Act of Union in 1707. This Act was commemorated on the coins by placing the English and Scottish arms

1703 crown of Queen Anne inscribed VIGO was struck from bullion captured in the Spanish port of that name.

Great Britain ❧ 205

side by side on one shield. Some of post-Union coins were struck at the Edinburgh Mint and a small E is placed below the bust. Distinctive Scottish coinage ceased after 1709. Anne's early coins are of great interest since a number of her silver and gold pieces of 1702–03 carry the inscription VIGO under the queen's bust. The coins were struck from bullion captured from Spanish ships at the Battle of Vigo Bay in 1702.

None of Anne's 17 children survived and her throne went to Elector George Louis of Hanover who became King George I of England (1714-27). The arms of Hanover have been added to the reverse shield of this 1726 5 guinea gold piece.

George I (1714–27), the first of the three Hanoverian kings, added the Hanoverian coat-of-arms to the reverses of many of his new coins. The obverses of some of his issues are inscribed with the initials SSC (South Sea Company) for the organization that supplied South American silver to the Royal Mint. Born in Germany, George I spoke only broken English during the 13 years he sat on the English throne.

During the reign of George II (1727–60), Admiral George Anson in 1744 brought back another sizeable haul of Spanish bullion. The scene of Anson's exploit was the Pacific Ocean where he relieved Spanish

The Georges used both their British and German titles on their coins. The many initials on the reverse of this 1758 shilling of George II and 1787 shilling of George III stand for Latin words which translate as "by the Grace of God, King of Great Britain, France and Ireland, Defender of the Faith, Duke of Brunswick and Luneburg, Arch Treasurer and Elector of the Holy Roman Empire."

George III's unusually large copper two pence of 1797 is often called a "cartwheel." Weighing a full two ounces, it measures 1½ inches in diameter.

galleons of some $3 million worth of gold and silver being brought back to Europe from Lima, Peru. The coins struck from this metal carry the inscription LIMA.

George III succeeded his grandfather in 1760 and during his long reign that lasted into 1820, several innovations were made in the coinage. The highest denomination struck was the guinea. One-third guineas were struck for the first time in 1797. Two new copper coins were also issued. Copper two- and one-pence pieces dated 1797 were struck by Matthew Boulton on a steam press produced in collaboration with James Watt, the inventor of the steam engine. These coins, weighing two ounces and one ounce respectively, were so expertly produced that forgery of them was virtually impossible. Commonly referred to as "cartwheels," these coins were only produced for one year because a copper shortage developed.

In 1797, a severe silver shortage led the Bank of England to buy Spanish pieces of eight which were countermarked with a tiny image of George III in an oval or octagonal frame, giving them an official value of 4 shillings and 9 pence.

Because counterfeiters imitated the counterstamped pieces, the Bank of England was authorized to issue "Bank Dollars" with the value of 5 shillings. The wall design over Britannia was intended perhaps to suggest the solidity for which the Bank of England is famous.

In 1816, a great recoinage took place with the introduction of the sovereign (valued at 20 shillings) and silver coins each with Benedetto Pistrucci's famous design of St. George and the Dragon. The Royal Mint was re-equipped with new steam-powered machinery and moved from its quarters in the Tower of London to a new site on Tower Hill.

William IV (1830–37) struck gold coins in ½, 1, 2, and 5 pound values, though the two higher denominations were not placed into circulation. In 1836, the groat or fourpenny piece in silver was revived with a Britannia reverse.

Coins of Queen Victoria's long reign can be divided into three distinct groups according to their portrait—young head (1837–86), Jubilee portrait (1887–1892), and older veiled bust (1893–1901). Under Victoria, as England increased its strength and influence as a world power, the British monetary system was established throughout the far-flung colonies.

Benedetto Pistrucci's famous sculpture of St. George and the Dragon first appeared in 1817, and is seen here on the silver crown of 1818. The Pistrucci design was used on a crown as recently as 1951.

208 ⚘ Great Britain

The silver crown of William IV (1830-37) was struck for specimen sets only, not for circulation, and is a very rare coin today.

Victoria's most attractive coin is the "Gothic" crown of 1847, so-called because of the queen's ornate dress and the Gothic letters in the inscription. A new denomination, the silver florin (equal to two shillings) was introduced in 1849 as the first step toward decimal coinage, a movement still not fully implemented.

The first florin issued was called the "Godless Florin," so-named because the obverse bore the simple title "Victoria Regina, 1849," omitting the customary "Dei Gratia, F.D." (By the Grace of God, Defender of the Faith). The offensive florin was immediately called in and replaced.

Victoria's most impressive set of coins was her Jubilee issue, first struck in 1887, to mark her fiftieth anniversary on the English throne. The coinage consisted of a gold five-pound piece, a double sovereign, sovereign, half-sovereign, silver crown, double-florin, half-crown, florin, shilling, sixpence, and three-penny piece. The five-pound and double

Queen Victoria's "Gothic Crown" was designed by William Wyon, the best known of a long and distinguished family of coin designers and engravers.

Queen Victoria, "young portrait"

Queen Victoria, "jubilee portrait"

Queen Victoria, "older portrait"

sovereign specimens were principally souvenirs rather than circulation pieces.

Edward VII (1901–1910) continued to issue the same denominations as his mother. The only novel design Edward used on his coinage was the standing, facing figure of Britannia on his florins.

Edward VII (1901-10) issued an unusual type silver florin with a standing, front-facing figure of Britannia.

The coinage of George V (1910–36) offered more variety due to there being two different reverse designs for most of the coins and some slight variations in the bust on the obverse. For the crown issued on the occasion of George V's Silver Jubilee in 1935, British coinage went modern, showing a sleek streamlined St. George in armor crushing a modernistic dragon. It is interesting to compare this design with Pistrucci's St. George.

The striking of sovereigns was suspended in 1917 because wartime emergencies made gold extremely scarce. In 1920, silver coins were reduced from .925 fine to .500 fine. By 1947, silver disappeared altogether from

The reverse of the 1935 Silver Jubilee crown struck for George V (1910-36) has a modernistic interpretation of St. George slaying the dragon.

regular British coinage with a copper-nickel combination being substituted. The only British coins being struck now in fine silver are the presentation Maundy coins.

Although dies were prepared for Edward VIII, who abdicated after being on the throne for only eleven months in 1936, the only coins struck were for various colonies (East and West Africa, Fiji and New

Brass 3-pence pieces dated 1937 with Edward VIII's portrait were already struck when the king abdicated in December, 1936. The coins were subsequently melted down, but a few rare specimens reached the hands of collectors.

Guinea). Since these coins were pierced with a center hole there is no portrait of Edward on them. A few twelve-sided nickel-brass threepence pieces, released as samples to vending machine operators did reach the hands of collectors. These coins were never officially released.

George VI (1936–52) issued two handsome crowns, the first in 1937, and the second in 1951. The latter commemorates the Festival of Britain—

George VI (1936-52) struck two differently designed shillings . . . the one at the left has an English crest; and the one at the right a Scottish crest. The Scottish design pays tribute to the ancestry of his Queen, Elizabeth.

Great Britain ❖ 211

a national exhibition of British achievements and industry. This crown, which reintroduces Pistrucci's St. George and the Dragon, also marks the 400th anniversary of the English crown first issued by Edward VI in 1551.

George introduced a Scottish shilling which was used to denote the Scottish ancestry of his Queen, Elizabeth. This coin features a Scottish lion seated above the crown, holding a sword in one paw and a sceptre in the other. At the sides are shields bearing St. Andrew's cross and the Scottish thistle. On the bronze halfpenny, Britannia yielded her place to Drake's *Golden Hind.*

Elizabeth II's 1953 crown struck to commemorate her coronation features the Queen on horseback, the first equestrian portrait of a British monarch since the reign of Charles I.

The 1953 coronation commemorative of Elizabeth II (1952–) shows the Queen on horseback, the first time a monarch has been shown in this manner since the reign of Charles I. The reverse, an equally striking design, has an elaborate crown of four shields. Another interesting crown piece of Elizabeth was minted in 1965 as a memorial to the late Sir Winston Churchill.

Elizabeth issued a few presentation gold pieces in 1953, and gold sovereigns sold for their bullion value have been struck for the general public in most years since 1957.

On March 1, 1966, the Chancellor of the Exchequer announced in the House of Commons the Government's decision to adopt a decimal

1968 gold sovereign of Elizabeth II with St. George and the Dragon reverse. Sovereigns have been issued in most years since 1957.

Elizabeth II's 1965 crown was issued as a memorial to Sir Winston Churchill, Britain's great World War II leader.

currency system in February, 1971. The pound will remain the major unit of currency but will be divided into 100 minor units called "new pence" instead of into twenty shillings each of twelve pence. The most controversial of the new decimal coins is the seven-sided 50 new pence piece released in 1969 as a replacement for the 10 shilling banknotes. The 50 new pence coin is about the same size and color as the 10 new pence and old 2 shilling pieces (worth only $\frac{1}{5}$ the face value) which has caused much confusion.

England's recently inaugurated decimal coinage includes the 10 and 50 new pence showing a more mature portrait of Queen Elizabeth. The 1954 florin at left is the same size and value as the 10 new pence piece which is destined to replace it in circulation.

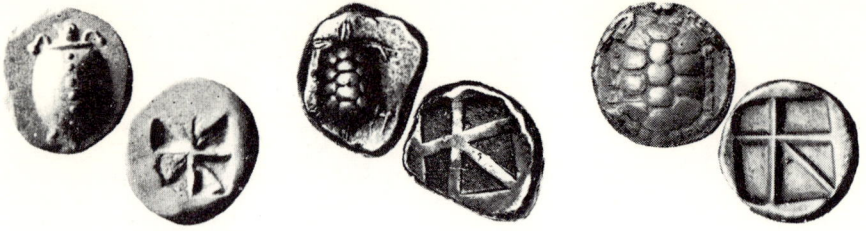

The badge of the island of Aegina was a sea tortoise, shown at left on a stater from c. 650 B.C. When the island declined in importance on the sea, a land tortoise took its place as on the staters at center (struck c. 450 B.C.) and right (struck c. 375 B.C.).

Greece, Ancient

While the world's first coins were probably produced about 700 B.C. by the ancient Lydians of Asia Minor, the Greeks, who struck their first coins about a half-century later, were the first people to circulate coins widely as a medium of exchange. The coins of the Greek city-states were of a standard shape, size, content, and value established by the authority. The word "standard" must be qualified, however, for the ancients did not have the precise machinery we use today for making coins. The Greeks produced their coins with the simplest of tools.

The Greeks used a hammer for striking coins and this tool was the main instrument for coin manufacture until about A.D. 1500. The die itself was embedded in an anvil, the planchet set against it, a punch placed on top and a blow struck with the hammer. Despite these rudimentary methods, the Greeks turned out some of the most beautiful and artistic coins ever made.

The earliest true Greek coins were minted about 650 B.C. on the island of Aegina, which lies some ten miles south of the present-day Piraeus, the port of Athens. A trading base of great importance in early times, ships from Aegina called regularly at the ports of the eastern Mediterranean, including Lydia. The mariners soon brought the idea of coins back to Greece.

Aegina's first coins, oblong silver staters, bore a sea tortoise, the emblem of the island. The reverse design consisted of four incuse compartments. At first the tortoise was plain-appearing, but later, probably about 550-40 B.C., it was decorated with a row of dots down the middle of the shell and across the top. These coins, commonly referred to as "turtles," were accepted in trade throughout the Eastern Mediterranean and in Egypt where there was a great demand for silver.

Corinth's silver stater from 400-335 B.C. shows the head of the city's goddess Pallas Athena. Pegasus, the sacred winged horse, is shown in flight on the reverse.

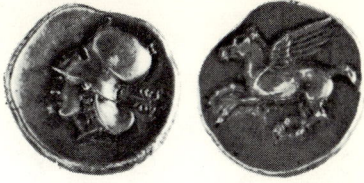

Corinth was the first of the mainland Greek city-states to strike coins, its first issues appearing about 600 B.C. Standing near the narrow isthmus connecting northern Greece and the Peloponnesus, Corinth is just a few miles from both Aegina and Athens. This strategic location gave Corinth commercial and military importance. Its navy was for a long time the strongest in Greece and Corinthian settlers founded colonies over a wide area, including Syracuse in Italy.

The earliest Corinthian coins portrayed the sacred winged horse Pegasus, while the reverse bore a pattern of incuse triangles. Like the "turtles" of Aegina, the Corinthian silver staters circulated throughout the Mediterranean world and were commonly referred to as "colts."

During the fifth century B.C., Corinth began minting two-sided coins. Pegasus remained on the obverse while the reverse showed the head of the patron goddess, Pallas Athene, wearing a Corinthian style helmet. The Corinthian moneyers also introduced a scheme for signifying different denominations by modifying the emblem. The stater had the complete figure of Pegasus, the half stater showed only the forepart, and an even smaller denomination (the obol) showed only a horse's head. This scheme made it possible for a trader in any part of the world to tell at a glance what a coin was worth in Corinth.

Many of the most beautiful Greek coins came from Athens, the greatest of the city-states. The Athenian coins eventually overshadowed those of Corinth in commercial importance. Because of the continuing

Athens was probably the first coin-producing state to use a regular design instead of punch marks on the reverse of its coins. Athena, the goddess of wisdom and patroness of the city, with her emblems, the owl and the olive branch, are portrayed on these tetradrachm from c. 550 B.C. (left) and c. 450 B.C. (right).

Greece, Ancient ⚘ 215

Athenian dekadrachm c. 480 B.C. and triobol (½ drachm) c. 450 B.C. Compare their size with the tetradrachm shown on the preceding page.

interest in Athens as the center of ancient Greek civilization, its coins have been studied more closely than any other series.

The earliest coinage of Athens has been placed at about 575 B.C. The first coins bear a wine jar or amphora, a reference to the oil, wine and pottery for which the city was famous. These specimens were relatively crude but the mint at Athens was probably the first to use an upper die in place of a punch, thus inscribing a second design rather than an incuse mark on the reverse side.

At the outset of the sixth century B.C., Athens introduced a new device on its coinage that remained in use for several centuries. The new coins portrayed the profile head of Pallas Athena wearing a crested helmet and a round earring. This goddess, famous in ancient mythology and later known to the Romans as Minerva, possessed many attributes—patroness of agriculture, industry and the arts. She was also Goddess of Wisdom, and among those things she held sacred was the owl. Consequently, the reverse of these silver tetradrachms portrayed the owl standing with wings closed, and in front the first letters of the city—AθE.

This silver stater of Athens from c. 150 B.C. still carries the head of Athena and an owl, a modification of the earlier types.

These "owls," as the coins were popularly called, were readily accepted in trade throughout the Mediterranean world. The purity of their silver content and their consistent full weight made them often the *only* acceptable coins in many cities and towns. Over the years, the Athenian owls were struck in many denominations, ranging down to the minute hemitartemorion which was equivalent to $\frac{1}{8}$ of an obol (1/192 part of a tetradrachm).

During the century and a half period from 500 B.C. to 350 B.C., distinctive coinages appeared for more than 1,000 communities. Every independent city, every nation or tiny state had its own coinage. As with the devices chosen by Aegina, Corinth and Athens, these coins carried distinctive designs, usually of local significance, to identify the issuing authority. Since the origin of a city was often attributed to some divine being, a likeness of the city's protecting god or goddess frequently identified the community. By about 400 B.C., however, so many cities had issued coins that an emblem was no longer adequate for identification. The name of the city, or at least its abbreviation, had to appear as well.

Elis, Zeus—King of the gods

Elis, Hera—Queen of the gods

Apollonia, Apollo—God of sunlight, manliness, music and poetry

Aenus, Hermes—Messenger of the gods

Delphi, Demeter—Goddess of agriculture

Greece, Ancient 217

ACRAGAS
(Crab)

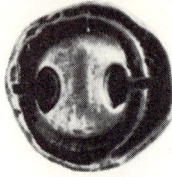

BOEOTIA
(Shield)

CYRENE
(Silphium plant)

ELIS
(Eagle)

EPHESUS
(Bee)

ERETRIA
(Octopus)

METAPONTUM
(Corn head)

RHODES
(Rose)

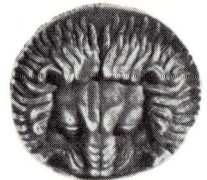

SAMOS
(Lion's scalp)

Greek city-state symbols on coins

The term "Greek coinage" actually covers a wide range of time and place. It includes the coinage of all the lands where Greek culture penetrated through trade and migration. Greek settlements in southern Italy, including the island of Sicily, became known as "Magna Graecia."

A coin of Syracuse, struck about 412 B.C., has been called "the most beautiful coin ever minted." This magnificent silver dekadrachm (ten drachmas) piece commemorates a Syracusan victory in 413 B.C. over Athenian forces that invaded at the height of the Peloponnesian Wars between Athens and Sparta. The exceptional coin was designed and struck

This magnificent dekadrachm of Syracuse, struck c. 410 B.C., was issued to celebrate the defeat of an invading Athenian army. The head of Persephone is surrounded by three dolphins with the engraver's signature EYAINE below the lowest dolphin. On the reverse, is a quadriga with Victory flying above.

as awards for the winners of the games and races held in celebration of the great victory. Among the many varieties of the dekadrachm are several signed by Kimon and others by the artist Euaenetus, the first instance we know of where the designer was honored on a coin.

Silver didrachms of Tarentum (the present day Taranto), located at the instep of the Italian boot, were struck from 400 to 300 B.C., picturing a jockey riding on a horse. The reverse has Taras riding on the back of a dolphin. Dozens of variations of this design type are known, indicating that once a device became widely recognized and accepted, the cities feared that any change would be rejected.

These four didrachms of Tarentum represent just a few of the many known variations of the same basic design struck c. 400-300 B.C. The Tarentines were renowned as horsemen and the reverses show Taras (the legendary founder of the city) riding on the back of a dolphin.

Greece, Ancient ❧ 219

These coins of Alexander the Great of Macedon (336-323 B.C.) are (left) a silver tetradrachm portraying Herakles and (right) a gold stater with a helmeted head of Athena. The reverses show Zeus seated and a winged Victory.

In the late fourth century B.C., the conquests of Alexander the Great spread Greek culture across Egypt, Persia, Mesopotamia and into India. The silver tetradrachm of Alexander the Great became the most widely circulated of all the Greek coins. It portrays Herakles (Hercules) in a lion's scalp, while the reverse has Zeus seated on a throne with an eagle. These coins circulated throughout Alexander's vast empire and coins of the same design were issued by his successors for some 200 years after his death in 323 B.C.

Alexandria in Egypt which had been planned by Alexander himself, was also equipped with an imposing mint, a facility that began operations in 326 B.C. Continuing even under the Romans, the mint at Alexandria produced coins in the name of the emperors until the time of Diocletian (A.D. 300).

Alexander's father, Philip II (382–336 B.C.) also struck an array of coins. When he took the town of Crenides from the Thracians in 356 B.C., he gained control of some of the richest gold mines in southern Europe. His gold staters became the dominant coinage throughout Greece and beyond. This coin shows a laureate head of Apollo, the god of manly youth, poetry and music, with a chariot on reverse. His silver tetradrachm shows the head of Zeus and on reverse a jockey on a race horse holding a

A head of Zeus appears on the obverse of this tetradrachm (left) of Philip the Great (359-336 B.C.), a head of Apollo on the gold stater (right). The reverses show Philip's horse and jockey commemorating a victory in the 105th Olympic Games and a biga, a chariot drawn by two horses.

Alexander the Great's successors, Ptolemy I (323-285 B.C.) in Egypt and Lysimachus in Thrace, broke all traditions by showing the likeness of an actual person, the deified Alexander, on their tetradrachms.

palm branch of victory. King Philip was a lover of horses and the design of the tetradrachm comes from a specific event. In 356 B.C., the king's own steed won the coveted first place at the 105th Olympic Games and in celebration, Philip directed that his horse and jockey be represented on his coins.

The ancient Greeks were deeply religious, and they often inscribed the images of their gods and goddesses on their coins. Alexander the Great's achievements in conquering so vast an empire must have seemed superhuman because Ptolemy, his successor in Egypt, altered the design of the tetradrachm—switching to an obvious portrait of Alexander himself, the first time in history that the undisguised likeness of a mortal person appeared on a coin. Alexander is shown wrapped in an elephant skin headdress, a reference to his conquest of India.

Lysimachus, a trusted general who became King of Thrace after Alexander, also issued a tetradrachm with an idealized head of the "Divine Conqueror." Alexander is shown wearing the ram's horn of Ammon, a symbol of immortality.

In about 300 B.C., Ptolemy I took the unprecedented step of using *his own* portrait on a silver tetradrachm, establishing a custom followed by monarchs and emperors down through the centuries. Ptolemy's four

Silver tetradrachm of Ptolemy I struck c. 300 B.C.—the first coin ever minted with the portrait of a living man.

tetradrachms in gold struck at the Alexandria Mint, circa 295 B.C., rank as one of the finest examples of Greek coinage art.

Eventually all three grand divisions of Alexander's empire fell into the hands of a new power whose force and influence spread out across Western Europe, finally into Britain. Macedon became a mere province of this emerging empire. Greece proper became a part of the Roman Empire in 146 B.C.

Roman coins struck and circulated in the East continued to carry inscriptions in Greek. This series is commonly called "Greek Imperial" or "Colonial." Though these coins are artistically sub-standard when compared with specimens of the Greek Classic Period, they are of great historical importance for the various types include views of statues now lost, representations of temples, and even portraits of famous personages such as Anacreon, Mitylene, and Sappho.

The ruined statue of Nike, the famous Winged Victory of Samothrace, now in the Louvre Museum in Paris, was pieced together by following the pattern on this silver coin issued in 303 B.C. by Demetrius Poliorcetes of Macedon.

Greek coinage also had its influence on moneys of neighboring lands such as Carthage. Situated in northern Africa near the site of modern Tunis, Carthage was founded in the ninth century B.C. as a trading post for Tyre and Utica. In the Second Punic War (218–201 B.C.), Hannibal, the daring Carthaginian general challenged the growing power of Rome. In 146 B.C., at the end of the Third Punic War, the city was utterly destroyed by Rome. Carthage was rebuilt by the Emperor Augustus and for several centuries remained a great Roman city.

Carthage first issued coins at the end of the fifth century B.C. A typical gold coin of Carthage minted in the fourth century portrayed the Phoenician goddess Tanit (she can be compared with the Greek goddess Persephone) and a prancing horse. Palm trees were also frequently inscribed on Carthaginian coins.

The story of ancient civilization's coinage is not fully known yet for countless hoards have been unearthed over the years, with new finds

The head of Persephone adorns this silver tetradrachm of Carthage. The reverse has a detailed horse's head and palm tree.

being made regularly even now. The largest find of the twentieth century occurred at Damanhur, Egypt, in 1905 where some 8,000 silver tetradrachms of Alexander, buried probably in 318 B.C., were brought to the surface.

Soldiers buried coins along the lines of march with the expectation of digging them up on the way back to Greece, but the knowledge of their locations died when Alexander's men were left isolated in Babylon. Much of this buried treasure has come to light again within the past century as archeological or accidental finds. One hoard in Sidon in Phoenicia, buried beneath the old city walls, revealed several copper pots filled with gold staters of Philip and Alexander. Two thousand pieces were saved by the government but the rest—and no one knows how many—went into the pockets of the workmen who made the discovery.

Greek treasure-trove law protects the country for no historical relics can be taken beyond its borders. All finds—ranging from massive pieces of sculpture, to coins and bits of pottery—belong to the government. Finders are paid a fee for their efforts but Greek museums have first rights to the treasures in all cases. Museums in the major Greek cities all have significant collections of Greek coins on display.

Struck about 425 B.C., this silver dekadrachm of Akragas is one of the masterpieces of Western Greek coinage.

Greece, Ancient ❧ 223

Minted in 1926, this 2 drachmai Greek coin with the helmeted goddess Athena recalls the country's ancient days of glory.

Greece, Modern

In early times, Greece produced the finest ancient civilization known to history. Subsequently part of the Roman and Byzantine empires, Greece was conquered by the Turks in 1453. The country did not regain full independence until 1828. Following World War I and a disastrous campaign against Turkey, it became a republic in 1924. In 1935 the monarchy was restored. The present King, Constantine II, was forced to leave the country in 1967, and Greece has been ruled by a combination of military officers and civilian political leaders ever since.

Though Greece has had a fairly regular coinage since becoming free of Turkish rule, coinage almost completely disappeared during the severe inflation following World War II. However, the monetary reform of 1954 established a new drachma (equalling 100 lepta) and 1, 2 and 5 drachmae values were struck in copper-nickel.

Since Greece has no mint of its own, its coins are produced on contract by other minting establishments, primarily the Paris Mint.

The Greek 30 drachmai of 1963 marks the centennial of the Dynasty. The five kings portrayed are (from the bottom): George I (1863-1913); Constantine I (1913-17, 1920-22); Alexander (1917-20); George II (1935-47); Paul I (1947-64). The reverse design is a map of Greece.

Hoards and Finds

Many of the ancient coins in collectors' hands today are in existence only because they were lost, hidden or buried centuries ago and have come to light unexpectedly in modern times. Significant finds of coins have been made in sunken treasure ships as well as in underground hiding places. In fact, wresting coins from the ocean floors has brought a tremendous amount of drama into numismatics during the past decade.

Most hoards, however, are discovered underground or in secret hiding places at ground level. One of the largest documented finds of ancient coins consisted of some 8,000 tetrodrachms of Alexander the Great (struck in 336–323 B.C.). This tetradrachm, with its head of Herakles and the seated figure of Zeus with his eagle and thunderbolt, was one of the most widely circulated coins of ancient times. Dug up at Damanhur, Egypt in 1905, the coins are believed to have been buried in about 318 B.C. Damanhur, situated 40 miles southeast of Alexandria, was one of the most important commercial centers in ancient Egypt.

Most ancient coins in existence today were buried in the ground centuries ago and came to light unexpectedly as a result of digging in the earth. The coin pictured is a silver tetradrachm of Ptolemy II of Egypt, struck in 254 B.C. It is the best preserved of 28 coins in a hoard uncovered in A.D. 1955 by a farmer near the modern Greek city of Kozani.

Hoards are usually found accidentally and they can turn up almost anywhere, at any time. In summer 1960, for example, a Roman urn containing several thousand coins was discovered in Gloucester, England. The urn, measuring 12 by 16 inches, was found by workmen digging in a basement, and the coins were immediately turned over to the Gloucester City Museum. Most of the coins, which included silver, bronze, and a few gold pieces, were struck in the third century A.D. during the Roman occupation of Britain and bore the heads of the Roman emperors Aurelian, Tacitus, Probus and Carinus.

According to English Treasure Trove law, those coins which are not required for the local museum—in this case the Gloucester City, or the British Museum in London—can either be kept or sold by the finder. A good percentage of the coins from this hoard were not required by the museums, and eventually found their way into the hands of eager collectors.

Treasure Trove laws in most countries cover coins made of gold and silver. Copper coins, however, regardless of how rare or valuable they may be, do not constitute treasure trove, nor do gold or silver casually lost or thrown away with no intention of reclaiming it later. In another recent case late in 1959, a 14-year-old boy, while plowing a field in Sussex, England with a tractor, uncovered 502 English copper, silver and gold coins dated in the 1650's and 1660's. The boy's parents contacted the Sussex Archeological Society, and the curator immediately went out to the field where he discovered several hundred more silver and copper coins in a big jar. The curator surmised that the coins were probably a life's savings hurriedly buried. The Sussex Archeological Society retained the hoard for its own display and rewarded the boy with a sum equal to

One of the largest coin finds in history occurred in England in 1831, when workmen unearthed 200,000 coins of Edward I and Edward II at one spot. As a result, coins such as this Edward I silver penny (1272-1307), with the "long cross" reverse, are readily available even today at modest cost despite their age.

the full market value of the coins. It is customary, though not legally required, to pay the finder the full value of the coins—thus insuring the preservation of numismatically valuable coins which might otherwise have been concealed and melted down for their metal value. A number of the rarer gold and silver pieces were later turned over to the British Museum's collection.

One of the most important of all finds of ancient coins in Britain occurred in 1878 at Carrawburgh, near Hadrian's Wall, on the site of a well dedicated to the ancient British water-goddess Coventina. More than 16,000 Roman coins were found, dating from A.D. 100 to 300, in addition to various types of pottery and jewelry. More than 300 of these Roman pieces were the interesting "Britannia" type struck by Hadrian (117–38) and Antoninus Pius (138–61). The Britannia coins commemorated Roman achievements in Britain.

Bronze 40 nummia of the Byzantine emperor Maurice (582-602) found in a hoard in the vicinity of Heliopolis (modern Baalbek, Lebanon) in 1959.

In 1833, at Beaworth, in Hampshire, a lead chest containing 8,000 to 9,000 silver pennies of William I and II was unearthed. The coins had been originally packed in rolls, and appeared to be strictly uncirculated. The majority of the coins were PAXS pennies of William I; as a result, this type, previously rare, became the most common. Perhaps the largest single find of coins in England occurred in 1831, near Tutbury (Staffordshire), where some 200,000 pennies of Edward I and II were unearthed by laborers engaged in deepening the River Dove.

Large-scale finds are still being made today as witnessed by recent reports from Madrid that antique dealers have been offering to sell Roman bronze coins by the tubful. A large hoard of Roman bronze pieces had been dug up near Toledo, 45 miles to the south and most of the coins remained to be cleaned—even in a most rudimentary way—and identified. These unattributed coins were priced to move and one antique dealer was offering them, as is, for only 15 pesetas (about 35 cents) each.

Archeologists often look to finds of coin hoards for clues to the economies and social conditions of past civilizations. A higher silver or gold content in coins, for example, denotes a prosperous economy, while thin, debased pieces usually indicate great economic stress.

Coin hoards can pose questions, however, as well as answers. Several hoards of late Roman and Byzantine gold solidi found in Sweden and Denmark, totaling more than 800 specimens, have puzzled historians for nearly a century. These coins were uncovered on three Baltic islands, Gotland and Oland, part of Sweden, and on Bornholm, part of Denmark.

A gold bezant issued by the Crusaders prior to 1251, found in 1965 in a small hoard near Marash in south central Turkey.

Hoards and Finds ❧ 227

These gold pieces were all struck during a period of a century and a half—from the death of Theodosius I in 395 to the latter part of the reign of Justinian I, *c.* 550. Scholars believe the coins were used originally by the Ostrogoths, the East Goths, who flourished in the region of the Black Sea at and around the headwaters of the Volga.

The 800-plus specimens is a large number considering the great distance between the Mediterranean world and the Baltic. From the location of the finds and the attribution of these coins, it has, of course, been determined that there was considerable contact between the Scandinavians and the Ostrogoths. This information, however, poses the question as to which of these two peoples were the carriers of the coins. It seems just as possible that the Scandinavians crossed the Continent to reach the Ostrogoths as it does that the Ostrogoths traveled back and forth between Scandinavia and their homelands.

The focal point for such discussions remains the same—the coins. As they are studied more intensively along with other scattered pieces of evidence, and perhaps additional finds of coins, the answers will be worked out.

Sunken treasure ships hold a special fascination for everyone, but numismatists in particular. One of the most electrifying finds of the twentieth century came in the spring of 1961 when salvage operations were completed on the Vasa, a ship which had rested on the bottom of Stockholm's harbor for 333 years!

In January 1625, King Gustavus II Adolphus (1611–32) ordered four warships to be constructed in Stockholm. The most powerful of these—the Vasa—set sail for the first time on the 10th of August 1628 in sight of a large crowd following vespers in Stockholm Cathedral. Suddenly, a small squall arose, the ship heeled over sharply to port and water entered the lower gun ports. Right in the harbor of the capital, Gustavus Adolphus' mightiest ship went down, all her flags flying. In 1644, divers were able to recover her valuable bronze guns in 100 feet of water. And then for more than three centuries the Vasa was allowed to lay almost forgotten.

Interest in the old ship stirred again in 1956 when a special Vasa Committee was formed to investigate the salvage possibilities. After many difficulties, the Vasa was raised in 1961 and was so well preserved, she was able to float on her own keel. Her mud-filled interior contained many archeological finds including some 4,000 coins in gold, silver and copper, which were immediately turned over to Stockholm's Royal Coin Cabinet for examination. The find has added much to the knowledge of Swedish numismatics. The copper coins, for example, were among the first struck in the country, for Sweden did not use copper coins until the early 1620's. These coins have also shed light on Swedish mints, for in the 1620's branch mints were in operation at Sater, Nykoping and Arboga in addition to the head mint at Stockholm. Though the coins had been in water for over 300 years, they are, on the whole, in remarkably good condition. Many of them can be viewed today at the Royal Coin Cabinet and at the Vasa museum where the ship itself is on display.

1626 emergency rectangular copper 2 ore klipping recovered from the wreckage of the Vasa. The coin has Gustavus Adolphus' crowned monogram on the obverse, the Vasa sheaf badge on the reverse.

When a large hoard of coins recovered from a wreck reaches the numismatic market, it might be expected to depress the price previously offered for that type of item. Actually, exactly the opposite usually happens—they command premium prices. A number of coins recovered in 1963–64 from the Gilt Dragon, a bullion-laden ship of the Dutch East India Company which sank mysteriously off the coast of Western Australia in April 1656, were offered at auction. Many of the coins,

These Mexico City mint cob 8 reales struck in 1649 and 1654 under the Spanish king Philip IV were recovered recently from the Gilt Dragon which sank off the coast of Western Australia in 1656.

which were mostly 8 reales silver cobs of the Spanish King Philip IV (1621–65), had unusually clear designs and dates. Many of the pieces offered brought several hundred dollars each, prices much higher than the standard catalogue values of ordinary Philip IV reales. Coins recovered from treasure ships are "pedigreed," known to be genuine, have a romantic history to them and are thus highly prized. Incidentally, gold coins especially are usually in like-new condition since gold is impervious to water and resists chemical reaction. Silver and copper coins salvaged from below the sea generally show some signs of corrosion.

230 ❀ Hoards and Finds

This Mexican cob coin, an 8 reales struck in 1612 under Philip III, was discovered in 1965 off the coast of the Bahamas in a wreck thought to be the Dutch ship *Van Lynden*, which sank in the early 1600's.

Treasures of the Dutch plate fleet which sailed under the notorious pirate Piet Heijn were found off the Bahamas in 1965. Thousands of Spanish colonial coins—probably from the ship Van Lynden—have been brought to the surface. Many of the specimens were struck in the period from 1612 to 1629 at the Mexico City and Potosi mints. A good percentage of the coins are easily identifiable as 4 and 8 reales pieces of Philip III and Philip IV. In recent years enthusiastic fortune hunters have been literally combing the Spanish Main (that part of the Caribbean through which Spanish galleons frequently sailed) for treasure.

Even a few coins from ancient times have been found in shipwrecks. In 1967, archeologist-diver Peter Throckmorton discovered the remains of a Roman ship in the Gulf of Taranto in southern Italy. While examining the ship, Throckmorton found a bronze coin of the Roman emperor Commodus (180–92), minted on the island of Lesbos, and he reported that "The Commodus bronze piece is really a telltale clue as to when this particular Roman ship went down," emphasizing again how numismatics particularly through the study of hoards and finds, has contributed to our knowledge of history.

In the mid-1960's an American salvage team brought this 1712 Lima gold 8 escudos up from a wrecked fleet of Spanish galleons that went down in 1715 off the Florida coast.

Hoards and Finds ❧ 231

Holy Roman Empire

Beginning with the coronation of Charlemagne on Christmas day in the year 800, the Holy Roman Empire existed for over a thousand years, ending with the abdication of Austrian emperor Francis II in 1806. This complex and long-lived empire was theoretically the secular counterpart of the Holy Catholic Church. The pope, elected by the princes of the church, stood at the head of society in its spiritual character. The emperor, also elected, was to stand above other rulers as the temporal chief of Christendom.

The post of elector was a high honor and from the 13th century on was hereditary to the Palatine of the Rhine, the Duke of Saxony, the Margrave of Brandenburg and the King of Bohemia. The Dukes of Bavaria and Brunswick-Luneburg (Hanover) were added later. The Archbishops of Mainz, Cologne and Trier were the ecclesiastical electors. The electors in practice named a German Kaiser who was confirmed Holy Roman Emperor by the pope.

Although the power of the emperor declined over the centuries outside of his own territories, he did have the right among others to grant the minting privilege, grant the status of "free city," and raise the rank of nobility.

1570 taler of Cologne issued in the name of Holy Roman Emperor Maximilian II (1564-76).

The Holy Roman Empire is sometimes called the German Empire because it included in general the German speaking people of central Europe. It did at various times embrace regions outside of modern Germany including parts of Italy. A study of the coins of the Empire is a study of the coins of several different countries, especially Germany and Austria.

Charlemagne (742–814), the founder of the Carolingian dynasty (800–911), ranks as one of the great men of history. By the time of his death his empire included most of Western Europe. To the Germans who claim him as one of their own, he is "Karl der Grosse," and to the French he is their own Charlemagne (from Carolus Magnus, "Charles the Great").

1572 taler of
Friedrich III,
Count Palatinate
of the Rhine.

Taler of Johann
Hugo von
Orsbeck
(1676-1711),
Archbishop of
Trier.

The electors of the Holy Roman Empire were granted the right to mint coins in their own names, a privilege that all of them exercised.

The successors of Charlemagne were not men of his caliber; they quarreled among themselves and eventually divided up his empire. In time, the modern states of France, Germany, Austria, Italy, Switzerland, Belgium and Holland arose from Charlemagne's Holy Roman Empire.

Otto I, "the Great" (936–73) of the House of Saxony (919–1024) did a great deal to revive the Holy Roman Empire and raise the esteem of the monarchial system in Europe. When he came to the throne in 936, Germany was a small country lying along the shores of the Rhine. Otto greatly increased the size of Germany by adding Bavaria, Bohemia, northeast Prussia and other territory to his dominions. Otto II (973–83) and Otto III (983–1002) established new imperial mints in such cities as Andernach, Bonn, Dortmund, Hildesheim, and Quedlinburg. The particular mint may be identified by the different saints portrayed in the reverse designs.

Henry IV (1056–1106), of the Salian and Franconian line (1024–1125) experienced great turmoil during his long reign. The bitter struggle between the emperor and the pope resulted in civil wars and weakened the position of the monarchy. The deteriorating economic situation led to a sharp reduction in the weight of the silver penny which gave rise to the coinage of bracteates.

Frederick I Barbarossa (1152–90), the greatest ruler of the Hohenstaufen line (1137–1254), aimed like Charlemagne to rule with a firm hand. Among other exploits, he led armies across the Alps six times to keep cities in Lombardy under imperial control. Barbarossa was a major figure in the Third Crusade as he proclaimed a universal peace in his dominions, placed the crown in charge of his son, and joined forces with Philip II of France and Richard of England to effect the recapture of Jerusalem from Saladin. Revitalizing the mint at Aachen, he made it one of the most productive of all the coin striking facilities in medieval Europe. On his coins, Frederick is portrayed seated, facing a globe on a sword. On the reverse, a building is inscribed ROMA CAPUT MUNDI (Rome, capital of the world).

Rudolf I (1273–91) was the first of the Hapsburgs to be Holy Roman Emperor. After the death of Rudolf, five different houses took turns at ruling for the next century and a half, but from 1438 until the Empire came to an end in 1806, the Emperor was always a Hapsburg.

During Rudolf's time both the bishoprics and imperial cities of the Empire struck their own coins. Rudolf minted various silver pieces bearing his portrait accompanied by his name "Rudolf" in full or the initial "R." He also introduced an eagle on the reverse of his coins which remained a characteristic of Austrian coinage throughout the country's history.

In 1519, Charles I of Spain, better known in history as Charles V (1519–56), was elected Holy Roman Emperor—he was only 19 at the time. He

234 ❧ Holy Roman Empire

The famous 1590 "dreikaiser" taler from the Hall mint in Tyrol. On the obverse are the portraits of Holy Roman Emperors Maximilian I (1493-1519), Charles V (1519-56) and Ferdinand I (1556-64).

succeeded in uniting Germany, Spain, the Netherlands, the Sicilies and Sardinia under one sovereign. As Holy Roman Emperor, Charles V struck a variety of coins throughout his domains. Many of his talers (silver dollar-size coins) had the imperial-eagle obverse and a cross and shield reverse. In 1556 Charles abdicated both the Spanish and Holy Roman thrones. His brother Ferdinand I (1556–64) succeeded him as ruler of the latter empire, his son Philip II taking Spain.

(Left) 1575 taler from the Kuttenburg mint of Emperor Maximilian II (1556-64) and (right) 1609 taler from the Hall mint of Emperor Rudolf II (1576-1612).

Holy Roman Empire ❧ 235

Gold 15 ducats struck in 1617 at the Kremnitz mint for Emperor Matthias (1612-19)

Silver taler struck in 1625 at Prague for Emperor Ferdinand II (1619- 37)

Taler struck in 1653 at Kremnitz for Ferdinand III (1637-58)

236 ☙ Holy Roman Empire

The Hapsburg Holy Roman emperors had their mints turn out prolific issues of talers. After the discovery of a rich silver mine at Joachimsthal (Joachim's Valley) in 1516, "thalers" or talers began to be struck in great quantities and circulated throughout Europe. In coin catalogues and auction listings, the coins of the emperors are usually listed under the name of the city or country that struck them but they must all be considered as issues of the Holy Roman Empire.

Undated double taler from the Hall mint, issued by Emperor Leopold I (1658-1705)

Coins of Leopold I (1658–1705) have long been of special interest to collectors because of the Emperor's unusual physical characteristic, his protruding jaw. Because of Leopold's decidedly grotesque appearance, he has been labeled as "The Hog Mouth," though the term was never used during his lifetime. Interestingly enough, however, the coin engravers apparently made no effort to "tone down" the jaw. Leopold's remarkable portrait is also shown on his many varieties of gold pieces. During his lengthy reign, he minted no less than 22 denominations of gold coins, ranging from the tiny 1/12 ducat piece to the large 30 ducats.

Even though the emperor's power eroded over the centuries, the wealth of the empire is apparent in the staggering number of varieties of talers and gold pieces minted. Charles VI (1711–40), for example, struck coins at some dozen-odd mints including Augsburg, Breslau, Graz, Hall, Kremnitz, Prague, Siebenburgen and Vienna.

Joseph II (1765–90) served as Holy Roman Emperor for 25 years and ruled the Austrian domains jointly with his mother, Maria Theresa, until

1705 taler from Munich of Emperor Joseph I (1705-11)

her death in 1780. Joseph is generally considered the embodiment of the spirit of the latter 18th century reforming monarchs known as the "benevolent," or "enlightened," despots. He established schools, hospitals and equalized taxation. Yet in spite of all his good intentions, his empire was threatened with dissolution at the time of his death.

Francis II (1792–1806) was the last of the Holy Roman Emperors. Francis was forced to give up the throne because radical political changes within Germany had removed the Empire's strongest supports. He

1713 taler from Steiermark of Emperor Charles VI (1711-40)

1790 taler from Vienna of Emperor Leopold II (1790-92)

continued, however, to rule Austria as Emperor Francis I until his death in 1835.

The Roman Empire and the Catholic Church were meant to be two aspects of one society. The Roman Caesar ("Kaiser" in German) was to stand at the head of this society in its temporal character as an empire. At its head in its spiritual character as a church, was the spiritual chief of Christendom, the Roman pontiff. Each claimed to rule by divine right and each was to be elected—the pope by the princes of the church, the emperor by the secular princes.

1806 taler from Vienna of Emperor Francis II (1792-1806). Under pressure from Napoleon, the Holy Roman Empire was formally abolished in 1806.

Holy Roman Empire ᛤ 239

Louis I, the Great (1342-82), issued this gold gulden at a time when Hungary was one of the most powerful states in central Europe.

Hungary

Little is known of the Hungarians, or Magyars, prior to their first appearance in Europe in the 880's. Starting from the Russian steppes, the Magyars swept into Europe, settling down in Hungary which corresponds roughly to the ancient Roman provinces of Pannonia and Dacia.

This ducat of Matthias Corvinus, king of Hungary (1458-90), minted at Kormocz-banya, portrays St. Ladislas holding a sceptre. The Madonna and Child appear on the coin's reverse.

King Stephen I (997–1038), declared a saint in 1087, invited Benedictine monks to his kingdom where they passed on to his unruly subjects their skill in farming and craftsmanship along with Christianity. Stephen I issued a series of silver deniers with both the obverse and reverse inscribed with a cross and the inscription STEPHANUS REX. Stephen's successors continued to produce the same type of coinage with the reverse inscription "Pannonia."

St. Ladislas on horseback is portrayed on this beautiful silver broad half-taler, dated 1506. Struck by Ladislas II, king of Hungary and Bohemia (1490-1516), the coin features an elaborate reverse arms.

George II Rakoczi, prince of Transylvania (1648-60), is shown wearing a fur cap on this 1655 gold ducat. During this period, Transylvania was an autonomous part of Hungary ruled by local princes called voivoides.

The main mint of the Hungarian kingdom was established at Kormocz-banya in 1326 by King Charles Robert (1308–42). Called Kormoczbanya by the Hungarians, Kremnitz under the Austrians, and Kremnica since it became a part of Czechoslovakia in 1918, a mint continues to operate in this city.

In 1526, at the Battle of Mohacs, the Turks won a decisive victory over the Hungarian army. Consequently, Hungary was broken up into three parts: (1) Turkish occupied Hungary; (2) the Principality of Transylvania; and (3) the Kingdom of Hungary, including the city of Kormoczbanya. King Louis II (1516–26) lost his life at Mohacs and the Hungarian throne went to the Hapsburg family, represented by Ferdinand of Austria. The Kingdom of Hungary was held intact throughout the entire span of the Hapsburg dynasty from 1527 to 1918.

As head of the House of Hapsburg, Maria Theresa also ruled as Queen of Hungary (1740-80) where she struck this 2 ducat gold piece of 1765 at Kormoczbanya ("KB").

One of the greatest of all the Hapsburg monarchs was Queen Maria Theresa (1740–80). The reverses for several varieties of Maria Theresa coins were inscribed with the Hungarian arms—two angels placing a crown on a shield. The Maria Theresa talers struck for Hungary during the 1741–80 period had on reverse a representation of the Madonna and child.

Hungary regained partial independence in 1867 when a dual monarchy was established. Through this arrangement Hungary was to be—at least theoretically—an equal partner with Austria in the empire. Emperor Franz Joseph (1848–1916) was crowned king of Hungary and swore to support

Hungary ❧ 241

5 korona Jubilee issue of 1907 was struck to mark the 40th anniversary of Franz Joseph's coronation as King of Hungary in 1867. The Austro-Hungarian Empires were united in that year.

the Hungarian constitution. The House of Hapsburg officially came to an end when Charles IV (1916–18) abdicated at the end of World War I.

Under the new Republic proclaimed in 1919, the Hungarian State Mint was relocated at Budapest. The new mint was temporarily housed at the

Franz Joseph's Hungarian coins such as this 1869 silver florin were similar to his Austrian issues except for the distinctive reverse.

Hungarian State Carriage and Wagon Works in the industrial section of Budapest. The first coins produced there were 10 and 20 filler coins in iron, dated 1920–22. Though they were struck at Budapest, the dies came from Kormoczbanya and still bore the mint mark "к-в."

Stephen I, patron saint of Hungary, was memorialized on this silver 5 pengo coin issued in 1938, the 900th anniversary of his death.

242 ⊛ Hungary

Franz Liszt (1811-86), the famous Hungarian pianist and composer, is portrayed on this silver 2 pengo of 1936.

In 1925, Hungarian mint officials began to convert the cavalry garrison near the city center into a modern coin striking facility. The first regular issues to come out of the new mint were the bronze 1 and 2 filler pieces of 1926–40, along with the copper–nickel 10, 20 and 50 filler denominations of the same date. The chief silver coin struck during this period was the 1 pengo. The mint mark of the Hungarian State Mint is "BP" for Budapest.

The Charles Bridge, pictured on the 1956 20 forint and the 1967 50 filler, spans the Danube River and connects the towns of Buda and Pest to form the united city of Budapest, capital of Hungary.

Today Hungary is nominally a republic under the influence of Russian Communism. Modern commemoratives struck at Budapest are of numismatic interest. Three silver pieces were minted in 1956: Hungarian National Museum, 10 forint; Szechenyi Bridge, Budapest, 20 forint; Hungarian Parliament, 25 forint.

Louis Kossuth (1802-94), leader of the 1848 Hungarian revolution, is portrayed on the current 5 forint coins.

Hungary ❧ 243

Indian gold stater of Chandragupta II (380-414), showing the King shooting an arrow at a lion. The reverse shows a goddess seated on a lion, holding a lotus blossom (a Hindu religious symbol).

India

India, the site of several great ancient civilizations, has produced such a variety of coins that no definitive catalogue has thus far been written on them. India's earliest known coin-like objects date back to at least the 6th century B.C.—during the early period, small silver ingots, marked only by three circular dots, circulated in the market places.

The country's "modern history" begins with the invasion by Alexander the Great in 327 B.C. The armies of Alexander eventually reached as far as the Indus River, spreading Greek culture through much of the Asian sub-continent. The coins of various districts, cities and rulers show real variety. Some pieces of the ancient rulers with idealized portraits reflect the Greek influence, while others have Indian sacred symbols. Elephants, trees, and swastikas abound, along with figures of the gods, horses, and even the rhinoceros. Indian coins produced up to the time of Christ are remarkable since many of the rulers' names and other information recorded on these specimens would have otherwise been lost to history.

At the end of the 1st century A.D., Greek influence began to give way to the Roman. At this time Roman gold was sent in enormous quantities to northwest India to be re-coined. Great hoards of Roman and Roman-type coins have been discovered in India, some of the hoards being uncovered only during the past decade. Interestingly enough, due to the mixing of cultures during this period, the deities of all the major religions of the time—the Greek, Roman, Zoroastrian, Hindu and Buddhist—were shown on the coins of India.

A square-shaped gold mohur of Quetbu-Edin Mubarak, Sultan of Delhi (1316-20). The coin has Indian legends on both sides.

244 ⊕ India

The later medieval dynasties of south India struck coinages primarily of gold, and rulers favored having their portraits, in heroic poses, engraved in coins. Animals were often represented on these coins. Elephants, for example, were common to coins of Malabar, those of the Deccan plateau had boars forming the central motif, while a few dynasties liked to have various species of fish in the coinage design.

Indian civilization rose to its greatest height when the Mohammedans conquered the country in 1526 and founded the Mogul Empire which endured, nominally at least, until 1857. The Mogul emperors established the greatest individual fortunes the world has ever known. The Moguls filled their giant treasure chests to the brim with gold coin, jewelry and precious stones.

One of the greatest Mogul emperors was Akbar the Great (1542–1605). Akbar made Agra the capital of India and built the massive Red Fort, a crescent-shaped structure of red sandstone. His grandson Shah-Jahan (reigned 1628–58) built the famed Taj Mahal, the "crown jewel" of

A round gold mohur of the Mogul emperor Akbar the Great (1556-1605). Indian legends are inscribed within an octagon on each side.

Indo-Islamic architecture, as a tomb for his wife Arjumand Banu. Akbar's mints were busy throughout India turning out coins in all metals. Many thousands of these specimens have survived to this day. Following orthodox Moslem tradition, Akbar did not allow his portrait to be engraved on his coins.

Akbar's son, Jahangir (1569–1627), the Emperor of Hindustan minted a remarkable series of gold mohurs bearing the signs of the zodiac. The mohur was the standard gold coin of India. Under Jahangir, moneys in gold, silver and billon were produced in great volume in Malwa, Kashmir, and elsewhere. His coins took on all sizes and shapes: round, square, diamond, rectangular, elliptical, triangular. The languages inscribed on his coins include Sanskrit, Urdu, Bengali and Punjabi.

In the early 1600's, the European nations became interested in India, the English established suzerainty in the 1760's. It was actually the British East India Company that gained power, establishing itself at

The remarkable gold mohurs of Mogul Emperor Jahangir (1605-27) show the signs of the Zodiac under which the coins were struck. The signs above are: Gemini (twins), Capricorn (goat), Libra (scales), Taurus (bull), Cancer (crab), Virgo (female), Aries (ram), Leo (lion), Scorpio (spider), Sagittarius (archer), Aquarius (water carrier), Pisces (fish).

coastal posts. To hold its ground against other European traders, the company raised a private army of Indian troops and British officers.

With the dawn of the 18th century, Indian coins in general became stereotyped as the engravers seemed to execute designs in an almost mechanical and routine way. For decades the English merchants followed native coinage types and did not mint along European lines until the beginning of the 1800's. As the Mogul Empire weakened, a group of so-called "Native States" came into existence. Most of these Native States struck their own coins until well into the 20th century. One of the most important independent mints was at Hyderabad, whose coinage was finally demonetized on April 1, 1955.

This gold mohur of Bengal, struck during the 1750-1820 period, was part of the coinage issued by the East India Company.

This crude, thick-planchet silver rupee was struck by the native state of Madras c. 1800.

The native State of Bikanir commemorated the 50th anniversary of Rajah Sri Ganga Singhji's reign on this 1937 rupee.

The coins were minted in India during the 1800's under the authority of the British East India Company. They were usually struck in silver with the portrait of Queen Victoria, who in 1876 was officially crowned "Empress of India."

By the beginning of the 20th century, a strong movement for independence had swept the country. After years of struggle, Britain granted dominion status to India in 1947, allowing the predominantly Mohammedan areas to split off into a new state called Pakistan. India is today a sovereign democratic republic within the British Commonwealth of Nations.

William IV, king of England, appears on the British East India Company's silver rupee of 1835.

Queen Victoria, who was proclaimed Empress of India in 1876, is shown on this 1877 rupee.

India ⚙ 247

Modern coins of India have been minted in a variety of unusual shapes . . . typical of these are the 1919 octagonal 4 annas, the 1924 square-shaped 2 annas and the 1924 scalloped-edge 1 anna.

Contemporary coins of India are attractive, come in several different shapes, and depict many of its animals. Among the animals portrayed are the sacred cow, the Bengal tiger, the horse and lion.

The two main government mints are situated at opposite ends of the country, at Bombay in the west and Calcutta in the east. These mints are among the most productive in the world since they strike a combined total of nearly two billion coins annually. Pakistan has its own mint at Lahore.

India's current 1 rupee coin shows the lions atop a famous pillar attributed to Emperor Asoka (259-232 B.C.).

Pakistan's 1 rupee of 1948, the first coinage of the newly created nation, features a toughra in wreath design. The reverse displays the star and crescent, another Moslem emblem.

In the partition of 1947, the sub-continent was divided into Pakistan (in two parts), formed out of predominantly Moslem areas, and the state of India, consisting of the mainly Hindu areas.

This unofficial Notgeld "emergency money" coin issued in inflation torn Germany in August, 1923, had a face value of a half million marks.

Inflation Coins

The most outstanding issues of inflation money originated in Germany during the period following World War I. All coins with intrinsic metal value virtually disappeared from circulation and money was produced using available materials such as shoe leather, cloth, porcelain, even newsprint. The costs for goods went sky-high and to keep pace with the rising prices, it was necessary to produce emergency coins having astronomical values. Coins were actually struck inscribed with values in millions of marks. One coin dated 1923 had the value of one billion marks!

Westphalia, an industrial region of Germany, was forced to issue coins with the astounding values of 50 million and 1 billion marks during the height of the inflation of 1921-23. Values as low as 5 marks were used at the beginning of the spiral.

Inflation Coins ❀ 249

Porcelain pieces were pressed into service in Germany to take the place of the regular metal coins that were hoarded during the economic crisis of the 1920's. Shown above are porcelain 25 and 50 pfennig values issued in 1921 at Freiberg and porcelain 20 and 50 pfennig and 1 mark values issued at Saxony in the same year.

Among the many unusual substitutes for metal coins are the porcelain coins issued 1920–23 during the height of the German economic crisis. These originated in Meissen, known for centuries as a center for the ceramics industry. Produced in denominations from 10 pfennigs to 20 marks, they circulated not only in Meissen but throughout Saxony and other parts of Germany as well.

Artistically designed, the Meissen porcelain pieces include representations of the German eagle, the horn of plenty, stalks of wheat, grapes on a vine, laurel wreaths, crossed swords, ships, oak leaves, fir trees, coat-of-arms, overhead railways, peasant farmers at work, soldiers at war, ambulance drivers, factory workers, miners, children playing, and religious themes such as madonnas, churches, crosses and steeples.

Inflation seriously affected some of the European coinages after the Second World War as well. The Italian 5 lire piece which was once the

Besides the base metal inflation coins, some of the earlier silver coins were counterstamped with higher values. This 1912 Bavarian 3 mark piece was revalued at 500,000 marks.

equivalent of a U.S. silver dollar shrunk to a small aluminum coin worth less than one cent. The current 500 lire coins are worth less than the old 5 lire pieces. In France, where a revolution took place in 1959, the postwar 100 franc coins circulate on a par with the new 1 franc issues.

By far the worst inflation occurred in Hungary where all coins simply disappeared from circulation. Paper money reached the fantastic value of 100,000,000,000,000,000,000 pengo (one hundred sextillion pengo). Brazil is currently in the grip of inflation and in spite of a revaluation making 1 new cruzeiro the equivalent of 1000 of the old, it has been impossible to keep even the new coins in circulation.

France's Liberty head coin of 1951 (left) was a 50 *franc* value but by 1963, under the new heavy franc system, the same size coin in the same aluminum-bronze metal was only 50 *centimes*, or half-a-franc—an example of what inflation does to coins!

Inflation Coins ❧ 251

The silver penny struck under Ireland's King Sihtric III (989-1029) is an imitation of a contemporary Saxon coin.

Ireland

The early history of Ireland is wrapped in delightful legends of warrior kings, their battles and councils. As far back as we can go in Irish history, these gifted people have been famous for their harpists and storytellers and even today, all coins of the Republic of Ireland picture a harp.

In the ninth century, a frightful period of Norse invasions began, coupled with intermittent civil war. The plundering and killing went on for four centuries. During Ireland's early history, most of its currency was imported from abroad, chiefly from England and the Scandinavian countries. The Vikings operated a mint in Dublin toward the end of the 10th century.

In 1172, England conquered the island. Under Henry II of England (1154–89) a regular Irish coinage began, struck in the name of Henry's son John who was created Lord of Ireland in 1177. John struck a series of crude portrait silver halfpennies in mints at Dublin and Waterford.

During the more than 700 years of English rule, Irish resentment frequently boiled up. One of these occasions produced that interesting oddity of coinage, the famous Irish "gun money." In 1688, when the English forced the tyrannical James II to abdicate, Ireland offered a welcome. Arriving in Ireland in June, 1689, James set about raising an army. In need of coinage to pay his troops, he issued emergency money struck from the metal of melted-down cannons, church bells—and anything else he could lay hands on. A curious feature of the "gun money" is that the coins show not only the year, but the month of issue as well, ranging from July, 1689 until June, 1690. In those days the year did not begin on January 1 but on March 25; consequently, the coins dated

This brass "gun money" half crown bears the portrait of James II, the deposed king of England. The reverse has a crown over crossed sceptres and the date August, 1690.

Following James, the British rulers through George IV continued a distinctive issue of "Hibernia" copper coins for Ireland. The 1736 bronze halfpenny portrays George II.

March, 1690, were issued only a few days after the coins dated March, 1689. In the same way, December, 1689 was followed by January, 1689. No doubt James intended to redeem the base metal coins with good silver on a month by month basis if his cause had been successful.

By the end of the First World War, it had become clear that England could continue to rule in Ireland only on a military basis. In December, 1921, following negotiations between the two countries, southern Ireland became the Irish Free State, while northern Ireland remained part of the United Kingdom. In 1937, it became officially known as Eire.

Although the currency denominations were taken over from English coinage, Eire is no longer a member of the British Commonwealth. Ireland has adopted a new decimal coinage which becomes official in 1971. Ireland's six new decimal coins will be of the same size, shape and metallic content as their British equivalents, but will retain distinctive Irish designs.

Ireland's modern coins carry animal, bird and fish designs. Here are a horse (half crown), salmon (florin), bull (shilling), wolfhound (sixpence), hare (threepence), hen and chicks (penny), sow and piglets (halfpenny), and a woodcock (farthing).

Modern Israeli coin designs were inspired by emblems used on coins of ancient Israel. The current issue shows the menorah (one pound), a lyre (25 agorot), a palm tree (10 agorot), pomegranates (5 agorot), and barley stalks (1 agora).

Israel

As a result of action taken by the United Nations, Israel came into existence as an independent republic on May 14, 1948. Previously it was a part of the British mandate of Palestine.

Although Israel is a new nation, its coin designs are replicas of emblems used on the coins of ancient Israel (c. 40 B.C.–A.D. 135). The dates, shown in Hebrew characters, are according to the Hebrew calendar, which is figured from the time of Adam. Thus, 1948, the year of independence, is given as 5708, and 1970 as the year 5730.

The silver 5 pound piece issued in 1958 commemorates the tenth year of Israel's independence.

The 1959 5 pounds marks the return of Jewish exiles to the new state of Israel.

The 1961 1 pound symbolizes the heroism of the founders of the state of Israel.

The menorah, or seven-branched candlestick, according to legend, brought into use by Moses and long an emblem of the Jewish people, is now the coat of arms of the new state and is featured in the design of several of its coins.

In addition to regular-issue coins produced for general circulation, Israel has issued numerous one-, five-, and ten-pound commemorative coins. Gold commemorative pieces in 20, 50 and 100 pound values have also been minted.

In 1960, Israel introduced a new coinage, based on a system of 100 agorot to the pound. Israel's coins are now being struck at a modern mint in Jerusalem, the capital.

The centenary of the birth of Dr. Theodore Herzl was commemorated on the 5 pounds of 1960.

Israel ֍ 255

Seafaring and the 15th
year of independence
are honored on the 1963
5 pounds.

The Parliament (Knesset)
building in Jerusalem
appears on the 1965
5 pounds.

The 1967 10 pounds
marks Israel's
astonishing victory
in the Six Day War of
June, 1967.

The 1968 10 pounds
commemorates the
reunification of
Jerusalem.

Luitbert, king of the Lombards (700-01), struck this gold ⅓ solidus. The coin carries his helmeted bust, with a representation of St. Michael on the reverse.

Italy

The early history of Italy coincides with that of Rome until A.D. 475 when the Gothic chieftan Odoacer (or Odovacar) became undisputed ruler of the Roman Empire in the West. As king of Italy, Odoacer made Ravenna his capital. Because Italy is situated at the crossroads of the Mediterranean basin, it has suffered the most invasions of any European country in the course of its long history.

The people of Italy have always maintained great pride in their own small towns, cities and regions and the history of Italy is quite complicated up to the date of unification in 1800. The history of Italian coinage is also extremely complex since most of the issues are local or regional. Italian coinage has been issued by successive conquerors, by independent city republics, great ruling houses, and papal authority. However, the Italian series is still one of the most carefully researched of all largely because of the vast project promoted through the efforts of King Victor Emmanuel III, a keen numismatist.

The Ostrogoths under their chieftan Theodoric took control of Italy after the assassination of Odoacer in 493. Theodoric (493–526) issued gold solidi in imitation of specimens of Anastasius I, the Byzantine emperor and a triple solidus bearing his own portrait. In 568, the Lombards swept down into Italy and soon occupied the great plain between the Alps and the Apennines, a region called Lombardy ever since. The Lombards controlled the destinies of most of Italy until they were defeated by Charlemagne in 774. Coins struck by the Lombardic kings

(Left) Silver denier of Charlemagne, first king of the Carolingian Dynasty (774-814) and (right) a denier of his grandson Lothair I (818-55). Charlemagne's coin is from the Milan mint, Lothair's from Pavia.

were at first imitations of Byzantine gold tremissis, but from the reign of Cunincpert (688–700), their coinage was distinctive in that each of the kings had his own portrait inscribed on his coins.

Pepin the Short twice invaded Lombardy, but it was his son, Charlemagne, who finally conquered the territory. On Easter Sunday in 774, Charlemagne visited Rome for the first time. His earliest Italian coins were tremisses in imitation of Lombardic issues, but they were inscribed with his name DN CAROLUS REX. Later he struck silver deniers at a number of Italian mints, including Florence, Lucca, Milan, Parma, Rome, Sienna and Venice. After his coronation by Pope Leo III on Christmas Day in 800, his deniers showing his laureate bust were inscribed KAROLUS IMP AUG. During the period of the coronation Charlemagne established new Italian mints at Pavia and Verona.

During this period, Venice started to become not only one of the most important cities in Italy, but in all of Europe as well. The Venice Mint struck quantities of coins for the Carolingian emperors Louis (814–40) and

This Venetian silver grosso of Doge (Duke) Peter Gradenigo (1289-1311), reflects a strong Byzantine influence. The coin shows the Doge and St. Mark, Christ seated on a throne on the reverse.

Lothair I (840–55), but beginning in the latter part of the ninth century, the engravers at Venice omitted mention of the emperor's name and instead used the inscription "PE SALVA VENECIAS." Venice continued to issues its own coinage for about a thousand years, until the latter part of the 18th century.

In 951, the German king Otto the Great invaded Italy and by 962, when he succeeded in deposing Berengarius II, King of Italy, he had himself crowned Holy Roman Emperor. The German Holy Roman emperors controlled the destinies of most of Italy through to the reign of Frederick II (1211–50). The Holy Roman emperors struck an important coinage of denarii up to the early 1100's, maintaining mints in northern Italy at Lucca, Milan, Pavia and Verona. These deniers were inscribed with the name of the emperor on obverse with the mint name being placed around a cross motif on reverse. There was a continuous struggle between the Holy Roman emperors and the papacy for control of Italy with the papacy becoming dominant after the death of Frederick II.

Gold florins showing St. John the Baptist and a lily, the city emblem, were struck in Florence from 1252 until 1422.

The developing Italian city-republics gained a good measure of autonomy after the defeat of Frederick I Barbarossa at Legano in 1176. This made it possible for many of them to issue their own coinage.

By 1192, Venice had augmented its denier coinage with the issuance of grossi, the earliest large silver piece of Italy. Gold coins also became more important during this period. The Dukes of Amalfi, including Duke Roger Borsa (1085–1111), Duke William I (1111–27), and Count Roger II (1105–54) struck undated gold tari. The Doges of Genoa also began issuing various types of gold pieces in about 1200.

Politically, the House of Savoy began to develop as a major force during this era. This dynasty which ruled over the territories of Savoy and Piedmont for nine centuries was founded by Humbert I "The Whitehanded" (1034–56), who gained control of the county of Savoy and the Alpine passes of Mount Cenis, Little and Great St. Bernard.

Florence became one of the first cities to make gold a standard currency with the minting of the famous *fiorini d'oro,* or gold florins, in 1252. The florin carried the figure of St. John the Baptist, and on reverse the lily, or *fleur-de-lis,* the badge of Florence, together with the legend FLORENTIA. Eventually, this coin circulated throughout Europe and the entire Mediterranean region.

In 1280, Doge John Dandolo issued the first Venetian gold coin, a *ducat.* The alternative name, *zecchino,* is derived from the Italian word for mint, *zecca. La Zecca* was the name of the palace which housed the Venetian Mint. This noteworthy gold piece shows on obverse the figure of Christ standing in glory, and on reverse the Doge receiving the gonfalone or

Gold ducat of Venice issued by Doge Francis Dona (1545-53), shows the Doge kneeling before St. Mark with a standing figure of Christ on the reverse.

Italy ❦ 259

The Renaissance brought realistic portraiture to coinage. The dies for the testone (left) of Duke Alessandro de Medici of Florence (1533-37), were engraved by Benvenuto Cellini. The reverse shows the standing figures of St. Cosimus and St. Damias. The 1575 testone (right) shows Francesco de Medici (1574-87).

sacred banner from St. Mark, the patron saint of Venice. Venetian ducats were struck for the next 700 years under more than 70 different rulers until 1797, when the Venetian Republic came to an end. The winged lion (symbol of St. Mark) appears on most Venetian silver coins.

Both the Florentine florin and the Venetian ducat were noted for the purity of their gold content and they were readily acceptable everywhere. By the mid-14th century, Florence had more than 80 banking houses.

Grand Duke Ferdinand I of Tuscany (1587-1608), issued this silver $\frac{1}{4}$ scudo portraying the Annunciation scene (the angel Gabriel telling Mary she will bear Jesus).

The most famous bankers of Florence were the Medicis, the richest men in 14th and 15th-century Europe. Their powerful bank had branches in France, England, the Low Countries, and the Levant. The Medicis became the rulers of Florence in the early 1400's, and they held that position for several centuries.

This silver testone of Duke Galeazzo Maria Sforza of Milan (1466-76) is a fine example of Renaissance portrait coinage. The Duke's helmeted arms are shown on the reverse.

260 ❧ Italy

Gold ducat of Giovanni Galeazzo Maria Sforza, duke of Milan (1476-81).

Silver testone of Giangaleazzo Sforza, duke of Milan (1481-97) and Ludovico Sforza, his uncle and regent.

Galeazzo Maria Sforza, Duke of Milan, in 1468 began striking the heavy silver piece, the testone, so-called from the importance given to the head of the ruler (testone in Italian for "large head"). The silver lira began to circulate in Venice during the mid-15th century, and by the time of Victor Amadeus I (1630–37) it was made the official monetary unit equivalent to 20 soldi.

The Age of the Renaissance had a significant effect on both Italian coinage and medallic art. Leonardo da Vinci designed many coins and a coining press, while Benvenuto Cellini (1500–71) engraved a variety of portrait coins and medals for Popes Clement VII, Paul III, and for Alessandro de' Medici, Duke of Florence.

The Renaissance also had a profound effect on the study and collecting of coins. In that age, with its rebirth of a passionate interest in Greece and

After Milan fell to the French in 1500, Louis XII, king of France, became ruler of the city-state. The reverse shows St. Ambrose.

Philip IV, king of Spain (1621-65), who struck this gold quadrupla (four ducats) also ruled Milan.

Italy ❧ 261

Silver testone of Savoy with the bust of Carlo I (1482-90). The arms of the Duchy—a plain white cross on a red shield—are on the reverse.

Gold doppia of Gianfrancesco Pico, Duke of Mirandola (1499-1533), with St. Francis of Assisi kneeling before the dove of peace on the reverse.

A goateed, bewigged Francesco II, Duke of Mantua (1484-1519), is portrayed on this silver testone.

On this gold quadrupla, Odoardo Farnese, Duke of Parma and Piacenza (1622-46), appears ornately dressed in a high ruff collar and epaulet. The Farnese arms, a she-wolf, is on the reverse.

Rome, cultivated persons were eager to possess ancient coins. This absorption in "living examples" of antiquity gave numismatics a powerful impetus. It is significant that the first printed book on the coins of ancient times appeared in 1489. Its author was Angelo Poliziano, a Florentine poet and friend of Lorenzo the Magnificent, one of the greatest Medicis.

The Duchy of Tuscany existed from the 11th century until 1861 when it became part of the Kingdom of Italy. From the 16th century until 1737, it was conferred on the Medici family. At that time the Duchy passed to the House of Hapsburg-Lorraine. Florence is the leading city in Tuscany; the other major cities are Leghorn, Pisa and Siena.

Ferdinand de Medici (1587–1608) issued a 14 scudo d'oro carrying his bust, with bees in flight on reverse. Cosimo III de Medici (1670–1723)

Silver testone of Louis II Di Saluzzo, Marquis of Carmagnola (1475-1504). The reverse shows an equestrian figure of Saint Constantine.

Ranuccio Farnese, Duke of Parma (1592-1622) struck this silver testone in 1604 as a memorial to his father Alessandro Farnese whose portrait it bears.

The bearded, armored bust of Alfonso I D'Este, Duke of Ferrara (1505-34), is shown on this handsomely engraved silver testone. The reverse inscription translates "Sweetness from Strength."

William II Paleologus, Marchese of Casale (1494-1518), is shown wearing a distinctive square cap on this silver testone.

issued many types of handsome coins, including a silver scudo showing his head in a spiked crown with the reverse having a view of Leghorn. Giovanni Gastone (1723–37), the last of the ruling Medicis, struck a handsome crown portraying his bust and, on the reverse, his crown over a stone fortress.

Beginning in the 16th century, there was a trend toward the growth of larger territorial units, and the less important local coinage gradually disappeared. Finally, there were five principal coin-issuing areas:

(1) The Kingdom of the Two Sicilies—the island of Sicily, and Naples (southern section of the Italian peninsula). (2) Papal States (central Italy). (3) Tuscany (west-central Italy). (4) Venice (northeast Italy). (5) Sardinia (northwest Italy and the Island of Sardinia) ruled by the House of Savoy.

This silver two scudi piece of Genoa struck in 1719 portrays the Virgin and Child.

In 1720, Sardinia passed to the House of Savoy. The kingdom was then ruled by Savoy descendants until 1861, when the King of Sardinia became King of Italy.

Charles Emmanuel II, Duke of Savoy (1638–75), issued several denominations of gold coins, all bearing his bust on obverse and his crowned arms on reverse. Charles Emmanuel III (1730–73) struck a wide variety of gold pieces. One type bore his bust on obverse with the oval shield of Sardinia on reverse. Victor Amadeus III (1773–96) also contributed a fine array of coins, including gold doppia specimens and silver

Ferdinand IV assumed the throne of Naples and Sicily in 1759 when his father, Charles III, gave up his Italian crown to become King of Spain. On this silver 120 grani, Ferdinand is shown in dual portrait with his Queen, Caroline. The reverse shows the Zodiac encircling the sun and earth.

264 ⸲ Italy

The large 30 tari struck for Sicily in 1791 shows Ferdinand IV, with a Phoenix rising out of ashes on the reverse.

scudi. The wealth of Sardinia is clearly shown through its extensive gold and silver coinage.

The kings of modern Italy—Victor Emmanuel II (1861–78), Humberto I (1878–1900), and Victor Emmanuel III (1900–46)—all struck portrait coins, including handsome gold pieces. Victor Emmanuel III issued several gold series during his long reign, including the 50 lire of 1911 marking the 50th year of the Kingdom. A 100 lire gold piece was minted in 1925 as a dual commemorative: to mark the 25th anniversary of Emmanuel III's reign and the 10th anniversary of Italy's entry into World War I. The

1684 silver scudo of Charles II, King of Spain and the United Kingdom of Naples and Sicily (1665-1700). The coin's reverse shows the Spanish crown above two hemispheres.

Tuscany, 1724 silver ducatone minted at Florence, portraying Grand Duke
Giovanni Gastone de Medici (1723-37). On the reverse is a view of the fortress
at Livorno (Leghorn), Tuscany's main port on the Tyrrhenian Sea.

Mantua, 1627 ducatone, portraying Duke Vincent II Gonzago (1626-27). The
Latin inscription around the large dog is FERIS TANTVM INFENSVS—"Hostile
only to the savage."

Venice, silver scudo of Doge Giovanni Bembo (1615-18). The obverse design
is a floriated cross, with a winged lion, the symbol of St. Mark, on the reverse.

266 ๑ Italy

Victor Emmanuel III (1900-46) appears in military uniform on this silver 5 lire of 1914. The reverse shows a quadriga of the type used in ancient Rome.

Rome Mint began using stainless steel (acmonital) for coins in the late 1930's and has continued to do so for lower and medium denomination pieces. Silver has now almost completely disappeared from Italian coinage, except for commemorative pieces. Under the Republic, beginning in 1946, the Rome Mint has utilized aluminum for 1, 2, 5 and 10 lire denominations. Aluminum-bronze has been used for the 20 lire value.

The designs of many modern Italian coins are taken from ancient motifs. The quadriga shown on the 500 lire silver 1961 unification centennial commemorative, for example, is certainly a modern interpretation of the ancient Roman didrachm. The 700th anniversary of Dante's birth was commemorated with a 500 lire silver coin in 1965.

The centennial of Italian unification is commemorated on the silver 500 lire of 1961.

The 700th anniversary of Dante Alighieri's birth is marked on the 500 lire of 1965.

Italy ❧ 267

Japanese "kanei tsuho" copper coin of the type issued from 1616 until 1769.

Japanese Coins

Although Japan's history stretches back into the deep mists of antiquity, her first known coins were not produced until A.D. 708 when a series of bronze specimens were minted. The first coinage was of cast bronze, usually with a center hole similar to contemporary Chinese moneys. (The early Japanese pieces are not nearly as common, however, as the Chinese since great quantities of coins were melted in the tenth century for the casting of statues of Buddha.)

For the next 600 years no government coins were issued and currency was supplied by the great nobles who merely ordered the making of imitations of contemporary Chinese coins. In 1599–1600, the Japanese government, dominated by the Tokugawa shogunate, once again assumed the power of coinage and began minting the copper kwan-ei, a coin that was to remain in general circulation for the next two centuries. During the early 1600's, rectangular silver pieces with the unusual names of "bu" and "shu" (meaning part and fraction) were introduced. These oblong silver pieces were circulating in Japan when Commodore Matthew C. Perry and his American naval squadron arrived in 1853 to open Japan to Western trade. The Tokugawa shogunate remained in power until 1867 when Shogun Yoshinobu Tokugawa was forced to surrender his authority in favor of the emperor who had held only ceremonial power since the twelfth century.

Japanese rectangular silver coins from about 1850 with the curious names of "ichibu gin" (1 bu), "nishu gin" (2 shu), and "isshu gin" (1 shu).

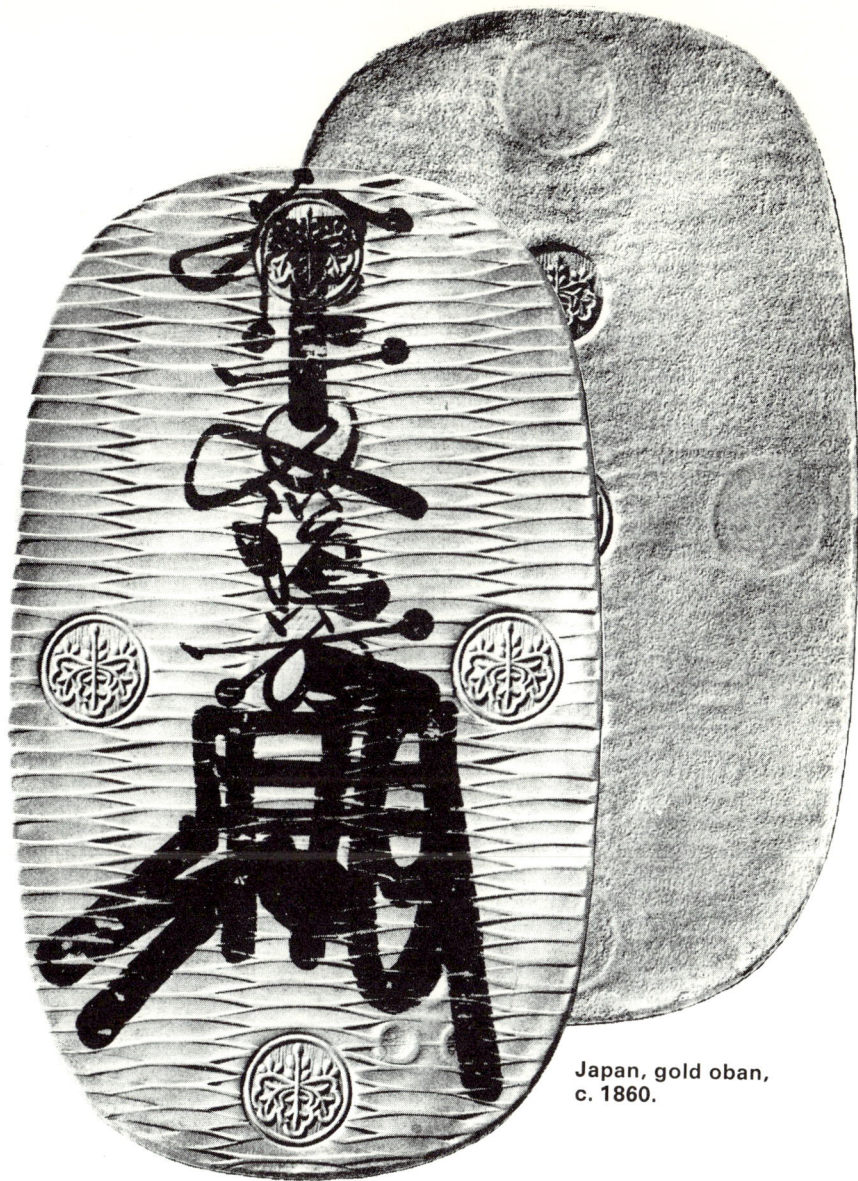

Japan, gold oban,
c. 1860.

This ten tael weight gold oban bears stamps denoting its value and era. The black India ink inscription, applied directly onto the gold, gives the name of the mint superintendent.

Japanese gold coins were first issued during the military dictatorship of Toyotomi Hideyoshi (1582–98). Hideyoshi's gold coinage was of "obans," flat, oval-shaped pieces with the kiri-flower crest on the edge, top and bottom. He had them inscribed with India ink showing their value and the signature of the mint superintendent. Obans were struck infrequently by Japanese mints for some 275 years, the last specimens being produced in 1860.

The oban, valued by weight at ten tael, measured about 150×100 millimeters. The goryoban, a five tael value current in the 1830's, measured 90×50 millimeters. The koban, a one tael value, measured 70×40 millimeters. The obans, goryobans, and kobans were all oval-shaped and similar in design. Smaller rectangular-shape gold pieces were also produced.

The 100 mon elliptically-shaped Tempo Tsuho coins were cast in both brass and copper and circulated in Japan between 1837 and 1870.

Emperor Mutsuhito, later called Mikado Meiji, acquired power in 1867. He favored modernization and during his reign the Japanese dropped their attitude of aloofness and began adopting Western methods.

The first modern gold coins of Japan, such as this rare 20 yen piece of 1876, were struck to the same standards of weight and fineness as the U.S. gold coins. This coin was thus the exact equivalent of a U.S. double eagle.

270 ๑ Japanese Coins

Among the first modern-type coins produced in Japan is this silver 1 yen piece, struck in 1870-72 during the reign of Emperor Mutsuhito. The obverse shows a coiled dragon, the reverse a radiant sun.

In 1869, a mint on European lines was established in Tokyo and regular round planchet gold, silver and copper coins have been issued from it regularly ever since.

By the 1920's, Japan followed the example of a good many other countries and began striking more and more of her coins from metals such as bronze, nickel and copper-nickel alloy. During World War II

The Japanese characters on the obverse of this 1900 50 sen coin read "dai nippon" (great Japan)'meiji era,'32nd year (it began in 1868).

the country was hard-pressed for metal and was forced to produce coins from such substitute metals as aluminum and tin. The increasingly acute wartime shortage of metal caused the mints to turn to a local material for which Japan has been noted for centuries—earthenware, a fired clay from which the Japanese make truly artistic pottery. An emergency issue of three denominations—one, five and ten sen pieces portraying Mount Fujiyama and the familiar chrysanthemum design—was manufactured

Mount Fujiyama, Japan's highest mountain renowned for its beautiful symmetry, is shown on the 1 sen of 1941-43.

Japanese Coins ⊙ 271

The silver 1,000 yen of 1964 commemorates the International Olympic Games held at Tokyo in that year. Mount Fujiyama is shown surrounded by cherry blossoms; the reverse has the Olympic emblem of five interlocking rings.

in June, 1945. The end of the war made their release unnecessary or undesirable; it is reported that the entire issue was scrapped in August, 1945. A few specimens of the earthenware coins have somehow survived, however, and bring high prices on the infrequent occasions when they are offered for sale.

In Japan today the minting of coins is centered at Osaka. The facility at Tokyo is considered a branch. Hiroshima also has a branch mint and much of the metal for use in coins is refined in a sub-branch at Kumamoto. With over a billion pieces struck annually, Japan is one of the top ten countries of the world in coin production.

Though Japanese coins of the past century have shown marked Western influence (denominations in Arabic numerals, regular round shapes, etc.) they still convey Oriental charm. Ever-present in the delicate designs are cherry blossoms, chrysanthemums, and the white dove of peace. To the people of Japan, the chrysanthemum has both sacred and patriotic meaning.

Japan's current 100 and 50 yen pieces, struck of copper-nickel alloy, portray cherry blossoms and chrysanthemums, Japan's national flower.

272 ❧ Japanese Coins

This 4 solidi jeton dated 1603 was used in Denmark as a counter for the calculation of accounts.

Jetons (Counters)

Counters or "jetons," the French name used by numismatists, are small, thin brass disks used in past centuries to facilitate the calculation of accounts. The French verb *jeter*, means to throw and the jetons are so-called because they were thrown about on a counting board or checkered cloth. As jetons were made to resemble coins, the word came to mean any form of imitation coin.

Prior to the 16th century, Roman numerals were widely used in Europe for all types of reckoning and accounting and normal procedures of multiplication and division as we know them were impossible. In France, for example, before the introduction of the decimal (based on 10's) system in 1794, 3 deniers were equal to 1 liard; 4 liards were worth 1 sol; 20 sols made 1 livre; and 24 livres were the same as a gold Louis. With such a system even straight addition was difficult.

To add using jetons, a merchant would place a pile of counters at one side of a board divided into compartments or a cloth marked off in sections. For each denier, a jeton was dropped into the first section. Whenever three pieces accumulated in the first section, one was advanced to the next area (3 deniers = 1 liard), the other two were removed from the board. When four counters accumulated in the second section, one was advanced (4 liards = 1 sol) and three were removed, etc. To read off the final sum, the merchant had only to count the number of jetons remaining in each section.

The earliest English counters were produced at London's Royal Mint during the reign of Edward I (1272–1307) from the same punches that were used for the silver pence. They were pierced to indicate they were not true coins. During the 14th and 15th centuries the English imported most of their counters from France, but later Nuremburg became the major source of supply. The most prolific manufacturer of the Nuremburg tokens was Hans Krauwinckel (1586–1635), whose name appears on many of them. Many varieties of the Krauwinckel counters have the emblem of the Holy Roman Empire, and since he also made large numbers for the French, another common device is the fleur-de-lis.

King Louis XV appears on this 1758 copper jeton, struck for use in Canada during the French regime. The reverse shows a flight of eagles at sea.

Counters often copy designs of contemporary coins and frequently reproduce one of the widely-used religious phrases such as "Ave Maria Gracia Plena" found on coins. Inscriptions on many counters are semi-illiterate and reproduce only in a general way the letters of the original phrases.

While some of the European counters were well-designed and struck with considerable finish, the majority of them tend to be strictly utilitarian. Some are even known to have been struck in gold or silver, but these are quite rare; brass was the usual metal employed. Brass card counters turned out by the sackful in Victorian England are often mistaken for old coins. The brass imitation of a spade guinea of George III has been inscribed with: "In memory of the good old times."

Jetons were liberally used in Canada during the French Regime. In the 1738–63 period (the final quarter century of French rule) the authorities brought over large quantities of jetons. The primary purpose of the jetons was to facilitate the reckoning of sums in the old French fractional currency, although, here as elsewhere, some did find their way into circulation as an unofficial type of small change. The general issues were produced in copper, while lesser numbers were struck in silver. A single specimen in gold was presented each year to the French king, Louis XV.

The French-Canadian jetons rank among the most attractive counters struck for any country. King Louis himself is portrayed on a variety of specimens. The reverse designs present various allegorical figures and scenes. Other types of jetons portray Indians, alligators, beavers building dams, and eagles in flight. Canadian numismatic specialists have a special fondness for these historic jetons; consequently, some of the scarcer specimens in choice condition catalogue more than $100 each.

So many types of counters have been produced by the countries of the world during the past six or seven centuries that no one has been able to compile anything resembling a definitive catalogue. Most varieties are available at very modest prices and three or four of them add a little extra interest to a numismatic cabinet.

Silver 16 ore diamond-shaped klippe of Eric XIV of Sweden (1560-68).

Klippe Coins

Klippe (from the Swedish *klippa*, to cut or clip) is the general name for any square, lozenge, or diamond-shaped coin. Many countries of Europe issued the unusual klippe coins, especially Sweden, the Netherlands, Poland and Germany.

The "klippings" were popular in Sweden and neighboring countries during the 1500's simply because they were easier to make than round coins. Under Gustavus I Vasa (reigned 1523–60), Sweden became one of the strongest military powers in Europe and there was a great need for an expanded coinage. Increased demand for coins placed severe strains upon the Swedish mints. At that time, when all striking of money was done by hand, cutting the flans square instead of round was an easy way to save time. The klippings were produced in large number, especially during wartime emergencies.

Swedish klippings were produced with a good deal of regularity through the reign of Gustavus Adolphus (1611–32) whose reign of 21 years was filled with wars. He constantly required emergency currencies. Erik XIV

Sweden's Gustavus Adolphus (1611-32) issued many "klippings" as wartime emergency currencies. Most were crudely struck like this copper 1 ore piece of 1626, produced at the time of the Thirty Years War.

Klippe Coins ❧ 275

Germany, city of Munster,
klippe taler of 1660.

(1560–68), John III (1568–92), Sigismund Vasa (1592–1604) and Charles IX (1604–11) all struck a variety of klippings in square, rectangular and diamond shapes.

A uniface square taler was struck in central Germany in 1567 during the siege of Saxony. Another unusual klipping-type specimen is the uniface octagonal siege taler struck in Leipzig by John Frederick during the siege of 1547.

A wide variety of strip talers came out of Hungarian Transylvania during the 17th century. Two or more talers were stamped onto a strip of silver and released into circulation without being cut. The strip talers have the appearance of being rectangular klippings.

John George I, elector of Saxony (1611-56), struck this klippe in 1614 to commemorate the birth of his son, John George II.

A klippe double taler struck in 1593 by Wolf Dietrich, Count Raitenau (Austrian Lands), to finance the war against the Turks. A saint is shown standing behind a shield, with a tower in the sea on the reverse.

Klippe pieces were often struck in later years as presentation or special commemorative issues. In this case, the square shape was meant simply to set the coins off from the normal, round issues.

This superb 5 taler klippe was struck in 1625 at the Graz (Austria) mint for Holy Roman Emperor Ferdinand II (1619-37).

Germany, 1669 Saxon shooting taler struck as a klippe. Young Hercules is pictured strangling a serpent.

Salzburg, 1625 klippe taler portraying the Madonna and Child above a shield with a cardinal's hat. St. Rupert is shown on the reverse.

Salzburg grew up around the monastery and bishopric founded there in about 700 by St. Rupert of Worms. Salzburg became an important archbishopric, issuing its own coins from about the year 1000 until it was secularized in 1803. Salzburg has been part of Austria since 1813.

Two mythological creatures, a phoenix and a dragon, are shown on the 5 chon and 5 yang pieces of Imperial Korea (1888-1910).

Korea

Situated on a peninsula between the Yellow Sea and the Sea of Japan, Korea was invaded by China in the 12th century B.C. and remained under partial Chinese control for many centuries. Subsequently, Korea was invaded by the Mongols, Manchus and Japanese, and this led to a policy of isolation so that the peninsula became known as the "Hermit Kingdom." Foreigners could not enter the country, and a ban on Christian missionaries was lifted only in 1882.

Korea produced its first coinage in the 11th century A.D. when cast copper and bronze pieces similar to those of the contemporary Sung Dynasty in China were issued. In modern times, coins were struck in the name of Korean emperors from 1888 until the country was annexed by Japan in 1910.

Liberated at the end of World War II, the nation was divided into North Korea (under Communist influence) and South Korea (under Western influence). The status quo was continued at the end of the Korea War (1950–53).

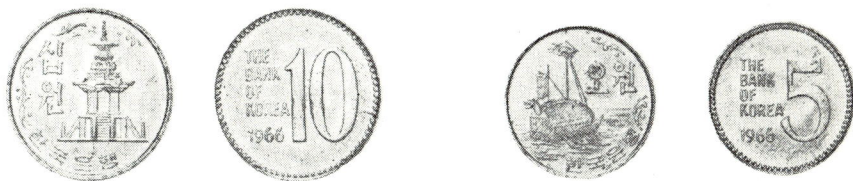

Korea's current 10 and 5 won coins show the Prabhutaratna pagoda and one of the famous 16th century armor-clad tortoise war galleys.

Korea ❧ 279

Luxembourg

Luxembourg, a grand duchy in central Europe covering 999 square miles, borders on Belgium, France and Germany. The country's numismatic history spans many centuries, its first coins silver deniers issued by Count Henry III (1136–96). In the 14th and 15th centuries, several Counts of Luxembourg were elected Holy Roman Emperors.

In the 14th and 15th centuries, several Counts of Luxembourg achieved royal rank . . . one of them, John, King of Bohemia (1310-46), sought death in battle after going blind. This 50 franc piece was struck in 1946, the 600th anniversary of his death.

From the 15th century, Luxembourg was attached to the Netherlands until 1890 when it became an independent grand-duchy. Luxembourg's currency is now keyed to that of Belgium, with 100 centimes equalling 1 franc. Both Belgian and Luxembourg coins circulate in the grand-duchy. In recent years most of its coins have been struck at the Brussels Mint.

Grand Duchess Charlotte (1919-64) retired in 1964 in favor of her son Prince Jean shown on this silver 100 francs of 1964.

Maundy set of Charles II (1660-85)—silver 4, 3, 2 Pence and 1 Penny. Though the Maundy ceremony dates back to the early 14th century, Charles was the first king to issue coins specifically for this purpose.

Maundy Money

Maundy Money, first issued during the reign of King Charles II in 1661, is a term for a series of small British silver coins, consisting of one, two, three and four pence coins.

According to legend, on Maundy (Holy) Thursday—the day before Good Friday—Christ washed the feet of his disciples and commanded them to follow his example. (The term "Maundy" is derived from the Latin *mandare*—to order). Among devout Christians it became a custom for kings, nobles and clergy to observe this day by washing the feet of beggars and poor people, and making them gifts of money, food and clothes. Edward II (1307–27) is perhaps the first English king to have observed this picturesque custom, but it was Charles II who, more than three centuries later, issued the first coins specifically for this purpose. The same silver one, two, three and four pence values were also used for general circulation. George II (1727–60) was the first monarch to strike presentation sets of Maundy coins for the Holy Thursday ceremony only, and since that time they have no longer doubled as current coin of the realm.

The Royal Bounty is given on Maundy Thursday to as many men and to as many women as the monarch has years. In each bounty (or bag) the number of pence is the same as the monarch's age. At the coronation of Elizabeth II in 1953, when she was 27, she gave 27 men and 27 women each 27 pence in Maundy Money.

Nowadays the Maundy ceremony probably attracts more public attention than it ever did before, and it ranks as one of the most impressive of all British ceremonies, attended by Royalty, guarded by Yeomen, and conducted by a host of romantically-named officials such as "Wandsmen."

Maundy coins have special numismatic significance because they are the only British silver coins currently being struck by London's Royal Mint. Maundy coins are relatively high priced to collectors since their mintages are extremely low.

Maundy Money ❧ 281

The first coins produced in the Western Hemisphere came from the Spanish mint at Mexico City during the reign of Charles and his mother, Joanna. The denomination of the 4 reales coin is indicated by a numeral, that of the 2 and 1 real pieces by two and one dots respectively.

Mexico

Hernando Cortez, a Spanish conquistador, captured the Aztec capital, Tenochtitlan (Mexico City), on August 13, 1521. A Royal Edict issued in 1535 by the Spanish king, Charles I (also known as Charles V, the Holy Roman Emperor) established a mint at Mexico City. According to the still-existing Mexico City Mint records, nearly 70 million gold coins and over two billion silver coins were produced there between 1537 and 1821. Even after this extensive exploitation of the country's silver, Mexico is still the world's leading silver producer, turning out approximately one-half of the total annual supply.

The first coins struck in Mexico under Spanish rule bore the names of Charles I and his mother Joanna. Produced during the period 1537–56, the 4, 2 and 1 reales silver pieces had two crowned pillars (representing

The Mexican ½ real of Charles and Joanna bears a large "KI," the monarchs' initials (Charles is "Karolus" in Latin).

282 ⊗ Mexico

the Pillars of Hercules, the Straits of Gibralter) and the inscription PLUS ULTRA—"More Beyond," proclaiming the New World. The reverse had a quartered arms design.

Mexico City's earliest coins were made with comparatively crude methods. A sheet of metal was rolled to the proper thickness, and planchets for the individual coins were cut out with heavy shears.

An 8 reales Philip IV (1621-65) struck on a square-shaped cob planchet. The main design is a crowned shield with the quartered arms of Castile and Leon on the reverse.

In about 1580, during the reign of Philip II, the mint began the coining of so-called "cob" money (from *cabo de barra*—"cut from a bar"). This type of money was made by chiseling off sections from crudely rolled silver bars and then hammering these crude planchets between a pair of dies.

Under Philip II (1556–98), Philip III (1598–1621) and Philip IV (1621–65) a range of coins from ½ to 8 reales was produced with the same design types. Since many of the coins of the three Philips were struck on irregularly-shaped flans, part of the inscription, particularly the king's ordinal number, is often missing. Exact attribution of the coins is thus quite difficult as many do not have dates on them either.

One of the famous gold doubloons, an 8 escudos of Philip V (1700-46).

The first Mexico City gold coins were struck under Charles II (1665–1700). The 4 and 8 escudo specimens are generally undated, but they were first minted in 1679. The rare 2 escudos is dated 1695. The Spanish milled dollar of 8 reales, better known as "pieces of eight," became the most widely circulated coin in the 18th century and early part of the 19th. First minted at Mexico City in 1732, it continued to appear until 1821. Some 441 million pieces were produced until 1772; all these featured two globes between the Pillars of Hercules. From 1772 on, a Spanish shield replaced the globes and the Spanish king's portrait took the place of the earlier coat-of-arms. About 880 million of these were issued to 1821.

This series of coins from the Mexico City Mint (8, 4, 2, 1, and ½ real values) all feature the globes and pillars design on the obverse. The reverse bears the arms of the Spanish king.

The Mexico City Mint used the portrait of Charles III (1759-88) on this 1790 8 reales of Charles IV (1788-1808) because dies with the new king's portrait had not yet arrived from Spain.

With its wide circulation, the famous piece of eight played an important role in the coinage of other countries as well. When the United States devised its coinage system in the 1790's, its silver dollar was modeled on the Spanish milled dollar struck in Mexico City. Interestingly enough, Mexican coinage remained legal tender in the United States until 1857— a tribute to the honest and high silver content of these coins. At the time the coins lost their legal-tender status, more than $2 million worth of Mexican currency was still in circulation in the United States.

Mexico's most dramatic and turbulent era came in the period between 1810–21, when its revolutionary leaders struggled against Spain for independence. Two humble parish priests, Miguel Hidalgo (1753–1811) and Jose Maria Morelos (1765–1815) are revered by Mexicans for their heroic roles in the war for independence. These two leaders were captured by the Spaniards, degraded and executed, but the courage of Hidalgo and Morelos served to inspire the Mexican people.

This provisional copper 8 reales piece was struck in 1813 by Jose Maria Morelos during the height of Mexico's revolt against Spanish rule.

Mexico ❧ 285

Ferdinand VII, the last of the Spanish rulers of Mexico (1808-21), is portrayed on this 8 reales dated 1822, the year after independence had been declared. Ferdinand opened a series of provincial mints, including one at Guanajuato where this specimen was struck, that continued striking regal coins for some time after Mexico City had stopped.

By 1820, a fiery leader, Augustin de Iturbide, came to the fore, and proclaimed the independence of Mexico in 1821. In the following year he declared himself Emperor of Mexico, but his reign was brief, and in 1823 Mexico became a republic.

During the decade of revolution about a dozen new mints sprang up in Mexico so that the revolutionaries could be assured of their own currency supply. These mints operated temporarily in such cities as Chihauhau, Durango, Guanajuato, Huaulta, Linares, Sombrerete, Tierra Caliente, and Zongolica. Coins struck from these mints were crude in comparison with those produced at Mexico City, but local provisional coinage was necessary since it was often impossible to get adequate supplies from the capital.

Augustin I Iturbide issued this 1822 portrait 8 reales piece during his brief tenure as constitutional emperor after Mexico proclaimed its independence from Spain.

286 ☙ Mexico

Once Mexico became free of Spanish rule, permanent new mints were constructed to serve as branches of the main facility at Mexico City, until there were a total of fourteen. Each of them was established for a special purpose. The Oaxaca Mint, in the heart of the silver country in southern Mexico, was built to be near the source of the metal.

This 8 reales of 1840 portrays a so-called "hook-necked" eagle, and a liberty cap. It was struck at Durango in central Mexico where a mint, identified by a "Do" mint mark, operated from 1811 to 1895.

These branch mints were gradually shut down, and by 1905, Mexico City was again the only Mexican mint. Coins with the mint marks of Guanajuato and Zacatecas are easily collectable, while specimens from the other branches—Alamos, Chihauhau, Culiacan, Durango, Estado de Mexico Guadalajara, Guadalupey Calvo, Hermosillo, Oaxaca, Potosi and Real de Catorce—are scarce or rare.

Another period of revolution followed the regime of Porfiro Diaz (1876–1911). During the six years of revolution, 1911–17, temporary mints were again established to strike emergency coin issues. Some of these mints were nothing more than converted blacksmith shops, and while the coins were often quite crude, they are of interest to numismatists and historians alike.

In 1864, Austrian Archduke Maximilian established an empire in Mexico. After three years, the ill-fated Maximilian, shown on this 1866 50 centavo piece, was executed by Mexican troops.

Mexico ❦ 287

Mexico marked its centennial of independence in 1921 by issuing this silver 2 peso coin featuring the figure of Winged Victory. The reverse has the Mexican eagle and serpent, Mexico's national emblem.

The 2 peso .900 fine silver specimen issued in 1921 marked Mexico's centennial of independence. This handsome coin bears on obverse the winged victory and the eagle on reverse. A similar type 50 peso gold piece was also struck in the same year and regularly issued up to 1947. The popular 20 pesos gold, produced in 1917–59, bears the elaborate Aztec calendar stone.

The Mexico City Mint struck a special .720 fine silver 25 peso coin in 1968 to commemorate the International Olympic Games which were held in the nation's capital in October of that year. This remarkable coin portrays on obverse a uniformed Aztec ball player superimposed upon an Aztec ball court. The Aztecs played one of the very earliest forms of basketball 500 and 600 years ago. The Olympic Games' symbol of five conjoined rings is shown underneath this design, while the inscription around the rim reads: "JUEGOS DE LA XIX OLIMPIADA MEXICO 1968."

Mexico's most attractive gold pieces are the 20 pesos showing the Aztec calendar stone and the 50 pesos, popularly called the "Centenario," portraying Winged Victory. The centenario was first issued in 1921, Mexico's centennial year.

The 1968 International Olympic Games 25 pesos coin portrays an ancient Aztec athlete.

An eagle holding a serpent in its beak is on the reverse. This emblem also derives from the Aztecs, for according to legend, the Aztec's god told them they should settle at the place where they found an eagle sitting on a cactus plant on a stone in the water and tearing a serpent apart with its beak and claws. The Aztecs saw this sight at Lake Toxcoco where they founded their city of Tenochtitlan, later known as Mexico City.

Each of the current Mexican coins displays the eagle and serpent design on one side. The 1 centavo has a wheat stalk on the reverse but the other denominations feature people from Mexico's history—Morelos (1 peso), Cuauhtemoc (50 centavos), Madero (25 centavos), Juarez (10 centavos) and Dona Josefa (5 centavos).

Honore II Grimaldi, Prince of Monaco (1612-62), appears wearing armor on this 1654 silver scudo. His lozenge arms are inscribed on the reverse.

Monaco

With an area of about 370 acres, Monaco, an independent principality, is the smallest country in the world. Located on the southern coast of France, Monaco has been ruled by the Genoese Grimaldi family since the 12th century.

French money is the official currency and the coins in daily use are those of France. Nevertheless, the Prince of Monaco has the right to issue coins, which he has done from time to time since the reign of Honore V (1819–41). The Monegasque coins are the same denominations and value as the French, with 100 centimes equalling 1 franc. All of Monaco's coins are struck at the Paris Mint.

The conjoined heads of Prince Rainier and Princess Grace appear on the silver 10-franc coin issued in 1966 to commemorate their tenth wedding anniversary. Princess Grace is the former Grace Kelly, the Philadelphia-born Academy Award-winning motion picture actress.

One of the earliest double talers, struck in 1509 by Maximilian I, Holy Roman Emperor and Archduke of Austria.

Multiple Talers

After the rich silver mines in Tyrol and Bohemia, including the famous mines of Joachimsthal, were opened in the early 1500's, large silver coins or "talers" were struck and widely circulated throughout Europe. By the late 1500's even larger, multiple talers appeared as silver took on added prestige as a circulating medium. Struck on heavier, broad planchets, the coins were usually the weight of two, three and even four normal talers.

Silver became such an important part of central Europe's economy during the late 16th century that the multiple talers served as a means of storing bullion in addition to acting as an exchange medium. During times of war or other necessity, the multiple talers were often called in by the local rulers who were careful to keep track of the large coins.

The German states in particular issued a huge volume of taler and multiple taler coinage. Many of these coins commemorate outstanding events, such as battles and peace treaties; others celebrated the weddings or deaths of minor princes.

Brunswick, a duchy located in north central Germany and now a part of Lower Saxony, issued many fine and artistic multiple talers during the Renaissance period. Several great silver mines were located in Brunswick during this time, so silver for coinage was plentiful. Duke Julius (1568–89) issued a whole series of multiple talers known as "Juliusloser." These

Some of the multiple talers were struck to commemorate historic occasions. This broad triple taler of John George I of Saxony was issued in 1650 to mark the peace of Westphalia which ended the Thirty Years War.

have two concentric lines of inscription, signs of the zodiac and a portrait bust on one side, with a shield and wildman supporters on the other. These highly unusual coins ranging from 1 to 10 talers in value are of great interest to numismatists.

The Brunswick silver triple taler of 1617 is one of the most famous of the multiples. On the obverse is Duke Friedrich Ulrich shown on horseback, with his elaborate coat-of-arms inscribed on the reverse. Brunswick's silver quadruple of 1685 is another noteworthy multiple. Labeled a

Brunswick, 1617 broad
triple taler.

Brunswick, 1655 broad
quadruple taler.

Multiple Talers ❧ 293

Brunswick, 1685
quadruple "mining"
taler. Mining talers were
struck at mints near the
mines, the dates often
marking years of
particularly good profits.

"Mining Taler," this specimen, as large as four standard U.S. silver dollars, portrays a lute player representing "Good Fortune" on a snail standing before the village and mine works of Lautenthaler, while the reverse has a coat-of-arms with five crests. Many interesting double talers were also struck by Brunswick. Typical among these is a 1662 specimen:

Brunswick, 1654 broad triple taler. The reverse shows a horse in flight over the city of Celle, the residence of the dukes of Luneburg-Celle, a branch of the ducal house of Brunswick.

forming the obverse design is a crowned monogram within a circle of arms, while the reverse has a free horse galloping above a mining landscape. Since the engravers had more space to work with on the large planchets of the multiples, many of these coins present intricately detailed designs.

Thick, wide, extremely heavy coin of Duke Julius of Brunswick-Wolfenbuttel (1568-89) with the value of 10 normal talers. The mark of value, a Roman "X", is on the orb of the reverse side.

Double speciedaler struck by King Christian IV (1588-1648) of Denmark.

Charles IX (1604-11), king of Sweden, holding sceptre and orb, appears on this large 20 marks specimen.

Multiple Talers ❧ 297

The 50 reales or "cincuentine" such as the 1628 specimen struck by Philip IV
(1621-65) is the largest silver denomination ever issued by Spain.

This gold piece equivalent to 100 ducats was struck in 1621 by King Sigismund III of Poland (1587-1632) the size and style of multiple talers. The size of a small saucer, this coin contains more than 12.5 ounces of pure gold and at the current rate has a bullion value of over $500.00.

Multiple Talers ❧ 299

Another multiple coin variety is the "strip taler," two or more talers stamped side-by-side onto a single piece of silver without being cut apart. The silver strip was struck twice between the dies, leaving two impressions of both the obverse and reverse. Most of these were produced in Transylvania during the 17th century. One of the best known Transylvanian strip talers was issued by King George Rakoczi II in 1653. On the obverse is the king holding a sceptre and wearing royal regalia; the reverse shows an ornate coat of arms. During Rakoczi's reign (1648–60) Transylvania was in her "Golden Age" and ranked as a major central European power.

1653 "strip taler" struck under George II Rakoczi, ruler of Translyvania (1648-60). Both the obverse and reverse 1 taler dies were impressed twice on the same piece of metal. This unique museum specimen was also impressed twice with the Madonna and Child dies for the gold denar of the same year.

Napoleon Bonaparte
issued this silver 5
francs piece as First
Consul. The coin is dated
year XI of the
Revolution (1803).

Napoleonic Coins

Napoleon I Bonaparte (1769–1821) deeply affected the history of France and the rest of Europe. For a brief period he was the virtual ruler of most of Continental Europe. After graduating from the Paris Military School in 1784, Napoleon at age 16 became a lieutenant in the French Artillery. Napoleon first came into prominence when he led the artillery that won Toulon from the British for the Revolutionists in 1793.

A powerful military leader during the latter part of the French Revolution, he became First Consul (1799–1804), and then Emperor of France (1804–14).

In 1812, he experienced one of his most disastrous defeats when he invaded Russia. As his forces arrived in Moscow they found that the Russian capital had been deserted and burned. In the retreat that followed thousands of his best troops starved or froze to death, while thousands more were slain or captured by the wild Cossacks.

Deposed by the foreign allies in 1814, Napoleon was banished to Elba, but he managed to escape, and became emperor again. However, he was defeated at the Battle of Waterloo in 1815 by the British forces under the Duke of Wellington, and then he was permanently exiled to St. Helena where he died.

Napoleon's portrait began to appear on French coins when he was First Consul. The 5 francs silver of the Year 11, reckoned according to the Revolutionary Calendar (inscribed on reverse as "AN XI," 1803), bore on its obverse the bare head of Napoleon with an inscription around the rim reading "BONAPARTE PREMIER CONSUL." The Napoleon portrait on this specimen is very reminiscent of the idealized portraits the Roman emperors inscribed on their coins.

Bonaparte issued two denominations of gold pieces (20 and 40 francs) during his tenure as First Consul in the Years 11 and 12 (1803–04). As on

Beginning in 1807, Napoleon's coin portrait changed from the bare headed to the laureate type, signifying his new station as Emperor of France. Beginning in 1809, the reverse inscription was changed from REPUBLIQUE FRANÇAISE to EMPIRE FRANCAISE.

the silver piece, they portray a bare head on the obverse. On the reverse they have the value and date, according to the Republican calendar, and the inscription "REPUBLIQUE FRANCAISE." Beginning in 1809, the inscription was changed to "EMPIRE FRANCAISE."

Napoleon issued a long series of gold coins bearing his portrait in 20 and 40 franc values during the decade that he was emperor. The earlier specimens of the period of the Empire (1804–07) show the idealized bare head, while the later coins (1807–15) have a laureate head. Total mintage of Napoleon gold pieces produced during the Empire runs into the many millions. They were struck not only at Paris, but at Bordeaux, La Rochelle, Lille, Nantes, Toulouse, at Genoa and Turin, Italy, and at other mints across Europe. During the Empire these gold pieces were popularly called "Napoleons" and since that time all 20 franc French gold pieces (including those minted during the first years of the 20th century) have been referred to as "Napoleons."

Napoleon also issued other types of coins, including a 10 centimes piece in billon, the series of 1808–10. Its obverse is inscribed with a large crowned "N." The reverse has the value with the inscription around the rim reading: "NAPOLEON EMPEREUR."

302 ◊ Napoleonic Coins

In 1798, France invaded and occupied Switzerland, reorganizing the country into the "Helvetic Republic." Napoleon in 1803, however, restored the Swiss Confederation. This 1801 4 franken, issued by the French for Switzerland, shows a warrior in a plumed helmet holding a flag and sword.

Napoleon and his invading armies created a string of republics which sometimes replaced and other times grouped together existing territorial units. The Piedmont region of Italy became a republic in 1798, and in 1796 Genoa was transformed into the Ligurian Republic. Napoleon was the founder and president of the "Republic of Italy" (which existed from 1797–1805). For the Republic he struck gold coins in ½ and 1 doppia values in 1803. These pieces featured his bare headed portrait on obverse. When the "Kingdom of Italy" was part of the French Empire in 1805–14, he utilized mints at Rome, Genoa, Milan and Turin to strike French type 20 and 40 franc coins but with distinctive mint marks.

The Emperor made his older brother Joseph Bonaparte (1768–1844) King of Naples and Sicily (1806–08) and King of Spain (1808–13). Joseph issued his own coins for both those countries. For Naples he produced a

Napoleon also set up a series of republics in Italy, including the Subalpine Republic (1798-1802) with its capital at Milan. On this 5 franc piece struck in the year 9 (1801), the standing figures symbolize France and Italy.

Napoleonic Coins ❧ 303

Joseph Bonaparte, Napoleon's older brother, was made King of Naples and Sicily, then King of Spain. Joseph appears (left) on an 1808 1 piastre of Naples and Sicily and (right) on an 1809 8 reales of Spain.

crown (a *piastre* of 120 *grani*) featuring his portrait and crowned arms. For Spain he issued a crown (a 20 *reales* piece) having similar designs.

Another brother, Jerome Bonaparte (1784–1860), was made King of Westphalia (1807–13), a vassal kingdom in Germany, and there he issued several types of gold and silver coins.

Napoleon's brother, Louis Bonaparte (1778–1846), was made King of Holland (1806–10) and he too issued coins in his own name, including

Jerome Bonaparte, youngest brother of Napoleon, struck this silver 5 franc piece while he was King of Westphalia, a vassal kingdom in Germany.

Louis Bonaparte, also a younger brother of Napoleon, issued this 50 stuivers in 1808 while he was King of Holland.

several varieties of gold and silver specimens. His crown (a 50 *stuivers* piece, series of 1807–09) was struck at the Utrecht Mint for presentation purposes only, and most of his other crowns saw generally limited circulation.

Elisa Bonaparte and her husband Felix Bacciocchi issued coins for the Italian principality of Lucca which they governed jointly in 1805-10. This 5 franc specimen shows their accolated busts.

For his sister Elisa Bonaparte and her husband Felix Bacciocchi, Napoleon in 1805 elevated the Tuscan towns of Lucca and Piombino into principalities. During the short time they ruled (1805–08), the two principalities enjoyed a great measure of prosperity.

Napoleon's brother-in-law was not forgotten either. In 1806, the German duchy of Berg was ceded to Napoleon, who expanded its boundaries, raised it to a grand duchy, and bestowed it on Joachim Murat. Murat ruled Berg until 1808 when he became King of Naples where he reigned for seven stormy years (1808–15). After Napoleon's fortunes declined, Murat fled Italy, tried to regroup his forces, but he was captured at Pizzo in October, 1815, court-martialled and shot.

Napoleonic Coins ⊛ 305

Joachim Murat, Napoleon's brother-in-law, and his most daring and brilliant cavalry marshal, issued the 1806 taler (left) while Grand Duke of Berg (1806-08) in Germany. As King of Naples (1808-15), Murat struck a series of coins, including the 5 lire of 1810 (right).

When Napoleon abdicated in 1815 he proclaimed his young son Francis Napoleon II emperor (1811–32), but the boy never reigned. Charles Louis Napoleon Bonaparte (1808–73), a nephew of Napoleon, became president of France during the Second Republic (1848–52), and then proclaimed himself Emperor Napoleon III, a title he held for eighteen years (1852–70). He was the last of the French emperors and the last of the ruling Bonapartes.

In 1815, the Duchy of Parma, Piacenza and Guastalla was assigned by the Congress of Vienna to Marie Louise of Austria, Napoleon's second wife, on condition that she never again see or correspond with her husband.

306 ❧ Napoleonic Coins

Silver grossus struck c. 1350 by the Bishop of Utrecht.

The Netherlands

Julius Caesar's forces advanced inside the present boundaries of Holland with the Romans exercising authority over the Germanic tribes in the area until the early fifth century A.D. Charlemagne included Holland within his sprawling Holy Roman Empire after he had been crowned emperor by Pope Leo III in 800. Gradually, small political units appeared and unified themselves into states. The semi-independent towns and counties of Holland, often nominally fiefs within the Holy Roman Empire, flourished for nearly 500 years, from about 936 to 1419 when the area fell under the control of Burgundy.

The earliest coins struck by mints in the Netherlands were probably done under Frankish authority in the sixth and seventh centuries at the cities of Duurstede and Maastricht. German kings and emperors continued to produce coins at Maastricht and at new mints constructed at Deventer, Tiel and Nijmegen. Beginning in the tenth century, however, coinage executed by local seigneuries and bishoprics replaced that of the imperial authority.

Philip the Good, duke of Burgundy (1419-67), struck this cavalier d'or as Count of Flanders. The inscription FLAD (for Flanders) appears below the rider.

The House of Burgundy controlled Holland for some 58 years (1419–77) and they in turn were succeeded by the Hapsburgs who ruled the country for just over a century (1477–1579). Through inheritance and marriage contract, the Dutch in 1506 became part of the immense Spanish Empire under Charles V (who was also Charles I, King of Spain).

The Netherlands ❧ 307

Philip II, King of Spain and ruler of the Netherlands, struck this 1561 portrait taler at Antwerp for Brabant, a part of the Netherlands. The reverse shows his crowned shield of arms on crossed batons.

In 1555, the dour and authoritarian Philip II inherited his father's crown. The new king set himself the task of wiping out Protestant "heresy"—along with regional freedom—in the Low Countries and the result was rebellion.

The uprising was sparked—rather like the American Revolution—by the imposition of certain taxes. Philip II chose as his army commander the Duke of Alva, who imposed a crushing 10 per cent sales tax and hanged shopkeepers on their doorposts if they did not pay it. He buried other victims alive, introduced the Inquisition, confiscated estates, and had thousands put to death after cities surrendered on his promise of merciful treatment.

The City of Leyden struck this 30 stuiver emergency coin during the Spanish siege of 1514. The reverse inscription means "God Save Leyden."

Silver necessity klippe struck in Amsterdam during a siege by the Spaniards in 1578.

An obscure but brilliant nobleman, William of Nassau, Prince of Orange, rallied a ragged force of Hollanders under his banner and thus became the country's George Washington. Called William the Silent, he attracted followers by his obvious integrity; he declined the throne of Holland when it was offered to him. In 1579, William united the seven northern provinces of the Netherlands into the Dutch Republic.

In their 80-year war against the mighty Spanish Empire (1568–1648) little Holland had certain advantages: a fine navy with which they repeatedly defeated Spain on the high seas; then, too, they received support on occasion from England. The so-called Eighty Years' War was actually a series of loosely connected campaigns, each more devastating and savage than the last. Many varieties of emergency coins struck inside besieged cities by the Dutch defenders appeared during this period.

1701 lion daler of Overyssel, one of the seven northern provinces that formed the Republic of the United Netherlands. Each of the seven provinces struck coins of this type with their individual arms on the shield—a lion in the case of Overyssel.

The Netherlands ❧ 309

During the course of the revolt the Dutch provinces in 1575 issued a series of "Leeuwendaalders" with types portraying on obverse a half-length armed figure holding a lion shield, and a rampant lion on reverse —there is no allusion to the king of Spain in the inscriptions. Each, however, shows the distinctive arms of the issuing province.

In 1648, the Spaniards gave in through sheer exhaustion. They recognized the Netherlands as an independent nation and Holland's "Golden Age" was ushered in. With a surge of dynamic energy and new self-confidence, Holland rose to a position of world power. Ships designed by great Dutch naval architects explored the four corners of the earth. A long list of newly-charted territories bore Dutch names: Cape Horn, Cape of Good Hope, Van Diemens Land (now Tasmania) and innumerable others, including New Amsterdam which eventually became New York City.

Dutch trading enterprises, such as the famous East India Company, became true empire builders, ruling vast overseas possessions like monarchs in their own right. Holland's Admiral Marten Harpertzoon

1735 rider daler of Gelderland. The reverse carries the arms of the United Provinces—a lion brandishing a sword and holding a bundle of seven arrows, each representing a province.

Gold coinage, too, was standardized with all the provinces striking similar pieces such as this 1653 double ducat of Holland.

310 ❧ The Netherlands

1612 silver ducatoon of Overyssel showing a knight holding a sword and lion shield. The legend means "By concord, small things increase."

1676 silver ducatoon of Westfrisia with a knight holding a sword and the provincial shield.

Silver ducatoon of Zeeland struck in 1690 portraying a soldier in armor (the personification of the Netherlands) holding a spear topped with the cap of Liberty.

The Netherlands ❧ 311

Tromp even tied a broom to his masthead and threatened to "sweep the English from the sea"—and he came very close to doing so!

William V (1751–95) reigned as the last ruler of the Dutch Republic. Holland was invaded and occupied by France in 1795, and the French controlled the country for almost 20 years. Louis Bonaparte, brother of Napoleon, ruled Holland between 1806 and 1810 when France annexed Holland outright.

1796 silver ducatoon of Overyssel struck during the era of the Batavian Republic (1795-1806) when the Netherlands was controlled by France.

The Congress of Vienna in 1815 created a new Kingdom of the Netherlands, which included Belgium and Luxembourg as southern provinces. A revolution occurred unexpectedly in 1830 and the two southern provinces broke away and achieved their independence.

The decimal currency introduced into Holland by the French was continued under the new kingdom, with a gulden of 100 cents as the

Kingdom of the Netherlands 1845 silver 2½ gulden of William II (1840-49).

Wilhelmina, young girl head
(1892-97)

Wilhelmina, young woman
head (1898)

Wilhelmina, mature head
(1925-33)

Wilhelmina, adult head
(1911-17)

basic monetary unit. The standard design for all but the lowest value coins has been the head of the reigning monarch with the coat-of-arms on the reverse.

The obverses of the current Dutch coins show the portrait of Queen Juliana (daughter of Wilhelmina) whose reign began in 1948. The orange blossoms on the reverse of the 5 cent piece recall that the ruling dynasty is the House of Orange.

Holland has also struck coins for her colonies. One of the most famous colonial coins was produced for the Dutch East Indies (now the Republic of Indonesia), a 1 ducat gold trade piece. This coin features an armored knight standing, with a plaque on reverse, a design that dates back to the United Province in the 16th century.

The modern 1 ducat gold trade coin of the Dutch East Indies features the armored knight design that was first used by the United Provinces in the 16th century. Struck from 1814 to 1960, the type did not change from ruler to ruler.

The Netherlands also produced coins for her New World colonies, Curacao, Surinam and the Netherlands Antilles. Coinage for circulation in Curacao and Surinam during World War II was struck in part at the Philadelphia Mint. While Curacao is now considered to be a part of the Netherlands Antilles, Surinam, situated on the northeastern coast of South America, is commonly referred to as Dutch Guiana.

Queen Wilhelmina appears (left) on Curaçao's 2½ gulden of 1944 (this World War II coin was struck at the Philadelphia Mint) and her daughter Queen Juliana is portrayed on a similar coin struck for the Netherlands Antilles in 1964.

Silver penning of Harald III Hardråde (1047-66). The design of this coin is similar to the Anglo-Saxon issues of the same period.

Norway

Norway was effectively united for the first time by Harold Haarfager (Fairhair), who ruled from 863 to 930, a period of 67 years. Before this each fiord had its own chief or "jarl," its war galleys and crews of Viking sea rovers. Probably the earliest true Norwegian coins are the crude silver pennies attributed to Earl Haakon in about 990. The obverse carries the portrait of the king and sceptre, while the reverse has a cross-like design.

It was Olav Tryggvesson (995–1000) who brought Christianity to Norway from England. Tryggvesson, usually called Olav I, did a great deal to make Norway a major European power in the brief five years of his rule. He was drowned in the year 1000 while in battle with the kings of Sweden and Denmark. Coins of Olav I were usually rather well struck and his name and title "Onlaf rex Nor" appear distinctly on his silver pennies.

During the 11th century, Norway became a powerful seafaring nation and shared with Denmark the conquest of England in 1016–18. Specimens of Harald Hardrade (King of Norway, 1047–66) thus bear a strong resemblance to contemporary coins struck by his English counterpart Edward the Confessor. Toward the end of the 11th century, the Danes and Norsemen lost their hold on England as the latter became fully independent.

1543 silver mark of Christian III (1534-59), King of Denmark and Norway, with the distinctive Norwegian arms, a crowned lion with St. Olav's axe, a design first used on coins about 1280.

Over the centuries, the Danish kings of Norway issued coins with distinctive Norwegian designs such as this 1647 taler of Christian IV (1588-1648). Coins of the normal Danish type were also produced at mints within Norway.

Norwegian history of the 12th century is clouded by domestic crises, and the 13th constituted the last period of early Norwegian independence and greatness. Haakon V (1299–1319) minted coins with a profile bust and cross fourchee, reminiscent of contemporary Scottish issues.

When the Union of Kalmar was effected in 1397, Norway was united with Denmark and Sweden. However, Norway was at a distinct disadvantage, and was eventually down-graded into a mere dependency of Denmark, a position in which it remained for more than four centuries.

When Denmark had to cede Norway to Sweden in 1814, the new union was accompanied by no small amount of friction. Finally, in 1905, the union was dissolved through mutual consent. Official approval for the separation came from Swedish King Oscar II, who caused Prince Carl, second son of the King of Denmark, to be invited to ascend the Norwegian throne. He was declared King Haakon VII by the Storthing or Parliament. Haakon VII ruled for more than a half-century until his death in 1957.

The Treaty of Kiel in January, 1814 transferred Norway from Denmark to Sweden. The union was one of two separate nations under one king and the Swedish kings continued the practice of issuing coins with the Norwegian lion arms. The crossed hammers on the reverse of this 1824 speciedaler are the mint mark of the Kongsberg mint.

316 ❧ Norway

This 1910 20 kroner coin and the 10 kroner piece of the same design are the only gold coins of independent Norway. The reverse shows St. Olaf, patron saint of Norway, holding the battle-axe which tradition says he used to drive heathen religion out of Norway.

Two of the 17th century Danish kings struck distinctive gold coins for Norway. The obverses carried portraits of the rulers, while the reverses all featured a lion on a sword. The only gold coins issued by Sweden for Norway under the Union were the 10 and 20 kroner specimens of King Oscar II struck from 1874 to 1902. Only one issue of gold coins has been struck by Norway since independence—the 10 and 20 kroner specimens produced at Kongsberg in 1910. The pieces depict the crowned bust of Haakon VII on the obverse, and the standing figure of St. Olav on the reverse.

1925 1 krone piece of copper-nickel composition, struck on center hole planchet, shows crowned monograms in the form of a cross on the obverse, the Order of St. Olaf on the reverse.

Haakon's first coins, minted in 1906–07, were bronze pieces in 1, 2 and 5 ore values. The obverse bears the Norwegian lion, while the reverse has the denomination within a circle of leaves. He also struck two commemorative 2 kroner silver specimens in 1906–07 to mark the achievement of independence.

For a quarter century Norway was one of the few countries in the world minting coins with holes in the center, some of which still circulate. World War II coins in nickel-brass struck for the Norwegian Government-in-Exile in London at the Royal Mint were also holed. The Scandinavian Mint Union required a specific metallic weight for each denomination and holing allowed the coins to be of larger diameter without exceeding the limits.

This 1964 silver 10 kroner piece was struck to mark the 150th anniversary of Norway's Constitution and shows the building, Eidsvoll Manor, in which it was signed.

King Olav V has reigned since 1957, and in this period the Kongsberg Mint has produced some of Norway's most attractive coins, featuring animals: a squirrel, rooster, moose, sparrow, dog, lion, bee and horse.

Norway's current coins below the 5 kroner value show a variety of animals; horse, elkhound, Lapland titmouse, moose, bee, grouse and squirrel. The obverses show King Olav's portrait or monogram.

This clay tablet of Babylonia is a due bill dating back to the 25th century B.C., one of the earliest known financial documents of man.

Odd & Curious Moneys

The field of odd and curious money includes any object or substance ever used as a medium of exchange. These are also called "primitive" or "strange" moneys.

One of the earliest objects exhibited by museums is the clay tablet due bill of ancient Babylonia dating back to about 2500 B.C. Financial records were inscribed on these tablets, and from them we may trace the evolution of modern banknotes and checks.

Though the ancient Egyptians did not produce coins, they did use forms of moneys, mostly gold rings shaped like bracelets. The ancient Chinese manufactured a variety of interesting moneys before round coins

Egyptian gold money ring (c. 1680-1350 B.C.). The use of such rings as currency was customary during this period.

Odd and Curious Moneys ❧ 319

(Left) Bronze "shirt money" of China from the 7th century B.C. and (right) "dress money" of the same period. Ancient Chinese coins were cast in the shape of the objects whose value they represented.

came into use. Early in the Chou Dynasty (1122–249 B.C.), replicas of barter goods began to play an important part in daily trade. Small bronze replicas of knives, hoes, spades and other implements were used as media of exchange in place of the actual goods.

Throughout China and Southeast Asia, silver bars and ingots have been used as currency for more than 2,000 years. Silver ingots called "sycee" (meaning a fine thread-like silver) circulated widely in China especially from the time of Kublai Khan, the Mongol emperor who ruled from A.D. 1260–95. Chinese sycee silver constituted legal tender until well into the 19th century. While China held vast treasures of silver, no silver coins were minted in 1866 when the British government set up modern minting machinery in Hong Kong.

320 ⊚ Odd and Curious Moneys

The object considered to be the world's largest silver "coin"—measuring $4\frac{3}{4}$ inches long, 3 inches wide, and $2\frac{1}{2}$ inches deep—with a weight of 4 pounds, is a 50 tael value piece of "boat money" produced in China in the 1850's. This piece, which is really a silver ingot, was made in a sand mold. This unusual boat-shaped money has special interest for the numismatist since it is stamped with the marks of several banks. "Sycee" money also came in a variety of other shapes, including the forms of miniature drums, boats and shoes.

A substance often becomes recognized as a medium of exchange because of its durability, appearance and scarcity. For example, gold has a high value in most areas of the world because it is attractive, durable and extremely difficult to wrest from the earth. In some societies, other items command values akin to that of gold. In certain areas, for example, a tiger claw is worth a great deal because it too is difficult to obtain. In Thailand, especially, various parts of the tiger's body were valued as currency: the claws, teeth, tail, tongue, etc. As this currency became more refined, replicas were made . . . i.e., "tiger tongues" of crude silver were

Odd and Curious Moneys ❧ 321

Siamese "tiger tongue" money,
a type of silver ingot.

produced and widely circulated. The history of Siamese tiger tongue currency stretches back for more than 1,000 years with several types still being circulated within recent years in the more remote sections of the country. Tiger tongue bars 3 to 7 inches in length were produced by the tens of thousands throughout those long centuries. As a result they can be readily acquired by collectors today.

Currency specimens shaped roughly in the form of bullets were introduced in Thailand as early as the 11th or 12th centuries, though they were most widely circulated early in the 19th. During the 1830's and 1840's, the

2 and 1 tical values of Siamese "bullet money." Last produced about 1860, these pieces were not finally demonetized until the 20th century.

country was being opened up for commerce with the West and a need developed almost immediately for a standard medium of exchange. Regular coins and banknotes were not readily available . . . thus, the government ordered the manufacture of the so-called "bullet" coins.

To produce these bullets, the Siamese coiner would begin with a bar of gold or silver. He would cut off chunks of various sizes depending upon the denominations and weigh each carefully. The tips of each piece were turned together so that the finished "coin" was nearly round. Each piece was of controlled weight and fineness. Most bullet coins bore two stamps: one indicated the Siamese dynasty, and the other bore the symbol of the King of Siam.

Bullet currency began passing out of circulation about 1860, when Thailand established its own modern mint at Bangkok with coin-striking machinery imported from Birmingham, England. By the mid-1860's the Bangkok Mint reached full production.

Siamese porcelain gambling tokens are so plentiful, colorful and inexpensive that many collectors have them. Chinese gambling houses in Bangkok and environs used these gambling tokens extensively in the 19th century. In the late 1850's and early 1860's, during a critical currency shortage in Siam, porcelain gambling tokens virtually replaced metallic currency among the merchants. Once the Bangkok Mint began producing regular coins in sufficient quantities, the tokens disappeared from circulation.

Porcelain gambling house tokens circulated as local currency in 19th century Siam.

Among Japanese odd and curious money, the rectangular silver coin issued in 1765 and called "Tanuma go momme gin" has an especially curious history. Tanuma, a high Japanese official, ordered all silver ornaments which he termed useless luxuries confiscated and minted them into coins. His decree naturally led to much resentment among the population and its strict enforcement was one of the causes leading to his assassination.

The Japanese money tree circulated widely in northeastern Asia. During the first several decades of the 19th century, coins were cast in tree-shaped molds. Coins were broken from the tree by mint employees,

18th century Japanese rectangular silver coins were called "Meiwa Go Momme Gin."

Odd and Curious Moneys ❧ 323

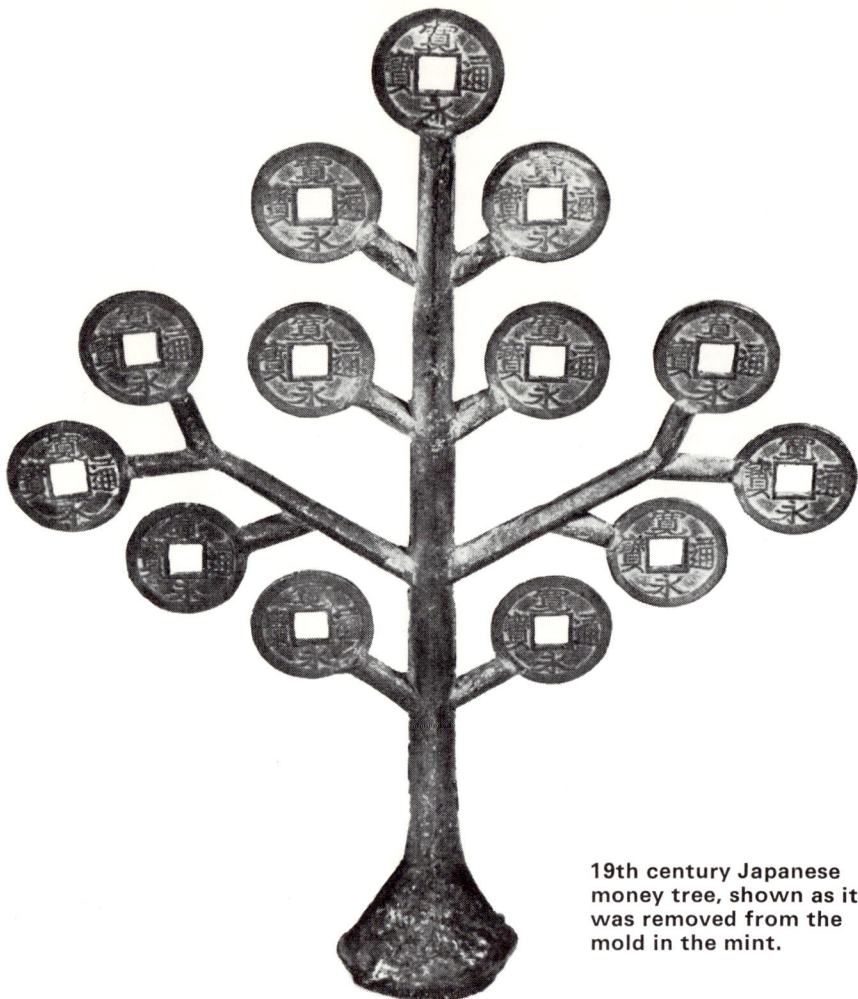

19th century Japanese money tree, shown as it was removed from the mold in the mint.

the stems returned to the melting pot. Many millions of these unusual pieces were produced . . . the number of coins on each tree varied. Tree money cast in Japan was employed in trade on Okinawa and on many other Pacific islands. The Chinese were also fond of tree money.

Japan's gold obans are generally regarded as the largest gold coins ever struck. The obans, oval-shaped 10 tael pieces, were minted infrequently from about 1591 to 1860. They average about 150 × 100 millimetres and are characterized by seals punched into the metal and by legends applied with ink. Smaller 5 tael pieces called "goryobans," and 1 tael specimens called "kobans" were also produced.

Japan, 1837 Tempo goryoban.

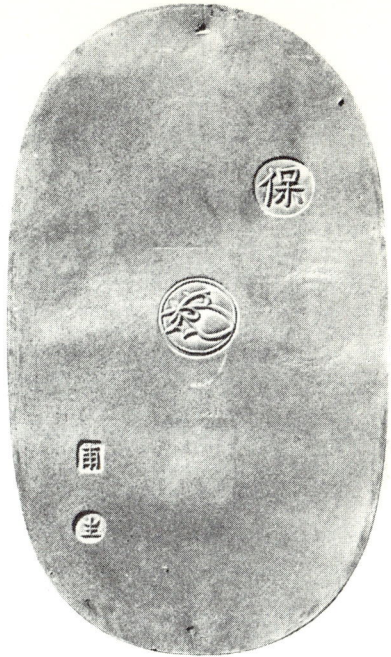

These hat-shaped pieces cast from native tin, are from the city of Penang in Malaya. They were designed to nest into one another and were usually holed on the rim for stringing.

For 900 years or more, tea cast into bricks was used as currency in China, Tibet and other Asian countries. These bricks were stamped with the value and the name of the issuing bank.

Asian brick tea money was circulated for more than 900 years. As late as the mid-19th century, tea bricks were given by the Chinese to the Mongols to pay for troops. The "standard tea brick" issued by Tibet in the 1800's weighed about 2½ pounds and was valued at approximately one rupee. The standard tea brick, fully inscribed with the value and name of the issuing bank, was mixed with wood to make it more durable. The bricks were frequently broken into smaller pieces to make "small change."

Dog tooth money was used as currency on New Guinea and other South Pacific Islands until recently . . . in fact, it is believed that dog teeth still may circulate in remote areas. The dog teeth were strung on necklaces for in this way they took on even a higher value. The necklaces were often given to prospective brides by their suitors.

Whale tooth money, produced from the teeth of the sperm whale, was once considered so rare in the Gilbert and Solomon Islands that only

Cowrie shells were used as currency the world over during ancient times.

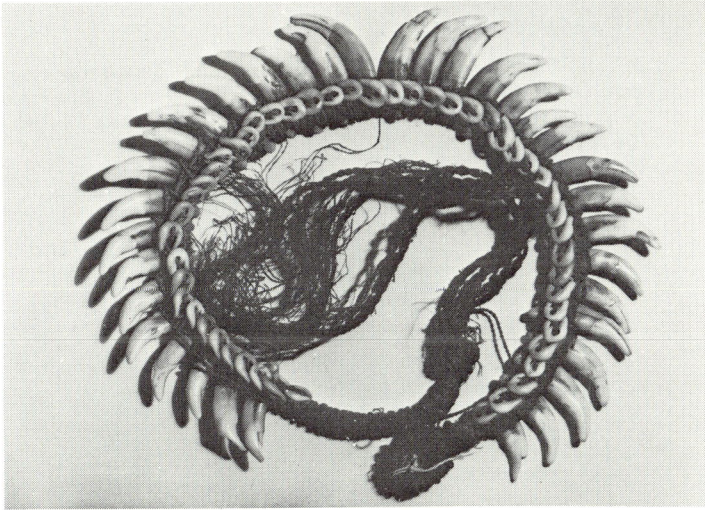

Dog tooth necklaces, given to prospective brides by their suitors, were highly valued in the market places of New Guinea during the 19th century.

tribal chiefs were allowed to wear them in necklace form. Eventually, sailors from over the world began to acquire whale tooth currency in such great quantity and circulated them to the point where financial panic was created on many of the Pacific islands. Sperm whale tooth money was often exquisitely painted and decorated by the islanders.

Odd and Curious Moneys ❧ 327

The largest "coins" in the world are unquestionably the stone money of Yap, an island in the South Pacific. These stone coins vary in size from small change of less than 9 inches in diameter to massive cartwheels 12 feet across. The largest piece to have left the island is this 875-lb. specimen.

Stone money of the island of Yap must be classified as the "biggest money" ever used by man. Yap, an island in the Carolines has been a United Nations Trust Territory under U.S. control since 1947. The stone money became valuable because the large discs of limestone necessary for its production had to be quarried on the Palau islands 200 to 400 miles away. Transporting the huge discs involved great danger . . . many of the Yapese who set out on the quarrying expeditions never returned. Once the stones reached Yap, they had to be worked, without being broken, into their round shapes. The hole in the middle, necessary so the "coin" could be carried on a pole, had to be carefully drilled. All this had to be done with crude and simple implements. The largest known specimens reached 12 feet in diameter and weighed over 4,000 pounds. It took as long as two years to carve out these huge stones.

Drums have been circulated as currency. Drums were used as a medium of exchange on Alor, a small island north of Timor. Kettle drums, called "mokos," and brass gongs were among the most highly valued possessions of the natives and served as the principal store of value. The most famous

This Swedish 1644 10 daler plate money piece is the world's largest metal coin, weighing 44 lb., measuring 14 inches by 24 inches by ½ inch (note 12-inch ruler in foreground). Its purchasing power was equal to two cows.

type of drum money is that of the Karen Tribes of Burma. The drum of this tribe, known as the "Kyee-Zee" drum, is noted for its frog design.

Odd and curious moneys of Africa have attracted the attention of numismatists, geographers, archeologists and scholars in associated

A specimen of "Kyee Zee" or drum money used by the Karen tribes of Burma. The top of the drum carries a frog-like design.

Odd and Curious Moneys ❧ 329

Various types of copper and bronze rings similar to this African specimen have served as currency, jewelry and as a store of wealth among native peoples.

fields. In many parts of Africa, brass and copper rings are still highly prized. They are valuable because they represent fine craftsmanship and possess ceremonial value. They also serve as a store of wealth among many African tribes. Originally, such rings were produced by the Africans themselves, but after the influx of European traders in the 19th century, many were manufactured in distant foundries.

Africa has given rise to some of the strangest types of currencies ever circulated. One of the most interesting of these is the "Gizzi Penny," often referred to as the "Penny with a Soul." Originated by the "Gizzi" or "Kissi" tribe in West Africa it has been used as an exchange medium for centuries. The iron "pennies" are about as thick as a lead pencil and up to several feet in length. One end is flattened to a wing shape and the other to a kind of double tail. If either end becomes broken the penny loses its "soul," and it must be reincarnated by the medicine man of the tribe. A small fee is charged for this particular service. Normally, two such pennies bought 20 oranges, a large bunch of bananas, or several Kola nuts. Enough of these iron ingots could be taken to the tribal blacksmith and easily converted into a cutlass, a hoe or some other piece of farming tool.

Spear money has been widely circulated in Africa over a period of centuries and commanded a high premium because a spear itself has intrinsic value. In the Camerouns on the African west central coast, the spears measure from two to three feet in length and are known as "wife money" since a dozen of them were sufficient for purchasing a wife. In West Africa, smaller spears were made for smaller purchases. Some of these are less than four inches long.

In another section of Africa, below Stanley Falls on the Congo River, an enormous spearhead, known as "liganda," measuring some 6 feet in length and weighing 5 pounds, is still thought to be used as a circulating medium as wife money, or for the purchase of small boats. Ten of these ligandas will buy a canoe 35 feet long, while 30 will pay for a wife.

When European traders began coming to Africa, beads became one of the most popular currencies . . . and they often served as a convenient means of making small change. A favorite currency among Southwest African tribes was the so-called bushmen's beads. They consisted of discs cut out of ostrich egg shells, pierced with an arrow and strung. While they were mainly used as ornaments, they also served as an exchange medium. A few tribes in Southwest Africa also used iron beads as a means of payment.

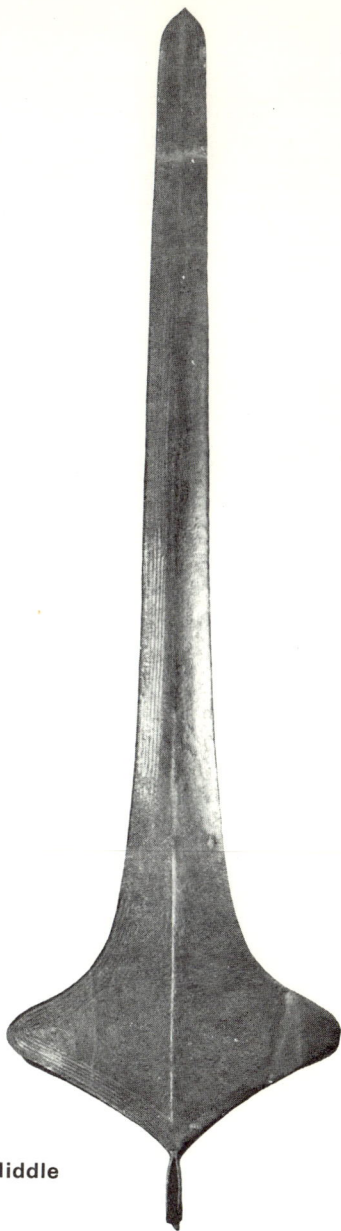

This iron spearhead, used as currency in the Middle Congo, is actually six feet long.

Odd and Curious Moneys ❧ 331

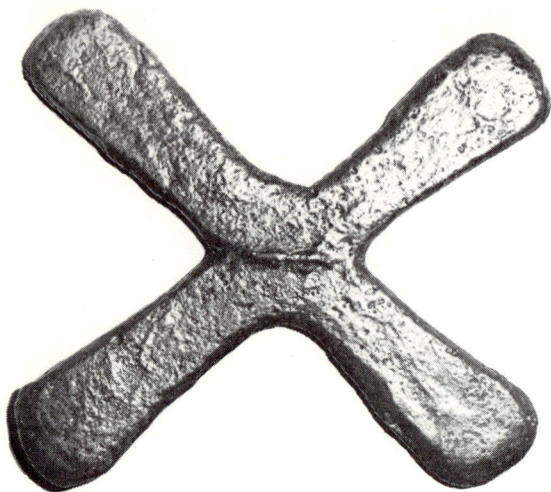

Copper, cast in the form of a cross, is still used to purchase brides among the peoples of isolated northern Rhodesia.

Among the best known odd and curious currencies, the Katanga cross has been produced in the old Katanga region of Central Africa for more than 350 years. They are still used as money to a limited extent among some of the peoples of Northern Rhodesia. These copper crosses, called "lunkana" by the natives, weigh from 2½ to 3 pounds and were frequently used for bride purchases by people of the Congo. The crosses were cast by digging a mold in the sand and pouring molten metal into it. About 20 crosses could be made from a single mold. They were usually worth from 15 to 25 cents in our currency and were carried in loads of nine or ten attached to a pole.

In the Western Hemisphere at the time of the Spanish conquest early in the 16th century, Mexico possessed an advanced economic system. In the Aztec civilization, gold dust constituted one of the most important exchange media. The gold dust was kept in transparent quills and in that form, or cast into bars, gold was used in payment of tribute by the southern provinces of the Aztec Empire.

Cacao beans also ranked as one of the key Aztec currencies. Travelers of the 18th century reported that value of cacao beans in Mexico was kept high through the restriction of cultivation of cocoa in the country. There were even debased cacao beans; the stone was removed and its place was filled with earth!

Hernando Cortez, in a message to the King of Spain, dated October 15, 1524, referred to hatchets used by the Aztecs as money. Their value had been established at 8,000 cacao beans. A number of historians have mentioned copper hatchets as one of the currencies of the Yucatan Indians. These copper hatchets, cut in small, T-shaped pieces, constituted the nearest approach to coined money. Cortez also found pieces of tin circulating as money in several provinces.

In North America, beaded ceremonial aprons were highly valued as currency by the Alaskan Indians. Several types of ceremonial aprons were brought to Alaska by Siberian Eskimos. The ornamental use of beads made the aprons so desirable that the natives often traded their valuable furs for them. When beads were scarce, a knife or a string of beads was worth 50 marten skins.

One of the most unusual currencies of the North Country was the "Copper Plate Money" made by the Indians inhabiting the northwestern coast of North America. The copper plates were utilized as an exchange medium before the Europeans arrived in the 17th and 18th centuries.

The earliest specimens were of solid native copper, but later, thinner sheet copper obtained from the traders was used. A ridge ran up the center of

American Indian wampum belts were used as currency during the 17th century in the British colonies of North America.

Copper plate money
currency was used by the
Indians inhabiting the
northwestern coast of
North America before the
arrival of the Europeans.

the plate's lower half and across the middle at the narrowest point, resembling the letter "T." Referred to as "taus," these copper plates sometimes
represented the total wealth of a tribe. The larger plates have been valued
as high as 35,000 blankets . . . the exact number was determined by the

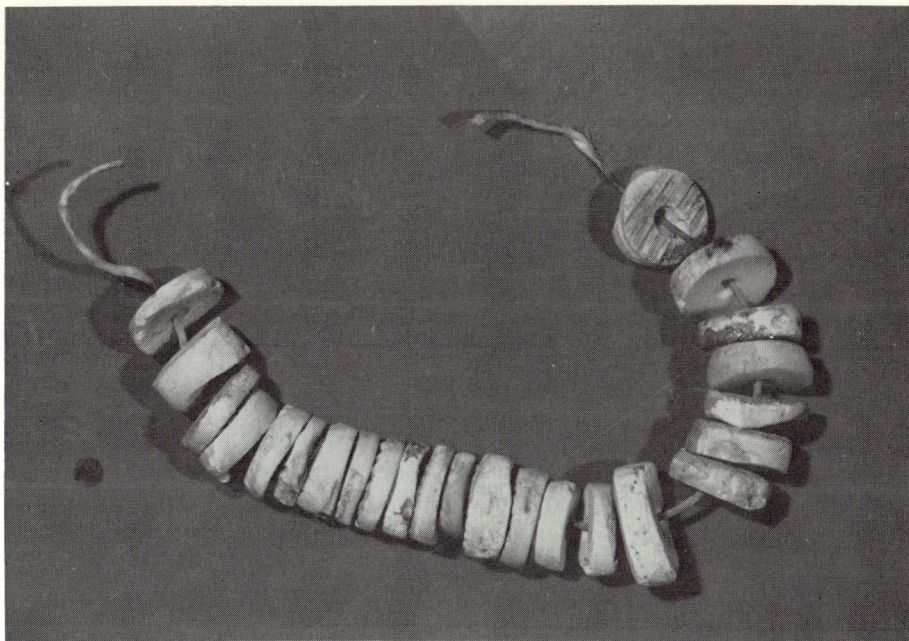

Originally produced by North American Indians as ornaments, shell discs on a string were later accepted by European colonists and the Indians themselves as money.

tau's age and history. The copper plates were usually elaborately etched or painted with the owner's totem or crest prominently displayed.

Shell discs, originally made by North American Indians as ornaments, were later accepted by both Indians and European colonists as currency. As coins gradually replaced shell discs in trade, shell money tended to lose its value. "Dentalia Shell Currency" was also liberally used for monetary purposes in the western part of the United States and Canada. A six-foot string of these horn-shaped shells once purchased one or two slaves. In the 19th century, one Dentalia shell was valued at $5.00.

Wampum is a form of money adopted by the white man from Indian designs. Wampum had passed its peak as a currency by 1700 although it is believed to have circulated in a few sections until the early 1800's. Wampum, beads made from various types of small polished shells, was usually strung together in strands, belts and sashes. Its value varied according to the quality and color of the beads and the artistry with which they were strung together. The Indians had no written language, so the wampum belt was used to record their history. Much time and skill was required to weave in images and the figures necessary to depict the

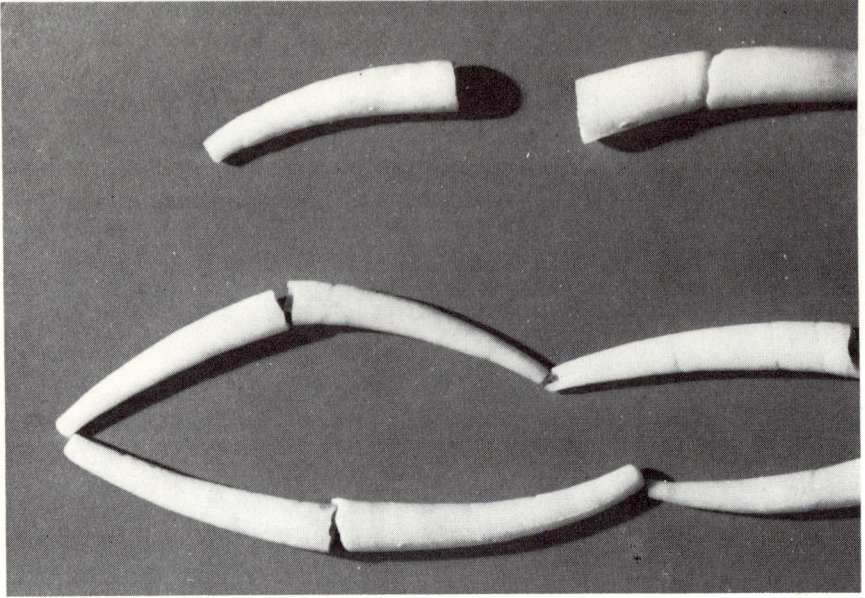

These horn-shaped "dentalia" shells once circulated as currency in the western United States and Canada.

important happenings of the tribes. Fine wampum belts could never be made in a hurry and the time involved in their production was a factor in assessing the value.

Among other forms of pioneer money in America were tobacco, bullets, gunpowder and "firewater." Since these commodities were desired by everyone and readily accepted in exchange for other items, all goods could be valued in terms of these "currencies." Tobacco, especially, was an important early form of currency in the southern colonies. The first law passed by the General Assembly of Virginia in 1619 was an act setting the price of tobacco. So vital was tobacco to these colonists that 23 years later a law was passed making it the sole currency. Eventually, tobacco notes were issued. They were certificates of deposit in government warehouses, and were declared to be acceptable for all tobacco debts within the warehouse district where they were issued. The tobacco notes consituted one of the most widely accepted currencies in the southern colonies during the 18th century. As colonies were settled these currencies began to be replaced by coins from the mints of Spain, France and England.

Struck under the aegis of Holy Roman Emperor Arnulf of Carinthia (887-99), this silver denier of Pope Stephen VII (896-97) has a monogram form of STEPHAN on the obverse with ROMA and ARNOLFUS MP on the reverse.

Papal Coins

Prior to 1870, the popes at Rome were temporal as well as spiritual rulers, and had their own coinage for use in the Papal States. From Adrian's time, the Papal States gradually grew in size and power so that by the 1600's they extended across the peninsula, dividing northern and southern Italy. During the 17th and 18th centuries they covered over 16,000 square miles of land area.

Comparatively little is known of the earliest Papal coins, but they were struck at the Rome Mint, mostly in silver and bronze. Their crude engraving and thinness is typical of the European coins produced during the Dark Ages.

Pope Clement VI (1342-52) struck this silver grosso at the Avignon mint.

The history of the Roman Catholic Church in the 14th and early 15th centuries was especially turbulent, a situation reflected on papel coins of the time. First, the popes were forced to reside at Avignon, France from 1309 to 1417 when there were two rival popes, one holding court at Avignon and the other in Rome. Starting in 1378, Urban VI was pope in Rome and Clement VII claimed to be pope in Avignon. In the early years of the 15th century, John XXIII claimed the papacy from Avignon while Gregory XII ruled as pope in Rome. Each of the rivals issued his own coinage.

On this gold ducat of Calixtus III (1455-68), St. Peter is shown in a ship (representing the church), with crossed keys (the Keys to the Kingdom of Heaven) over the papal arms on the reverse.

Papal Coins ❧ 337

The two archbishops who claimed the papacy in Avignon during the Great Schism were labeled as "anti-pope" or "pretenders" to the papal throne. (Thus, John XXIII is not recognized in the line of the "official" popes, the same name and ordinal number being taken over by Angelo Cardinal Roncalli when he was elected pope by the College of Cardinals on October 28, 1958.) The breach was healed through the extraordinary efforts of Martin V upon his accession to the papal throne at Rome in 1417.

Silver giulio of Julius II (1503-13) struck at the Bologna Mint shows St. Petronius, patron of the city, on the reverse.

During the past twelve centuries, papal mints have been located at nearly two-score Italian and French cities with the main coin-striking facility, however, nearly always being located at Rome. Some of the other papal mints were at Avignon, Bologna, Fermo, Ferrara, Modena, Parma, Ravenna, Reggio, Tivoli, and Umbria. Most of these also produced coins and medals for the various noblemen or petty kings who controlled them.

Bologna silver giulio of Leo X (1513-21) struck at Bologna. The coin's reverse has the inscription BONONIA MATER STVDIORVM—"Bologna, the mother of studies," in reference to its university, the oldest in western Europe.

Bologna for centuries had one of the busiest mints in Europe, operating for 670 years, from the time of King Enrico VI in 1191 to 1861 while Italy was in the process of federation. The mint came under the jurisdiction of Pope Innocent VI in 1360, and coins were struck there for many of the popes up to the time of Pius IX in the 1850's. St. Petronius was the patron saint of Bologna and coins from its mint are generally found with "S. Petronius Prot." honoring him as protector of the city.

Silver giulio of Pope Clement VII (1523-35). On the obverse are St. Peter and St. Paul. On the reverse are the six golden balls of the Medici.

The Ravenna Mint operated intermittently for nearly 1,300 years, from the time Rome fell in 476 until 1758 when Pope Benedict XIV died. Leo X (1513-21) issued many types of coins from Ravenna, including zecchini, julios and quattrini.

The Ferrara Mint began striking coins for the dukes d'Este in the middle of the 12th century. The first papal coins produced there were for Clement VIII (1598-1605). Like the mint at Ravenna, the Ferrara facility was closed at the death of Benedict in 1758.

Bevenuto Cellini, the renowned Florentine artist, designed this silver portrait giulio for Clement VII. On the reverse, Christ is shown with St. Peter.

Coins were issued at Parma for the emperor Charlemagne as early as 781. Julius II (1503-13) took possession of the city during the latter part of his reign and struck ducats there which were inscribed VIRGO FAVEAS PARMAE TVAE on the reverse—"Virgin, protect thy Parma" . . . this was a plea to the Blessed Virgin for aid in his battles. The Parma Mint also produced coins during the 1500's for various other popes.

During the Renaissance, the engraving of coins and medals was ranked on a par with other art forms. The popes, not to be outdone by the secular princes, tried to hire the best engravers available. The most

Gold scudo d'oro of Paul III (1534-49), struck at the Parma Mint, shows crossed keys over the papal shield, with Pallas Athena, goddess of wisdom, on the reverse.

Papal Coins ❧ 339

This silver testone of Gregory XII (1572-85) shows the manger scene with Mary, Joseph and the infant Jesus with the Christmas star above, all surrounded by the legend LETAMINI GENTES ("Rejoice ye nations").

renowned artist commissioned to engrave papal coins and medals was Benvenuto Cellini (1500–71). Cellini created a number of outstanding coins and medals for Clement VII (1523–34). He also designed coins for the Medici family in Florence.

In the 16th century, the popes began using their own portraits on coins. Prior to this, stylized figures of saints and Biblical themes dominated the coin designs. The themes include representations of The Three Magi, Two Apostles in a Ship, The Holy Door, The Lateran Church, Justice Standing, as well as the papal coat-of-arms.

Besides gold pieces issued from the time of John XXII (1316–34) the Papal States have, up to John XXIII (1958–63), also issued a regular series of silver crown-sized coins. Several varieties of crowns show the Crossed Keys, referring to "the keys of the Kingdom of Heaven," and alluding to the Popes, successors of St. Peter. Other typical designs with religious symbolism are an angelic figure representing the Church, St. Thomas and the beggar, Christ and the apostles in a boat, St. Michael hurling thunderbolts at Satan, the Infant Jesus in the Temple, even Noah's ark.

Silver scudo of Urban VII (1623-44) shows St. Michael battling Lucifer, the fallen archangel, who personifies the Devil.

340 ❧ Papal Coins

Innocent X (1644-55) silver scudo depicting Christ blessing St. Peter with the legend IN VERBO TUO—"In Thy word."

Alexander VII (1655-67) silver scudo with St. Thomas Aquinas aiding a beggar.

Innocent XI (1676-89) silver scudo with a view of St. Peter's Cathedral in Rome.

Clement IX (1667-69) silver scudo showing the throne of St. Peter.

Alexander VIII (1689-91), 1690 silver scudo, has a personification of the Church holding a basilica and standard.

Innocent XII (1691-1700), 1692 silver scudo has St. Michael hurling thunderbolts at Satan.

Innocent XII, 1699 silver scudo with a scene of the Jews gathering manna in the desert.

This 1704 silver scudo of Clement XI (1700-21) bears the Papal arms on the obverse, a representation of the Infant Jesus in the temple on the reverse.

342 ❧ Papal Coins

During the reign of Pius IX (1846-78), the Papal States lost their sovereignty to the Italian government. The Pope became a voluntary prisoner in the Vatican.

In 1870, the newly unified Italian government brought the Papal States under its sovereignty. In protest, the Pope remained a voluntary prisoner in the Vatican. This continued until 1929 when the Lateran Treaty created the 109 acre independent state of the Vatican City. Papal coinage resumed once more and has continued with annual issues up to the present time.

Since 1929 the Vatican coins have been struck at the Italian government mint in Rome, in denominations keyed to those of Italy itself. In 1940, the use of nickel for coinage was discontinued at the Rome Mint and a new metal known as "acmonital," a type of stainless steel, substituted. Acmonital has been used for striking Vatican coins ever since.

Besides gold, silver and stainless steel, several other metals have been utilized for Vatican coinage during the past 30 years. Brass was used during the war, while aluminum and aluminum-bronze have been employed for many of the contemporary issues.

In addition to the regular coinage of the popes, there are "Sede Vacante" coins issued to mark the interregnum periods between the death of one pope and the election of another. "Sede Vacante" literally means that the papal throne or Holy See is vacant. In modern times Sede Vacante coins

Special "Sede Vacante" coins are struck for the interregnum period between popes. This 1939 10 lire piece bears the arms of the chamberlain, Eugenio Cardinal Pacelli who became Pope Pius XII.

Gold 100 lire coins show portraits of three 20th century popes—Pius XI
(1922-39), Pius XII (1939-58) and John XXIII (1958-63).

were minted in 1939, 1958 and 1963. During the interregnum the papal
chamberlain takes charge and has the authority to issue Sede Vacante
coins bearing his own coat-of-arms. Most of the Sede Vacante coins of
the past two centuries have been similar in general design, the arms of the
pontifical chamberlain and the spirit of peace represented by a dove.

Vatican coins have the same value as the regular Italian coins and,
by arrangement with the Italian government, are legal tender throughout
Italy. While it is thus possible occasionally to find Vatican coins in circulation anywhere in Italy, you are much more likely to find them in Rome
or at the Vatican itself.

These 1967 coins of Pope Paul VI (1963-   ) show his portrait and (left) heads
of St. Peter and St. Paul, (center) St. Peter on throne and (right) St. Paul
on horseback.

344 ∿ Papal Coins

Paraguay's first coin, a copper $\frac{1}{12}$ real dated 1845, has a design taken from the national treasury seal.

Paraguay

Paraguay, settled by the Spanish beginning in 1535, became independent in 1811. Since that time dictators have ruled the republic and they have involved the country in several costly wars. Coins of Paraguay have been minted at Buenos Aires, London, Birmingham, and Switzerland. The country has never had its own mint.

Paraguay's earliest coinage consisted of a copper 1/12 real issue showing on obverse a lion standing in front of a staff surmounted by a Liberty Cap; the value is inscribed on reverse, along with the date, 1845.

The copper 1, 2 and 4 centesimos, struck in 1870, have a star between two branches, while the reverse is inscribed with the value and date. The silver peso of 1889, minted at Buenos Aires, portrays a seated lion; the reverse has a star.

The seated lion and Liberty Cap design, taken from the national treasury seal, was also employed on several other issues of Paraguayan coins, including the last coins issued, dated 1953. Virtually all coins have disappeared from circulation because of their low face value and they have been replaced by paper money. The 1 guarani value (which equals 100 centimos) is not represented by a coin, but by a banknote.

The 1889 silver peso is Paraguay's only crown-sized coin. Several of the country's coins have been struck on scalloped planchets which are difficult to counterfeit.

This 1698 2 escudo gold piece with a C mint mark was struck at a temporary mint that operated in Cuzco only during that one year.

Peru

The Inca Empire, one of the greatest civilizations ever developed by a primitive people, flourished from about A.D. 1100 (Cuzco, their capital, was founded at that time) until 1532 when Peru was conquered by Francisco Pizarro. Although the Incas used no currency whatsoever, the Inca kings were enormously rich, and all the land, gold, silver and jewels belonged to them.

This silver 2 reales was struck in Lima (L mint mark) during the reign of Charles II (1665-1700).

The Spanish established a mint at Lima which began striking coins in 1565 with design types similar to those established at Mexico City. Peru issued its first coins as a republic in 1822–23, although Spanish rule did not end completely until 1824. These were silver 4 and 8 reales pieces struck at the Lima Mint. They show Virtue and Justice on obverse, and

Officials of the Lima mint produced coins for the new King, Ferdinand VII, before the arrival of portrait dies from Spain by creating a "fantasy" portrait of their own. Compare the head on this 1810 8 reales piece with the coin at the top of the next page.

346 ◦ Perù

The 1819 silver 4 reales of the Lima (MAE mint mark) shows Ferdinand VII's true likeness.

the new national arms, consisting of a llama, a tree, and a cornucopiae on the reverse.

After independence became officially recognized, Peru produced a wide variety of coins, struck mostly at the Lima Mint, but mints also

Peru's 1822 8 reales piece was minted just as the country was emerging as a republic. It shows a pillar between standing figures of Virtue and Justice.

operated for a time at Arequipa, Cuzco and Pasco. Both the Lima and Cuzco mints struck 1 to 8 escudo gold pieces during the 1826–55 period. These specimens feature Liberty standing holding a shield and pole on obverse; reverse has the national arms.

A standing figure of Liberty holds a shield and Liberty cap on a pole on Peru's 2 reales of 1826.

Peru's Liberty is shown seated on 1925 silver sol. The reverse shows the Peruvian arms symbolizing the country's natural riches—fauna, flora and minerals.

In 1857, a new decimal coinage was instituted with the silver sol (equalling 100 centavos) as the monetary unit. The silver specimens usually featured a seated Liberty and arms design. The nickel and bronze pieces were generally inscribed with a sun. These basic types continued

An Inca Indian's portrait is featured on Peru's gold libra of 1913. Peru has struck great numbers of gold coins during the 20th century.

through the rest of the 19th century and were carried over into the first part of the 20th.

Peru utilized a number of world mints from the 1860's to the 1940's to supplement its own coinage production (including those at Philadelphia, San Francisco, Brussels and London), but the Casa Nacional de Moneda

Manco Capac, the first Inca chieftan, appears on Peru's gold 50 soles of 1930-31. According to legend, the Sun god who created Manco Capac instructed him to teach the arts of civilization to all the other Indians.

at Lima is now able to provide the country with all its coinage needs. Total production is over 70 million pieces per year.

Peru has issued a relatively large number of gold coins during the 20th century. These include the $\frac{1}{5}$ libra (1906–55), $\frac{1}{2}$ libra (1902–13), and 1 libra (1898–1929) specimens showing an Inca Indian head on obverse and the arms on reverse. The five piece gold set, series of 1950–57 (5, 10, 20, 50 and 100 soles values) shows Liberty seated facing right, with the national arms on the reverse.

This 20 soles is one of a set of coins struck in 1965 to commemorate the 400th anniversary of the Lima Mint. The obverse design is a replica of an 8 reales coin of the type struck at Lima in 1565.

The 20 soles of 1966 displays the Our Lady of Victory statue that stands in Lima and was struck to mark the centenary of the Spanish bombardment of Callao, the port of Lima on the Pacific.

The coins now in general circulation (brass 5, 10 and 25 centavos, and $\frac{1}{2}$ and 1 sol values) all have an arms in wreath obverse; the centavos specimens have the value and flowers on the reverse, while the two higher denominations have the value and a llama.

Peru's current 1 sol shows a vicuna which, related to the llama and alpaca, provides a fine and highly prized wool. A cantuta flower is shown on the 25 centavos.

A 4 pesos gold piece of the type issued in 1861-68 by Spanish Queen Isabella II for the Philippines.

Philippine Islands

A group of more than 7,000 islands in the southwest Pacific, the Philippines were ruled by Spain from about 1565 until the end of the Spanish-American War in 1898, when they passed to the United States. The Philippines gained partial freedom in 1935 and became completely independent in 1946.

These 1903 coins of the Philippines portray a standing female figure representing "Filipinas," with the Mayon volcano in the background and a workman with an anvil. Both coins, inscribed with the American shield on the reverse, were struck at the Philadelphia Mint.

Spain first issued a distinctive coinage for the Philippines under Charles III in 1766 in the form of copper quartos. The quartos featured a crowed castle design and the inscription "CIUDAD D MAN(ILA)"; the reverse had the arms of the Philippines consisting of a lion with sword, and crown. During the early 1800's, Philippine coinage continued to be mainly of

General Douglas MacArthur, under whose command American armies liberated the Philippines from the Japanese in 1944, is honored on the silver 50 centavos and 1 peso coins of 1947.

This 1967 peso commemorates the 25th anniversary of the ill-fated American-Filipino defense of Bataan Peninsula on the island of Luzon, one of the most heroic actions of World War II.

copper quartos, the usual types having a crowned lion on the obverse, and the Spanish arms on the reverse.

Isabella II (1833–70) and Alfonso XII (1875–85) both strengthened Philippine coinage by issuing silver and gold pieces. Isabella struck 1, 2 and 4 pesos values in gold, while Alfonso struck a 4 pesos gold. The silver peso of Alfonso XIII, dated 1897, was the last Spanish coin minted for the Philippines.

The Islands' coins for 1903–19 were struck at the Philadelphia and San Francisco mints, and since 1920 they have been produced at the new mint in Manila.

The Filipino Heroes issue of 1967 shows some of the patriots who fought for Philippine independence during the 400 years of Spanish rule. The coins picture Marcelo H. del Pilar (50 sentimos), Juan Luna (25 sentimos), Francisco Baltazar (10 sentimos), Melchora Aguino (5 sentimos) and Chief Lapu-Lapu (1 sentimo).

Philippine Islands ✌ 351

Platinum Coins

Following the discovery of platinum in the Andes Mountains of South America (in the Choco district of Colombia, then under Spanish control) in 1735, Spain became the first country to use this precious metal for coinage. Since that time, a number of other countries—including Denmark, France, Germany, Great Britain, the Netherlands, Poland, Russia and the United States—have used the white metal for the striking of coins, patterns, or medals; but Spain's record of 18 different coin issues between 1747 and 1904 is unmatched. Many collectors, however, classify the Spanish pieces as patterns.

When first discovered, platinum was highly prized because it could be produced only in small quantities, though less than a century later, it became so plentiful many mines were actually abandoned because they produced too much platinum. Over the past two centuries the price of platinum has fluctuated wildly. A decade ago the metal was worth approximately three times as much as gold, or about $105.00 per ounce. In July, 1968, the price of platinum was quoted at $300.25 per ounce, an all time high, but since that time the price has settled to approximately $150.00.

Platinum, commonly referred to as "white gold," is slightly heavier than gold. The name is derived from the Spanish word "platina," diminutive form of "plata," silver. Like gold it may be hammered into thin sheets and drawn into a slender wire.

In 1819, large quantities of platinum were discovered in the Ural Mountains of Russia, and for a 17-year period, from 1828 to 1845, a regular issue of platinum coins was struck at the Leningrad Mint. Denominations were 3, 6 and 12 rubles. At this time, however, platinum had a bullion value of only about $7.50 per ounce, and thus a 3 ruble piece had a face value of about $2.32. Today the bullion value of that coin is over $50.00—this same item also has a collector's value of more than $200.00.

Russia produced nearly 1,400,000 platinum coins during those 17 years, and finally stopped all coinage in that metal because these coins never really became popular with the people, and also because the bullion value was gradually sinking. Moreover, platinum was not suited for large-scale mintage because the metal was difficult to melt and not easily wrought. Counterfeiting became a major problem. Russian platinum pieces were plated with gold and passed off as the then more valuable gold coins of the same size. It was possible to fool even the most alert bank tellers

Czar Nicholas I's platinum coins were similar to his gold pieces but the denominations were different. The inscription around the reverse of the platinum pieces means "pure platinum of the Urals." Mintages for the 1829 6 rubles and the 1832 12 rubles were low (628 and 1,102 pieces respectively), but 50,002 specimens were struck of the 1845 3 rubles piece.

and merchants with these counterfeits since platinum and gold were of nearly the same weight.

Even more remarkable is the fact that platinum counterfeits of United States $5 and $10 gold pieces were made in the middle of the 19th century. Platinum was used as the "base" metal, and then plated with gold.

After 1880, however, the price of platinum began skyrocketing in value, and this type of counterfeiting came to a sudden end. By 1900, when platinum's value tripled that of gold, counterfeiting in a few cases went the other way. Gold coins were plated with platinum and passed off as genuine platinum coins.

Regular issue platinum coins were never struck by the United States Mint, but many varieties of commemorative medals in platinum have been issued by an assortment of private companies.

Platinum is now so expensive, that no country has made coins of this metal for the past two-thirds of a century, and chances are slim that it will ever be used again. The few coins struck of platinum thus hold a unique place in numismatics.

The silver denier (left) of Prince Mieszko I, struck at Poznan in 963, is Poland's first coin. Interestingly enough, Mieszko is shown a thousand years later with his Princess, Dabrowka, on the 100 zlotych (right) struck at the Warsaw mint in 1966 commemorating Poland's millennium as a Christian state.

Poland

The first coin issued by Poland was a silver denier struck by Prince Mieszko I at Poznan in 963. Mieszko (960–92) was the country's first effective ruler and succeeded in unifying and Christianizing Poland during the years that he was in power.

Boleslav I Chrobry, "The Brave," son of Mieszko I, succeeded his father in 992 as ruler of Poland. It was Boleslav who firmly established his nation as an independent kingdom. He extended the boundaries of Poland from the Baltic Sea on the north to the Black Sea on the south, and established the western borders in the vicinity of the present day Berlin, while the eastern boundaries were near Moscow. He thus created one of the largest and most powerful states Europe has ever known. He had himself crowned as Poland's first king in 1025.

The appearance of Poland's coins depended largely on how the state was prospering at the time. The bracteates of the 12th and 13th centuries, for example, are so thin that they usually must be picked up with a pair of tweezers. Poland's early bracteates were generally struck from silver

Another interesting contrast is provided by the silver denier (left) of Boleslaw I Chrobry, "the Brave," struck about A.D. 1000 and the 10 and 20 zlotych gold pieces of 1925 which mark the 900th anniversary of his being crowned the first king of Poland.

354 ❧ Poland

and uniface. The bracteates were in vogue until the latter part of the 14th century when they were supplanted by the groschen.

The first solid Polish silver "groszy" were produced under Casimir III, "The Great" (1333–70), who established mints throughout Poland to augment the work of the crown or royal mint at Krakow.

This silver groschen of 1531 minted at Gdansk (Danzig) bears the portrait of Sigismund I (1506-48).

This 1549 silver ½ groschen was struck for Lithuania by Sigismund II August (1548-72) at a time when the crowns of Poland and Lithuania were united.

Although King Ladislas Lokietek struck Poland's first gold coin in about 1310, it was not until the time of Sigismund III that gold coins were minted on any large scale. As Poland prospered during the Renaissance and into the modern era, it continued to issue a wide variety of gold coins from several mints. John Casimir (1648–58), for example, struck a handsome set of five gold pieces ranging in denomination from a half ducat to ten ducats.

Sigismund III (Vasa) (1587-1632) shown on this 1627 taler struck a magnificent series of gold and silver portrait coins during his reign, in which Poland reached its peak as a European power.

Poland ❧ 355

The half-length armored figure of King Vladislav IV (1632-48) is shown on this ornately engraved taler.

John III Sobieski (reigned 1674–96) revitalized Poland's coinage during his 22 years on the throne. Best known for his great victory over the Turks at Vienna in 1683, he struck many medals in commemoration of that achievement.

John III Sobieski is shown on the 1679 silver orte (18 groschen).

Poland's talers of the 17th and 18th centuries are of particular interest. Many have square (referred to as a "klippe") or hexagonal shapes. One of the most unusual of all the talers is the famous "Butterfly" specimen

King Augustus III struck this unusual "butterfly" taler in 1733 as a memorial to his father Augustus II. The butterfly's triple wings symbolize the cycle of life—birth, life and death.

struck in 1733 by order of King Augustus III after the death of his father, August II. The symbolic butterfly on the coin's obverse is triple-winged with the wings representing the cycle of life—birth, life and death.

By the end of the 18th century, Poland's political fortunes had waned and in a series of three partitions—in 1772, 1793 and 1795—the country was divided up between Russia, Prussia and Austria with the largest

This 1825 silver 10 zlotych portrays Russian Czar Alexander I although it was struck at the Warsaw mint, and inscribed in Polish for circulation in Poland.

share going to Russia. At first the Russian czars permitted Polish inscriptions on the coinage, but after the insurrection of 1830–31, Czar Nicholas II discontinued anything that resembled a separate Polish coinage. After the third revolt in 1863, Czar Alexander II succeeded in completely shutting down the Warsaw Mint.

The BOZEDOPOMOZ inscription on the 6 groszy siege coin struck for the Zamosc fortress in 1813 means "God Help Us!"

Poland ❧ 357

A number of siege coins were issued during this troubled period. Among the most famous Polish siege pieces are those struck for the fortress at Zamosc during both the 1813 and 1830–31 insurrections. The 10 groszy specimen in billon of 1831 has the inscription, "BOZEDOPOMOZ," meaning "God Help Us!"

The silver 10 zlotych of 1932 was struck during the brief period between the two World Wars when Poland was an independent republic. The white eagle is the country's national emblem.

Poland regained its sovereignty in 1918 at the end of World War I. During the past half-century Poland has produced an array of fine coins, both regular and commemorative issues with the Warsaw Mint now one of Europe's busiest. A number of commemorative pieces were minted in the 1930's. These include: the 5 zlotych silver of 1930 to mark the centennial of the revolt against the Czar in 1830; the 10 zlotych silver of 1933 to celebrate the 250th anniversary of Sobieski's victory over the Turks at Vienna; a 10 zlotych silver in 1933 to recall the 70th anniversary of the insurrection against the Czar in 1863; and the 5 and 10 zlotych silver of 1934 to commemorate the 20th anniversary of the founding of Marshal Pilsudski's Rifle Corps in World War I.

The 250th anniversary of John III Sobieski's victory over the Turks in 1683 was recalled with the silver 10 zlotych struck in 1933.

358 ⚬ Poland

The 1966 10 zlotych piece marks both the 700th anniversary of Warsaw and the 200th anniversary of the city's mint.

The Polish astronomer, Nicolaus Copernicus (1473-1543), portrayed on the 1959 10 zlotych, proved that the earth revolved around the sun.

The Polish scientist Marie Curie, the first woman to win a Nobel Prize, is honored on the 1967 10 zlotych piece marking the centennial of her birth.

Poland's commemoratives of recent years include: the Kosciuszko and Copernicus portrait pieces of 1959; two varieties issued in 1964 to mark the 600th anniversary of the founding of the great Jagiellonian University at Krakow; and two varieties struck in 1965 to commemorate the 700th anniversary of Warsaw. All are 10 zlotych coins minted in copper-nickel.

Marie Sklodowska-Curie was portrayed on a 10-zlotych portrait piece in 1967. This coin, issued to mark the centenary of Madame Curie's birth, pays tribute to one of Poland's greatest scientists. Among her many achievements, Madame Curie discovered the elements radium and polonium, and she became the first two-time winner of the Nobel Prize.

The legend inscribed on the 1957 1 zloty piece is POLSKA RZECZPOS-POLITA LUDOWA—the "Polish People's Republic."

Portugal

Portuguese coinage dates from the establishment of the kingdom by Alfonso I (1139–85). In 1139, at the battle of Ourique Alfonso defeated the Moors and took the title King of Portugal. He established Portugal as a free and sovereign state and founded a dynasty that held the throne for 460 years.

Though Portugal is a relatively small country, her position on the western section of the Iberian Peninsula led her to become one of the world's greatest sea powers. Portugal's age of discovery began through the dynamism of Prince Henry the Navigator (1394–1460).

The caravel shown on this 1964 5 escudos is the type of ship used by the Portuguese to win a vast overseas empire. Prince Henry the Navigator, the guiding genius of Portugal's efforts to master the oceans, is shown on the 5 escudos struck in 1960 to mark the 500th year of his death.

Prince Henry was fascinated with the idea of sending ships down the west coast of Africa in an attempt to find a passage to India and the Spice Islands. Prince Henry's ambition was to eliminate the Arab and Italian middlemen, who up to that time were indispensable in bringing spices to Europe, and to concentrate this trade through Portugal's excellent harbors on the Atlantic. He planned many expeditions—every ship sent out to Africa between 1418 and his death 42 years later was under his supervision.

The great Portuguese navigators Bartholmew Diaz and Vasco da Gama continued Prince Henry's work of exploration. Diaz in 1487 rounded the

John II (1481-95) struck this cruzado of gold taken from Guinea on the African coast. The inscriptions give his title as "King of Portugal and Algarve, Lord of Guinea."

tip of Africa at the "Cape of Storms," a name he changed later to the Cape of Good Hope. When da Gama arrived on the Malabar (west) coast of India in 1498, he crowned his nation's efforts of almost a century.

Portuguese exploreres under Pedro Alvares Cabral headed for the New World as well, founding Brazil which remained a Portuguese colony until 1822.

Philip II, Spanish ruler of Portugal (1580-98), struck this gold tostao for his Portuguese domains bearing the reverse inscription IN HOC SIGNO VINCES— "By this sign, thou shalt conquer."

Despite the technical skills of the Portuguese in navigation, they were unable to retain a pre-eminent position as a world power for any length of time. At the death of King Henriques the Cardinal in 1580, Portugal fell under Spanish rule for 60 years.

The 4 escudos gold piece, such as this 1822 specimen issued by John VI (1816-26), was commonly referred to as a "half Joe" because of its inscription (from the Portuguese word Joao for John). 8 escudos was a "Joe."

Portugal ❧ 361

The Napoleonic Wars led to a long period of unrest in Portugal; as a consequence Brazil was lost as a colony early in the 19th century. After a great deal of political strife, Portugal became a republic in 1910.

Since the time of Sancho I, Portugal has produced a wide variety of gold coins at its various mints. Its gold coinage covers a period of approximately eight centuries with the last specimen, a 5 escudos piece, being struck in 1920.

After the discovery of gold in Brazil in 1690, vast quantities of the yellow metal were brought back to Lisbon where a good deal of it was converted to coin at the Mint, the "Casa da Moeda." Peter II (1683–1706), John V (1706–50), and Joseph I (1750–77) all had many gold pieces minted. It was John V who began the practice of having the monarch's portrait placed on coins.

The Casa da Moeda managed to survive Lisbon's historic earthquake of 1755. Many of the mint workers were cited for bravery in assisting persons who were trapped in wreckage, for helping to quell fires, etc.

Portugal's silver crowns have long been popular with collectors because of their beauty. The crowns, like the gold pieces, constitute a regal coinage, with the monarch's portrait and the coat-of-arms on the reverse.

Maria II (1828-53) appears wearing a fashionable, upswept hairdo on this 1835 4 escudos gold piece.

The silver 1 escudo struck in 1914 commemorates the founding of the Portuguese Republic in 1910. The figure of Freedom on the obverse carries the torch of liberty in her right hand.

The earlier silver coins usually carry a crown-type obverse rather than the monarch's portrait.

Many of the modern Portuguese coins recall the country's long and proud history. The 200, 500 and 1000 reis silver pieces of 1898 mark the

The completion of the new Salazar Bridge spanning the Tagus River at Lisbon was commemorated on this silver 20 escudos of 1966.

400th anniversary of the great Voyages of Discovery. The 10 escudos silver of 1928 commemorates Alfonso's victory over the Moors at the Battle of Ourique. The 5, 10 and 20 escudos silver specimens of 1960 mark the 500th anniversary of the death of Prince Henry the Navigator.

Over the centuries, Portugal has also struck many coins for her overseas territories.

The 1 escudo showing the head of the Republic has been current in Portugal since 1927. The coat-of-arms on the 20 centavos shows the Cross of Redemption (Quinas Cross) made up of five shields arranged in a diagonal cross.

Portugal ❧ 363

Rarities

In recent years, numismatic rarities have commanded considerable attention in the world numismatic press as record-breaking prices have been realized in both public auctions and private sales.

In regard to American coins, three factors have been of paramount importance. These are: (a) the stress on trying to assemble a complete series of a given type; (b) variations in the annual amounts issued by the mints, making some dates and/or mint marks much more inaccessible and expensive than others; (c) the strength of the demand for the coins, often expressed in a lifelong specialization in a single series. For these reasons, American numismatics abound in glamorous rarities. Following is a partial list of some of them, along with estimated valuations for specimens in the best possible condition available:

Cent: 1793 Wreath type; (strawberry leaf variety); 1856 Flying Eagle; 1914-D Lincoln Head. Standard catalogues simply label the strawberry leaf varieites as being "extremely rare" without placing an exact valuation. The 1856 Flying Eagle catalogues for nearly $3,000.00 in proof condition, while the 1914-D goes for nearly $600.00 in uncirculated. Though the mintage for the 1914-D was 1,193,000, its rarity in uncirculated condition determines the value. The 1909-S, V. D. B. Lincoln cent (mintage, 484,000), although more valuable in used condition catalogues for only about $225.00 in uncirculated.

Two cents: 1864 small motto. This piece catalogues for nearly $300.00 in uncirculated. The common large motto variety brings $25.00 in new condition, about $2.50 in good.

Nickel five cents: 1913 Liberty Head (unofficial issue). Only five specimens are known. One of them was purchased by a U.S. dealer for

A mintage of 10,000 1876 Carson City 20¢ pieces was recorded but only a few copies are known since most of them were melted at the mint. One specimen brought $12,750.00 at a recent auction.

$46,000.00 at the 1967 American Numismatic Association convention auction sale.

Dime: 1894-S Liberty Head. Mintage, 24. One of the few specimens extant sold for $12,250.00 at the 1965 "Century Sale."

Twenty cents: 1876-CC. Though the mintage was 10,000, few copies are known. One of the finest known specimens brought $12,750.00 at the 1966 "Waldorf Sale."

Although mint records show that some 4,000 turban type quarters were struck in 1827, only six or seven specimens are actually known.

Quarter dollar: 1827 Turban type; 1873-CC Liberty Seated type without arrows at date. Only six or seven of the 1827 "curled base" Turban types are known, and standard catalogues usually do not attempt to give exact valuations. The Carson City Mint struck 4,000 quarter dollars of this 1873 variety and a specimen in uncirculated condition would likely realize $3,000.00.

Half dollar: 1838-O Turban Head type; 1853-O, 1866 (unique proof) Liberty Seated type. Only 20 specimens of the 1838-O Turban Head type were struck; one of them sold for $14,000.00 at the Charles Jay Sale in

Only twenty 1838 New Orleans half-dollars are believed to have been minted for presentation purposes (no official record exists).

Rarities ⚜ 365

The "King of American Rarities," the 1804 dollar.

1967. The 1853-O is simply listed as "extremely rare," while the 1866 unique proof realized $15,500.00 at the 1961 Hydeman Sale.

Dollar (silver): 1794, 1804 Bust type; 1836–39 Gobrecht design; 1851; 1866 (no motto), 1870-S Liberty Seated type. Mintage for the 1794 dollar was 1,758; an uncirculated specimen catalogues for over $12,500.00. The 1804 "original" dollars were actually struck at the Philadelphia Mint between 1834–35 for use in presentation proof sets. The 1804 dollar, called "The King of American Rarities," has an estimated value of approximately $50,000.00.

The 1836–39 Gobrecht dollars are classified as patterns. In value they are catalogued at well over $3,500.00 to "extremely rare." The 1851 "original" dollar, mintage 1,300, has a value in excess of $2,500.00 in proof. Only two specimens are known of the 1866 "no motto" dollar. One of them realized $15,000.00 at the 1967 Charles Jay Sale. No mintage figures are given for the extremely rare 1870-S dollar; one specimen realized $12,000.00 at the 1963 Wolfson Sale.

Trade Dollar: 1884, 1885. These were not known to numismatists until 1908. It has been determined that 10 proof copies were struck in

Only five 1885 trade dollars were struck, all in proof condition.

1884, and 5 in proof for 1885. The 1884 specimen brought $8,750.00 at the 1963 Wolfson Sale, while the 1885 piece is catalogued at about $9,000.00

Dollar (*gold*): 1849-C Liberty Head type. Only two specimens of the Charlotte Mint 1849 "Open Wreath" gold dollars are known. One of those specimens brought $6,000.00 at the 1956 A. N. A. Sale. The value is undoubtedly higher today.

Only two specimens of the 1870-S $3 gold pieces are known to have been minted, one placed in the cornerstone of the old San Francisco mint and never recovered. The specimen illustrated is now in the Eliasberg Collection.

Three-dollar gold: 1870-S (unique); 1875. Only two three-dollar gold pieces were struck at San Francisco in 1870. The only known specimen is held in a private collection. The 1875 three-dollar gold in proof (mintage, 20) brought a record $24,000.00 at the 1968 A. N. A. Sale.

Four-dollar gold: All issues (Stella patterns). There are four varieties of the four-dollar gold pattern pieces: 1879 "Flowing Hair" (mintage, 415); 1879 "Coiled Hair" (10); 1880 "Flowing Hair" (15); and 1880 "Coiled Hair" (10). Though standard catalogues don't usually assign exact valuations to these pieces, they often realize up to and well over five figure prices when they are offered at public auction.

The recorded mintage for the 1879 "coiled hair" variety four-dollar "Stella" pattern is 10 pieces.

Half Eagle ($5 *gold*): 1815, 1822, 1829 (large and small dates) Turban Head type; 1854-S Coronet type. The 1815 (mintage, 635) has a valuation of $6,500.00 upwards. Though mint records indicate that some 17,796 half eagles were struck in 1822, only three specimens are known. The 1829 small date brought $21,500.00 at the 1963 "Florida Sale." The 1854-S (mintage, 268) fetched $16,500.00 at the 1963 Wolfson Sale—this was for a specimen in extremely fine condition.

Eagle: 1798 overstrike on 1797 Liberty Cap type; 1858 Coronet type. The 1798 overstrike on 1797, 7 stars left, 6 right (mintage, 842) is valued

Production of the $20 double eagle began in 1850 but two pattern specimens dated 1849 were struck. Only one is now known and this unique piece is now on display at the Smithsonian Institution's Hall of Coins and Medals in Washington, D.C.

at some $8,500.00 in uncirculated. The 1858 (mintage, 2,521) is rated at about $6,000.00 in uncirculated.

Double Eagle: 1849, 1861-S (Paquet reverse) Coronet type; 1907 plain edge, large lettering on edge—Saint-Gaudens type. The 1849 double eagle is unique and is housed in the U. S. Mint Collection. The 1861 Paquet reverse specimen is classified as "extremely rare." The 1907 Saint Gaudens, large letters on edge, in proof, is unique.

Among the coin rarities of other countries, the following list are especially noteworthy:

Rome, Emperor Maximianus, ten-aurei gold, struck at Trier in A.D. 303. This gold portrait coin, issued by Maximianus as a presentation piece, realized $38,660.00 at a 1965 Lucerne auction, a record for any ancient coin.

Dies were prepared in 1877 for a $50 "half union" coin but only two pieces were struck in gold. These two pieces, fully an $\frac{1}{8}$th of an inch thick, are now at the Smithsonian, but were at one time held privately. Now priceless, they were sold in 1909 for $10,000.00 each, then a world's record price for a single coin.

Russia, Konstantine, 1825 silver ruble. In 1825, a silver ruble was struck at St. Petersburg bearing the portrait of Grand Duke Konstantine Pavlovich. This was done immediately after the death of Konstantine's brother Czar Alexander I (1801–25), but within a few days a younger brother, Nicholas I, succeeded to the throne. The excessively rare Konstantine ruble was never released for circulation and only a few specimens are known. One specimen sold for $11,650.00 at an October, 1964 Lucerne, Switzerland auction, and another brought $41,000.00 at a November, 1965 New York City auction. Until the sale of the 1913 Liberty nickel in 1967, this was the highest price ever paid at public auction for a coin.

Russian Grand Duke Konstantine Pavlovich is portrayed on an extremely rare 1825 silver ruble. This specimen brought $41,000.00 at a November 1965 New York auction.

Great Britain, William IV, 5 pounds, 1831. Not placed in circulation, specimens of this rare pattern catalogue at $7,500.00.

Spain, Philip IV, 100 escudos gold, struck in 1633 at the Segovia Mint. The obverse of this famous and extremely rare coin carries Philip's ornate and crowned arms, while the reverse has a cross with castles and lions in the angles. One of the finest known specimens of this gold piece sold for $37,200.00 at a June, 1968 Amsterdam auction.

Poland, Sigismund III, 100 ducats gold, 1621. The obverse portrays Sigismund III in damascened armor, wearing the collar of the Golden Fleece; the reverse has the king's highly ornate crowned shield. This is most likely the largest European gold coin ever struck, its weight of 348 grams equal to about 230 Dollars U.S. gold. A V.F. specimen was offered at $9,000.00 in 1956 but would likely realize several times that amount if offered today.

Rarities ❧ 369

Bohemia, Ferdinand III, 100 ducats gold, 1629. One of the largest gold coins ever struck, and one of Europe's outstanding rarities, this specimen has on obverse the portrait of Ferdinand in high ruff collar and armor; reverse has the king's arms. Ferdinand was King of Hungary 1625–57, King of Bohemia 1629–57, and Holy Roman Emperor 1637–57.

This unique gold 100 ducat piece was struck in 1629 for the coronation of Ferdinand III, King of Hungary and Bohemia.

Rare coins of all sorts command attention in the numismatic press and are often the topic of conversation among collectors. Even if most of them are beyond the resources of the ordinary collector, they are seldom out of his dreams.

The Roman "aes signatum" from 350-300 B.C. are generally regarded as Rome's earliest recognizable form of money. The obverse of this specimen which weighs about five pounds shows an elephant, the reverse the figure of a pig.

Rome

The Romans struck so many coins—literally millions of them—that they are now still common among collectors. Ancient Rome produced coins for more than 800 years, from about 350 B.C. until the fall of the Empire in the West in A.D. 476.

Rome minted its first coins with identifying marks in the middle of the fourth century B.C. the first known specimens are the so-called "aes signatum" (the Latin "*aes*" means bronze), which was really more of an ingot than a coin. Measuring about 3 and $\frac{3}{4}$ by 7 inches, and weighing nearly 5 pounds, these rectangular bars had designs on both sides. The designs had meaning for the Romans. Among the symbols used was an ox. Cattle had such a high value in early Rome that they constituted the chief barter item. Because of great difficulties in transporting cattle, these cast bronze bars representing them came to be recognized as a medium of exchange.

Shortly after the "aes signatum" pieces were produced, the Romans made their first round moneys, the "aes grave," or "heavy bronze," which weighed a Roman pound (or "libra") equalling 12 ounces. (Our own abbreviation for pound, "lb." comes from this libra.) The aes grave pieces, which were also cast, showed the figure of Janus, the two-headed god of beginnings and endings for whom the month of January was named. The reverse shows the prow of a ship, a tribute to Rome's power on the sea.

This large cast bronze coin of 325-275 B.C., is called an "aes grave," meaning heavy bronze.

The Semis

The Triens

The Quadrans

The Sextans   The Uncia

The denominations of the Roman *aes grave* series are indicated by the dots
. . . each dot signifying 1/12th part of the *as*.

Rome ❧ 373

The earliest Roman coins were of cast bronze since this metal was readily found throughout the Italian peninsula. As Rome grew in importance, it required a silver coinage that would be recognized not only in Italy, but throughout the Mediterranean area as well. For a time Rome emulated the issues of other countries, particularly Greece. The Greeks had long used the silver drachma, a coin accepted everywhere.

The silver didrachm was the standard silver coin during the period 222-187 B.C. The Janus head obverse was borrowed from the early bronze coins, but the reverse design showing a quadriga or four-horse chariot reflects the Roman's love of racing.

Rome's first silver coinage, the didrachm was produced in 269 B.C. These were soon replaced by the silver denarius and sestertius. The denarius was equal to ten bronze asses and the sestertius was worth $2\frac{1}{2}$ asses. The silver quinarius, which came a little later, had a value of 5 asses.

The silver denarius served as the principal silver coin of Rome from 187 B.C. until about A.D. 300. The first issues portrayed Roma, guardian of the city and, on the reverse, the Dioscuri or Heavenly Twins ("Dios of Zeus," meaning "Boys of Zeus"), who were sacred to Rome. The two boys, known as Castor and Pollux, are credited with having led Roman armies to victory. Castor and Pollux are shown on horseback charging with levelled spears, their mantles flowing behind them and their conical hats surmounted by a star, emblematic of morning and evening.

The denarius, equal in value to ten of the large bronze pieces, was the principal silver coin of Rome from 187 B.C. until about A.D. 300. This specimen from c. 150 B.C. shows the goddess Roma and the Dioscuri, the Heavenly Twins.

At the end of the Punic Wars (the series of three wars against the Carthaginians which were fought intermittently from 264 to 146 B.C.), Rome was on the verge of bankruptcy, with the result that the weight of the coinage was constantly being reduced. The cast bronze aes shrunk from a coin nearly three inches in diameter to less than one inch.

Because of inflation, the Roman cast bronze coins were steadily reduced in size and weight. Compare this bronze aes, from about 200 B.C., with the original size of the denomination shown on p. 372.

The ultimate Roman victory over Carthage made a reorganization of the coinage possible. From this point on, all coins were struck from dies, no more of them were cast. The silver denarius became the basic coin and gold pieces were struck for the first time.

Silver denarius of the Cassia family struck in 57 B.C. portraying the head of Vesta, goddess of Family Life, with her temple on the reverse.

This silver denarius from 100-91 B.C. portrays Mars, the war god, with a legionnaire battling a barbarian on the reverse.

Under the Republic (which lasted for nearly five centuries, from 509 to 27 B.C.), the Roman Senate was vested with the authority to issue coins. Actual production of moneys was given over to three officials, the triumvers. They were appointed annually to one-year terms and their chief responsibility was to supervise the state slaves who struck the coins.

At first the denarii gave no sign of the individual moneyer's name. These are called "consular coins," since they were probably issued by authority of the consuls themselves. By about 150 B.C., however, the name or initials of the mint masters began to appear on the coins. Names were probably used to ascertain responsibility in the event underweight, debased, or counterfeit coins were discovered. On the other hand, they also served as a mark of honor to the moneyer and his family. Nearly 200 families' names appear on coins minted in the period 150–27 B.C.

Rome ⚜ 375

Denarius of Lucius Roscius Fabatus (58-55 B.C.) with serrated edges meant to show that the coin was precious metal throughout, not just silver plated.

Roman moneyers sometimes issued their coins with "nicked" or serrated edges so that anyone could tell at a glance they were made of solid gold or silver, not merely plated. These serrations were made by hand, a time-consuming task with more than twenty of them on each coin. The nicked edge also discouraged counterfeiting and was a fore-runner of the milled edge, so common on precious-metal coins minted in recent times.

Gold aureus of L. Cornelius Sulla, dictator of Rome (82-79 B.C.), with the helmeted head of Roma and Sulla himself in a quadriga being crowned by Victory.

Denarius with a bareheaded portrait of Pompey the Great issued by his sons after his death in 48 B.C. On the reverse is a galley with sails and rowers.

When Roman armies were conquering all of the world known in the second and first centuries B.C., the Senate bestowed the title "Imperator" on the generals in command of the legions. They were also given or they assumed the right to strike coins from captured bullion. Thus, in many cases, the legions became the armies of the commanding generals rather than armies of the state. This struggle between legion commanders and the state eventually led to the establishment of the Empire.

Defying the Senate's order not to bring his army into Italy, Julius Caesar crossed the Rubicon in 48 B.C. and soon after established himself as dictator. He continued to mint his own coins, thus assuring the con-

Silver denarius of Julius Caesar struck c. 49 B.C. The elephant trampling a serpent is symbolic of Caesar's victory in Gaul, which brought present-day France and Belgium under Roman control.

Silver denarius of 44 B.C. showing the head of Julius Caesar. The Roman Senate granted him the extraordinary honor of being the first living man portrayed on a Roman coin.

tinued loyalty of his troops. Julius Caesar, who named the month of July for himself, struck a great volume of coins in gold, silver and bronze. During the last year of his life he took for himself the extraordinary honor of showing his portrait on the current coinage struck at the Rome Mint. These were the first Roman coins to show the likeness of a living man. The coin also bore the inscription CAESAR DIVUS ("Caesar God"). Caesar was assassinated on the Ides (15th) of March, 44 BC., as he entered the Senate Building to receive yet one more title.

Shortly thereafter, Brutus, one of the assassins, issued an historic coin with a dagger on the reverse which served as a public declaration of the murder of Caesar.

This silver denarius of c. 42 B.C. bears the head of Brutus. The reverse shows a liberty cap between two daggers with the inscription EID(ibus) MAR(tiis), meaning the "Ides of March"—the day on which Caesar was assassinated.

In the struggle for power that followed Caesar's death, the principal antagonists were Mark Antony, Caesar's most trusted general in Gaul, and Octavian, Caesar's grandnephew and adopted son and heir. Antony and Octavian were forced to share power and the Empire was divided between them. In a showdown at the naval battle of Actium fought in 31 B.C., Octavian won a great victory, leaving him undisputed master of the Roman state. Octavian (who took the name Augustus) received the title of Emperor in 29 B.C.

Mark Antony and Octavian are shown on this Roman denarius of c. 42 B.C.

This denarius of 32-31 B.C. was struck to pay the troops of Mark Antony. The reverse of each coin was inscribed with the number of a legion, ranging from LEG 1 to LEG XIX.

Rome ❧ 377

Bronze as of Tiberius (A.D. 14-37), with laureate head of the emperor and a globe with rudder attached on the reverse. This coin reveals that the Romans knew the world was round.

Gold aureus of Caesar Augustus (27 B.C.-A.D. 14) showing the emperor's laureate head. The reverse shows Caius Caesar, the emperor's adopted son, on a galloping horse.

Ruling for 43 years, Augustus struck a great variety of coins. One of his first measures had been to set up a series of 18 mints throughout the Empire. The initials "s.c.," were inscribed on the reverses of bronze coins issued by Augustus. In 2 B.C., Augustus abolished the office of the *monetarii*; taking over the coinage of gold and silver as a privilege of the emperor, while leaving the striking of bronze to the Senate. This privilege was denoted by the letters "s.c.," to the Senate, meaning literally by order of the Senate. These letters also served to differentiate the bronze coins of Rome from those issued in the provinces.

A comet is depicted on the reverse of this portrait denarius of Augustus Caesar struck to commemorate the deification of Julius Caesar. The inscription DIVVS IVLIVS means "Divine Julius."

Augustus' successor, Tiberius, who was emperor during the time of Christ, was a just and able ruler during the first portion of his reign, but in his old age, fearful of plots against his life, he carried on a brutal reign of terror. All Rome breathed a sigh of relief when the lonely and sinister old man finally died at the age of 79. A common type silver denarius of Tiberius (A.D. 14-37) is known as the "Tribute Penny" because of its connection with a Biblical text (see Biblical Coins). Augustus reorganized the coinage completely, with bronze coins again playing an important part in the monetary scheme. The largest coin was the sestertius worth one-fourth of a silver denarius. A smaller brass coin, the dupondius, was valued at half a sestertius. A third coin, a bronze as, was equal to half a dupondius.

Bronze sestertius of Caligula (37-41). On the reverse, Caligula is shown addressing a group of soldiers.

Caligula (37–41) was one of the cruelest emperors in Roman and world history. He went completely insane and is said to have named his horse a Consul. In A.D. 41, when he was only 29 years old, Caligula was assassinated by the Praetorian Guard.

Nero's bad reputation is well known even today. He persecuted the Christians, poisoned the nobleman Brittanicus, had his wife Octavia murdered, poisoned his mother Agrippina, and climaxed his career by participating in a series of wild orgies. He was accused of setting fire to Rome and finally forced to commit suicide by the Praetorian Guard in A.D. 68. Nero's coins quite clearly show his huge head and great bull neck.

Brass dupondius of Nero (54-68) with a seated figure of Roma, the "genius" or spirit of Rome, on the reverse.

The Roman Empire reached its greatest extent under Trajan (98–117). In an age without newspapers or photographs, coins served to circulate the Emperor's likeness throughout the vast reaches of the provinces. During his reign, Trajan's portrait was unquestionably the best known in the entire world. The reverse of one of his sestertii shows the famous Circus Maximus. This great arena had a seating capacity of at least 140,000 during Julius Caesar's time, but over the years it fell into bad repair. Trajan ordered the structure restored, increasing the seating

Rome ❧ 379

The reverse of this bronze portrait sestertius of the Emperor Trajan (98-117) shows the Circus Maximus, the scene of the great chariot races. The huge arena seated 260,000 spectators.

capacity to 260,000. Some of Rome's greatest gladiatorial contests and chariot races were staged here during Trajan's reign. Most Roman citizens were unable to read so the Emperors often used the designs on their coins to advertise their victories and good deeds.

The Colosseum, whose ruins still stand in the heart of Rome, is seen on this sestertius of Titus (79-81).

The great baths in Rome whose ruins can be visited today were constructed during the turbulent six-year reign of Caracalla (211–217). Caracalla first ruled as joint emperor with his brother Geta although he later had him murdered. His one great constructive achievement was to declare all the males of the provinces Roman citizens. One of the results of this policy was to subject them to inheritance taxes, which could be levied only on Roman citizens. He introduced a new silver coin, the antoninianus, equal to two silver denarii but only $1\frac{1}{2}$ times the weight.

Antoninianus of Caracalla (211-17). This denomination was equivalent to two denarii and although struck of fine silver at first, its content was later greatly debased.

The year 238 was a most turbulent one in Roman politics for, in the course of those twelve months, no fewer than six men held the title of Emperor. Maximus Thrax, who had been in power since 235, was assassinated; Gordian I Africanus, his successor, a Proconsul in Africa, committed suicide; Gordian II, son of Gordian Africanus, was slain in battle; Balbinus, elected by the Senate as joint emperor with Pupienus was assassinated; Pupienus Maximus was also assassinated—in fact Balbinus and Pupienus were killed on the same day! Finally, Gordianus III Pius, grandson of Gordian I, became emperor in December 238 and he managed to remain in power for almost six years before he too was assassinated. All six of these emperors managed to strike coins during their brief reigns.

Maximinus Thrax, shown on this silver denarius, was one of six emperors to hold power in the year 238.

Denarii of Gordian I Africanus (left) and his son and co-emperor Gordian II Africanus (right).

Sestertius of Balbinus with the ironic legend "Concord among the Caesars."

Denarius of Pupienus (left) and an aureus of Gordianus III Pius (right), the only survivor of the bloody year 238.

Diocletian (284–305) is one of the few rulers in Roman history who "resigned" as emperor. On May 1, 305 he formally abdicated and retired to his palace on the Dalmatian coast where he lived quietly until his death in 316. He established an elaborate system of government known as the "Dominate" and had as many as three joint emperors ruling with him.

Diocletian also made some innovations in the coinage, revaluing the gold aureus and introducing a new, thinner bronze coin commonly called a "follis." The follis was the principal bronze coin for many years thereafter.

Constantine the Great (305–337) is best remembered as the first Roman emperor to embrace Christianity. Constantine also divided the Empire into two parts with a new, eastern capital in Byzantium which he renamed Constantinople (now Istambul). Constantine administered his division of the empire from his new capital, with an assistant emperor ruling in the West. In 312, he introduced a new gold piece, the solidus, at seventy-two to the pound (the aureus was only 60 pieces to the pound).

Gold aureus of Constantine the Great (305-37) struck at the Ticinum (Pavia) mint in northern Italy.

Gold solidus of Constantius II (337-361) struck at the mint in Constantinople.

In 395, the Roman nation was permanently divided into two independent empires. The Western Empire steadily declined and during its latter stages, mints in Italy were active only at Rome, Ravenna and Milan.

Romulus Augustulus, the last of the emperors, reigned until 476 when he was defeated by Odoacer, a Gothic chieftan. The Eastern Byzantine Empire, however, survived until 1453.

Arcadius (395-408) emperor of the Eastern Roman Empire at Constantinople, struck this gold solidus.

The Imperial Roman coins present a realistic portrait gallery of the 86 emperors from Augustus Caesar to the fall of the Empire under Romulus Augustulus in 476 B.C. In several cases the only representation we have of a Roman emperor is his portrait on a coin.

Other portraits have come down to us as well since members of the emperor's family were often depicted on coins. Julia (lived 39 B.C.–A.D. 14), daughter of Augustus who became the wife of Tiberius, was honored with her own coin. Several other emperors showed their wives, adopted heirs, daughters, sons, brothers, sisters or mothers on coins. Elagabalus (218–222) even issued a coin with the likeness of his grandmother.

Many emperors portrayed members of their families on coins, including the women of the court. These Roman ladies are: Julia Maesa, grandmother of Elagabalus (218-22) on a sestertius; Faustina the Younger, daughter of Antoninus Pius (138-61) on an aureus; and Otacilia Severa, wife of Philip I (244-49) on a dupondius.

Rome ❧ 383

The Romans often hid their money for safekeeping, and even armies on the march buried their captured gold and silver, expecting to pick it up after the battle. If they didn't return, however, the coins were not recovered. Thus, to this day their moneys are being unearthed, either through deliberate study and search along the Roman armies' lines of march, or by accident. Construction workers in England, farmers in France, and roadbuilders in Italy have brought Roman coins to the surface with pick, shovel and hoe. A typical hoard of more than 2,000 Roman silver denarii was unearthed in the summer of 1966 at the ancient city of Cosa, 70 miles north of Rome. The recovery operations for these coins was directed by the American Academy in Rome.

Roman coins often represent actions or ideas personified, that is, in human form. These personifications are: Fortuna—fortune, holding a cornucopia or horn of plenty; Pax—peace, with an olive branch; Fecunditas—fertility, holding two infants; Libertas—liberty or freedom, holding a pileus or cap of liberty; Pietas—piety or dutifulness, holding a patera, a sacrificial bowl, and a sceptre; Moneta—money or minting, holding a scale and cornucopia—of particular interest to numismatists.

Gold piece of Vladimir I, Grand Duke of Kiev (988-1015), shows a seated figure of the ruler and the bust of Christ crowned with a halo. Russian coins of this period were of Byzantine style.

Russia

Russia is by far the largest country in the world in respect to land area—over 8,000 miles wide and 5,000 miles deep at some points. Its history begins in the ninth century A.D. when the Russian Slavs began organizing a political community. The ruling house came to be known as Varangian with many of the Varangians believed to have been Viking Norsemen. The Varangians moved to Kiev in 972 where they ruled as

Silver coins of Vladimir I were similar to the gold pieces, but were struck on thinner, wider planchets. Vladimir, called "the Saint," helped introduce Christianity into Russia.

Dukes of Keiv. The Varangian princes of Kiev began to strike gold and silver coins in imitation of currencies of the Byzantine Empire.

Gold pieces are attributed to Vladimir I (988–1015) with the obverse showing his seated figure holding a sceptre accompanied by his name and title. The reverse has a facing bust of Christ with cross in nimbus. Vladimir also issued a series of silver coins, which, like the gold specimens,

Yaroslav I, Grand Duke of Kiev (1016-54), issued this silver piece bearing the portrait of Christ.

This gold piece was issued by Ivan III the Great, Grand Duke of Moscow (1462-1505), with the ruler and his sceptre on the obverse, a royal shield on the reverse.

were of a generally flat, spread fabric. In addition to coinage, Russia took from the Byzantine Empire its religion, its Greek-type alphabet (Cyrillic), its tendency toward autocratic government, and its imperial symbol of the double eagle.

Until the mid-15th century, the country was fragmented by a succession of internal disputes into small principalities. A number of native states and duchies (especially Moscow, Novgorod, Pskov, Tver and Riasan) achieved enough independence so that they were able to mint their own coins from sometime in the mid-1300's. These coins were mostly the eccentrically-shaped silver "wire" dengi. There are countless varieties of the wire dengi . . . in the principality of Muscovy they were to become the sole currency until the introduction of the ruble by Peter the Great. These specimens usually bore a rough portrait of St. George and the Dragon.

Silver "wire" denga of Basil III (1505-33) and a silver kopek of Ivan IV, "the Terrible" (1533-84). Both of these crude coins portray St. George and the Dragon, with Cyrillic alphabet reverse legends.

Ivan IV, "The Terrible" (1533–84), grandson of Ivan III, became Grand Duke of Moscow at the age of 3. He struck a series of undated gold coins . . . in values of 5 ducats, and in ½, 1, 2 and 4 grivnas. The 5 ducats specimen had the Russian eagle on both sides, while the others showed the eagle on obverse only, and the Czar's inscriptions on reverse. Though Ivan IV was possessed of terrifying lusts for blood and power—he also suffered from an acute persecution mania—he succeeded in laying the foundations for Russian sovereignty in Asia through the conquest and colonization of the vast reaches of Siberia.

Boris Godunov (1598–1605), brother-in-law of Fyodor, was elected by the boyars (nobles) as czar. The House of Godunov was short-lived since Fyodor II was murdered by the boyars shortly after he succeeded his father to the czardom. The period that followed (1605–13) was a time of great political unrest and is generally referred to as the "Times of Troubles" in Russian history. Boris Godunov struck a handsome ducat showing his bust with sceptre on obverse and the eagle on reverse. Boris' colorful reign became the basis for Pushkin's verse-drama *Boris Godunov*, which was later adapted by Mussorgsky as the basis for his famous opera *Boris Godunov*.

This gold 3 ducats of Michael I Romanov (1613-45), carries a crowned double eagle on each side. The center shield on the obverse depicts St. George on horseback, while the reverse shield has a riderless horse.

Michael Romanov became Czar in 1613, though his father, Patriarch Philaret, was the actual ruler until his death in 1633 . . . then Michael ruled in his own right for the next 12 years. The House of Romanov was to hold imperial power for more than 300 years until 1917 when Nicholas II, the last of the Romanovs, was overthrown by the Russian Revolution and subsequently executed.

Despite the fact that the czars always struck their own coinage, there were never really enough gold and silver pieces to go around during this period. Various gold ducats and silver talers of Western Europe saw wide circulation in Russia. In the period of Czar Alexei Mihailovitch (1645–76) especially, there were many types of foreign talers overstruck to produce silver rubles. The overstrike design sometimes consisted of the czar mounted on horseback on obverse and the double eagle within a square on reverse.

Peter I, "The Great" (1682–1725), the greatest of all the czars, instituted a full scale modernization of Russian coinage. A new mint was constructed at Moscow in 1711, and for the first time in the country's

Peter I "the Great" established a uniform coinage in 1704 based on a silver ruble standard, a coin which he first issued in that year.

history, coins were produced by mechanical means. In 1719 Peter ordered the minting machinery moved to his new capital at St. Petersburg where another mint was established. (St. Petersburg, now Leningrad, to this day remains the site of Russia's main mint.)

Peter, who structured a uniform coinage in all metals, issued Russia's first authentic silver ruble in 1704. This coin was divided into 100 kopecks and became the standard unit of currency throughout the huge country. He struck a set of gold coins in nine values, ranging from 1 to 12 ducats, all bearing his laureate bust, the crowned double eagle on the reverse. Under Peter, all coins were regularly dated in Arabic numerals for the first time.

Peter the Great's many gold coins include this 4 ducat specimen of 1714 showing the czar as a young man.

Elizabeth (Elizaveta) Petrovna (1741–62), a younger daughter of Peter the Great, issued new gold denominations in the form of 5, 10 and 20 ruble pieces.

Catherine II the Great (1762–96) ruled with considerable ability during her 34 years in power as she added new territories to Russia, including the Crimea at the expense of Turkey. Catherine maintained mints at

Silver ½ ruble of Catherine II (1762-96), also called "the Great." Catherine proved to be as ruthless as any of the czars.

St. Petersburg, Moscow, Ekaterinburg, Kolyvan and other cities. Her 5 and 10 ruble gold pieces have her bust facing right on obverse and an ornate cross of four shields on reverse. Catherine's most distinctive coin— one that is most frequently found in collections—is the large 5 kopecks copper with crowned monogram on obverse, and an eagle reverse having a scroll below inscribed in Russian with the coin's value.

Catherine's most distinctive coins are large copper 5 kopecks. This 1773 specimen is from the Kolyvan ("KM") Mint in Siberia.

Alexander I (1801–25) who led the Russian armies against Napoleon, gained a prestige that lasted for a good part of the 19th century. His 5 and 10 gold rubles, series of 1802–09, have on obverse an ornate cross of four shields, while the reverse has a four-line legend.

Nicholas I (1825–55) introduced Siberian platinum into Russian coinage, with platinum coins in 3, 6 and 12 ruble values being struck during the 1828–45 period. The total mintage reached nearly 1,400,000 pieces and this is the only time in numismatic history when any nation minted platinum coins for actual circulation. The obverse design features the

Russia ๑ 389

This 1836 1½ ruble coin struck in honor of the imperial family shows Czar Nicholos I (1825-55), Czarina Alexandra and their seven children: Alexander, Marie, Olga, Constantine, Nicholos, Michael and Alexandra (all grand dukes and grand duchesses).

Russian eagle with a triple crown; the reverse has simply the value, date and a rim inscription. Value of platinum at this time was rated at only little more than $7.00 per ounce, a far cry from the $105.00 and more per ounce it has commanded in recent years. This experimental coinage was not a success. Platinum was not really suited for large scale mintage because it was difficult to melt, the metal was intractable, and the supply was generally not plentiful.

Alexander II (1855–81), who was assassinated by terrorists at St. Petersburg, issued gold pieces having an eagle obverse in 3, 5 and 25 ruble values. However, the 25 rubles specimen was not placed into circulation. His copper and silver coins were struck with either his monogram or portrait on obverse.

Nicholas II (1894–1917) was the last czar of Russia. Nicholas struck a number of commemorative silver rubles, including a 1912 coin marking the centenary of the victory over Napoleon, and a 1913 commemorative

The tercentenary of the Romanov dynasty is marked on this 1913 ruble with its dual portrait of Nicholas II, who turned out to be the last of the Romanovs, and Michael Feodorovich, the first Romanov czar.

The 1924 ruble and 50 kopecks of the Union of Soviet Socialist Republics show workers standing before a brilliant dawn and a blacksmith hard at work. The reverses bear the Communist emblem, a hammer and sickle representing industry and agriculture.

celebrating the tercentenary of the Romanov dynasty. This coin has the dual portrait of Michael Romanov and Nicholas II.

Coins of Russia—since it became the Union of Soviet Socialist Republics in 1917—are inscribed with the initials "cccp" and with the sickle and hammer, symbols of the revolution. The only gold coin struck by the U.S.S.R. is the 10 rubles ("Tchervonetz") of 1923.

Aluminum-bronze, copper-nickel, brass and nickel-silver have constituted the country's chief coinage metals in recent years. Through a currency revaluation which became effective on January 1, 1961 a New Ruble is now equivalent to 10 Old Rubles.

Nikolai Lenin, the founder and first premier of the Soviet Union, appears on this 1967 ruble marking the 50th anniversary of the Socialist Revolution.

The wreath surrounding the hammer and sickle on this 1961 ruble is wrapped with a ribbon with one band for each of the 15 republics of the U.S.S.R.

Russia ❧ 391

The Dutch city of Leyden issued this 14 stuiver emergency coin while under siege by the Spaniards in 1574.

Siege Coins

Siege coins, sometimes called OBSIDIONAL money, have frequently appeared in times of war or revolution. Armies had to be paid regularly and when no regular coinage was available, as sometimes occurred in the case of a beleaguered city or province, an emergency coinage had to be improvised. One of the easiest ways to accomplish this was to cut up pieces of silver plate, or even gold, into small pieces and stamp them with a value based on their metal content.

Siege coins were produced on a wide scale beginning in the 16th century, especially in the Netherlands (which then included Belgium). Many provinces were controlled by the Spanish king and there were frequent battles for independence and battles between the Catholics and Protestants. Many towns and cities had fortified walls at the time, so battles frequently meant a siege. During the 16th and 17th centuries,

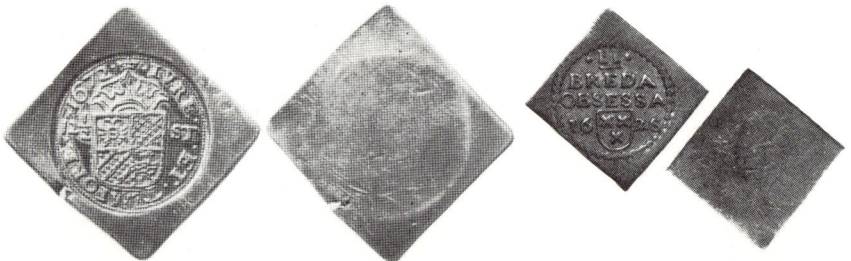

These diamond-shaped uniface siege pieces are 12½ stuivers issued by the town of Groningen in 1672 while under siege by the Bishop of Munster and 2 sols from Breda in the province of north Brabant, struck in 1625 while under siege from Spanish forces.

The city of Breisach in south Germany came under Swedish siege during the Thirty Years War. Its Austrian defenders struck this emergency klippe taler (48 batzen) in 1633.

more than 250 beleaguered towns and cities in the Netherlands and its environs issued some type of emergency money.

Emergency moneys were produced in England during the time of the Civil War, 1642–49. The English siege pieces were mostly silver, and were minted at Carlisle, Colchester, Newark, Pontefract, and Scarborough. Because the siege coins were cut from silver plate, and valued according to their weight, many bear strange denominations such as 7, 8, 9 and 10 pence. Those issued at Newark and Pontefract were more regularly struck, mostly on lozenge-shaped blanks. The irregular-shaped pieces from Scarborough have a rough design of the castle and value stamped on them. Since the English emergency coins were so crudely made and cut in irregular shapes, they have been counterfeited in profusion.

Siege coins were struck at Newark, during the English Civil War of 1642-49. The city was for Charles I and endured three sieges during the "Great Rebellion." These 30 pence and 9 pence specimens are from 1646.

Siege Coins ❧ 393

The English town of Pontefract struck this octagonal-shaped emergency 10 shilling in 1648 while besieged by Parliamentary forces.

Irish siege pieces were produced during the troubled times of the 1640's. The major issues are the *Inchiquin*, *Kilkenny*, and *Ormonde* pieces.

James Butler, Marquis of Ormonde and Viceroy of Ireland, struck emergency coins like this 1642 half crown to pay the supporters of Charles I in Ireland.

This irregular piece of silver plate stamped with its weight, 19 pennyweight and 8 grains (5 shillings), was issued in Ireland by Lord Inchiquin, also to pay troops supporting King Charles I.

In many cases where the coins were made from cut-up silverware, fragments of borders and ornaments still show through. Most have a design impressed on one side only. Coins struck under adverse conditions,

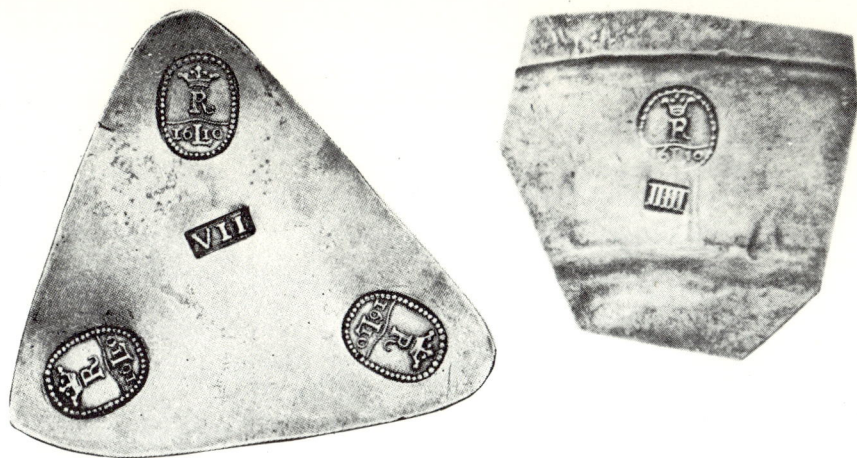

Johann von Rauschenberg, governor of the city and duchy of Julich in Germany's Rhineland region, produced these odd-shaped 5 and 7 gulden pieces from silverware while the city was besieged by the Dutch in 1610.

often on or near the field of battle, of silver from platters, plates, even spoons, often with dies prepared by blacksmiths, seem very crude in comparison. The siege coins may lack beauty but they are among the most fascinating of all coins, however, as each can be linked to a specific historic time and place.

This 1813 5 francs coin with its cannon design was struck by the French defenders of Cattaro in Italy, a town they had occupied since 1807. The French were forced to evacuate, and in 1814 the Congress of Vienna awarded Cattaro to Austria.

Siege Coins ❧ 395

Southeast Asia

Ruled for centuries by native kings, the peninsula of Southeast Asia came under European influence during the 19th century. The British obtained trading concessions in Siam (called Thailand since 1939) while the French established protectorates in Annam, Cambodia, Cochin-China, Tonkin and Laos. Thailand maintained its independence but the remaining states, grouped together as French Indo-China, remained under French control until their partition in 1953.

The earliest known currency of Siam consisted of various silver objects, mostly bracelets, which circulated as early as the seventh and eighth centuries. The well-known silver "tiger tongue" bars were first used about A.D. 1000, and bullet-shaped silver pieces formed an important part of the country's monetary system from the 12th century through the early part of the 19th.

Thailand's silver 2 ticals of 1863 shows the ornate Siamese crown on the obverse, an elephant on the reverse.

A modern mint was established at Bangkok, the capital, in 1860, with coin-striking machinery imported from Birmingham, England. Thus, the nation's coinage became Westernized in appearance although the design remained obviously Asian.

A three-headed elephant, a Buddhist religious emblem, appears on Thailand's 20 satangs struck under King P'ra Paramin Maha Chulalongkorn (1868-1910).

King Phumiphal Adulyadet and Queen Sirikit are shown on this 1961 1 baht struck to hail their safe return from a world goodwill tour.

Since nearly 95 per cent of the people are Buddhist, Buddhist symbols and inscriptions appear on many issues. The elephant, which is revered in Siam, is also seen on numerous coins. The three-headed elephant on some specimens represents the three bodies of Buddha, a triad corresponding to the body of law, the body of bliss, and the body of transformation. The triad also represents wisdom, discipline and compassion, and perhaps even the past, present and future.

A double portrait of King Phumiphal Adulyadet (Rama IX), the present king, and Queen Sirikit on the 1 baht copper-nickel piece of 1961 commemorating their safe return from a world tour. The date on this coin, in Siamese numerals, is 2504 given according to the Buddhist Era which begins in 543 B.C. To convert a B.E. to an A.D. date, it is only necessary to subtract 543 (2504–543 = 1961).

Today the Royal Mint of Thailand is one of the major coin-striking facilities in the Far East, employing 400 workers and producing nearly 100,000,000 coins annually.

The first coins for French Indo-China were struck at the Paris mint in 1885 and show a seated figure of Liberty similar in concept to the American Statue of Liberty which was erected in New York harbor in

The seated figure of Liberty on the 1 piastre pieces struck at the Paris mint for French Indo-China is done in a style similar to the American Statue of Liberty which was also designed in Paris.

Southeast Asia ❧ 397

1886. The final issue was dated 1947. The first issues of independent Cambodia, Laos and South Vietnam were all struck in aluminum and appeared in 1952–53. Communist North Vietnam's first regular issues appeared in 1958.

Cambodia's first independent coinage included this 1953 20 centimes portraying a ceremonial urn.

Laos' 1952 20 centimes shows three elephants in a monument motif.

South Viet Nam's 1953 10 xu carries three female portraits representing the constituent states of Cochin-China, Annam and Tonkin.

South Viet Nam's 20 dong FAO coin shows a farmer working in a rice field. In 1968 the Food and Agricultural Organization of the United Nations launched a "Freedom-from-Hunger campaign" asking the nations of the world to use their coinage to publicize the project. Over 40 countries issued special FAO coins and the profits from the sale of these pieces was used for agricultural development.

398 ❧ Southeast Asia

Spain

The Carthaginians were active both militarily and commercially in Spain before the Romans arrived in 209 B.C. The Iberian peninsula was then part of the Roman Empire for over six centuries. Roman coinage in Spain consisted mostly of military-type issues. C. Annius Luscus, the Roman proconsul in Spain, struck a special coinage for the province in 81 B.C., and Pompey the Great produced an issue in 49 B.C. Galba, the Roman commander of the Spanish Legions, minted a series of denarii and aureii for the province shortly before he succeeded Nero as emperor in A.D. 68.

During the fifth century A.D., the Visigoths, a German tribe, established themselves in Spain after Rome became powerless to hold on to its provinces. The Visigothic coinage is an imitation of late Roman gold. The Visigoths eventually established mints all across the country, the most important being at their capital, Toledo.

By 711, these "West-Goths" were conquered by a Moorish army from North Africa under Arab leaders. The Moors (Moslems of mixed Berber and Arab ancestry) held a grip on the Iberian peninsula for nearly eight centuries. The old Visigothic coinage continued to circulate as the Moors solidified their hold in Iberia, but Carolingian deniers and Arab dirhems became important exchange media. Toward the middle of the eleventh century, the resurgent Christian states—Leon, Castile, Aragon and Navarra—began to strike their own billon dineros and obols.

Alfonso VIII (r. 1158–1214), King of Castile, did much to break Moorish power in Spain. He struck a rather remarkable gold morabitin

Spain ❧ 399

with an Arabic legend on each side. The obverse, however, is inscribed with a cross and a statement of the Christian faith. The reverse relates that the coin was minted by Alfonso VIII, son of Sancho III, at Toledo.

Castile and Leon were permanently united in 1230 by Ferdinand III, "The Saint," whose silver dineros were of a uniform type.

Ferdinand V of Aragon and Isabella of Castile, whose marriage unified Spain, struck this silver 8 reales piece about 1497. The obverse bears the quartered arms of Castile, Leon, Aragon and Sicily, with the arms of Granada below. The reverse has Ferdinand's personal symbol, the yoke, and that of Isabella, a bundle of arrows.

By 1480 the Moors were confined to the small kingdom of Granada in the south. Twelve years later, in 1492, Moslem rule in Spain ended completely with the capture of the city of Granada by Ferdinand of Aragon and Isabella of Castile. The marriage of Ferdinand II (who became Ferdinand V) and Isabella in 1469 led to a single united kingdom of Spain which included the entire Iberian peninsula with the exception of Portugal. Isabella, who died in 1504, sponsored the great voyages of Columbus, and Ferdinand, who died in 1516, was also interested in extending Spanish power.

Modern Spanish coinage begins with Ferdinand and Isabella. In 1497 a new and efficient monetary system was inaugurated with a new coinage in all metals. The new gold unit was the "excellente" struck in multiples of 2, 4, 10 and 20. Later $\frac{1}{2}$ and 1 excellente specimens were issued. The

The gold double excellente of Ferdinand and Isabella shows their crowned facing busts, a design that was later copied in other countries. The "G" mint mark on the reverse shows the coin was struck at Granada.

obverses of the gold pieces carry dual, facing portraits of Ferdinand and Isabella which were continued even after Isabella's death.

Charles I (grandson of Ferdinand and Isabella) inherited the throne of the Spanish Empire in 1516, and took the throne of the Holy Roman Empire as Charles V three years later. He thus became ruler of a domain that was enormous even in comparison with the Roman Empire of ancient times although not nearly so wealthy or powerful. The lands in the New World required settling and developing. Charles drained the homeland of men, revenue, and resources in order to fight for the complex interests of the Holy Roman Empire. Spain, under Charles, was almost constantly at war with France since he felt he could not allow France to take over Italy and his Sicilian granary or let Spain be isolated from Austria.

As King of Spain for 40 years (1516–56) Charles struck gold and silver pieces with inscriptions reading "Ioana et Carolus," for Charles and Johanna, his mother, who was his co-ruler. The silver 1, 2 and 4 reales struck at the new Mexican mint in their names show the Spanish crowned arms. The reverses show the crowned Pillars of Hercules, representing the Straits of Gibraltar, with the motto "plus ultra," meaning "more beyond," a reference to the discovery of the New World. The legend around reads "Hispaniarum et Indiarum," meaning "Rulers of Spain and the Indies."

During the century following Columbus' explorations, the Spanish conquistadores and navigators raised the Spanish flag over vast sections of South America, Mexico, the Caribbean islands, the southern shores of North America, and over the Philippines and other scattered islands in the Pacific. Under Philip II (r. 1556–98), son of Charles I, Spain reached its peak of power. Philip II initiated the New World coinage of that fabled coin, the 8 reales or "piece of eight." Mints were established at Lima (1565) and Potosi (1572) continuing the design type initiated at Mexico City. The coins struck at the mints in Spain proper have an elaborate shield of arms on the obverse, the castles and lions common to the New World coinage on the reverse.

The gold 2 escudos of Philip II (1556-98), struck at the Seville ("S") mint, has a Jerusalem cross on the reverse.

The copper 8 maravedis of Philip III (1598-1621) has the castle emblem of Castile on the obverse and the lion of Leon on the reverse. The term "maravedis" is derived from Murabitin, the name of a Moorish dynasty that flourished in Spain during the Middle Ages.

This cob type silver 4 reales of Philip IV (1621-65) was struck at Seville. The castle and lion emblems are alternated within the angles of the reverse cross.

During the reign of Philip V (1700–46), the "dos mundos" or "two worlds" dollar (struck only at the American mints) first appeared. It was better known to North American colonists as the "pillar" or "Spanish milled" dollar. The design is a refinement of the devices on the earlier pieces, and the coin has a milled or "grooved" edge which prevented the unauthorized clipping off of metal.

The pillar type "dos mundos" or "two worlds" dollar exemplified by this 1739 Mexico mint issue was first struck under Philip V but only by Spain's mints in the New World. The 1734 Seville mint dollar with the royal shield and quartered arms types is the design used at mints in Spain.

With the striking of this 1729 8 escudos gold piece at Seville, Philip V became the first Spanish monarch since the time of Ferdinand and Isabella to have his portrait placed on coins.

A new silver coinage with a bust of the reigning king was started under Charles III (1759–88). Fractional parts of the 8 reales dollar-size were also minted—4, 2, 1, $\frac{1}{2}$, even a $\frac{1}{4}$ real.

When Spain was made a part of the French Empire in 1808, Napoleon placed his brother, Joseph Bonaparte, already King of Naples, on the Spanish throne. During the Peninsular War that lasted for six years, the French were eventually driven out by Spanish guerrilla forces aided by British armies. Joseph Bonaparte struck a handsome series of gold and silver coins during his brief rule.

Charles III (1759-88) was the first Spanish king to have his portrait placed on coins of all metals, beginning with the recoinage of 1772. These pieces are a silver 8 reales of the Seville mint and a copper 4 maravedis of Segovia (aqueduct mint mark).

With the restoration of the hereditary monarchy under Ferdinand VII (1814–33), Spain's political difficulties continued. The unsettled conditions in Spain led to a series of revolts in the colonies, resulting in the loss of territories in Mexico, Central America and South America.

For the next century and a quarter Spain's history was marked by a long series of civil wars alternating with uneasy periods of peace. The Spanish monarchs, for example, struck portrait coins in gold and silver: Isabella II (1833–68), Amadeo I (1871–73), Alfonso XII (1875–86), and Alfonso XIII (1886–1931). The intermittent civil wars gave rise to various types of revolutionary and emergency currencies.

Spain's 19th century gold coins present an interesting portrait gallery of its rulers. This 1822 gold 320 reales of Ferdinand IV (1808-33) shows the king with his hair uncombed.

Isabella II (1833-68) presents a variety of hair styles on her coins, appearing with her hair combed up in 1845, combed down in 1850, and tied with ribbon in 1860.

Alfonso XII (1875-86), a handsome young king on his 1878 gold 25 pesetas, died at the early age of 28.

404 ❧ Spain

The coinage of Alfonso XIII (1886-1931) who was proclaimed king at birth is distinguished by its series of portraits. These four gold 20 pesetas show the king as a baby (1889), a child with curly hair (1892), a boy (1899) and a young man (1904).

After the civil war of the late 1930's, General Francisco Franco was appointed head of state for life. He has made plans for a restoration of the monarchy after he steps down. Franco is portrayed on the current 5, 25 and 50 pesetas copper-nickel coins.

Francisco Franco, "Caudillo" or head of state, appears on most of the current Spanish coins. The holed planchet 50 centimos shows the shilds of Castile, Leon, Aragon and Navarre, devices that have been used in the Spanish coat-of-arms since 1516.

Sweden

At the dawn of the Christian era the area was populated in the north by the "Svea," or Swedes, and in the south by the "Gota," or Goths. The Swedes eventually prevailed over the entire country, with the migratory and adventurous Goths moving on to Germany and Russia, their descendants in turn invading the Roman Empire. Roman influence on Sweden and its environs is apparent because of significant Roman coin hoards found there. Worn silver denarii found on the island of Gotland, for example, demonstrate clearly that Roman moneys served as an important exchange media.

Regular minting of coins in Sweden did not begin until about the year 1000 under Olov Slottkonung "Tax King" (995–1022), son of Eric "The Victorious," and considered by historians to be the first true king of all Sweden. Christianity was introduced into Sweden in the middle of the ninth century, but the struggle between the forces of paganism and Christianity raged for at least 300 years before the latter finally prevailed.

Like most European states which began their basic monetary systems in the 11th and 12th centuries, Sweden patterned its coins on previously established systems. As an example, the type with a king on obverse and

The 1542 silver daler of Gustavus I Vasa (1523-60) is called a "Salvatorsdaler" because the figure of Christ is represented on the reverse with the legend SALVATOR MVNDI ADIVVA NOS—"Saviour of the world, help us."

1570 silver ore of Johan III (1568-92), son of Gustavus I Vasa.

a cross (with the word "CRUX" spaced in the corners of a cross on reverse) is taken from Anglo-Saxon issues.

The Swedes weren't too happy with their position in the Union of Kalmar of 1397 which united Denmark, Norway and Sweden into a single monarchy under the Danish court. They organized their own legislative assembly, the "Riksdag," in 1435, but it wasn't until 1521–23 that Sweden under Gustavus I Vasa broke away from the Union and became independent. As King, Gustavus I Vasa (1523–60) was a brilliant administrator who re-established civil order in the country and broke the monopoly that the Hanseatic League exercised over Swedish trade. At his death in 1560, Sweden ranked as one of the most powerful nations on the European Continent. The story of modern Swedish coinage begins with Vasa's accession to the throne in 1523.

Gustavus Adolphus (1611–32), grandson of Gustavus I Vasa, made Sweden an even greater European military power and is himself ranked as one of the greatest soldiers in all history. Adolphus laid the groundwork for the Swedish American colonization of New Jersey and Delaware that commenced in 1638. In 1938, Stockholm's Royal Mint marked the 300th anniversary of the occasion with a silver 2 kroner coin. The U.S.A. also struck a half-dollar commemorative coin to mark the tercentenary of the Swedish settlement at Delaware. This half-dollar portrays the "Kalmar Nyckel," the ship in which the Swedes crossed the Atlantic. The reverse shows the old "Swede's Church" in Wilmington.

During the 17th century, the Swedish mints struck copper klippings such as this 1625 1 ore value of Gustavus II Adolphus (1611-32).

The obverses of these copper pieces of Gustavus II Adolphus bear the coat of arms of the monarch, including the Vasa badge and a wheat sheaf. The reverse arms indicate the source of the metal—an eagle for Arboga, griffin for Sodermanland, and crossed arrows for Dalarna.

During parts of the 17th and 18th centuries, Sweden's monetary system was based in large part on a copper standard. This phenomenon was due to the fact that Sweden had enormously productive copper mines, and as a result, the bulk of its coinage was struck in copper.

While Sweden was on its peculiar form of a mixed copper and silver standard, from 1644 to 1768, the Swedish mints struck the famous "copper plate money." Ranging in denomination from ¼ to 10 daler pieces, the value of those copper plates was fixed by weight in definite

Silver taler of Queen Christina (1632-54), daughter of Gustavus Adolphus.

ratios to silver and gold. The copper plates were produced in a roughly rectangular form. They were usually inscribed with five official stamps —the four corner ones gave the name of the ruler, the one in the center indicated the value. The largest amounts of Swedish copper plate money were struck at the mints in Avesta and Dalarna, and smaller quantities were produced at the Husa, Kengis, Ljusnedal and Semlan mints. When the copper mines began to run out, production of the copper plate pieces also declined.

During Christina's reign great quantities of copper coins, including huge pieces of copper plate money, were issued. This 1644 ten daler specimen weighs 44 pounds and its actual size is 14 inches by 24 inches, and $\frac{1}{2}$ inch thick.

This 1 daler copper plate piece dated 1656 was struck under Charles X and measures 6 inches by 7½ inches. Approximately 25,000 pieces of plate money were issued between 1644 and 1768.

Because copper plate money was so hard to handle, Sweden issued bank notes in their stead and became one of the first European countries— if not actually *the first*—to do so. In 1661, Stockholm's "Banco" (predecessor of the Central Bank of Sweden) released a number of credit notes for fixed denominations. Over the years the Swedes preferred to

The 1707 silver taler portrays a youthful Charles XII (1697-1718). Although he was only 25 at the time, Charles XII was already a veteran of Europe's political and military wars . . . shortly before this taler was issued he dethroned Augustus II of Saxony, King of Poland.

spend their banknotes while holding onto their silver "riksdalers". Before 1855, the unit of coinage was the silver, dollar-size riksdaler

Charles XII's wars nearly drove Sweden into bankruptcy and in 1709 the government called in all silver coins, replacing them with copper coins carrying the legend, "One Daler Silver Money." Old Father Time with his scythe in one arm, an infant in the other was one of several designs used.

equal to 96 ore or 48 skillings. With the introduction of decimal currency, the unit was made up to 100 ore. Early gold coins were mostly ducats.

The 1821 taler of Charles XIV John struck to commemorate the 300th anniversary of the Reformation in Scandinavia has medallion portraits of Gustavus Vasa, Gustavus Adolphus, and Frederick I (rulers in 1521, 1621 and 1721).

The small 10 ore silver piece issued by Oscar II in 1887 approximated in value the much larger copper 4 skilling coin struck under Charles XIV in 1852. When Sweden went on the decimal system in 1855, silver coins largely replaced copper coins in circulation.

No gold coins are used now in Sweden. The last gold piece produced was the 20 kronor of 1925 with the portrait of King Gustav V.

Silver coinage in circulation today is the 1 krona piece, first issued in 1952, bearing the portrait of King Gustav VI. Gustav VI also appears on

Sweden's last gold piece was this 20 kronor of 1925 with the portrait of King Gustav V.

the 2 and 5 kronor regular issue silver pieces of 1952-55. Commemorative silver 5 kronor coins were issued in 1952 and 1962 to mark the 70th and 80th birthdays of King Gustav.

Sweden's contemporary coins are known for the originality of their design, an angular "modernistic" portrait of the king and incuse design and lettering on the minor values.

The 300th anniversary of Swedish settlement in America was marked in 1938 with this 2 kronor piece portraying the *Kalmar Nyckel,* the ship in which the Swedes made the Atlantic crossing.

A handsome silver 5 kronor specimen was struck in 1959 to commemorate the sesquicentennial of Sweden's Constitution of 1800. In 1966 the Stockholm Mint struck a silver 5-kronor commemorative to mark the centennial of Swedish parliamentary reform.

This 1962 silver 5 kronor commemorates the 80th birthday of King Gustav VI (1950-). The reverse portrays Athena holding an owl and a shield.

The 150th anniversary of the Swedish Constitution which made the country a constitutional monarchy was celebrated with this 1959 silver 5 kronor.

Sweden ◈ 413

Switzerland

Switzerland's history stretches well back into antiquity. Between 58 B.C. and A.D. 15, the Romans conquered the two chief Celtic tribes— the Rhaetii in the east and the Helvetii in the west—and used them as a buffer against the Germans. The Latin name *Helvetia* is still used today on Swiss stamps and coins.

The powerful Hapsburg dynasty, which dominated the Holy Roman Empire for centuries, had its origins in Switzerland, and Switzerland eventually came under Austrian rule. Rebelling against this domination, the Swiss won their independence at the Battle of Sempach in 1386. The national legend of William Tell, who is shown on the current 5 franc coins, springs from this period.

The various cantons or districts of Switzerland formed an anti-Hapsburg self-defense organization called the "Everlasting League." By 1513, the League included 13 states. Swiss independence from the Holy Roman Empire was fully recognized in 1648 at the Peace of Westphalia which formally ended the Thirty Years War.

This 1512 taler from the Free Imperial City of Zurich is one of the earliest of the Swiss large size silver coins. On the obverse are the beheaded patron saints, Felix, Regula and Exuperantius. The arms on the reverse, parted per bend, are the black (a grid) and white (no lines) of the city and canton with the double headed eagle of the Holy Roman Emperor above.

At St. Gall coins were issued both by the city and from the abbey in the name of the abbot. The rampant bear was used as an emblem by both authorities. At left is a 1776 ½ taler piece of the abbey; at right a 30 kreuzer issue of the city.

In 1798, France invaded and occupied the country, and subsequently reorganized Switzerland into the "Helvatic Republic." Napoleon increased the number of cantons to 19 in 1803 and to 22 in 1815, the present number. At the Congress of Vienna in 1815 Switzerland was declared an independent republic and her perpetual neutrality was guaranteed by the major European powers. For the first time in history the country developed a strong central government. The cantons did, however, retain their individual languages and today Switzerland has four official languages—German, French, Italian and Romansch.

Although one of the smaller cantons, Zug had a regular coinage from about 1550 until 1805. This 1612 dicken, equivalent to the Italian testone and the English shilling, shows the Archangel Michael and the imperial eagle.

1810 silver 2 batzen of the canton of Schwyz. This canton eventually lent its name to the whole nation.

Switzerland ❧ 415

This undated 18th century taler of the Swiss canton of Basel shows a view of the city on the Rhine River with the twin spires of its 11th century cathedral dominating the skyline. The inscription on the reverse, DOMINE CONSERVA NOS IN PACE means "Lord preserve us in peace."

The earliest Swiss coins were minted in about A.D. 500 after Helvetia was incorporated in the Frankish kingdom of the Merovingian kings. Gold tremisses bearing the name of the engraver and the mint were produced at a half-dozen mints in Switzerland, including Basel, Geneva, and Zurich. The Zurich mints coined silver deniers for the successive German emperors, including Otto I (936–73).

During the Middle Ages various emperors granted coinage privileges to ecclesiastical foundations as a means of gaining support in the prolonged conflicts between emperor and pope. These ecclesiastical coins

Geneva's interesting coat-of-arms, half of a black eagle and a gold key, are shown on this 1623 ½ taler.

Berne is famous for its bear pits even today. Not surprisingly, the arms of the city shown on this gold doppelduplone of 1795 are a black bear on a gold band across a red shield.

416 ◦ Switzerland

10 batzen of the Helvetian republic of 1798-1803 formed during the French occupation under Napoleon. The Republic introduced a uniform, decimal coinage for Switzerland. This 1801 issue is from the Berne (B mint mark) mint.

(which were usually silver deniers and bracteates) were struck at Lausanne, Geneva, Basel and Sitten, and at abbeys at Frauenmunster-Zurich, and St. Gallen, as well as in other towns.

Ruled as a subject territory by the three forest cantons of Uri, Schwyz and Unterwalden, Ticino was admitted to the Swiss Confederation as a full canton in 1803. The inscriptions on this 1814 4 franken piece are in Italian, the language of the canton.

Beginning in the 13th century, the growing cities gained coinage rights: including Berne in 1228; Basel, 1373; St. Gallen and Lucerne, 1415; and Zurich, 1514. Over the years as Switzerland worked toward unification, the various cantons and cities, and even bishoprics, maintained their independent coinages. It wasn't until 1850 that a truly national coinage

After the Swiss Confederation of 1848, the country adopted a uniform national coinage based on the decimal French franc system.

Switzerland ⟐ 417

The current coins of Switzerland show William Tell, Switzerland's national hero, leader of the 1291 alliance of the first three cantons formed to resist the Austrians, a figure and head of Helvetia and a Helvetian cross.

and currency system was fully instituted. The system adopted was identical to the French, the basic monetary unit being the franc, divided into 100 centimes. Since 1850, the silver coinage has been made up of $\frac{1}{2}$, 2 and 5 franc values. Gold coins, first minted for the Confederation in 1871, have circulated freely in Switzerland since there has been almost literally a free market in gold in the country for many years. The modern Swiss Federal Mint is in Berne, the capital.

Gold coins of the Swiss Confederation have been struck in great quantity since 1871 and they have circulated freely because Switzerland has few restrictions on the trading of gold.

The Swiss cantonal coinage is particularly rich in silver talers or crowns. The talers, which took hold in Europe as an important currency early in the 16th century, were especially artistic in Switzerland. The city-view talers of Basel are typical of this coinage—a detailed, panoramic scene complete with clouds in the sky with the arms of Basel within an elaborate shield on the reverse.

Shooting festival talers such as this 1857 Berne 5 franc piece were struck primarily as prizes, but were also used in circulation for a brief time.

Berne's 1885 shooting taler shows figure holding a sword and standing with a bear and Berne's city shield.

Issued for the 1934 Fribourg Shooting Festival, this 5 franc piece portrays a Swiss Guard. Swiss Guards have protected the Pope in Rome for centuries.

This commemorative 5 francs of 1963 marks the centennial of the founding of the International Red Cross by the Swiss humanitarian Henri Dunant.

Switzerland ◈ 419

The first dollar-sized coin was the silver guldengroschen ("large gulden") issued by Archduke Sigismund of Austria in 1486. It contained silver equal in value to the gold in the widely circulated gold gulden.

Talers

Near the end of the 15th century, the increasing volume of trade in Europe created the need for heavier silver coins than had been current previously. Newly discovered silver mines made silver more plentiful and, since gold had become relatively scarce, dollar-sized coins were a logical step.

The first of these pieces called a *guldengroschen* ("golden penny"), was produced in 1486 by Austria for the province of Tyrol.

In 1516, the famous mines at Joachimsthal (Joachim's Valley) in Bohemia were opened up, resulting in the broad and heavy silver dollars which were first minted in 1518 by Stephen, Count of Schlick, under the authority of Louis, King of Bohemia, whose legend appears on the

Bohemia undated Joachimsthaler of Louis I (1516-26) with a standing figure of St. Joachim (father of the Virgin Mary) and the rampant double-tailed lion of Bohemia.

1659 taler of Munster issued by Bishop Christoph von Galen, showing the miraculous crucifix of the Lambertskirche in Coesfeld.

reverse of the coin. Count Stephen issued these silver pieces in considerable quantity during the seven-year period, 1518–25. The coin shows the standing figure of St. Joachim (father of the Virgin Mary) for whom the valley containing the silver mine was named. The reverse features the crowned, rampant Lion of Bohemia. Most of these coins were issued without dates, although some pieces inscribed 1525 are known.

First known as "Joachimsthalers," the coins soon had their name shortened to "thalers." (The modern spellings are "Joachimstal" and "taler.") Rulers of the Holy Roman Empire issued a steady stream of

The 1626 taler of Saxe-Altenburg portrays the three brothers who ruled jointly—Johann Philip I, and on the reverse Johann Wilhelm IV and Friedrich Wilhelm II.

This 1614 double taler was issued by Archduke Maximilian (1588-1618) of Austria as Master of the Teutonic Order of Knights.

Called a patagon, this 1627 Brabant taler was struck by the Spaniards at Maastricht during the reign of Philip IV.

Saxony, 1630 taler of Elector John George I commemorating the 100th anniversary of Luther's Augsburg Confession.

The "man in the moon" design on this 1547 taler of Luneburg, Germany, is a pun on the city's name (the Latin word for moon is luna).

This taler of Berne, Switzerland struck about 1660 portrays the bear emblem of the city. Bears, which supposedly gave the town its name, have been maintained in pits there since 1513.

talers up to the time of that Empire's dissolution in 1806. As the taler became popular everywhere in Europe, it was imitated under the names of *dollar, daler, tallero,* etc. Other names given to this type of large silver coin are *peso, ecu, crown, ruble, scudo,* and *piastre.* For some 400 years, the taler was the standard unit for European silver coins. The larger size coin provided the engraver sufficient space for composition. Portraits could be larger with finer details, complete dates and the ruler's full title, could be shown. The taler was readily acceptable everywhere because of its convenient size, weight and metal content.

In England, the first dollar-sized coins (commonly referred to as *crowns*) were struck in 1551 during the reign of Edward VI. A completely new design type shows a portrait of the king dressed in mail, holding a

Talers ❧ 423

1558 taler of the Deutz mint struck by John Gebhart von Mansfield, Archbishop of Cologne. St. Peter is shown holding the Keys to the Kingdom of Heaven and the Book of the Gospels.

This 1568 taler issued by Daniel Brendel von Homburg, Archbishop of Mainz, depicts St. Martin offering his cloak to a beggar.

Karl Kaspar von der Leyen, Archbishop of Trier, issued this 1659 portrait taler.

St. Stephen in ornate robes appears on this 1691 taler of the Bishopric of Halberstadt.

1723 taler of Brunswick-Luneburg struck by George I, who was also King of England. The "Wild Man" emblem came from the name of a rich silver mine in the Harz Mountains that was the source of silver for many coins.

sword, astride a galloping horse. Below the horse is the date, 1551, the first appearance of an Arabic numeral on an English coin.

In the New World, the Spanish peso (an 8 reales coin, or "Piece of Eight") circulated throughout Latin America. After the United States came into existence, the American Dollar followed the taler tradition through the direct influence of the Spanish "Pieces of Eight."

Crown-sized coins are still being produced by many countries of the world today, especially for commemorative purposes. Because of the sharply increased prices on the world silver market, however, many of the modern crowns are not struck in fine silver as they used to be. Crowns are often minted in silver only .500 fine, or entirely from base metal alloys.

This 1679 taler of Strasbourg struck to commemorate the Peace of Nymegen shows Noah's Ark floating on water. The obverse legend is a chronogram containing the date.

1689 piastra of Naples and Sicily showing the bust of Charles II of Spain. At this time the kingdom of Naples and Sicily was united with the Spanish crown.

Kuang Hsu, Emperor of China (1875-1908), struck this portrait tael for the province of Szechuan.

King Kalakaua I (1874-91) is shown on this 1883 Hawaiian silver dollar.

Great Britain issued trade dollars for the Far East during the 1895-1935 period, all with the same Britannia design.

King Taufa'ahau Tupou IV appears on Tonga's 1968 1 pa'anga value. Situated in the South Pacific Ocean, Tonga is a self-governing kingdom under the protection of Great Britain.

England, gold noble of Henry VI (1422-61). At this time, the moneyers placed small distinctive markings on coins which they changed periodically. The authorities, in checking the weight and fineness of a particular coin, could thus tell at what period it had been struck. This specimen displays an annulet (small circle) near the king's wrist and in one spandrel on the reverse.

Trial of the Pyx

Judging from the uniform weights and fineness of the coins that have come down to us, even the ancient Greek authorities kept a close check on their coin makers. The Romans used mint letters on some coins as a check but so much official debasement of the coinage went on that any real regulation must have been difficult. In Anglo-Saxon England, laws approved by Ethelred at London in 1002 provided heavy penalties for any mintmaster who took his tools to a secret place—a forest is suggested —and "there, out of sight of all witnesses, struck coins which were unsatisfactory in weight and metal."

After the Norman Conquest of England, the weight and purity of the King's pennies showed a marked decline. To correct the situation, Henry I in 1124 levied severe punishment on all the moneyers of England. His harsh decrees were carried out on some 94 hapless individuals, and one chronicler's report indicates there was a great scarcity of money the following year due to a lack of moneyers.

A more sociable gathering took place in 1208 when King John summoned to Westminster his moneyers, who brought their workmen, assayers, and dies with them. This was apparently for a general assize and verification of issues. Records tell also of an assembly in 1248 of moneyers, "custodes cuneorum" (die mechanics), and the assayers of all the mints. The meeting was attended by King Henry II, the Mayor of London, and other high government officials, at which time a jury of professional goldsmiths made assays of two wedges of silver, one of pure metal and one of the standard coinage metal.

The Trial of the Pyx became established as a continuous and regular ceremony during the reign of Edward III (1327–77). By his proclamation, it was provided:

"So soon as the moneys are coyned and compleate, the Warden to receave yt as the Master receaveth yt from the moneyers, and putt yt in one chest shut with two keys. And before the moneys bee paid to the Merchant, at the request of the said Master, the Warden shall make a tryall of yt, and if yt shall not bee so good as yt is undertaken, yt shalbee retorned to the said Master to bee remolten at his owne proper costs."

The tradition has been continued with a control test each March held at Goldsmith's Hall, the London meeting place of the Worshipful Company of Goldsmiths.

In the United States, an annual Assay Commission meets early in February at the Philadelphia Mint to review the past year's coinage. This commission was first proposed in 1791, before actual coinage began, by Alexander Hamilton, first United States Secretary of the Treasury. In his report to Congress on the establishment of the mint, he stated that "a remedy for errors in the weight and alloy of the coins must necessarily form a part in the system of the Mint; and the method of applying it will be regulated."

Composed of about a dozen citizens serving by special appointment, the Assay Commission weighs and tests selected samples of the coins and passes approval on the minting process. Each member receives a medal specially struck for the occasion.

1940 U.S. Assay Medal. Franklin D. Roosevelt and view of the first U.S. Mint at Philadelphia.

Two quarters and two half-dollars are taken from every 50,000 coins in the "pyx", as well as two dimes from every 100,000 struck. The coins are weighed on sensitive scales calibrated to 1/500th of a milligram. The coins are then cut up and dissolved in acid to determine whether they conform to the prescribed degree of fineness.

1901 U.S. Assay Medal with portrait of William McKinley and a scene depicting the assay process.

1928 U.S. Assay Medal showing Calvin Coolidge and a coiner using a screw press of the type used at the mint in 1793.

500 piastres "harem" gold piece of Sultan Abdul-Hamid II (1876-1909) struck in 1909.

Turkey

At its peak, the empire of the Ottoman Turks stretched from Hungary to the Indian Ocean, from northern Africa to central Asia. This Empire, the greatest of the Moslem states, was named for Osman I (1299-1326), the first outstanding ruler of the Ottoman Turks. Originally Tatar tribesmen of the Asiatic steppes, the Turks wandered westward, finally settling in Asia Minor, where they were converted to Mohammedanism about A.D. 900.

20 piastres of Sultan Mohammed Reshat V (1909-18) struck in 1918. The last line of the reverse inscription has the A.H. date 1327 (A.D. 1909), the year of his accession, while the small 9 below the toughra on the obverse shows the coin was struck during the ninth year of his reign, A.D. 1918. Designs of all Turkish coins were similar to this until 1933.

Turkey ❧ 431

In 1453, the Turks captured Constantinople and destroyed the Byzantine Empire. They remained a constant menace to Europe beyond the borders of the Balkan Peninsula for 250 years.

In the days of its decline, during the 19th century, the Ottoman Empire lost one province after another. World War I left Turkey with only a small area in Asia Minor and a much smaller area in Europe. In 1921, a revolt deposed the last Sultan, and Turkey became a republic.

All Turkish coins under the sultanate carry the toughra, the Sultan's calligraphic emblem, on the obverse. In most cases the value appears directly under the toughra. On the bottom of the reverse appears the date on which the reigning Sultan began his rule. (The dates follow the Mohammedan system of beginning with A.D. 622 as the year 1.)

Since Ataturk came to power in 1923, all Turkish coins have carried the country's crescent and star emblem. The current coins show a figure of Ataturk, a peasant woman and stalks of wheat.

432 ◦ Turkey

"Half Joe" or 4 gold escudos struck in Brazil in 1773. These coins were used extensively in colonial America and were legal tender until 1857 in the United States.

United States

By an Act of Congress on April 2, 1792, the first U.S. mint was established in Philadelphia, then the capital city of the United States. In the following year, the first coins for general circulation, cents and half cents, were struck and issued. Of course, many kinds of coins had been in circulation in the American colonies under British rule prior to the Declaration of Independence and, in fact, these continued in use along with the products of the new U.S. mint for the better part of a century before they were finally withdrawn from use.

COLONIAL COINS

The early settlers in New England conducted transactions among themselves by barter, but traders arriving from other countries with goods to sell demanded payment in coins. Any nation's coins were acceptable since the English government had not provided its colonists with a coinage of their own. Thus, although the English colonists used the British money of account—reckoning values in pounds, shillings and pence—there were French, Dutch, German and assorted Spanish coins in actual use. Spanish milled dollars valued at 8 reales, the so-called "pieces of eight," from Spain's silver-rich colonies in Mexico and South America, were by far the most common coins in the American colonies. The milled dollars served as the standard monetary unit throughout the entire colonial period and the subsequent coinage of the United States was based primarily upon this coin.

English colonists in America used the British money of account, reckoning values in pounds, shillings and pence. This shilling of James I (1603-25) was the type current in England at the time of the Pilgrims.

Spanish milled dollars, such as the 1765 eight reales from Mexico were the chief coin of the American colonists. Small silver coins were scarce so the dollars were sometimes cut into fractional pie-shaped parts as small as an eighth, worth one real and called a "bit." The cut sections shown are "four bit" and "two bit" pieces with counterstamps showing they originated from islands in the West Indies.

Not all of the colonists in North America were British. Settlers from other European nations brought supplies of their national coins along to the New World and these eventually passed into circulation in the colonies. Dutch settlers, for example, following closely behind the Pilgrims, founded a colony on Manhattan Island in 1626. It is generally believed that Peter Minuit purchased the island from the Indians for trinkets (not coins) worth $24, but the Dutch did bring coins to the New World. Before New Netherlands was lost to the English in 1664, one type of coin which came over in fair quantity was the so-called "dog," actually a "lion" dollar, made of base silver. Most of the specimens still in existence are so poorly struck, it is easy to see how such a misidentification could occur.

1648 base silver ducatoon of the type brought to America by the Dutch.

The nearly blank planchets of New England (Massachusetts) silver shillings invited clipping. Though the penalties for clipping were severe—offenders often had both ears cut off, were stood for hours in the pillory, heavily fined, etc.— the practice was still widespread.

As the assortment of foreign money circulating in the colonies was always of uncertain fineness and value and since England ignored the colonies' need for coins, the settlers decided to take some action of their own. The General Court of the Massachusetts Bay Colony in 1652 granted authority for a local coinage to be produced by John Hull, a goldsmith who had come from England in 1635 at the age of 10. The Court provided the tools and put up a mint building on land owned by Hull in Saugus, Massachusetts, just outside Boston.

The first coins struck in the American colonies were the crude NE (for New England) pieces produced between June and October, 1652. Shillings, sixpences and threepenny bits were made from planchets cut more or less round from thinly hammered strips of silver. The blank planchets were placed on an anvil; a punch with NE engraved on the end was held against it and hammered a few times. The planchet was then turned over and the value XII, VI or III hammered into the other side. With so much of the planchet blank, it was too easy for unscrupulous characters to clip off metal without anyone being able to tell it had been taken, short of weighing the coin. This problem led to minting of the better-known willow, oak and pine tree coins whose design covered the whole planchet.

Though John Hull minted his famous silver "tree" coins for some 30 years, they are all dated 1652. These are the Oak Tree three pence, the Willow Tree sixpence, and the Pine Tree shilling.

United States—Colonial Coins ⚹ 435

1723 one penny and halfpenny tokens struck for use in America portray King George I of England. The reverse legend ROSA AMERICANA UTILE DULCI means "the American rose—the useful with the pleasant."

The Massachusetts Bay Colony mint operated for 30 years and the various "tree" coins were struck until 1682. Curiously, however, they all bear the same date, 1652. King Charles II who came to the throne in 1660 objected to the coinage on the grounds that it was an infringement on the

Hibernia tokens such as this 1722 halfpenny were unpopular in Ireland, so most of them, with George I's portrait, were sent to America.

royal prerogative. Although he strongly disapproved of Colonial coinage, he could not very well prove issues to be unauthorized if they were all dated 1652, before his reign began.

Copper money was especially scarce in the colonies, and as time went on, many different tokens were pressed into service for small transactions

Imitation copper coins called "bungtowns" were pressed into service in Britain's American colonies. These false coins resembled the contemporary halfpenny design but used different legends, thus protecting their makers from prosecution as counterfeiters. (Left) Regal halfpenny of George III and (right) bungtown halfpenny showing the head of the king and Britannia with the legends GIVE US PEACE, PITT FOR EVER.

436 ⊚ United States—Colonial Coins

and for making change. A series of Rosa Americana tokens were circulated in the colonies during the 1700's by one William Wood who obtained a patent from George I to supply copper tokens for Ireland and America. Other anonymous tokens and outright counterfeits of the current English half-pence, called "bungtowns," appeared as well. The idea behind the bungtowns was to make imitations just different enough from the originals (by means of distorted legends) to avoid prosecution under the counterfeit laws, but enough like true regal coins to appear identical at first glance. Most of the copper tokens and counterfeits that circulated in the colonies were produced in England. Since they were all underweight, they provided considerable profit to the coiner and, in the case of the patent coins, to the Crown as well.

With the Revolution, the Continental Congress acted to propose a new dollar. It was the first coin ever produced for the United States, or more

The 1776 Continental Dollar, a pattern of a coinage proposed for the United colonies following the American Revolution.

correctly, the United Colonies as they called themselves until 1777. The 1776 Continental Dollar was a pattern issue only, never reaching circulation. Struck primarily in pewter, the coin shows a sun dial and the legend, "Fugio, mind your business." This does not mean what it seems, but "I (Time) fly, therefore mind your business." Benjamin Franklin, famous among many other things for his *Poor Richard's Almanac,* is believed to have been influential in adopting this legend. On the reverse is the legend, "American Congress, We Are One," surrounded by an endless chain of 13 links each inscribed with the name of one of the original colonies. The chain motif was used again later on the first U.S. large cent.

United States—Colonial Coins ❧ 437

The State of New Jersey issued copper cents produced by private contractors, 1786-88.

Connecticut also issued copper cents produced by private contractors, 1785-88.

Vermont produced copper cents from 1785 until 1788. The VERMON AUCTORI legend means "Under the authority of Vermont."

The Commonwealth of Massachusetts established its own mint, producing cents and half cents in 1787 and 1788.

STATE COINAGE

Following the Revolution, no immediate attempt was made to create a national coinage. The Articles of Confederation which preceded the present Constitution granted the individual states the right to issue coinage. Three states and Vermont (independent until 1791 when it became the 14th state) actually did produce their own coins during the period 1785–88. Vermont, Connecticut and New Jersey issued copper cents. Massachusetts issued both cents and half-cents.

The Fugio cents of 1787 were made in New Haven, Connecticut, and possibly other cities under contract with private coiners.

The New Jersey cents carried the "E Pluribus Unum" legend featured on many later U.S. coins. "Nova Caesarea" is an allusion to the ancient name of the Island of Jersey in the English Channel from which New Jersey derives its name.

Private contractors were employed to strike Vermont, Connecticut and New Jersey coins, but Massachusetts established its own mint. The Massachusetts cent was valued at 1/100 of a Spanish dollar. The Massachusetts cent piece was the first official coin in the world struck on a strictly decimal basis in line with a 1785 Congressional resolution. When the United States adopted "cent" from the Latin word "centum," meaning hundred, as a unit of its coinage, it created the forerunner of all the cents, centavos, centimes and centimos that are used in the nations of the world today.

The first national coins issued by authority of the United States, the Fugio cents, appeared in 1787. The Treasury Board entered into a contract with one James Jarvis to coin 300 tons of copper into cents. The design specified in the Congressional resolution was similar to that of the previously proposed dollar. A mint was set up in a store in New Haven, Connecticut, and the coins were struck there. Copper for the Fugio cents came from the copper bands which held together the kegs of gunpowder sent to America by the French during the Revolutionary War. With the Fugio cent's obverse legend reading "Mind Your Business," this coin is often referred to as the Franklin Cent.

This 1791 one cent token showing President George Washington is a token prepared as a pattern by a British firm seeking a minting contract for a proposed national U.S. coinage.

United States—State Coinage ❧ 439

This halfpenny Washington portrait piece of 1795 bears the American shield on the reverse with the patriotic legend **LIBERTY AND SECURITY.**

Much discussion ensued concerning the establishment of a U.S. mint, but no other coins were struck in America during the next six years. Tokens were still in use during this period. A series starting in 1783 showed the portrait of George Washington on the obverse. The Washington pieces of 1791, especially, are thought to be designs presented as proposals for a national U.S. coinage by British firms seeking minting contracts. President Washington, however, rejected the use of his portrait on coins as being too much like the coins issued by monarchies.

The reverse of this 1783 one cent token inscribed UNITY STATES OF AMERICA, bears a striking resemblance to designs later adopted for U.S. coinage.

ESTABLISHMENT OF THE U.S. MINT

The proposals of the English coiners to strike coins for the United States on contract spurred Congress in the direction of establishing a mint. Secretary of State Thomas Jefferson strongly expressed the opinion that coinage was an attribute of sovereignty and was not to be tampered with. On March 3, 1791, Congress passed a resolution definitely authorizing a mint to be set up and the President to engage artists and purchase coining machinery.

The "Act of Establishing a Mint and Regulating the Coins of the United States" was finally passed and signed into law by Washington on April 2, 1792. The law provided that the mint be established at the seat of government (Philadelphia). It authorized gold eagles ($10), half eagles ($5), and quarter eagles ($2.50); silver dollars, half dollars, quarters, dismes (original spelling of dime) and half dismes; copper cents and half cents.

A small trial coinage of half dismes was struck at the Philadelphia mint in December, 1792, from silver plate supplied by George Washington himself. The obverse legend LIBERTY PARENT OF SCIENCE AND INDUSTRY was never used on regular U.S. coins.

The devices and legends were specified: on one side an impression emblematic of liberty, and the year of coinage; on the reverse of each gold and silver coin a figure or representation of an eagle with the Inscription, "United States of America" and on the reverse of the copper coins, an expression of the denomination of each piece. On the obverse of the first U.S. coins is a "wind-blown" head of Liberty with the date, 1793. On the reverse is an endless chain of 15 links representing the 13 original states plus Vermont and Kentucky, which had been admitted to the Union in 1791 and 1792, respectively. The die engraver added the word, LIBERTY, to the obverse although no such legend had been specified in the coinage law.

1793 chain cent, the first regular issue United States coin.

Large cents were to be struck for a period of 64 years at the Philadelphia mint, from 1793 to 1857, in a total of seven major types, including the chain and wreath flowing hair types produced in 1793. The others were: Liberty cap type, 1793–96; draped bust type, 1796–1807; turban head type, 1808–14; coronet type, 1816–39; and the braided hair type, 1839–57. The rising cost of copper made the large cents impractical and they were superseded by the small cents. The various types of half cents were fashioned after the large cents, but lagged a few years behind in changing designs.

United States—Establishment of the U.S. Mint ⚓ 441

Only two denominations, cents and large cents, were struck in 1793, the first year of U.S. coinage. Both of these coins were designed by Adam Eckfeldt.

The Liberty cap design was introduced on U.S. large cents in late 1793. Joseph Wright designed this type cent, Robert Scot the half cent.

Gilbert Stuart, the American painter, is credited with designing the draped bust of Liberty that appeared on both copper and silver coins.

The "turban" head portrait of Liberty used on both large cents and half cents is credited to John Reich.

New equipment at the mint following a fire in 1816 produced a more uniform coinage. The numerals of the date were still punched in by hand, however, as evidenced by the widely spaced numerals on this 1817 large cent.

The first regular silver coins were produced at Philadelphia on October 5, 1794. Half dollars and half dimes dated 1794 soon followed. The dollars and half dollars were seldom struck sharply as they were minted in presses designed for stamping out cents and small coins.

The 1794 silver coins have obverses very much like the original chain cents, the liberty head with long flowing hair facing right, LIBERTY above, and the date below. An addition to the design was a circular arrangement of eight stars at the left, seven stars at the right—another reminder that by 1794 the thirteen original colonies had become fifteen states.

No gold pieces were struck until 1795, and then only eagles and half eagles were minted. The part of the law regarding devices on the new U.S. coins specified an eagle as the emblem for the reverse of all gold and silver pieces. The "eagle" also provided the official name for the standard gold coin, but in actual use, it has always been regularly referred to as a "$10 gold piece," the "half eagle" as a "$5 gold piece."

U.S. silver coinage began in 1794 with dollars, half dollars and half dimes. The obverse of Liberty with long flowing hair is similar to the design used on the original chain cents.

United States—Establishment of the U.S. Mint ❧ 443

U.S. gold coinage began in 1795 with the eagle ($10) and half eagle ($5). The design consists of a draped bust of Liberty wearing a tall cap and a fledgling eagle.

The head of Liberty on the obverse of the gold coins is quite different from that on copper and silver coins. Liberty is shown with a draped bust rather than as a severed head. Her hair is carefully arranged and she wears her cap upon her head. As on the silver coins, there are 15 six-pointed stars on the obverse, LIBERTY and the date.

In 1796, the fourth year of U.S. coinage, three new denominations were added —the quarter dollar, dime and the quarter eagle ($2.50). None of the early U.S. coins had their value marked on them.

The remaining three authorized denominations, the dime, the quarter dollar and quarter eagle made their appearance in 1796, the fourth year of coinage. The reverses of the silver dime and quarter are the same type as the 1794 silver coins, also without mark of value but the obverses show a completely different, new head of Liberty, the so-called draped-bust design. Liberty is shown without a cap, her hair fastened with a ribbon bow at the back of her head.

By 1805 the heraldic type eagle had replaced the original natural-looking bird on all U.S. gold and silver coins as on the 1805 quarter dollar and half eagle gold piece above.

Coinage of silver dollars and gold eagles was suspended in 1804 and 1806 respectively by President Thomas Jefferson for the very good reason that these desirable coins were disappearing from sight as fast as they could be produced. The silver dollars were being demanded in exchange, one for one, for old, worn, underweight Spanish milled dollars which still made up the bulk of coins in circulation. The full weight American dollars were then melted down for export, yielding a small percentage of profit to the manipulator.

The so-called "turban" head of Liberty replaced the draped bust types shortly after 1800 on U.S. gold and silver coins.

For the first time, the denominations were shown on all the coins, inscribed below the eagle on the reverse.

United States—Establishment of the U.S. Mint ❧ 445

Prior to 1834, U.S. gold coins, valued at 15 to 1 in relation to silver, were worth more as bullion than their face value in silver. As a result, the majority were melted down by profiteers. The 1834 revaluation at 16 to 1 eliminated this profit potential and the newly designed quarter- and half-eagles remained in circulation.

MODERN U.S. COINAGE

Steam, in 1836, replaced horsepower and manpower for driving the mints' machinery and because of the greater pressure, the complete design of the working dies, except for the date and mint mark, could be stamped at one time from one master hub. From this point on, in the U.S. coin series, it is usually not possible to distinguish between coins struck from different dies although we occasionally see a variation in the size or placement of the digits in the date or mint letter.

The new coinage act of January 18, 1837, completely revised and standardized the mint and coinage laws. Legal tender, weight tolerance, a bullion fund, standardization of purity for gold and silver coins at

The 1836 pattern silver dollar designed by C. Gobrecht has his name on the base of the figure, the only instance of an engraver of a U.S. coin signing his work with his full name. The soaring eagle motif was adopted years later for the one cent piece.

Christian Gobrecht's seated Liberty design (with 13 stars inscribed around the obverse) became the principal device on U.S. silver coins for more than a half century, discontinued finally in 1891.

900 thousandths fine, were provided for and changes in type were made for the various coin denominations. Resumption of coinage of the eagle and silver dollar occurred shortly thereafter.

After gold was discovered about 1830 in Georgia and North Carolina, the mines in these states became the chief source of gold for coinage. In 1835, Congress acted to establish the first branch mints, locating them near the source of the gold in Charlotte, North Carolina, and Dahlonega, Georgia. Both branches began operations in 1838. The Dahlonega and Charlotte mints coined gold only, half eagles and quarter eagles; later on, they coined gold dollars and at Dahlonega one date of a $3 gold piece. Both of these gold mints were closed during the Civil War, in 1861, never to be reopened. Then as now, dies for branch mint coinage were sent out from Philadelphia and coins struck at the branches have their own mint marks for recognition—"C" for Charlotte and "D" for Dahlonega.

United States—Modern U.S. Coinage ☙ 447

These coins carry mint marks showing they were struck at the branch mints established in 1838. The 1838 Charlotte quarter eagle has a "C" above the date; the 1859 Dahlonega quarter eagle a "D" below the eagle; and the 1855 New Orleans half eagle an "O" below the eagle.

A third branch mint in New Orleans also started operations in 1838. The New Orleans branch, in contrast to Charlotte and Dahlonega, was not restricted to gold, but at intervals struck all denominations from 3 cent pieces to $20 gold pieces between 1838 and 1861, when it, too, was closed during the Civil War. Coinage resumed, however, in 1879 and lasted until 1909 when the mint was closed down permanently. New Orleans issues have an "o" mint mark.

Congress authorized two new gold denominations in 1849, the one dollar and the twenty dollar pieces although the latter was not minted until 1850. The great volume of gold coming from California after 1848 called for a coin of higher value than the eagle.

Two new gold denominations were adopted in 1849, the dollar and the $20 double eagle although regular coinage of the double eagle did not start until 1850. A new silver denomination, the 3¢ piece, appeared in 1851. This unusual denomination was made necessary because the postal rates for a letter had been lowered to 3¢ in the same year. With the

448 ❧ United States—Modern U.S. Coinage

Both the 3¢ silver piece and $3 gold piece were issued after the postal rate for letters was lowered to 3¢. The 3¢ silver is the smallest size coin ever circulated in the United States.

establishment of the 3¢ letter rate it was somehow thought that a $3 coin would be convenient in postal transactions and $3 gold pieces were struck in generally small numbers from 1854 until 1889.

The letter "S," shown below the eagle on the reverse of this 1866 half dollar, is the mark of the San Francisco mint that was opened in 1854.

A branch mint was organized in San Francisco in 1854 in recognition of the state's material wealth and growing population. In those days of transportation around the Horn by ship, a mint was essential near the source of the gold. Before long the San Francisco Mint (with an "s" mint mark) was outproducing Philadelphia in mintage of gold coins, but it also struck most other denominations as well. The San Francisco Mint moved into new buildings twice to increase its capacity, continued regular operations until 1955, became an assay office only for over a dozen years, and then resumed striking coins in 1968.

The Coinage Act of February 21, 1857, decreed that Spanish silver coins still in circulation, mostly quite worn down, had to be redeemed within

The design on this 1855 pattern was a forerunner for the flying eagle cents of 1857-58. Its size is intermediate between the large cents then in use and the small cents later adopted.

United States—Modern U.S. Coinage ৯ 449

The first U.S. small size cent was the flying eagle type of 1857-58. Patterns dated 1856 are rare. Although regularly issued for only two years, more than 42 million pieces were struck.

two years, after which time they would no longer be legal tender but worth bullion value. The coin used to redeem the Spanish silver was the flying eagle cent created by the same law. During their two years of regular issue, 1857 and 1858, more than 42 million flying eagles in copper-nickel were struck. The small cent was redesigned in 1859, nevertheless,

The U.S. Indian head cent was first issued in 1859. On this coin, engraver James B. Longacre portrayed the goddess Liberty in Indian headdress.

probably because of the difficulty of striking up the fine detail in the eagle's feathers in the hard nickel alloy. The famous Indian cent followed although this is actually a misnomer since the portrait is of Liberty shown wearing Indian headdress. Copper-nickel was used from 1859 to 1864 when a switch was made to bronze. Indian cents were struck continuously through 1909, a total of 50 years.

Indian head cents were struck in copper-nickel from 1859 to 1864, and then in bronze until the series ended in 1909.

The act of April 22, 1864 authorizing the bronze cent also created a bronze 2¢ piece. A great coin shortage existed toward the end of the Civil War and the reasoning was simply that a coin press could produce just as many 2¢ pieces as 1¢ pieces in a given time, but at double the value

450 ᐒ United States—Modern U.S. Coinage

as small change. The short-lived two-cent piece (issued 1864–73) is best
remembered because it was the first U.S. coin to carry the motto, IN GOD
WE TRUST.

This 1863 2¢ piece with the head of
Washington and motto GOD AND
OUR COUNTRY predates the regular
use of the 2¢ denomination by a year.

A new 3¢ nickel piece made from an alloy of 25% nickel and 75%
copper made its appearance for the first time in 1865. One of the proper-
ties of nickel is that its color dominates its alloys so that even though the
new coins had three parts of copper to each part of nickel, the new
composition was nearly as white as silver. The nickel 3¢ piece was
intended originally to redeem the 3¢ paper notes issued during the Civil
War.

The first U.S. coin struck in nickel was a 3¢
piece introduced in 1865, a year before the
5¢ coin of the same metal.

Another nickel coin, the 5¢ nickel piece followed in 1866. Like the 3¢
piece it was intended for redemption of the 5¢ paper notes issued during
the Civil War rather than to compete with the silver half dime. Both
nickel coins, however, did soon replace the corresponding silver issues.
The design chosen for the 5¢ piece was a shield similar to the one in use
on the 2¢ pieces with minor modifications.

The first nickel 5¢ pieces were introduced in 1866. There were two varieties of this shield type—with rays between the stars on the reverse (1866-67) and without rays (1867-83).

A fifth branch mint was established in 1870 at Carson City, Nevada, 14 miles from the great gold and silver mines of the Comstock Lode at Virginia City. Coins struck at Carson City are distinguished by a "cc" mint mark. This facility was constructed to save Nevada producers the expense of shipping their precious metal 300 miles to the mint at San Francisco, but many of them continued to do so despite the new mint. Most "cc" coinages are comparatively low, ceasing entirely after 1893.

The fifth U.S. branch mint was established in Carson City, Nevada, in 1870. Coins struck at Carson City are distinguished by a "CC" mint mark, as on the reverse of this silver dollar. Most "CC" coinages are low and there are many scarce issues.

The shortest lived U.S. coin, the 20¢ piece, was authorized on March 3, 1875 and was discontinued on May 2, 1878. There were general complaints about its similarity in design and size with the quarter dollar. The 20¢ piece was largely promoted by silver mine owners who wanted to use up some of the large surplus of silver on hand at the time.

The 20 cent piece was the shortest-lived U.S. coin denomination, regularly issued only in 1875 and 1876.

452 ৭ United States—Modern U.S. Coinage

The Liberty head silver dollar introduced in 1878 is usually called the "Morgan head" type after its designer George T. Morgan. The rarest date is the 1895 which has a recorded mintage of 12,000 pieces, of which only a small fraction are known.

Another effort of the silver promoters to create a constant market for large quantities of the metal resulted in the Bland-Allison Act of 1878. By law, the Treasury was required to buy a minimum of $24 million one dollar coins, the profit going to the Government. This profit, the difference between metal value and face value (called "seignorage"), increased as silver became more plentiful and prices went down.

The new dollar was designed by George T. Morgan, after whom it is usually called. The Morgan design, with slight modifications, was utilized until the new Peace design was adopted in 1921.

In working out the designs for the new silver dollar coinage, a number of patterns were prepared with various combinations of obverse and reverse.

The 1877 pattern half dollar designed by William Barber shows Liberty wearing a helmet.

United States—Modern U.S. Coinage ❧ 453

This 1882 pattern half dollar had Liberty facing to the right as on the design adopted for the new coinage of 1892.

In 1883, shield type nickels were discontinued for a Liberty head design. The Liberty nickel closely resembled the head on the Morgan dollar except that the goddess is not wearing a cap and there is no legend on the obverse other than LIBERTY on the coronet. In the style of the nickel 3¢ piece, a large Roman numeral, V, dominated the reverse surrounded by a wreath with UNITED STATES OF AMERICA around the rim. The Liberty head nickel continued as a regular issue through 1912.

When the Liberty head nickel 5¢ piece was introduced in 1883, it had a large Roman numeral V on the reverse as a mark of value but no indication of denomination. Unscrupulous people began gold-plating them and passing them off on the unsuspecting as the "new" $5 gold piece. To remedy the situation CENTS was added to the later issues of 1883 and all subsequent dates.

In 1885, the mint experimented with center hole planchets for the nickel 5 cent pieces. Pierced planchets had the advantage of being easily identifiable.

Since the American people had apparently tired of the Liberty seated design which had appeared on silver coins since the 1830's, a whole new series of dimes, quarters and half dollars was inaugurated in 1892.

Chief Engraver Charles E. Barber returned to a design using just the head of Liberty, as on pre-1837 coins, but he turned her around to face right as on the first silver coins of 1794. On the reverse of the half and quarter dollar is an eagle taken from the design of the Great Seal.

454 ⚙ United States—Modern U.S. Coinage

A new series of coins first minted in 1892, show the head of Liberty facing to the right. For more than 50 years Liberty had been portrayed in a seated position. The new type was designed by Charles E. Barber

The year 1892 also saw the issue of the Colombian Exposition half dollar, the first of a series of United States commemorative coins. Altogether the mint has issued 48 different types of commemorative half dollars plus one quarter and one silver dollar. A variety of commemorative gold coins have also been struck in values ranging from $1 to the $50 round and octagonal specimens issued for the Panama-Pacific Exposition in 1915.

The first U S. commemorative coin was a Columbian Exposition half dollar of 1892. The 1893 Isabella quarter, also issued for the Columbian Exposition, is the only U.S. commemorative of this denomination. The 1900 Washington-Lafayette piece is the only U.S. silver dollar commemorative and the first U.S. coin to portray an American president.

United States—Modern U.S. Coinage ❧ 455

These commemoratives extol American leaders and recall historic occasions, some of national importance, others with local meaning. Special legislation was passed for each issue and all commemoratives have been sold originally at a premium above their face value. The commemoratives have many admirers, and each tells an interesting story, but they are not significant as coins because they have had only limited circulation.

The Panama-Pacific Exposition held at San Francisco in 1915 was staged to celebrate the opening of the Panama Canal. Five coins were struck at the San Francisco Mint to commemorate the event—a silver half dollar, and $1, $2.50, and two $50 gold pieces. The round and octagonal $50 coins are the highest denomination coins ever struck by the U.S. Mint.

1918 Illinois Statehood Centennial.

1920 Pilgrim Tercentenary.

1921 Missouri Statehood Centennial. The first coins minted have 2★4 incused on the obverse, indicating that Missouri became the 24th star in the flag.

1922 Grant Memorial. A star appearing on the first issues was later removed.

United States—Modern U.S. Coinage ❧ 457

1923 Monroe Doctrine
Centennial.

1925 Lexington-Concord
Sesquicentennial.

1925 Stone Mountain
Memorial.

1925 California Statehood
Diamond Jubilee.

1926 Sesquicentennial of American Independence commemorative half dollar
and quarter eagle.

1926-39 Oregon Trail Memorial.

1927 Vermont Independence Sesquicentennial.

1928 Hawaiian Sesquicentennial.

1934-38 Texas Independence Centennial.

1934-38 Daniel Boone Bicentennial.

1935 Connecticut
Tercentenary.

1935 Hudson, New York
Sesquicentennial.

1935 Old Spanish Trail
400th Anniversary.

1936 Cincinnati Golden
Anniversary as a musical
center.

1936 Bridgeport,
Connecticut Centennial.

1937 Roanoke Island, N.C. 350th Anniversary.

1937 Battle of Antietam 75th Anniversary.

1946 Iowa Statehood Centennial.

1946-51 Booker T. Washington Memorial.

1951-54 Booker T. Washington-George Washington Carver Memorial.

United States—Modern U.S. Coinage ❧ 461

The sixth branch mint was established at Denver in 1906. Denver issues are distinguished by a"D" mint mark, also used prior to 1861 at Dahlonega. The Denver Mint for years outproduced Philadelphia because of its more modern facilities and proximity to sources of metals. However, a brand new mint at Philadelphia, dedicated in August, 1969, is equipped with the most modern, high-speed machinery.

A sixth branch mint was established at Denver, Colorado in 1906. This 1912 quarter shows its "D" mint mark below the eagle on the reverse.

The coinage of the United States had been extremely conservative for over a century. In this respect, President Theodore Roosevelt (1901–09) asked the famous sculptor Augustus St. Gaudens to design a coin for the United States that would be comparable to those of the ancient Greeks in beauty. The result was a new high standard of art on U.S. coins.

This 1907 Roman numeral, high relief double eagle designed by Augustus St. Gaudens is usually regarded as the most beautiful coin ever produced at the U.S. Mint.

St. Gaudens first design was for the 1907 double eagle—a forward-facing full length figure of Liberty holding a torch and an olive branch, stepping out of a sunrise with the Capitol building in the background. On the reverse is an eagle in flight above a rising sun. The first issues show the date in Roman numerals and are struck in very high relief.

The obverse of the St. Gaudens $10 gold eagle shows the head of Liberty crowned with an Indian war bonnet below a semi-circle of 13 stars. On the reverse is a majestic standing eagle.

462 ❧ United States—Modern U.S. Coinage

President Theodore Roosevelt objected to the Deity's name on U.S. coins and the $20 gold pieces of 1907 and some of 1908 were issued without the IN GOD WE TRUST motto. Congress restored it during 1908 and on all succeeding issues it appears above the sun on the reverse.

The 1907 and some 1908 $10 gold pieces were also issued without the motto. When it was restored in 1908, it was added to the design just in front of the eagle.

The design of the quarter- and half-eagles introduced in 1908 was a departure from all previous tradition—the design was cut down into the planchet rather than standing out in relief.

New designs for the half- and quarter-eagle were prepared by another distinguished sculptor, Bela Lyon Pratt. On the new type, the design and lettering are cut down into the planchets. The planchets do not have raised edges so the highest point of the design is below the surface.

United States—Modern U.S. Coinage ❧ 463

The Lincoln head cents, designed by Victor D. Brenner and first issued in 1909, are by far the most popular coins for beginning U.S. collectors.

As 1909, the centennial of Lincoln's birth approached, President Roosevelt had the idea of issuing a special coin to commemorate the martyred 16th President. He had seen and admired a plaque bearing a portrait of Lincoln done by an engraver named Victor D. Brenner, and so he commissioned him to design the Lincoln cent.

On the first 1909 coins, Brenner placed his initials, V.D.B., on the lower reverse. Protests arose, although there was ample precedent for an engraver initialling his work. In fact, all of the coins then current showed their engraver's initials. None, however, were as prominently placed as Brenner's. In spite of the precedent, the initials were removed in short order and not restored until 1918 when they reappeared on the obverse below Lincoln's shoulder.

James Earl Fraser's design for the head on this nickel was a composite of the features of three actual Indians. The buffalo or bison on the reverse was modelled after "Black Diamond" in the New York City Zoological Gardens.

The new nickel 5¢ piece, introduced in 1913, continued the attractive style of art set by St. Gaudens' gold coins. The designs were by James Earl Fraser, also a sculptor, and have an Indian head on the obverse and an impressive buffalo (an American bison) on the reverse.

The so-called "Mercury" head dime of 1916-45 looks very much like an ancient Roman silver denarius issued 20 centuries earlier.

The dime, quarter and half dollar designs introduced in 1916 were all strongly influenced by ancient coin motifs. The dime, designed by A. A. Weinman, has been universally known as the "Mercury head dime" after the Woman god of commerce and grain, who is traditionally shown wearing a winged helmet. What the dime actually shows, however, is just another representation of Liberty, the wings of her cap symbolizing liberty of thought. This motif does come from a Roman coin, but from the goddess Roma rather than from Mercury. On the reverse are a laurel branch and the "fasces," a bundle of rods with an ax projecting, used as a badge of authority in Roman times, and probably meant to emphasize the rule of law and authority in the days just prior to America's entry into World War II.

Sculptor Herman A. MacNeil used a World War I Red Cross nurse as the model for the figure of Liberty on his quarter which first appeared in 1916.

The standing Liberty quarter, designed by the sculptor Herman A. MacNeil, also shows the menacing approach of war. In her right hand, Liberty offers the olive branch of peace while the shield on her left arm, from which she is withdrawing the cover, shows her unmistakable intention of protecting herself, reflecting the national sentiments of the times.

A. A. Weinman also designed the 1916 walking Liberty half dollar. The director of the mint described the new half dollar design as "a full figure of Liberty, the folds of the stars and stripes flying to the breeze as

The half dollar type of 1916-47 shows a walking figure of Liberty on the obverse with a natural-looking eagle on the reverse. The dime, quarter and half dollar designs introduced in 1916 were all strongly influenced by ancient coin motifs.

a background, progressing in full stride toward the dawn of the new day, carrying branches of laurel and oak symbolic of civil and military glory. The hand of the figure is outstretched in bestowal of the spirit of Liberty. The reverse of the half dollar shows an eagle perched high on a mountain crag, his wings unfolded, fearless in spirit and conscious of his power."

United States—Modern U.S. Coinage ❖ 465

The silver dollar type of 1921-35 was proposed as a peace commemorative celebrating the end of World War I.

A proposal made at the 1920 convention of the American Numismatic Association ultimately led to the so-called "peace" type dollar, first issued late in 1921. This coin, designed by the medalist Anthony De Francisci, shows the Goddess of Liberty with rays around her head, another device borrowed from the Romans who used the radiate head-dress to symbolize the immortality of the emperor. The naturalistic eagle perched on a rocky crag maintains the classical theme, being reminiscent of eagles pictured on old Greek and Roman coins. The last silver dollar coinage was in 1935.

George Washington finally appeared on a regular issue U.S. coin in 1932, the 200th anniversary of his birth. On the reverse is a standing eagle with spread wings, maintaining an unbroken series of eagle reverses on U.S. quarter dollars since the first issue of 1796.

The current U.S. quarter design, introduced in 1932, shows a bust of George Washington prepared by John Flanagan who based his engraving upon a 1785 marble bust by Jean Antoine Houdon.

In 1933, the issuance of U.S. gold coins came to an end. An order by President Franklin D. Roosevelt on March 6th discontinued the coinage, prohibited banks from paying out in gold or gold certificates, and removed gold coins from circulation by making it compulsory to turn in all such coins to the Treasury. Gold was thus kept for reserve purposes in support of U.S. paper money.

The last U.S. gold coins to be struck were the 1933 $20 and $10 gold pieces. None of the 1933 double eagles were released, however, so 1932 is the last collectible date of this denomination.

A law of 1890 specified that coinage designs were not to be changed oftener than every 25 years and special legislation was necessary to introduce the Washington quarter in 1932. In 1938, however, the buffalo nickel was eligible for change and mint officials decided to follow the precedent and place the third U.S. president, Thomas Jefferson, on the 5¢ piece. The reverse shows Monticello, Jefferson's home near Charlottesville, Virginia.

The current Jefferson 5¢ piece, first issued in 1938, is by Felix Schlag whose design was chosen in a competition of 400 artists.

The first specimens of the dimes portraying Franklin D. Roosevelt were released on January 30, 1946, the date of the late president's birthday and less than a year after his death. This was the first U.S. coin to show an actual person so soon after death. On the reverse is the torch of liberty, placed between an olive branch of peace, on the left, and an oak branch, signifying strength and independence on the right.

Benjamin Franklin has the distinction of being the only non-president to appear on a regular issue U.S. coin, the 1948–63 half dollar. The Liberty Bell is featured on the coin's reverse. Alongside the Liberty Bell is

The Roosevelt dime was introduced in 1946, the year following the President's death. Designed by John R. Sinnock, this was the first U.S. coin to portray a person so soon after his death.

The Franklin half dollars of 1948-63 were cut short to make way for the Kennedy memorial coin. U.S. coin designs may not be changed oftener than every 25 years without special Congressional approval.

the eagle, a device required by law on silver coins above ten cents in value, but for the first time it is small and subsidiary to some other device. On the Liberty Bell the celebrated crack is clearly discernible.

The most recent design change on a U.S. coin occurred in 1964. Since Franklin had been on the half dollar for less than 25 years, special legislation was again necessary to make the change. President Lyndon B. Johnson asked Congress for such legislation less than three weeks after the assassination of his predecessor, John F. Kennedy. One notable reason for selecting the half dollar was that it was the only subsidiary coin not bearing the likeness of a President.

The first specimens of the new coins were stamped at both the Philadelphia and Denver mints on February 11, 1964. The chief sculptor of the U.S. Mint, Gilroy Roberts, had prepared the die for the Kennedy medal in the mint's presidential series. The coin portrait was adapted from Roberts' medal. The reverse design is by Frank Gasparro (now the mint's chief engraver), based on the coat-of-arms of the President of the United States. The 13 original states are represented in the number of olive leaves, berries, arrows, clouds and stars above the eagle. The 50-star ring around the eagle represents all the states.

The Kennedy half dollar is not a special commemorative but a regular issue with a design that by law will now remain in effect for at least 25 years unless Congress specifically authorizes a change.

Although millions of Kennedy half dollars have been struck since 1964, nearly all were put aside as mementos. Gilroy Roberts designed the obverse, Frank Gasparro the reverse.

468 ❧ United States—Modern U.S. Coinage

Through the provisions of the U.S. Coinage Act of 1965, the composition of dimes, quarters and half dollars was modified to eliminate or reduce the silver content of these coins. The new "clad" or "sandwich" dimes and quarters are composed of an outer layer of copper-nickel (75% copper and 25% nickel) bonded to an inner core of pure copper. The clad half dollar contains an outer layer of 80% silver bonded to an inner core of 21% silver, with a total silver content of 40%.

The enlarged obverses of this 1968 proof set—coins specially struck for collectors with brilliant surfaces, sharp edges, and perfect detail—clearly show the "S" mark of the San Francisco Mint where they were produced. The arrows point to the designer's initials on each coin.

The rayed sun face design was featured on Uruguay's coins for a full century, from its first issues of 1840 until 1941.

Uruguay

Uruguay, once part of the Spanish vice-royalty of La Plata and later a province of Portuguese Brazil, declared its independence on August 25, 1825. In 1828, with the assistance of Great Britain, Uruguay was recognized as an independent republic, a buffer state between Argentina and Brazil.

Before striking its first coins in 1840, Uruguay used currency of Argentina, Brazil and other countries. All coins dated 1840–55 were minted at Montevideo. These include the copper 5, 20 and 40 centesimos having the sun obverse and the value on the reverse. Since the Monte-

These three coins were struck in 1930 to mark the centennial of the establishment of the Republic. The gold 5 pesos portrays Jose Gervasio Artigas, Uruguay's national hero; the 10 centesimos has the head of Liberty, with a jaguar on the reverse; the 20 centesimos shows Liberty seated, with wheat stalks on the reverse.

The Uruguayan 1961 10 peso coin honors the Gaucho heroes of the 1811 revolution against Spain.

video Mint was closed in 1855, various world mints have struck coins for Uruguay, including those at Buenos Aires, Santiago, Birmingham, London, Vienna, Utrecht, Paris and Lyon.

Jose Gervasio Artigas, the national hero who led the Uruguayan fight for liberation in the critical 1810–20 period, has been portrayed on many coins. Artigas has also been portrayed on the country's only regular issue gold coin: the 5 pesos of 1930, struck to commemorate the centennial of Uruguay's Constitution.

One of the most attractive recent issues is the silver 10 pesos Gaucho Heroes Sesquicentennial commemorative struck at London in 1961. The Gauchos (cowboys of mixed Indian and Spanish ancestry) fought for Uruguayan independence during the Artigas' era.

During the early 1960's, coins almost disappeared from circulation in Uruguay because of a severe inflation. Numerous substitutes for currency appeared such as scrip, tokens and postage stamps. However, the new aluminum-bronze Artigas coins, struck at the Santiago Mint in 1965, brought about the return of a regular metallic coinage.

Artigas appears on the current coins of Uruguay. The national coat-of-arms is on the reverse of the higher values. In the arms' upper quarters are a balance representing justice and a mountain as an emblem of strength. In the lower quarters are an untamed horse symbolizing liberty and an ox for cattle raising, the chief industry. The sun at the top of the shield is a reminder of Uruguay's former association with Argentina.

Valuation

The word, "value," itself has several different meanings. There is, first of all, an intrinsic value, the worth of the metal a coin is made of. Then there is the face value, the officially set quantity of goods and services that a coin will buy. Not too long ago, gold and silver coins contained precious metal in an amount exactly equal to the denomination stamped on them. Nowadays, however, the base metal alloy or "sandwich" planchet coins have an intrinsic value that is almost nil. Interestingly enough, the values of gold and silver have gone up to the point where some of the older coins are now worth more as metal than as circulating money. A U.S. $20 gold piece contains about $35 worth of gold. Even the U.S. silver coins struck as recently as 1964 are worth a small percentage over their face value as melted down metal.

Nearly every coin, however, even including some of those that can be found in daily circulation, has another even greater value. This is its value to collectors, what is usually called a coin's market value. This market value is determined by the "law" of supply and demand—which depends on how many collectors would like to own any given coin, opposed to how many of that coin are available, and how frequently the coins are offered for sale.

One factor that does *not* have much effect on values is age. Many coins from the ancient Roman Empire cost less than some modern issues of the past few years. Why? Because the number of people buying ancient coins is infinitesimal in comparison to the number of collectors buying modern issues. A factor that does have an enormous effect on value is condition—how much or how little wear a particular specimen shows. Coins in new, uncirculated condition—just as they left the mint—are obviously more attractive than worn or battered coins. So much more attractive, in fact, that ardent collectors will sometimes pay several times as much for a perfect coin as they would for the same issue in average condition. Similarly, mutilated or bent or holed coins are worth little or nothing to a collector even as "space fillers."

Really rare coins are usually sold at auction and spirited rivalry can drive the price up quickly. Common and even moderately rare coins are generally offered by dealers at fixed prices. Dealers buy and sell from each other at frequent coin meetings and organization conventions and thus have a good idea of how plentiful a particular coin is, how much call there is for it and, thus, at what price it can be sold. Dealers compete sharply for collectors' business and most of them would rather sell a coin quickly at a modest profit than to keep it in stock, unsold, at a high price.

If you have coins to sell, it's usually not so easy to find a collector who wants just the coins you want to sell. So, in most cases, people sell their individual coins, or collections or accumulations to a dealer as a single lot. Coin dealers, like other businessmen with overhead expenses and a living to earn, cannot, of course, pay as high a price as they charge. Everyone knows that hardware stores, clothing shops and department stores mark up their merchandise—but it is amazing how many people profess surprise or disappointment when a coin dealer offers to pay them less than his asking price for coins they want to sell!

The fact is that coin dealers will pay a fair price for material they have customers for or can use in their stock. (The price a dealer pays when he buys a coin is called the premium value.) A dealer who specializes in the series that you have to sell is the man most likely to have customers for your coins and can probably afford to pay more than a dealer with a general stock. The price dealers will pay is usually 50% to 60% of the current retail price. For very rare coins or coins in great demand that can be sold right away, dealers will often work on an even smaller margin. On the other hand, if you have large quantities of the same item or accumulations of coins taken from circulation—coins that many collectors are likely to have already—then the dealer may offer a lower price, if he will buy the coins at all.

If you can sell directly to another collector, in a club or elsewhere, you can probably settle on a price somewhere between a dealer's buying price and selling price. This would be a bargain for both collectors.

Collectors have to be realistic about the difference between buying and selling. One of the greatest attractions of the hobby, however, is that collectors have that law of supply and demand working in their favor. The supply of most coins is constantly decreasing as more and more of them go into collections, and demand is building as more and more people take up the hobby.

Coin catalogues generally list the approximate market value of coins, arrived at by consulting with dealers, studying their price lists, and recording the prices realized at coin auctions. For information on specific American coins, see *Coin Collector's Handbook;* for foreign and ancient coins, see *A Catalogue of the World's Most Popular Coins*, both by Fred Reinfeld and revised by Burton Hobson.

The Venezuelan 1858 silver 5 reales portrays Liberty wearing a headband.

Venezuela

Venezuela was a part of the Spanish vice-royalty of New Granada when the Spanish governor was deposed in 1811. At first a part of Gran Colombia, Venezuela became an independent state in 1830. A few silver ½ real and 1 real pieces were struck at Caracas in 1812 after the Spanish

Venezuela's 1852 Liberty head copper centavo was struck at Paris as were many of the early issues.

governor was overthrown. A number of quarter real silver pieces were also produced in Caracas in 1821–22 when Venezuela was part of the federation.

Venezuela's first coins as a republic were produced in 1843 at London's Royal Mint. These ¼, ½ and 1 centavo copper pieces (designed by William

The silver 1876 Venezolano was patterned after the French 5 franc value. Bolivar is shown on the obverse, the national arms on the reverse.

474 ☙ Venezuela

The values of Venezuela's gold pieces are expressed on the reverse by the weight of the coins in grams as on the 100 and 10 bolivares shown above.

Wyon) have a Liberty Head with the value and date on the reverse. When the country adopted the new title of "Estados Unidos de Venezuela" (The United States of Venezuela) in 1871, a new monetary unit was also adopted, the bolivar, divided into 100 centimos. The unit was named, of course, after Simon Bolivar, "The Liberator." Since this time Bolivar's portrait has appeared on many Venezuelan coins, including a set of six gold pieces, ranging in value from 5 to 100 bolivares, which were intermittently struck from 1875 to 1930.

Nearly all Venezuelan coins have been manufactured abroad, except for the 1886–89 silver ½ and 1 bolivar, and 2 and 5 bolivares which were struck at Caracas. Mints used for Venezuelan coinage, in addition to London, include: Birmingham, Paris, Philadelphia, Denver, San Francisco, Brussels and Berlin.

Bolivar's portrait appears on the current (series of 1965) 25 and 50 centimos, and 1 and 2 bolivares being struck in pure nickel.

The current Venezuelan coins look much like those issued nearly a century ago. The coat-of-arms displays a sheaf of corn (unity and fertility), two flags with swords (a victory trophy) and a wild horse (liberty). The 12½ centimos denomination (one-eighth of a bolivar) is a holdover from colonial days when the Spanish dollars were divided into 8 reales.

Venezuela ◈ 475

West Indies

Christopher Columbus named the islands of the Caribbean and the southern Atlantic the "Indies" because he thought he had entered the waters surrounding the subcontinent of India. He called the people he found there "Indians," but Columbus wasn't in the East Indies as he believed—he was in the West Indies!

The Europeans established their first New World colonies in the West Indies and the Caribbean became the great sea highway for the fabulous treasure galleons from the rich cities of the Spanish Main to the Atlantic—en route to home bases in Europe. Numerous bands of pirates also set up their "head offices" in the West Indies.

An enormous market developed in Europe for coffee, sugar, cocoa and rum and this in turn led to a power struggle. By the 18th century, the islands had been divided up between the great colonial powers. In the past decade many of the colonies have achieved independence but each follows the traditions, customs and language of its mother country. The West Indies have become one of the world's great tourist destinations.

British Islands

THE BAHAMAS

Scattered over more than 70,000 square miles of sea, the Bahamas are composed of nearly 700 islands and several thousand cays (reefs) and rocks. Only 20 of the islands are inhabited. Nassau, the capital of this British possession and its principal port, is on the island of New Providence. In 1492, Columbus landed on Watling Island, also known as San Salvador. The British acquired the islands in 1783.

The earliest coin struck for the Bahamas was the copper half-penny dated 1806, bearing on its obverse the portrait of King George III. The reverse has a three-masted "Man-o-War" and a Latin motto meaning "By expulsion of pirates, commerce is restored." Early in Bahamas

Bahamas' copper halfpenny of 1806 bears the portrait of George III and a three-masted man-o'-war.

history, the islands were a favorite haunt for pirates. Here the buccaneers auctioned off cargoes to smugglers and other traders.

The first full set of coins were struck for the Bahamas in 1966 by the Royal Mint in London. The set of nine decimal values is made up of the 1 cent in nickel brass; the 5, 10, 15 and 25 cents in copper-nickel; and the 1, 2 and 5 dollars in silver.

Bahama's new decimal coins with Queen Elizabeth II on the obverse present a panorama of island motifs—the coat-of-arms, flamingos, a conch shell, a leaping marlin, a sailing sloop, a hibiscus blossom, bonefish, a pineapple and a starfish.

BERMUDA

The Bermuda Islands are geographically north of the West Indies, but their coins are usually considered in this group. The 300 islands of "Bermuda" cover 21 square miles, with the largest island being 20 miles. long and having a maximum width of 1 mile.

Bermuda was discovered by the Spaniard Juan de Bermudez in the early 1500's but it remained unsettled until 1609, when the ship of Admiral Sir George Somers was wrecked on the reefs while bringing settlers to Virginia. The survivors found the islands over-run with hogs, a welcome source of food.

Silver shilling struck in 1616 for the "Sommers Islands" (Bermuda).

The islands were subsequently named the "Sommers Islands" and coins for them were struck in 1616. These coins, known as "Hogge Money" or "Hoggies," constituted the first coinage produced for the English-American colonies. This currency, made of lightly silvered brass, features a hog on the obverse, a full-rigged galleon with flags on the reverse.

The copper penny issued for Bermuda in 1793 portrays King George III, with a three-masted fighting ship of the line on the reverse.

Bermuda became a British Crown Colony in 1684. A copper penny with the bust of George II and a sailing ship was also produced for Bermuda in 1793. The first modern coin, struck in 1959, commemorated the 350th anniversary of the settlement of Bermuda.

478 ⚙ West Indies—British Islands

The 350th anniversary of the founding of Bermuda was commemorated on a 1959 crown. The sailing ship at the top is a Bermuda sloop; the one at the bottom is a Bermuda "fitted dinghy."

BARBADOS

Barbados, the easternmost of the West Indian islands, is an integral part of the Eastern Group of British Caribbean Territories, along with the Leeward Islands, British Guiana, Trinidad and Tobago, and the Windward Islands. Regular British coins were used on these islands until 1955 when a distinctive, decimal coinage was started for this group of British Caribbean Territories.

The Barbados copper penny of 1788 portrays a native with a crown and plume of three ostrich feathers; the reverse shows a large pineapple.

Neptune on a sea chariot is portrayed on the reverse of the Barbados copper penny dated 1792.

The British found Barbados uninhabited when they reached it in 1605. In its early history, Barbados too was a favorite pirate lair; cotton and tobacco were often used as currency. The British issued a copper penny for Barbados in 1788 whose obverse portrayed a Negro head with a crown and plume of three ostrich feathers, along with the inscription "I serve," the motto of the Prince of Wales. The reverse has a pineapple and the words "Barbadoes Penny."

Distinctive coins were first issued for the British Caribbean Territories in 1955. The reverse of the 50 cents value portrays Britannia above the arms of her territories, while the reverse of the 25 cents value portrays Sir Francis Drake's flagship the *Golden Hind*.

JAMAICA

Jamaica, the largest island of the British West Indies group, covers an area of 4,411 square miles. Discovered by Columbus in 1494, the island belonged to Spain until its capture by an expedition sent out by Oliver Cromwell in 1655. During the 17th century, the harbor of Port Royal was a favorite pirate rendezvous.

Jamacia has had its own coinage since 1869. During the past century mints at London, Birmingham and Ottawa have produced the Jamaican

Jamaica's first coinage under Queen Victoria is exemplified by this 1871 copper halfpenny.

coins. The first coins were the 1869 penny and halfpenny specimens. These denominations bearing the portrait of Queen Victoria, were issued regularly until 1900. A Queen Victoria farthing was also produced beginning in 1880.

Jamaica became an independent member of the British Commonwealth in 1962. Jamaica's recent halfpenny and penny values carry the portrait of Queen Elizabeth II. A special 5-shilling piece was minted in 1966 to commemorate the Commonwealth Games.

The 8th British Empire and Commonwealth Games held at Kingston, were commemorated on Jamaica's 5 shillings of 1966. The reverse bears the Jamaican shield of arms—a cross with five pineapples, supported by a West Indian woman with a basket of fruit and flowers and a West Indian warrior holding a bow. The crest above the shield is an alligator on a log. The scroll at the bottom reads INDUS UTERQUE SERVIET UNI—"Both the Indies [East and West] serve the same ruler."

TRINIDAD AND TOBAGO

Columbus named the island of Trinidad, most southerly of the West Indies, after its "trinity" of three mountain peaks. The tiny island of Tobago, situated some 20 miles northeast, has been combined with Trinidad for administrative purposes. Since 1962, Trinidad and Tobago have been independent members of the British Commonwealth.

Trinidad and Tobago's 50 cents of 1966 is the highest denomination in a similarly designed set of five coins.

Trinidad was acquired by Great Britain from Spain in 1797. Under Spanish rule, various types of pieces of eight, cut moneys and counter-marked coins were utilized. Coins countermarked for use in Trinidad had special monograms. Countermarked Spanish 8 reales pieces were still widely circulated in Trinidad under British rule in the early 1800's.

Spanish Islands

CUBA

Cuba, the largest island of the West Indies, was discovered by Columbus on his first voyage in 1492. Havana, the capital, is an Atlantic Ocean port of more than a million population. The first Spanish settlements were founded in 1511. The Cubans fought from 1817 until 1898 to throw off the Spanish yoke. The Spaniards brutally crushed one Cuban insur-rection after another until United States intervention in the Spanish-American War of 1898 assured an independent Cuba.

During their fight for freedom against the Spaniards, Cuban revolutionaries struck this silver souvenir peso in 1897 with the inscription PATRIA Y LIBERTAD—"Fatherland and Liberty."

Jose Marti (1853–95), who is considered the outstanding Cuban national hero, devoted his life to his country's fight for independence. He was killed in battle in the insurrection of 1895. Marti's portrait can be seen on many varieties of Cuban coins.

Jose Marti, Cuba's national hero, is portrayed on the country's only gold coins, a set of six values struck in 1915-16 that includes this 5 peso piece.

El Morro Castle, built by the Spaniards in the 16th century to protect the Bay of Havana, appears on Cuba's 1952 40 centavos.

Cuba's only issue of gold coins—a set of six values (1, 2, 4, 5, 10 and 20 pesos) struck in 1915–16 features his portrait. The centennial of Marti's birth was marked with a set of four portrait coins in 1953.

Cuba's 20 centavos of 1962, struck under the Castro regime has a bust of Camilio Cienfuegos and the inscription PATRIA O MUERTE—"Fatherland or death."

PUERTO RICO

Puerto Rico enjoys the unique status of being a commonwealth in association with the United States—its full title is the Commonwealth of Puerto Rico (Estado Libre Asociado de Puerto Rico).

Columbus discovered Puerto Rico in 1493, and Ponce de Leon established the first settlement there in 1506—primarily to serve as a defense for the Spanish in the adjacent island of Hispaniola. Ponce de Leon gave the island its name, which means "rich port."

Puerto Rico's only distinctive coinage was the five value issue of 1895–96 under Alfonso XIII of Spain. All types of Spanish gold pieces, reales, cob and cut money circulated on the island, however, for more than three

This silver peso, with the child portrait of Alfonso XIII, was struck in Spain for Puerto Rico in 1895.

West Indies—Spanish Islands ❧ 483

centuries. The island became a possession of the United States after the Spanish-American War of 1898, and United States currencies have been used since then.

French Islands

HAITI

A country occupying the western third of the island of Hispaniola, Haiti is the only independent French-speaking nation in the Western Hemisphere and was perhaps the first Negro republic in the world. The Dominican Republic occupies all of eastern Hispaniola. All of Hispaniola originally was controlled by the Spaniards, but by the Treaty of Ryswick in 1697, the western third was ceded to France. During the 18th century, Haiti became France's richest colony; so many Negro slaves were imported from Africa that by 1760 Haiti had over 200,000 Negroes to only 15,000 whites.

After the outbreak of the French Revolution in 1789 with its cry of "Liberty, Equality and Fraternity," the island's slaves rose against their French masters, forcing France to abolish slavery in 1793. Toussaint l'Ouverture, a former slave who had become a general, seized the colony in 1801, appointing himself governor.

Henri Christophe, first President and later Emperor of Haiti (1811-20), appears in military uniform and cocked hat on this 1807 copper 1 centime.

Henri Christophe, Toussaint's eventual successor, was another brilliant amateur general who was a remarkable statesman as well. He succeeded in building up Haiti's finances in an ingenious way. First he requisitioned every green gourd (a kind of vine fruit) in the country. When the coffee crop was ripe, he had the dried berries shipped to Port-au-Prince, the capital. Paying the planters in gourds, Christophe sold the coffee in Europe, and with the gold he received in return, he was able to establish the foundation for a sound currency. At this time Haiti's unit of currency came to be called the "gourde," French for gourd. Christophe was portrayed on a copper centime struck in Haiti in 1807.

Haiti's silver gourde portrays the draped head of Liberty, with the Haitian arms on the reverse. The arms consist of a palm tree surmounted by a Cap of Liberty, with a drum in front and at each side three flags, three rifles, a cannon and a pile of cannon balls.

Throughout the 19th century, Haiti's history was a turbulent series of dictatorships and uprisings. Dr. Francois Duvalier, who has been president of Haiti since 1957, is portrayed on the current 5 and 10 centimes specimens.

Dr. Francois Duvalier, president of Haiti since 1957, is seen on this nickel-silver 10 centimes value of 1958.

DOMINICAN REPUBLIC

The Dominican Republic lies on the eastern two-thirds of the island of Hispaniola which it shares with Haiti. Hispaniola was discovered by Columbus on December 6, 1492, and he founded a settlement near the present city of Santo Domingo, now the capital of the Dominican Republic.

The Dominican Republic's copper-nickel 5 and 2½ centavos coins of 1877 show the Book of the Gospels and a cross.

West Indies—French Islands ⚜ 485

Liberty in a feather headdress is featured on the Dominican Republic's peso. The reverse shows the national arms, a shield bearing a white cross with an open Book of the Gospels, a small cross above, all surrounded by a trophy of lances and flags.

Santo Domingo, one of the oldest cities of the Americas, was for over three centuries one of the focal points of Spanish power in the New World.

When the Dominican Republic won its independence from Spain in 1822, it was promptly seized by Haiti and did not become fully independent until 1844. The first coins were issued in 1844, bronze one-quarter reals.

Since the 1890's most regular coinage issues of the Dominican Republic have been struck at the Philadelphia Mint.

MARTINIQUE AND GUADELOUPE

Martinique, a volcanic island, and Guadeloupe, popularly called the Emerald Isle, have belonged to France since the 17th century. In 1730 the French government decreed a special coinage for the "Isles du Vent" —the Windward Islands, that is Martinique, Guadeloupe, Grenada and St. Lucia. This silver coinage consisted of two denominations, 6 and 12 sols. Numerous varieties of Spanish reales, countermarked, and cut coins also saw wide circulation on both Martinique and Guadeloupe.

Martinique had its own limited coinage during the 1897–1922 period. During that span of 25 years its copper-nickel 50 centimes and 1 franc

Martinique's 1897 copper-nickel franc portrays a native woman, with the reverse having the value and date inscribed within a wreath.

A native woman in local headdress appears on Guadeloupe's 1903 nickel 1 franc piece. A palm tree is shown on the reverse.

pieces were struck at the Paris Mint. Since 1947, Martinique has been a department of France and the French franc forms the basis of the island's currency system.

Guadeloupe consists of two islands separated by a narrow channel. It too had its own coinage for a brief period—from 1903 until 1921, also copper-nickel 50 centimes and 1 franc pieces minted at Paris.

Danish Islands

THE VIRGIN ISLANDS (DANISH WEST INDIES)

The 1740 silver 12 skillings struck under Christian VI for the Danish West Indies bears the king's crowned monogram, with a sailing ship reverse. The inscription FOR DE DANSK AMERIC INSULER means "For the Danish-American Islands."

The Virgin Islands, situated off the Puerto Rican coast, cover some 132 square miles and have a population of nearly 50,000. The Dutch were the original settlers, though the islands were also held for a time by Spain and England. St. Croix, the largest island, belonged for a time to the Knights of Malta.

The Danes seized the islands in the 1670's and held them until 1917, when the United States purchased them for $25 million. Spanish, Dutch

In 1859, Danish West Indies coins were keyed to the U.S. dollar, and then in 1905, under Christian IX, they were also keyed to the French franc. This Christian IX 1905 gold 4 daler piece was worth $4 or 20 francs, while the 1905 silver 40 cents was valued at 2 francs.

West Indies—Danish Islands ❧ 487

and Danish coins circulated here for more than three centuries. The Danish kings issued a distinctive currency for the islands, including gold coins from 1868 to 1913.

Christian IX's portrait 20 cents of 1878, has a sailing ship on the reverse. The 5 "bits" or 1 cent bronze issued in 1913 under Christian X shows the king's crowned monogram.

Dutch Islands

CURACAO

Curacao along with the islands of Aruba and Bonaire make up the Netherlands Antilles group in the West Indies. Formerly a Dutch colony, the Netherlands Antilles have been autonomous since 1954, an integral part of the Kingdom of the Netherlands.

The copper-nickel 5 cents coin (left) was struck in 1948 for Curacao, while a similar specimen (right) was struck in 1957 for the broader domains of the Netherlands Antilles. The obverse design shows an orange branch within a circle.

Spain settled Curacao in 1527, but lost it to the Dutch in 1634. Peter Stuyvesant was the first Dutch governor. Like most of the Caribbean territories, Curacao made use of counterstamped and cut Spanish silver coinage until the early 1800's. Curacao had its first coinage in 1813 under King William I of The Netherlands. The Philadelphia Mint struck coins for the island during World War II.

APPENDIX

GUIDE TO COIN IDENTIFICATION

Most modern world coins are easy to attribute. A sizable proportion of them, including those from most of the British colonies and Commonwealth nations (but *not* Britain itself) show the name of the issuing country in English. Then, too, many countries are known in English by the same name as in their native languages. Spanish is the official language in most of Central and South America, but you will recognize coins of Argentina, Bolivia, Chile, Colombia, Costa Rica, Cuba, Ecuador, Guatemala, Honduras, Nicaragua, Panama, Paraguay, Peru, El Salvador, Uruguay, Venezuela, and others right away because we use their Spanish names when we speak and write English. The same is true also of some other coin-issuing states, such as Haiti, Madagascar, Mali, and Timor, that use languages besides Spanish. To identify these coins, all you need to know is your geography so that you recognize the country name when you see it.

Another large group of countries issues coins on which the name in the native language is close enough to English for you to guess with some confidence where they are from. Here are some foreign country names from the Coin Finder list which you will probably recognize right away: Belgique (Belgium), Brasil (Brazil), Cabo Verde (Cape Verde), Ceskoslovenska (Czechoslovakia), España (Spain), Filipinas (Philippines), Island (Iceland), Kibris (Cyprus), Norge (Norway), Polska (Poland), Sverige (Sweden). If you want to double-check your guesswork on such coins, just look up the names in the

Argentina

Mali

Norway

Appendix ❧ 489

Poland

Germany

Hungary

Albania

list of key words that follows for verification (or correction) of your deduction.

Other countries issue coins that are not so easily identified until you know certain key words. You may need help, at least the first time, to know that "Deutsches Reich" is Germany, "Helvetia" is Switzerland, and "Magyar" is Hungary. It is almost certain you will not recognize "Euzkadi" as the Viscayan Republic, "Suomi" as Finland, or "Shqipni" as Albania. Some of these key words are written on coins with the Greek or Cyrillic alphabets and can only be approximated using English characters. These words, such as PYbAb on Russian coins or CBbNJA on Serbian coins are preceded by an asterisk (°) in the key-word list.

When you have an unknown foreign coin, study its design and inscriptions for clues to its identity. Check first of all to see whether the name appears anywhere in English or is close enough to English to be recognizable. Be sure not to pass over the name of some small colony or new nation without realizing it is the very name you are seeking. If reading the inscription on a coin doesn't tell you what country it is from, you'll have to find the key word or design element in the tables that follow. Pick the word that looks most promising and look it up. If you find it listed, the table will give you the name of the issuing country, plus the heading under which you will likely find the coin described in standard coin catalogs, as for example, BRAUNSCHWEIG – Brunswick (Germany). If the word you choose first isn't listed, keep trying until you find one that is. Generally, words such as "republic," "colony," "king," and their foreign equivalents and popular denominations like "cent" and "shilling" are no help — being common to so many coins, they are not diagnostic in identification. Words that seem unusual are likely to be the distinctive key words.

INSCRIPTIONS ON COINS

Words written with the Greek or Cyrillic alphabets can only be approximated when using English characters. These words are preceded by an asterisk (*) in the following key-word list.

AARGAU — Argau (Switzerland)
ACVNVM — Ancona (Italy)
*AEBA — Bulgaria
*AENTA — Crete, Greece
AFRICA PORTUGUEZA — Angola
AFRIQUE DE L'OUEST — West African States
AFRIQUE EQUATORIALE FRANÇAISE — French Equatorial Africa
AFRIQUE OCCIDENTALE FRANÇAISE — French West Africa
AFRIQUE ORIENTALE — Mozambique
AGLIA — England (Great Britain)
AGRIPPINA — Cologne (Germany)
AGVIS — Aachen (Germany)
AICHSTADIVM — Eichstadt (Germany)
AISSINDIA — Essen (Germany)
ALGARBIORUM — Algarve (Portugal)
ALGERIE — Algeria
ALOSTENSIS — Alost (Flanders — Belgium)
ALSATIA — Alsace (Germany)
ALWAR — India (Native State)
AMBIANIS — Amiens (France)
AMERICA CENTRAL — Costa Rica
ANDEGAVIS — Anjou (France)
ANDVSIENSIS — Anduse (France)
ANGL — Great Britain
ANH — Anhalt (Germany)
*ANHAPA — Serbia, Yugoslavia
AN HWEI — China
ANTILLEN — Netherlands Antilles
ANTVVP — Antwerp (Brabant — Belgium)
ANVERS — Antwerp (Brabant — Belgium)
*APAXMAI — Greece

Greece

Portugal

Great Britain

APOSTOLORVM PRINCEPS — Papal States (Italy)
APPENZELL — Switzerland
AQVENSIS — Aachen (Germany)
AQVIS — Aachen (Germany)
AQVITANIA — Aquitaine (France)
ARAGONE — Aragon (Spain)
ARAVSID — Orange (France)
ARENBERGAE — Arenberg (Germany)
ARGAU — Switzerland
ARGENTORATVM — Strasbourg (France)
ARGOVIA — Argau (Switzerland)
ASSINDIA — Essen (Germany)
ASTENSIS — Asti (Italy)
AUSTRIAE — Austria
AVGVSTAS VINDILICORVM — Augsburg (Germany)
AVINIO — Avignon (France)
AVRASIGE — Orange (France)
AVRELIANVS — Orleans (France)
AVTIOCERCI — Auxerre (France)
BAD — Baden (Germany)
BAHAWALPUR — India (Native State)
BALEARES — Balearic Isles (Spain)
BAM — Bamberg (Germany)
BANK DEUTSCHER LÄNDER
    — Germany (Western Zone)
BARCANONA — Barcelona (Spain)
BARCINO — Barcelona (Spain)
BARRI — Bar (Lorraine — France)
BAS CANADA — Quebec (Canada)
BASILEA — Basel (Switzerland)
BAV — Bavaria (Germany)
BAYERN — Bavaria (Germany)
°BbATAPNR — Bulgaria
BELGEN — Belgium
BELGES — Belgium
BELGIE — Belgium
BELGIQUE — Belgium
BELGISCH CONGO — Belgian Congo
BERNENSIS — Berne (Switzerland)
BIKANIR — India (Native State)
BISONTIVM — Besançon (France)

Papal States

Basel

Berne

BITERIS — Beziers (France)
BITVRICES — Bourges (France)
BLEDONIS — Beldo (France)
BLESIS — Blois (France)
BOGOTA — Colombia
BOHEM — Bohemia (Austria)
BOHMEN UND MÄHREN — Bohemia & Moravia
   (Czechoslovakia)
BOLIVIANA — Bolivia
BOLVNENE — Boulogne (France)
BONNENSIS — Bonn (Cologne — Germany)
BONONIA — Bologna (Italy)
BORNEO — British North Borneo
BORUSSORUM — Prussia (Germany)
BRAB — Brabant (Belgium)
BRABANTIE — Brabant (Belgium)
BRAND — Brandenburg (Germany)
BRASIL — Brazil
BRASILLIAE — Brazil
BRAUNSCHWEIG — Brunswick (Germany)
BREGA — Brieg (Silesia — Austria)
BREMENSIS — Bremen (Germany)
BR ET LUN — Brunswick (Germany)
BRITANNIARUM — Great Britain
BRITANNIE — Brittany (France)
BRITT — Great Britain
BRVNESVICVM — Brunswick (Germany)
BRVXELENSIS — Brussels (Brabant — Belgium)
BUENOS AYRES — Argentina
BUNDESREPUBLIK DEUTSCHLAND —
   Germany (Federal Republic)
BVILLONAEVS — Bouillon (France)
BVINA — Bonn (Germany)
BVLLON — Bouillon (France)
BVRDEQILA — Bordeaux (France)
BVRGVNDIA — Burgundy (France)
°BYTA HANPAMAAX MOHTOA APAYAC — Mongolia
CABILON — Chalons (Burgundy — France)
CABO VERDE — Cape Verde Islands
CAMBODGE — Cambodia
CAMERACENSIS — Cambrai (France)

Bohemia-Moravia

Bologna

Brunswick

Mongolia

Cape
Verde

CAMEROUN — Cameroons
CAMPEN — Kampen (Netherlands)
CANTON — Switzerland
CARTIS — Chartres (France)
CATALUNA — Catalonia (Spain)
CAYENNE — French Guiana
°CCCP — Russia
CECHY A MORAVA — Bohemia and Moravia
   (Czechoslovakia)
CELE — Celles (France)
CENOHANNIS — Maine (France)
CENTRAFRICAINE — Central African Republic
CENTRO DE AMERICA — Costa Rica (mint mark CR),
   Guatemala (mint mark NG), Honduras (mint mark T)
°CEPEbPOMb — Russia
CESKOSLOVENSKA — Czechoslovakia
CHERIFIEN — Morocco
CHING KIANG — China
CHUCKRAM — Travancore (India — Native State)
CLIVIA — Cleves (France)
°CNbNPCKAR — Siberia
COCHIN CHINE FRANÇAISE — French Cochin China
   (Indo-China)
COESFELD — Koesfeld (Germany)
COLONIA — Cologne (Germany)
CONFLUENTIA — Koblenz (Trier — Germany)
CONGO BELGE — Belgian Congo
CONSTANCIA — Constance (Germany)
CORBECIA — Corvey (Germany)
CORDOBA — Argentina
COTE FRANÇAISE DES SOMALIS — French Somaliland
°CPBCKII — Serbia
°CPbHJA — Serbia
°CPbNJA — Serbia
°CTOTNHKN — Bulgaria
CUMHURIYETI — Turkey
CVGN — Cugnon (France)
DALPhS — Dauphiné (France)
DANIA — Denmark
DANMARK — Denmark
DANSK AMERIKANSK — Danish West Indies

Catalonia

Morocco

Siberia

Serbia

DANSKE — Denmark
DANSK VESTINDIEN — Danish West Indies
DAVANTRIA — Deventer (Netherlands)
DEMERARY & ESSEQUEBO — British Guiana
DEUTSCHE DEMOKRATISCHE REPUBLIK —
   German Democratic Republic (Eastern Zone)
DEUTSCHES REICH — Germany
DEUTSCHLAND — Germany
DEUTSCH OSTAFRIKA — German East Africa
DEUTSCH OSTAFRIKANISCHE GESELLSCHAFT —
   German East Africa Company
DEWAS — India (Native State)
D'HAITI — Haiti
DHAR — India (Native State)
D'ITALIA — Italy
DIVIONESIS — Dijon (Burgundy — France)
*DNHAPA — Yugoslavia
D.O.A. — German East Africa
DOMB — Dombes (France)
DOMINICANA — Dominican Republic
DRETMANNA — Dortmund (Germany)
*EAAADOE — Greece
*EAAHNIKH AHMOKPATIA — Greece
*EAAHNIKH ILLOAITEIA — Greece
EESTI — Estonia
EIRE — Ireland
EISTADIVM — Eichstadt (Germany)
ELVANCENSIS — Ellwangen (Germany)
EMPIRE CHERIFIEN — Morocco
EQSTRIV — Lausanne (Switzerland)
EQVITAS — Sicily (Italy)
ERFORDVM — Erfurt (Germany)
ERYTHR — Eritrea
ESPANA — Spain
ESSEQUIBO & DEMERARY — British Guiana
ESTADO DA INDIA — Portuguese India
ETABLISSEMENTS FRANÇAIS DE L'OCEANIE —
   French Oceania
ETAT FRANÇAISE — France (Vichy)
ETRVRIA — Tuscany (Italy)
EUZKADI — Viscayan Republic

Danish West Indies

Greece

Estonia

Ireland

Viscayan Republic

EYSTETTENSIS — Eichstadt (Germany)
FER — Ferrara (Italy)
FILIPINAS — Philippines
F.K. CUSTOM HOUSE — China
FLANDRIA — Flanders (Belgium)
FLORENTIA — Florence (Italy — Tuscany)
FOEDERATI BELGII — Netherlands
FOO KIEN — China
FRANÇAISE — France
FRANCOFORDIA — Frankfurt (Germany)
FRANCKISCHEN CRAIS — Franconian Circle
FRAN ET NAV — France
FREIE STADT DANZIG — Danzig (Germany)
FR ET NAV — France
FREYBURG — Fribourg (Switzerland)
FRIBVRGVM — Freiburg (Germany)
FRIDBERG — Friedberg (Germany)
FRISIA ORIENTALIS — East Friesland (Netherlands)
FRISING — Freising (Germany)
FUN — Korea
FUNG TIEN — China
G — Guatemala
GALLIARVM — Lyon (France)
GANDENSIS — Ghent (Flanders — Belgium)
GEDANENSIS — Danzig
GELRIA — Gelderland (Netherlands)
GENEVENSIS — Geneva (Switzerland)
GENV — Genoa (Italy)
GERVNDA — Gerona (Italy)
GHANIENSIS — Ghana
GOA — Portuguese India
GOSL — Goslar (Germany)
GR (counterstamp) — Jamaica
GRAND LIBAN — Lebanon
GRAUBUNDEN — Grisons (Swiss canton)
GRIQUA TOWN — Griqualand
GRONLAND — Greenland
GUINE — Portuguese Guinea
GUINEÆ — Angola
GUINEE — Guinea
GUYANE FRANCAISE — French Guiana

Florence

France

Guatemala

Danzig

Jamaica

GVLIACVM – Jülich (Germany)
GVLICH – Jülich (Germany)
HABILITADA POR EL GOBIERNO (counterstamp) –
Costa Rica
HALAE – Hall (Germany)
HANONIE – Hainault (Belgium)
HASSIA – Hesse (Germany)
HELVETIA – Switzerland
HELVETICA – Switzerland
HERBIPOLIS – Würzburg (Germany)
HIBERNIA – Ireland
HILDES – Hildesheim (Germany)
HISPANIARUM – Spain

Spain

HISPANIARUM ET INDIARUM REX – Spanish-American
mints. Exact country of origin determined by mint mark
in legend – M (Mexico), G or NG (Guatemala), LM
or MAE (Peru), S (Santiago, Chile), PTS (Potosi,
Bolivia), P or PN or NR (Colombia)
HISPANIARUM REX – Spain
HOHENLO– Hohenlohe (Germany)
HOL – Holland (Netherlands)
HOLLANDIE – Holland (Netherlands)
HOLSATIA – Holstein (Denmark)
HO NAN – China
HOND – Honduras
HOSP ET S. SEPVL HIERVS – Malta
HRVATSKA – Croatia
HUNG SHUAN – China

Peru

HU PEH – China
HU POO – China (Empire)
HVNGARIA – Hungary
HWAN – South Korea
IEVER – Jever (Germany)
*ΠАРА – Montenegro

Montenegro

*ΠΡΗΕΤΟΡΕ – Montenegro
ILE DE LA REUNION – Reunion Island
ILES DE FRANCE ET BONAPARTE – Mauritius
INDIA PORTUGUEZA – Portuguese India
INDIE BATAV – Netherlands East Indies
INDO-CHINE FRANCAISE – French Indo-China
*IONIKON KPATOE – Ionian Islands

Ionian Islands

IPRA — Ypres (Netherlands)
ISLAND — Iceland
ISLES DU VENT — Windward Islands
ITALIA — Italy
IVLIACVM — Jülich (Germany)
IVNGHEIT — Aachen (Germany)
IVVAVIA — Salzburg (Austria)
°JUGOSLAVIJA — Yugoslavia
°JYPOCIIABNJE — Yugoslavia
°JYTOCNABNJA — Yugoslavia
KATANGA — Congo
°KBAXEBHHA — Montenegro
KIANG NAN — China
KIANG SEE — China
KIANG SOO — China
°KIBRIS — Cyprus
KIRIN — China
°KOIIEEK — Russia
°KONbEKb — Russia
°KPHTH — Crete
°KPHTIKH — Crete
KWANG SEA — China
KWANG TUNG — China
°KYTIPIAKH — Cyprus
L — Lima (Peru)
LATVIJAS — Latvia
LEO — Leon (Spain)
LEODIENSIS — Liège (Belgium)
LETZEBURG — Luxembourg
LIBANAISE — Lebanon
LIETUVAS — Lithuania
LIGNICIVM — Liegnitz (Germany)
LIGURE — Ligurian Republic (Italy)
LILLA — Lille (France)
LIMBVRGIE — Limburg (Germany)
LIMOVICENSIS — Limoges (France)
LINGONIS CVTS — Langres (France)
LIPSIA — Leipzig (Germany)
LIPP — Lippe (Germany)
LM — Lima (Peru)
L'OCEANIE — French Oceania

Iceland

Yugoslavia

Lithuania

Peru

LOMBARDO VENETO — Lombardy-Venetia (Italy)
LOTHARINGIA — Lorraine (France)
LOVANIEN — Louvain (Brabant — Belgium)
LOWENST — Löwenstein (Germany)
LUBECENSIS — Lübeck (Germany)
LUCENSIS — Lucca (Italy)
LUZERN — Lucerne (Switzerland)
LVCDVNVM — Lyon (France)
LVCENBGENSIS — Luxembourg
LVGDVNVM — Lyons (France)
LVGDVNVM BATAVORVM — Leyden
  (Netherlands)
LVNEBVRGVM — Lüneburg (Germany)
LVXEMBVRG — Luxembourg
M (on rectangular coin) — Mozambique
M — Mexico
MACUTA — Angola
MADEIRENSIS — Madeira
MAG BRIT — Great Britain
MAGYAR — Hungary
MANCHURIAN PROVINCES — China
MANTOVA — Mantua (Italy)
MARCHIE — Marche (France)
MAROC — Morocco
MECHLENB — Mecklenburg (Germany)
MEDIOLANVM — Milan (Italy)
MEGAPO — Mecklenburg (Germany)
METENSIS — Metz (Lorraine — France)
METVLLO — Melle (France)
MEXICANA — Mexico
MILETA — Malta
MIMIGARDEFORT — Münster (Germany)
MLI — Milan (Italy)
MOCAMBIQUE — Mozambique
MOGONCIA — Mainz (Germany)
°MOHETA PYbAb — Russia
MONASTER — Münster (Germany)
MONOEGI — Monaco
MUTINA — Modena (Italy)
NAMVRCEMSIS — Namur (France)
NANCEII — Nancy (Lorraine — France)

Lyons

Mozambique

Great Britain

Hungary

Russia

NANTIS — Nantes (Brittany — France)
°NAPA — Montenegro, Serbia
NAVARRA — Navarre (France)
NEAP — Naples (Italy)
°NEBA — Bulgaria
NEDERLANDEN — Netherlands
NEDERLANDSCH INDIE — Netherlands East Indies
NEDERLANDSE ANTILLEN — Netherlands Antilles
NEV GUINEA COMPAGNIE — German New Guinea
NG — Guatemala
NIVERSCIS — Nevers (France)
NORGE — Norway
NORIMBERGA — Nuremberg (Germany)
NORTHVSIA — Nordhausen (Germany)
NORVEG — Norway
NOUVELLE CALEDONIE — New Caledonia
NR — Nuevo Reino, Santa Fe de Bogota (Colombia)
NUEVA GRANADA — Colombia
OESTERREICH — Austria
OLOMVCEN — Olmütz (Germany)
ONCA (on rectangular coin) — Mozambique
ORANJE VRYS STAAT — Orange Free State (Orange
   River Colony)
OSNABRVGA — Osnabrück (Germany)
OSTAFRIKANISCHE — German East Africa
OSTERREICH — Austria
PADERB — Paderborn (Germany)
PAPIA — Pavia (Italy)
PARMAE — Parma (Italy)
PASSANIA — Passau (Germany)
PECUNIA INSULANA — Azores
PECUNIA MADEIRESIS — Madeira
PEI YANG — China
PENNIA — Finland
PFALZ — Palatinate (Germany)
PICTAVIENTSIS — Poitou (France)
P.M. (counterstamped) — Mozambique
POLSKA — Poland
POLSKIE — Poland
PONTISIENSI — Pontoise (France)
PONTIV — Ponthien (France)

Bulgaria

Colombia

Austria

Poland

PONT MAX — Papal States or Vatican City
PORTUGALIÆ — Portugal
PORTUGUESA — Portugal
POTOSI — Bolivia
PREUSSEN — Prussia (Germany)
PROCENIE — Forcalquier (France)
POVINCIA — Provence (France)
PROVINCIAS DEL RIO DE LA PLATA — Argentina
PTS (superimposed on one another) — Bolivia
°PYbAb — Russia
QUETZAL — Guatemala
QUINDAR — Albania
QVOCVNQVE IECERIS STABIT — Isle of Man
RATISBON — Regensburg (Germany)
REDONIS — Rennes (France)
REGNUM ITALICUM — Eritrea
REMIS — Reims (France)
RENAV — Château-Renaud (France)
REP CENTRAFRICAINE — Central African Republic
REPUBLIQUE FRANÇAISE — France or colonies
REPUBLICA PORTUGUESA — Portugal or colonies
R.F. — France
RIGSBANK — Denmark
RIO DE LA PLATA — Argentina
RODES — Rovergue (France)
ROMANA — Rumania
ROMANIA — Rumania
ROMANIEI — Rumania
ROMANILOR — Rumania
ROM IMP — Holy Roman Emperor (Austria)
RUANDA URUNDI — Belgian Congo
S — Santiago (Chile)
SAARLAND — Saar
SABAUD — Savoy (Italy)
SABAVADI — Savoy (Italy)
SACHSEN — Saxony (Germany)
SAILANA — India (Native State)
SALISBVRGVM — Salzburg (Austria)
SALVTIARVM — Carmagnola (Italy)
SAORSTAT EIREANN — Ireland
SARDEGNA — Sardinia (Italy)

Papal States

Bolivia

Château Renaud

Chile

SAXONIA — Saxony (Germany)
SCHLESIEN — Silesia
SCHLESW-HOLST — Schleswig and Holstein (Denmark)
SCHWEIZER — Switzerland
SCI DIONYSIM — St. Denis (France)
SCOTORVM — Scotland
SEDE VACANTE — Papal States or Vatican City
SHANG TUNG — China
SHQIPERI — Albania
SHQIPNI — Albania
SHQIPTAREVET — Albania
SICILIAE ET HIERVSALEM — Naples and Sicily
SILESIAE — Silesia (Austria)
SLOVENSKA — Slovakia (Czechoslovakia)
SLOVENSKYCH — Slovakia (Czechoslovakia)
S.M. — Sweden
S. MARINI — San Marino
S. MARINO — San Marino
SOMALIA ITALIANA — Italian Somaliland
SOMALIS — French Somaliland
SOMMER ISLANDS — Bermuda
SOSATVM — Soest (Germany)
S. TOME E PRINCIPE — St. Thomas and Prince Islands
STYRELSE GRONLAND — Greenland
STYRIAE — Styria (Austria)
SUD — Mexico (Revolutionary)
SUID AFRIKA — South Africa
SUOMEN — Finland
SUOMI — Finland
SURINAME — Surinam
SVECIAE — Sweden
SVERIGES — Sweden
SVESSIONIS — Soissons (France)
SYRIE — Syria
SZE CHUEN — China
TAI CH'ING TI KUO — China (Empire)
TAI WAN — China
TASAVALTA — Finland
TAZHTAIE — Ionian Islands
THEROTMANNI — Dortmund (Germany)
TICINUM — Pavia (Italy)

Saxony

Sicily

Sweden

Sweden

TIGVRINAE — Zürich (Switzerland)
TIROL — Tyrol (Austria)
TOKYO — Japan
TOLETO — Toledo (Spain)
TOLOSA — Toulouse (France)
TORNACVM — Tournai (Netherlands)
TOSCANA — Tuscany (Italy)
TRAIECTVM — Utrecht (Netherlands)
TRAJECTVM AD MOSAM — Maastricht
    (Netherlands)
TRANSISVLANIA — Overijssel (Netherlands)
TRANSYL — Transylvania (Austria)
TRAVANCORE — India (Native State)
TRECAS — Troyes (Champagne — France)
TREMONIA — Dortmund (Germany)
TREVERIS — Trier
TSINGKIANG — China
TUNISIE — Tunisia
TÜRKIYE — Turkey
TVCIVM — Deutz (Cologne — Germany)
TVLLV — Taul (Lorraine — France)
TVRENA — Turenne (France)
TVRICVM — Zürich (Switzerland)
TVRINGIA — Thuringia (Germany)
TVRONVS — Tours (France)
TVVCIVM — Deutz (Cologne — Germany)
TYR — Tyrol (Austria)
*UPHETOPE — Montenegro
UPPER CANADA — Ontario (Canada)
VABARIIK — Estonia
VALENCERENSIS — Valenciennes
    (Burgundy — France)
VALENTIAI — Valence (France)
VALLS D'ANDORRA — Andorra
VATICANO — Vatican City
VEDOME — Vendôme (France)
VENASINI — Avignon (France)
VENECIAS — Venice (Italy)
VENETVS — Venice (Italy)
VENT — Windward Islands
VERDA — Werden (Germany)

Utrecht

Overijssel

Venice

Inscriptions on Coins ⚜ 503

VESTINDIEN – Danish West Indies
VIGO – Great Britain
VINDELICORVM – Augsburg (Germany)
VINDOBONA – Vienna (Italy)
VIRDVNCM – Verdun (Lorraine – France)
VIROMENDI – Vermandois (France)
VNGARIE — Hungary
WERDINVM – Werden (Germany)
WESTFRI – West Frisia (Netherlands)
WESTPHALEN – Westphalia (Germany)
WON – Korea
WRATISLAVIA – Breslau (Germany)
WURTEM – Württemberg (Germany)
YANG – Korea
YEN – Japan
YUN NAN – China
ZAR – South African Republic
ZEELANDIA – Zeeland (Netherlands)
ZEL – Zeeland (Netherlands)
ZUID AFRIKA – South Africa
ZUID AFRIKAANSCHE REPUBLIEK –
  South African Republic

Great Britain

Hungary

West Frisia

South African Republic

INDEX